A CULTURAL HISTORY OF MEMORY

VOLUME 6

A Cultural History of Memory
General Editors: Stefan Berger and Jeffrey Olick

Volume 1
A Cultural History of Memory in Antiquity
Edited by Beate Dignas

Volume 2
A Cultural History of Memory in the Middle Ages
Edited by Gerald Schwedler

Volume 3
A Cultural History of Memory in the Early Modern Age
Edited by Marek Tamm and Alessandro Arcangeli

Volume 4
A Cultural History of Memory in the Eighteenth Century
Edited by Patrick Hutton

Volume 5
A Cultural History of Memory in the Nineteenth Century
Edited by Susan A. Crane

Volume 6
A Cultural History of Memory in the Long Twentieth Century
Edited by Stefan Berger and Bill Niven

A CULTURAL HISTORY OF MEMORY

IN THE LONG TWENTIETH CENTURY

Edited by Stefan Berger and Bill Niven

BLOOMSBURY ACADEMIC
LONDON · NEW YORK · OXFORD · NEW DELHI · SYDNEY

BLOOMSBURY ACADEMIC
Bloomsbury Publishing Plc
50 Bedford Square, London, WC1B 3DP, UK
1385 Broadway, New York, NY 10018, USA
29 Earlsfort Terrace, Dublin 2, Ireland

BLOOMSBURY, BLOOMSBURY ACADEMIC and the Diana logo are trademarks
of Bloomsbury Publishing Plc

First published in Great Britain 2022
Paperback edition first published 2024

Copyright © Bloomsbury Publishing, 2022

Stefan Berger and Bill Niven have asserted their right under the Copyright, Designs
and Patents Act, 1988, to be identified as Editors of this work.

Cover image: © ODD ANDERSEN / Staff / Getty Images

All rights reserved. No part of this publication may be reproduced or transmitted
in any form or by any means, electronic or mechanical, including photocopying,
recording, or any information storage or retrieval system, without prior permission
in writing from the publishers.

Bloomsbury Publishing Plc does not have any control over, or responsibility for, any
third-party websites referred to or in this book. All internet addresses given in this
book were correct at the time of going to press. The author and publisher regret
any inconvenience caused if addresses have changed or sites have ceased
to exist, but can accept no responsibility for any such changes.

A catalogue record for this book is available from the British Library.

A catalog record for this book is available from the Library of Congress.

ISBN: HB: 978-1-4742-7352-7
       PB: 978-1-3504-0864-7
       Set: 978-1-4742-7384-8

Series: The Cultural Histories Series

Typeset by RefineCatch Limited, Bungay, Suffolk
Printed and bound in Great Britain

To find out more about our authors and books visit www.bloomsbury.com
and sign up for our newsletters.

CONTENTS

List of Illustrations — vi
General Editors' Preface — viii
   Stefan Berger and Jeffrey Olick

Introduction — 1
   Stefan Berger and Bill Niven

1. Power and Politics — 17
   Jay Winter

2. Time and Space — 31
   Chris Lorenz

3. Media and Technology — 51
   Wulf Kansteiner

4. Knowledge: Science and Education — 75
   Nick Tosh

5. Ideas: Philosophy, Religion, and History — 95
   Stefan Berger

6. High Culture and Popular Culture — 115
   Patrick Finney

7. The Social: Rituals, Faith, Practices, and the Everyday — 139
   Jeffrey Olick

8. Remembering and Forgetting — 155
   Bill Niven

Notes — 173
Bibliography — 175
Notes on Contributors — 207
Index — 209

ILLUSTRATIONS

INTRODUCTION

0.1	Carl Gustav Jung	2
0.2	Maurice Halbwachs	3
0.3	Aleida and Jan Assmann on receipt of the Peace Prize of the German Book Trade in 2018	4
0.4	Pierre Nora	11
0.5	Berlin's Memorial to the Murdered Jews of Europe	15

CHAPTER 1

1.1	Commonwealth War Graves Commission Cemetery, Lone Pine, Gallipoli	21
1.2	French War Cemetery, Hellespont, Gallipoli	21
1.3	German War Cemetery, Bayeux, France	22
1.4	The Cenotaph, London	23

CHAPTER 2

2.1	"France" as Hexagon	38
2.2	"France" unlike the Hexagon	38
2.3	History beyond memory	41
2.4	*Moses and the Promised Land*	46
2.5	"Beloved Stalin is the People's Happiness"	46
2.6	Vancouver Westside condo prices	47

CHAPTER 3

3.1	*Black November* poster	52
3.2	*Assassin's Creed Odyssey*	54
3.3	*T-Men*	57
3.4	Cover of *Der Spiegel*, 1979	63
3.5	*This War of Mine*	70

CHAPTER 4

4.1	Sigmund Freud, *c.* 1921	79
4.2	Santiago Ramón y Cajal in 1899	87
4.3	ENIAC, *c.* 1950	88
4.4	John von Neumann in 1956	90
4.5	*Aplysia californica*	92

CHAPTER 5

5.1	Hans Draeger, *Anklage und Widerlegung*, book cover	96
5.2	Resistance Memorial in Dachau	100
5.3	Boris Kustodiev, *The Bolshevik*	101
5.4	Mass exhumation of the bodies of those killed in the Spanish Civil War	104
5.5	May Day, Belfast, 1984	106
5.6	Brexit campaign	108

CHAPTER 6

6.1	Soviet postage stamp	116
6.2	*Strike*, 1925	121
6.3	Japanese child's propaganda kimono	125
6.4	*Gunsmoke*	128
6.5	Warrior armored personnel carriers of the Irish Guards	133
6.6	Exhibition in the Tallinn Museum of Occupations and Freedom, Estonia, 2012	135
6.7	Performance art event "We're here because we're here . . ."	137

CHAPTER 7

7.1	Herbert Spencer	140
7.2	Bust of Emile Durkheim in Paris	142
7.3	Ernest Renan	147
7.4	Portrait of Karl Marx	150
7.5	Memorial to Theodor Adorno in Frankfurt	150

CHAPTER 8

8.1	*The Bronze Soldier*, Tallinn, Estonia	159
8.2	Berlin Wall, border crossing Oberbaumbrücke in 1987	161
8.3	Robert E. Lee Memorial, Richmond, Virginia	162
8.4	Pictures and newspaper clips of *desaparecidos*	163
8.5	Memorial at Choeung Ek	169
8.6	National Holocaust Centre and Museum near Laxton, Nottinghamshire	171

GENERAL EDITORS' PREFACE

STEFAN BERGER AND JEFFREY K. OLICK

Any project titled *A Cultural History of Memory* begs a number of questions from the very beginning. For instance: What does it mean that this project is a *cultural* history, rather than some other kind of history? (What other kind of history might it have been?) In turn, what makes memory a feasible and interesting topic for such a history? (It certainly isn't immediately obvious that it would be.) Finally, why a cultural history rather than *the* cultural history? (After all, with forty-eight chapters spread over six volumes, how many more cultural histories of memory could one imagine?)

CULTURAL HISTORY

A Cultural History of Memory is but one entry in a series of cultural histories already and soon to be published by Bloomsbury, including cultural histories of Animals, the Human Body, Food, Gardens, Women, the Senses, Dress and Fashion, the Theatre, Work, Law, Money, and Hair, among many others. The publisher has taken a light hand in prescribing the orientation of these projects, leaving the definition of cultural history to each project's senior editors. And this is very well, as there are many different ways to inflect the idea of cultural history, and different approaches are likely appropriate to the different subject matters. In turn, we have not imposed any particular definition on the editors of the six volumes in this current project, nor have they on the authors of the forty-eight chapters that comprise the total product. That being said, we have relied on a broadly shared understanding of the purposes and tools of cultural history in framing this particular entry in the series, and it is clear that its many authors have as well, though perhaps with occasional divergences.

Namely, contemporary cultural history, at least as it has been practiced in and on the West (and this is one of the important limitations on the project we will discuss below), has defined itself in contrast to at least three other approaches (on the historiographical developments sketched in the following pages see in greater detail Berger, Feldner, and Passmore (2020)). First, there is a broadly defined "traditional" political historiography, dominant in the nineteenth century, that wrote the story of states, their leaders, and their wars. These "high politics" approaches, of course, fully advanced the claim to "objectivity," particularly since the matters they studied—states, their leaders, and their wars—have been quite well documented. These approaches, nevertheless, not only studied the world of nation-states and their high politics but were often part of defining the claims of those states and glorifying the achievements of their leaders, so their claims to be value-free and scientific were obviously dubious ones.

Following this, though at different times in different parts of the world, and only partly under the influence of Marxist perspectives, there developed a vibrant interest in "economic" and "social" history alongside, and sometimes in contrast to, the traditional political histories: the stories not of the "great men" and the great achievements, but of economic processes and social structures. Like political history, this was often presented in national containers and sometimes served the purpose of highlighting the particular "achievements" of nations in the economic and social spheres. Only later did a nascent Marxist historiography, often relatively weak in the universities before the 1970s, come to understand this study of history to be part of a struggle not merely to interpret or understand history, but to change it, as Marx famously put it in his eleventh thesis on Feuerbach.

A stronger concern for ordinary people in social history, however, only occurred with the turn to "history from below," sometimes also referred to as history of everyday life, micro-history, or historical anthropology. This was largely a development that gathered momentum from the 1970s onwards. "History workshop" movements that often became supporters of this new, more human-agency centered understanding of social history, critiqued older forms of social history for being too focused on structures and processes and thereby for ignoring human agency. Furthermore, these approaches criticized the adherence of much of social and economic history to modernization theories and teleologies of progress that appeared to many practitioners of historical anthropology as outdated. The interest of these historians in the everyday had made them turn to anthropology and, inspired by anthropological methods and theories, they set out to change understandings of the social and cultural. As Robert Darnton has put it, "The anthropological mode of history [. . .] begins from the premise that individual expression takes place within a general idiom" (quoted in Hunt 1989: 12). In other words: history had to start from individual human agency and then locate it within a wider collective field.

More difficult to understand is the next form of "traditional" historical interest that was always a lesser strand when compared to political and economic/social history: namely, intellectual history or the history of ideas. Like "traditional" forms of history that focused on states, wars, and high politics, intellectual history has often focused on a narrow slice of life as well: the thoughts and ideas of other great men than politicians (though sometimes them too), mainly artists, scientists, philosophers, and others whose writings are seen to have captured, defined, and led the "spirit" of an age. To be sure, intellectual historians are quite interested in the contexts and structures that enabled the great thinkers to produce their great works, as well as in how those great works affected the less great thoughts of the cultures and societies that produced them. The recent influence of the so-called "Cambridge school" around Quentin Skinner and J.G.A. Pocock is a good example of such contextualization of great thinkers. Internationally even more influential has been the "history of concepts"—shaped seminally by the German historical theorist Reinhart Koselleck. Conceptual history is now a truly global undertaking and one that takes seriously the belief that we need to thoroughly historicize our key concepts in order to understand how people made sense of the world and how they consequently acted in the world.

Next to political history, economic and social history, historical anthropology, and intellectual history, cultural history now forms one of the great traditions of historical writing, reaching back to the very beginnings of professional historiography. Jacob Burckhardt and Johan Huizinga are just two examples of classical representatives of cultural history that can still be read with great pleasure and benefit by contemporary cohorts of students. However, older cultural history often had a strong emphasis on studying "high culture" and thereby distinguishing what was "true" and "worthwhile" culture from "popular culture" or simply "trash." When a "new cultural history" began to conquer history departments in the 1980s, it democratized older forms of cultural history by redefining culture in broader and more inclusive terms. Furthermore, many of its practitioners were much influenced by the "linguistic turn" and theories associated with poststructuralist approaches (Toews 1987: 879–907). Like historical anthropology the new cultural history was dissatisfied not only with an older political history interested mainly in "high politics" but an older social and economic history reducing the past to structures and processes. Unlike an older intellectual history, it was also not so much interested in "great ideas" but instead in ordinary thoughts and practices. Whilst the initial interest in language led cultural historians to study discourses, many soon realized that discourses had to be related back to practices. Furthermore, practices had much to do with things and objects, in other words, materials that needed to be considered to have an agency of their own in history. The history of material culture could thus build on the linguistic turn and practice theory, but it carved out a niche of its own in a field of cultural history that became increasingly compartmentalized as we enter the new millennium after 2000.

Marxist social historians like E.P. Thompson and Geoff Eley spearheaded new understandings of the history of society that took on board many of the insights of the new cultural history without ever abandoning an appreciation of the Marxist understanding of social developments. Thompson, for example, focused not only on the economic condition that made the English working class, but on "the way [. . .] material experiences are handled . . . in cultural ways" (Merrill 1972: 20 f). This happened, according to Thompson, through "cultural and moral mediations." In turn, however, Gareth Stedman Jones moved the discussion even farther afield from economic reduction when he declared that "We [. . .] cannot decode political language to reach a primal and material expression of interest since it is the discursive structure of political language which conceives and defines interest in the first place" (Stedman Jones 1983: 21-22). For the "new cultural historians" in this tradition, then, what they, in part following Emile Durkheim among others, called "representations" became of primary interest. And, as Roger Chartier put it, "The Representations of the social world themselves are the constituents of social reality" (Chartier 1982: 30). This is because, as Lynn Hunt writes, "All practices, whether economic or cultural, depend on the representations individuals use to make sense of their world" (Hunt 1989: 19). The goal of cultural history is thus, as again Chartier defines it, to show "how, in different times and places, a specific social reality was constructed, how people conceived of it and how they interpreted it to others" (Chartier 1998: 4). In this, Chartier followed Lucien Goldmann, who had defined worldviews—the true subject for intellectual historians who were interested in culture more broadly—as "the whole complex of ideas, aspirations and feelings which links together the members of a social group [. . .] and which opposed them to members of other social groups" (Goldmann 1967: 17). And this is indeed the approach that most of the authors in these six volumes have taken, though in an obviously wide variety of ways in and for a wide variety of contexts.

MEMORY

The turn toward memory, especially understood as a collective or cultural phenomenon, can in fact be seen as—though not only as—another inflection of the new cultural history (Berger and Niven 2014). Its interest in representations and discourses encouraged an interest in memories as constituting those representations and discourses. Whether it was written in pursuit of a nostalgic longing for a great national past, as is evident in some of the contributions to Pierre Nora's seminal seven-volume study on the realms of memory of France (Nora 1981–7), or whether it was conducted in the search for understanding and possibly overcoming the consequences of traumatic events in the past, like genocides or wars, memory history has linked contemporary memories to processes of sense-production in the present that gave rise to very different and always contested understandings of the past.

It should already be obvious, then, that the cultural history of memory undertaken in the forty-eight chapters that follow is not just about recall or other basic cognitive processes. Though the concept of memory employed across these six volumes is sometimes the lay understanding of memory as what and how people can recall in different times and places, the majority of the chapters take memory to be something broader. Memory may seem to take place within individual minds, yet for most of the last century numerous scholars both within and beyond cultural history have understood memory more broadly (Olick, Vinitzky-Seroussi, and Levy 2011). Individual memory always takes place within social contexts, with social materials, from social positions, and in response to social cues. So whatever neurological or mental processes it involves, these are obviously deeply embedded in structures and contexts that extend far beyond the individuals whose minds engage in remembering, traditionally understood. Individuals, moreover, employ many technologies of memory—for instance, chanting or writing—which exist outside of themselves and are not part of their brains, and which vary across social settings and in their impacts on individual mnemonic processes. In this way, it becomes perhaps clearer why memory is such a rich terrain for cultural (and other!) forms of history.

However, many of the chapters that constitute this cultural history of memory take yet another step beyond the mind—that is, beyond what Maurice Halbwachs, one of the key figures in contemporary thinking about memory, called the social frameworks of memory, to see memory as an inherently social activity (Halbwachs 1950). We often—even most often—remember together. Social psychologists understand that there are significant differences between remembering alone and remembering in a group, whether this is a matter of simple recall (e.g. when a group of individuals can reconstruct memorized lists more completely than the sum of individuals alone via cuing and other social processes) or in narrative process (e.g. when a family retells a story of an experience they have shared, and the complete narrative emerges from the many voices involved, which bring different pieces than everyone necessarily would have recalled). However, some scholars argue that groups themselves remember; for instance, they build libraries and fill them with materials, they curate representations of the past in museums and elsewhere in ways that transcend the resources of individuals, and they preserve knowledge that very few individuals recall (Assmann 1992). As such, scholars often refer to social, collective, or cultural memory—the forms and traces of the past that transcend the capacities or even interests of individuals—and many do not believe these forms of memories are merely metaphors (see Erll 2008). The field of memory is thus a vast one, and it is clear that understanding all the different forms of memory—from the neurological to the museological—requires, and is an appropriate subject for, all the resources of cultural history.

Having said that, the development of memory studies since the 1980s has been characterized by the gradual constitution of a new discipline that was self-consciously transdisciplinary. Of all the disciplines that constituted this new field, historians were arguably in a minority. Literary scholars and sociologists were far more numerous, and, as all six volumes in this series demonstrate, a cultural history of memory cannot do without referencing a range of literary, sociological and other disciplinary approaches to memory.

Apart from its characteristic transdisciplinarity, which had a major impact on memory history, however, the latter also remained, for quite some time, tied to the national container that, as we have already discussed, had been so strongly established in the historical sciences in the century roughly between 1850 and 1950. The move of memory history to *transnational* forms of memory has only been a relatively recent development, following a general trend in historical studies to criticize "methodological nationalism" and move to more transnational forms of historical writing, emphasizing interlinkages, adaptations, and transfers. However, as a perusal of any of the hugely successful conferences of the Memory Studies Association will show, most scholars today still focus on national memory.[1] Transnational, let alone global memory is not practiced very widely,[2] which also reflects a major difficulty for a cultural history of memory; there are simply not enough scholars who can truly synthesize vast amounts of work on a particular theme in a global perspective. Here we can only trust that our failure will be an inspiration to future generations of scholars to move to more global perspectives on memory history.

Where our six volumes have hopefully been more successful has been in moving histories of memory away from their fixation with trauma, especially national trauma. The huge body of work on the memory of genocides, in particular the Holocaust, and the equally massive amount of work on the memory of wars, especially the two world wars, but also the Vietnam war and a range of civil wars, is an indicator of to what extent memory scholars have homed in on traumatic events in the past. Undoubtedly, much of this work has been incredibly valuable and inspirational, but the six volumes that we introduce here, whilst not ignoring genocides and war, also intend to highlight a range of other areas in which memory history can be usefully applied.

If *A Cultural History of Memory* tries to escape memory history's bias toward "methodological nationalism" and toward traumatic events in the past, it also deliberately—and structurally—seeks to introduce a longer-term perspective and to show how memory history is a relevant and intriguing exercise for older periods of time. Once again, looking from a bird's eye perspective over the field of memory history, we see a massive concentration of work in the modern period, basically from the late eighteenth century to the present day. But the first four of our six volumes underline to what an extent the history of memory benefits from considering older time periods. As general editors, we particularly hope that modernists (of whom we are culpable examples) may delve into the writings on pre-modern times, as it will reveal not only substantial differences, but also, and certainly more striking to us, amazing similarities when considering the role of memory for cultural sense-production.

A CULTURAL HISTORY

Finally, what of the definite article "A" Cultural History of Memory. In the first place, across a work as extensive as this one (or these ones), it is obvious that there are many different approaches to the subject matters. Though all contributing to this cultural history, the authors come from numerous different disciplines and specialties, have different foci, bring to bear different interests and expertise even within this "one" work. We do so, moreover, from numerous different countries, languages of origin, and periods of study, though the list, however extensive, is still limited in significant ways. In the second place, however, much as the publishers did not lay a heavy hand on the forms of cultural history to be employed, they did determine that all the volumes should have the same structure. Hence, we came up with eight themes that had to be the same across all six volumes. In choosing broad themes—power and politics, media and technology, knowledge: science and education, time and space, ideas: philosophy, religion, and history, high and popular culture, the social: rituals, practices, and the everyday, and remembering and forgetting—we sought to give the volume editors the space to adapt those themes to the particular foci appropriate to different times and geographies. As any reader of the six volumes will realize, the editors made good use of that leeway, but this also leads to the phenomenon that different authors have put the emphasis of their respective chapters differently and usually in line with their own specialisms.

The publisher also dictated the epochal labels we employed, and they determined that the eight topics addressed in each chronologically constituted volume should be nominally the same as the topics in the other volumes. Much as we appreciated the reasons for this—for instance, so that a particular theme could be followed across the epochs, or that someone interested in a particular epoch could recombine the history of memory we have produced for that epoch with the history of something else addressed in other entries in the series—this constraint did raise concerns for us and our colleagues. For instance, no single chronology labeling applies uniformly for different areas of the world (e.g. not every society or culture identifies the same antiquity, or an antiquity at all). And the present chronology is a very Western one indeed. Moreover, the application of these labels can be anachronistic. After all, the people whose forms of memory we are studying in a particular age did not understand themselves as having that particular place in history (e.g. the people in the antiquity we have studied did not think of themselves as inhabiting an ancient world). Finally, had we not understood the imperative of recombination of themes and periods, the editors of each epochally-defined volume might have wanted to label the eight chapters differently from the editors of the other volumes, since the same relevances did not necessarily obtain in the same ways in different periods.

Nevertheless, much as the ground we have collectively covered here is vast indeed, we might still hope—if not for other, at least for additional work in this vibrant field on this fascinating subject. We hope that, despite the additional works that might be possible—and that we hope will be produced—what we have to offer here will be of use to as many as possible. The field of memory studies is a relatively new one. But the sophistication of the chapters (and volume introductions) we have the pleasure of presenting here shows that much as the field has a long way to go, it is well on its way.

Introduction

STEFAN BERGER AND BILL NIVEN

THE DEVELOPMENT OF MEMORY STUDIES IN THE TWENTIETH CENTURY

A cultural history of memory in the twentieth century is at first the history of an intense psychological interest in memory. Hermann Ebbinghaus, working at the end of the nineteenth century, is known for his experimental research into the capacity of memory to retain information, but also into the rate at which it forgets (learning and forgetting curve) (Ebbinghaus 1885). On the eve of the First World War, Sigmund Freud, the father of modern psychology, published an essay on "remembering, repeating and working through" in which he focused on psychotherapeutic methods to help patients access and process repressed memories (Freud 2018). Ebbinghaus and Freud were interested in memory at an individual level, its functionality, its limits, and its susceptibility to a range of psychological pressures. So, too, was Carl Jung, but rather than understand the unconscious mind purely in terms of suppressed memories, Jung argued that we need to distinguish between the "personal unconscious" and the "collective unconscious." The contents of the latter, he believed, were not individually acquired, but inherited; they took the form of universal and archaic archetypes, or, in the words of Lucien Lévy-Bruhl, "collective representations" (Jung 1936: 55; see also Lévy-Bruhl 1910). Some have linked Jung's ideas to the ideas of Plato, such as anamnesis, or the writings of Darwin, with Jung's notion of the collective unconscious demonstrating that natural selection existed in the mind as well as the body (Lawson 2008). Others have connected them to the catastrophic *völkisch* and racist ideas of Nazism (Dohe 2016). More modern notions of genetic memory can also be traced back to Jung (Bullock and Stallybrass 1977: 258). Wherever one places Jung's ideas, without doubt his conceptualization of consciousness as having a collective as well as an individual dimension chimes with the arguments which sociologists were advancing around the same time.

It was, perhaps, ultimately the work of sociologists that were to prove most central to the way we have come to understand memory. Karl Mannheim's theory of generations from 1928 posited that people are fundamentally shaped by their immediate sociohistorical environment; shared experience, and therefore shared memories, are the basis for the formation of social cohorts and a key factor in behavioral motivation (for the English translation, see Mannheim 1952). A few years earlier, in 1925, Maurice Halbwachs laid the foundations for cultural memory studies when he suggested there existed a "mémoire collective," a collective memory which was, essentially, socially constructed. But there is more than one such memory: as Lewis A. Coser, the editor and translator of Halbwachs' work puts it, "there are as many collective memories as there are groups and institutions in a society" (Lewis 1992). Unlike Jung, Mannheim and Halbwachs placed the emphasis not on a quasi-mythical phylogenetic inheritance, but on the determining influence of the environments into which individuals were born and within which they

FIGURE 0.1: Carl Gustav Jung. Credit: Wikimedia Commons (Public Domain).

were subsequently socialized. If Halbwachs often had in mind more the established traditions and values of, say, the family, or social classes, Mannheim seemed interested more in the influence of contemporary events and the immediate political environment. When memory studies emerged forcefully on the scene in the 1980s and 1990s, it was Halbwachs' idea of "collective memory" that caught the imagination of most scholars. The idea of a suprapersonal memory of which all individuals partake may seem counterintuitive, but that twentieth century developments could be understood in terms of the generation of such group memories, usually often in the interests of nationalism, was an interpretation that found support in Halbwachs' ideas.

In the interwar period, the intense interest in memory did not just comprise the disciplines of psychology and sociology, but it also extended to history. Here, in particular the Annales school, by focusing on the history of mentalities, highlighted not just the importance of collective representations, symbols, and myths, but also the importance of memory (Confino 2010: 79–84). Art historian and cultural theorist Aby Warburg also developed a theory of collective memory that was rooted in proper attention to culture, socialization, and customs (Assmann 1995). If memory studies had their intellectual origins in the interwar period, they were all but forgotten again after the end of the Second World War and had to be practically rediscovered by French historian Pierre

Nora, himself a member of the third generation of the Annales school, in the 1980s. The context of their rediscovery points to the proximity of group memories and questions of national identity, for Nora came back to the question of French national collective memory in the context of a deep crisis of the republican consensus on national identity during the 1980s (Jackson 1999). Nora's (1984–92) seven volumes on the "realms of memory" in France were an attempt to stabilize and give meaning, in other words, bolster a canon of French national history and identity. What Nora did not foresee and what, in fact, he spent some time fighting by insisting that his project was one that could not be replicated outside of France, was the huge success that his concept of the "realms of memory" would have not only with regard to other national histories, but also with regard to other spatial and non-spatial entities. Thus, we have by now not only innumerable "realms of memory" on specific cities and regions, but also on transnational entities, such as empires, the European Union, or larger history regions, such as the Iberian peninsula, Scandinavia, or the Balkans. And furthermore, we have realms of memory that relate to religion, class, labor and other social movements such as the women's movement. Political parties and trade unions are exploring their "realms of memory" and there seems no end in sight to the memory boom that has gripped not only the academic world but also larger publics since the 1980s (for a review of the concept of "realms of memory" as one of the most important key concepts in cultural studies, see Berger and Seiffert 2014).

FIGURE 0.2: Maurice Halbwachs. Credit: Wikimedia Commons (Public Domain).

Indeed, over recent years, memory studies has become one of the fastest growing and most popular fields of studies in the humanities and social sciences. The Memory Studies Association, founded only in 2016, has already gathered thousands of scholars from across the globe indicating not only a vast geographical spread but also an impressive disciplinary breadth (MSA 2019). Sociologists and psychologists are still prominent among its ranks and they have been joined by historians, literary scholars, political scientists, art historians, archaeologists, anthropologists, and many other disciplines who have all turned to memory over recent years. Leading theorists of memory have emerged, including Jan and Aleida Assmann, Jeffrey K. Olick, Marianne Hirsch, Astrid Erll, Wulf Kansteiner, Ann Rigney, Michael Rothberg, Jay Winter, and many others who have all added important concepts and theoretical insights on the workings of memory (Pethes 2019; Berger and Niven 2014; Rossington and Whitehead 2007).

The massive turn to memory in the last two decades of the twentieth century cannot simply be explained with Nora's success and the crisis of French national memory—of major importance was also a key shift in time regimes in the 1980s. The modern time regime until then was oriented toward the future and operated with notions of progress and progressive time. Yet by the 1980s, the future seemed more and more problematic. Looking increasingly bleak, it ceased to be the resource for hope for something better (Hartog 2015; Lorenz 2019). Hence, the past became more attractive as an anchor point for the search for meaning which also explains the explosion of interest in memory. Furthermore, the rise of oral history that coincided with the rise of memory history also played an important role in making subjectitivites and their views on the past attractive as an object of study (Thompson 2000). Last but not least the rise of interest in narrativity and narration inspired scholarship to ask about how scholars

FIGURE 0.3: Aleida and Jan Assmann on receipt of the Peace Prize of the German Book Trade in 2018. Credit: Wikimedia Commons (Public Domain).

had constructed the past which in turn led straight to questions of memory (Hutton 1997).

The most prominent public debates in memory studies have, for a long time, been national debates. This has had a lot to do with the strength of nationalism producing a multitude of traumatic memories within many nations around the globe (Berger and Storm 2019). One might think of nationalism as a nineteenth-century development, but the First World War can be understood as its global explosion, while the emergence of new states after 1918, and the injuries nursed by old ones, led to a proliferation of nationalist causes that played no small part in developments leading to and during the Second World War. Nations found justifications for their politics by streamlining or rewriting history so that it appeared to corroborate contemporary positions (Berger with Conrad 2015). To take one key and obvious example: Nazi Germany's destructive antisemitism and territorial aggression were underpinned by the constant telling and retelling of a historical narrative in which Jews—in various guises—were portrayed as the long-standing enemies of Germans (Confino 2014). Tendentious, or quite false versions of history could be called upon to bolster ethnic solidarity and antagonisms towards supposed internal and external enemies—nationalism's perennial target. Ideas about memory's collective character evolved in nationalism's shadow, and in the wake of mass political movements and industrialization. Far from ending in 1945, nationalism merely remodeled itself. The history of postwar Europe is a history of nations—regardless of whether they had experienced occupation, defeat or victory—striving to reconstruct themselves on the basis of a refound solidarity. This was achieved by remembering the Second World War as a time of national sacrifice, victimhood, anti-Nazi resistance, the clandestine support of persecuted Jews, and unity of purpose (Bauerkämper 2012). Perpetration, collaboration, territorial greed, antisemitism, and internecine conflicts between nationalist factions (for instance in Poland and Ukraine) were written out of the picture or played down. Memory politics played a particularly strong role in the Soviet Union, where the Red Army's campaign against Hitler was framed as the "Great Patriotic War" (Zhurzhenko 2015). Such a celebratory reading was designed to rally the Union's diverse ethnicities and regions behind the Soviet leaders, and to crush alternative understandings of the role of the Red Army—regarded in the Baltic states, for instance, as a savage occupation force.

The collapse of the Soviet Union ushered in another nationalist phase in European history as countries released from the grip of Soviet communism—whether in the form of independence or true self-determination—set about rewriting their histories to emphasize decades of victimhood at the hands of both the Soviets and the Nazis (Iordachi and Apor 2019). Such twentieth century national memory trends bear out the idea of collective memory as something forged, or constantly being forged and reformed, in the interests of contemporary national politics. But scholars do not always subscribe to this "presentist" view, at least not in all respects. In an important study, Anthony D. Smith outlined the various theories that have been offered to explain the history of nations. Smith (1999: 3–28) distinguishes between primordialism (the belief that nations exist as elements of nature), perennialism (the view that nations have existed throughout recorded history, but not as part of the natural order), modernism/post-modernism (according to which nations are communities constructed in the name of homogeneity), and his own theory of historical ethno-symbolism. For Smith, nationalism's power resides in the myths, memories, traditions, and symbols of ethnic heritage and the ways in which the popular living past can be rediscovered and reinterpreted—an idea which recalls the ideas of Jung.

Accepting for a moment then that there can be a collective memory, is it really simply something that is fashioned and refashioned as the state wills? Or is there, conversely, for each nation a historically established set of collective self-understandings which shape reactions in the present? The truth might be somewhere in between. Zionism was informed by a biblical narrative which had played a key part in Jewish religion, thinking, and ritual for centuries. It is a narrative that can be found particularly in the first books of the Hebrew Bible, about Jewish liberation from slavery, a Mosaic covenant, and a return to a promised land. But when this "memory" was invoked by Zionists (around the turn of the nineteenth century and with increasing intensity thereafter), it was shaped to support and legitimize a very contemporary secular political and colonial vision (Zerubavel 1995).

While the relationship, then, between collective and national memory is essential to any understanding of the twentieth century—and twentieth century "memoriography"—that relationship is complex. Quite in keeping with Halbwachs' idea that there are as many memories as there are collectives, scholars have pointed out that official state memory cannot simply be equated with memory on the ground. In this respect, John Bodnar (1992), in a study of memory in America, distinguished between official and vernacular memory. Rather than merely explore official memory, scholars have come to "investigate intangible memory practices, vernacular traditions of collective memory, and popular culture as a means to preserve memory" (Marschall 2013: 79), as well as the dynamics influencing the interaction between different group memories, generational memories and state memory (Erll 2005). Yet there was always a risk that presupposing the existence or desired existence of national collective memories might itself play a part in trying to inspire or sustain these. The dividing line between analytical description and prescriptive projection was a thin one.

THEMES AND AGENDAS OF MEMORY HISTORY IN THE TWENTIETH CENTURY

This volume, like all others in the series, considers the study of memory from the optic of power and politics, time and space, media and technology, knowledge, ideas, culture, the social, and the tension between memory and forgetting. One major theme, as implicit in our discussion above, is the relationship between the nation and memory. While the nation emerged strongly in the nineteenth century, it reached its zenith in the twentieth as the motor of modernity, only to come under increasing pressure from processes of globalization. Contributors explore the power of the nation as a framework for the operation of collective memory, but in line with recent memory theory they also warn against the pitfalls of what has been termed "methodological nationalism" which risks subsuming society under the rubric of the nation-state (Beck 2007). Contrasting his views with those of George Mosse (1975), for instance, Jay Winter argues that we should be cautious of seeing memory as always state-driven: twentieth century commemoration demonstrates the refusal of the "voices and memories of the many" to be orchestrated or homogenized (see Winter's article in this volume). In the end, commemoration is a dialectic between state and civil society (Wüstenberg 2017). Chris Lorenz makes us aware that Nora's "realms" or "sites" of memory project actually reflects the loss of a connection between society and national history, such that one needs to be generated: one could almost argue that the sites of memory are a last-ditch attempt to shore up national history against forgetting. Lorenz also points to the increasing trend towards memory "multiscalarity": memory is no longer contained by the nation-state. Rather it is constantly "on the move" (Erll 2011a), more and more "cosmopolitan" (Levy 2002) or "multidirectional" (Rothberg 2009), a fluid process whereby transnational memory flows interact with national, regional and local memory patterns ("glocalization") (Roudometof 2016). In his chapter, Stefan Berger makes clear in his analysis of the memory activism of historians that they have not only provided historical interpretations which help to support state memory—as in the case of foundational narratives around revolutions—but also written studies which challenge such memory. More globally, the work of the historical sciences have both fed into processes of decolonization, or served to resist them and justify Western imperialism. Through all this, the nation nevertheless serves as a focal point for memory studies: either as an example of Halbwachs' collective memory writ large, of the top-down shaping or bottom-up contestation of images of the past, or as the site of an increasingly porous memory container as memory "spills" from one nation to another under the pressure, for instance, of large-scale migration.

Another topos addressed in several of the chapters in this volume is the Holocaust. It would be hard in fact to imagine a cultural history of twentieth century memory which did not accord the Holocaust a central place in that history. As modernity grew increasingly conscious of its risks and deficits, remembering the Holocaust became the focal point of an intense, cautionary and well-orchestrated memorialization. Several contributors identify Marvin J. Chomsky's TV series *Holocaust* (1978) as a key milestone in the development towards Holocaust commemoration. Jay Winter reminds us in his contribution that half the adult population of West Germany watched it, galvanizing civil society and, ultimately, politicians into addressing injustices associated with the Holocaust. The influence of culture, then, on memory cannot be underestimated. Both Wulf Kansteiner and Patrick Finney show in their discussions of film and television how important *Holocaust* was. For Kansteiner, it helped to usher in what he terms the "cultural externalization" of memory in the form of memorials, museums and film, as well as the turn towards victim-centered memory and the shift in the direction of cosmopolitan memory: as Daniel Levy and Natan Sznaider have argued in an important study, memory of suffering in the Holocaust has in recent decades been instrumental in informing transnational commitment to the protection of human rights (Levy and Sznaider 2004). The result has been a shifting away from the heroic memory long typical of national takes on the Second World War. In his contribution, Bill Niven situates his discussion of the Holocaust within wider patterns of remembering and forgetting in the twentieth century. The prevalence of Holocaust memory today alongside continuing genocide and ethnic cleansing has prompted some to ask how effective cosmopolitan memory is (Rieff 2016a). While all agree the Holocaust must be remembered, in recent years scholars have begun to give consideration to the healing quality of forgetting. The importance of memory should not necessarily lead to a stigmatization of forgetting, as if it were in itself a vice. Recent theories around agonistic memory (see below) also point to the failure of cosmopolitan memory to resist the challenge of antagonistic memories, particularly at a national level (Bull and Hansen 2015).

One key question which emerges in several of the chapters in this book is periodization: how should we conceive of patterns in memory over the course of the twentieth century? For Winter, the shifting dialectical relationship between state and civil society memory actors can be imagined in terms of three separate periods: the first surrounded the two world wars, the second the wars of decolonization, and the third—ongoing—began roughly in 1980 (with the onset of Holocaust memory). Lorenz, focusing more on ideas around memory itself, divides the century into a "foundational period" (identified with the work of Halbwachs), a "memory boom" phase (identified with Nora) and a present-day period of transnational and transcultural memory. These he sets in relation to ideas around the evolution of time: are we stuck in traumatic, non-progressive, non-linear time, always looking back at the past? Is the present characterized by an insatiable thirst for memory (Hartog 2015)? Does "the past" exist, any more than the future, other than as a construction of the present (Assmann 2013)? Stefan Berger, in looking at the influence of historians as memory agents, identifies six broad themes around which this influence has particularly crystallized in the twentieth century: the two world wars, the history of civil wars, the history of revolutions, the histories of decolonization and of de-industrialization. Several contributions make clear that significant changes in memorial cultures occur when there are fundamental shifts in political systems—witness the impact of the end of the Cold War—although contributors are equally aware that such changes are themselves prepared and anticipated by civil actors or culture.

The development of memory over the course of the twentieth century raises questions, too, about its relationship to history. Jeff Olick in his survey of social and collective memory draws our attention to the fact that many of the forces which shaped collective memory—the family, religion, institutions—are gradually losing their binding force in an increasingly fragmenting modernity. It was Nora's idea that the loss of memory as an organic connection to these forces had led to its affiliation instead to history—yet as Olick writes, while the modern world may have become a world of history, this history is itself a form of "dead memory" to which we also have no organic connection. It is cultural memory, the transmission of images of and ideas about history, sometimes in iconic form, which persuades us that we do. In this situation, historians have become even more important, not less so, as Stefan Berger's contribution makes clear. Then again, as Wulf Kansteiner argues, there has been a certain parting of ways between professional academic history and popular culture in the twentieth century. For Kansteiner, and also Patrick Finney, visual culture has become a particularly powerful vector of memory and of the transmission in particular of visions of a shared past—an idealization from which professional historians may often feel the need to distance themselves.

As with all volumes in the current series, the present volume has a broad geographical scope, covering several continents. Many developments in memory across the globe are connected by the fact that political, social, and cultural forces in the twentieth century have been and remain global in reach. One might think of nationalism, for instance, in terms of a purely national framework, but if, as in the twentieth century, many nations are defining their identities in national terms, then they are doing so in demarcating relation to other nations, and often following similar dynamics. National memorialization in one country mirrors that in another. Throughout the current volume, the reader will identify patterns in the national commemorative narratives used to "shore up political projects," as Jay Winter puts it when discussing Saddam Hussein's attempt to fabricate a direct lineage between his rule and ancient Babylon. Global developments which fundamentally impacted on memory in the twentieth century include the two world wars, the end of empires, decolonization, and the Cold War. In his chapter, for instance, Stefan Berger explores the connections between wider histories of decolonization and memory cultures in Britain, Germany, Algeria, and India, and for Jay Winter wars of decolonization (in China, Korea, India, and Palestine, for example) played a key role in twentieth century collective memory. The impact of the Cold War on memory around the world, or of the end of the Cold War, is reflected upon in the chapters by, among others, Bill Niven (South Korea, Estonia), Stefan Berger (Indonesia), and Patrick Finney (the USA). Another, particularly tragic global trend in the twentieth century was genocide in its various forms and with its various motives. Memory of the Holocaust features throughout this volume, as does memory of violence and mass killing elsewhere such as in Rwanda and Cambodia (Bill Niven, Wulf Kansteiner, Chris Lorenz), or Indonesia and Spain (Stefan Berger). Last but not least, the volume also includes a discussion of the relationship between global threats such as climate change or pollution, and memory. Wulf Kansteiner writes of "catastrophes of the anthropocene requiring a new type of anticipatory memory culture."

While most chapters in the current volume consider memory at the social and collective level (see particularly Jeff Olick), Nick Tosh provides us with a discussion of memory science in the twentieth century which illuminates theories of individual memory, from the ideas of philosopher Hermann Ebbinghaus (Ebbinghaus 1885), through to those of Eric Kandel (Kandel 2006). Tosh shows how the development of computing technology went hand in hand with discussions and theoretical reflections around the relationship between the workings of human memory and the functioning of computers: thus for John von Neumann, the nervous system was essentially digital, and he also believed that there existed in the brain a memory system separate from the neuron network, in analogy to computers (Neumann 1958). Even if this idea has not worn well, computer technology has proven and does prove vital for memory research, as well as providing a rich source of analogies. Other contributors also discuss key links between technology, media, and memory. Patrick Finney, for example, as well as Wulf Kansteiner and Jay Winter discuss the importance of television, or cinema, for the transmission of cultural memory. Kansteiner also investigates the significance of video games and social media, with their "immediacy, mobility, flexibility and interactivity" (Hoskins 2014: 55). Thanks to virtual reality, we can now conjure up images of pasts near and far, and offer users both a high level of immersion in these pasts and, through gaming technology, the chance to participate in them and even influence them. It remains to be seen what effect this will have on the way we remember.

Eight chapters dealing with specific themes in memory studies can obviously not cover the entire cultural history of memory in the twentieth century. Hence, it was always going to be inevitable that there would be gaps in this attempt to provide a broad overview. Despite the fact that authors have made an attempt to deal with non-Western forms of memory history, there still is a considerable bias toward Western concerns and memorial practices reflecting the fact that all of the contributors are ultimately specialists in Western memory history. They have tried to expand their remit to include other parts of the world, but here still lies a challenge of twentieth-century memory history—to decenter Western forms of memory and ask about the functioning of non-Western forms of memory. Thus, for example, Latin America has witnessed the mobilization of memory in relation to political violence, dictatorships, and the disappearance of oppositional voices, but also in relation to poverty, drugs, and social conflict (Allier-Montaño and Crenzel 2016; Villalón, 2017). Violence has often caught the attention of those dealing with memory in other parts of the non-Western world, such as Africa and the Middle East (Makdisi and Silverstein 2006). In black Africa, memories of constructions of modernity by the colonizing west need to be deconstructed in order to overcome the West's denial of Africanness as modern and to allow Africa to begin to shape its own destiny free from the conceptual shackles of centuries of colonialism often perpetuated by postcolonial states following their independence (Diawara, Lategan, and Rüsen 2010).

In the Far East, in China, Japan, and the Koreas, memories of the Second World War, of imperialism and communism loom large over historical consciousness and have been the center of attention in cultural histories of memory (Matten 2012). The strength of postcolonial histories of the Indian subcontinent has led to an abundance of studies on the memory of colonialism and its impact on the postcolonial states (Rhashkow, Ghosh, and Chakrabarty 2018). However, the histories of communism and of communalism, including communalist violence, the trauma of partitioning and the story of the many ethnic minorities within the Indian sub-continent have also all produced rich streams of work on memory (Saikia 2004).

Apart from the ongoing Western centrism of this volume, it also lacks proper engagement with a number of themes that would merit greater attention. Let us just pick out three that could have been dealt with more extensively. First, there is the memory of migration. When Pierre Nora published his "realms of memory" in France, Gérard Noiriel, the French historian of migration in France, argued powerfully that the memory of migrants in France were generally excluded from national memory (Noiriel 1996). And this has been true not only for France. Given the strength of national memory cultures throughout the twentieth century, memories of migration tended to be sidelined, as it often meant that something different and foreign was coming into a national culture often constructed as homogeneous and unitary (Glynn and Kleist 2012). Studies, first championed in the context of Franco-German studies, that highlighted the importance of transfers for the constitution of constructed national cultures helped pave the way for greater attention to the importance of migratory processes in the construction of national realms of memory (Werner and Zimmermann 2006). Migration always involved a sharing and fusion of cultures, although migrants often also sought to retain elements of what they regarded as their own culture against attempts to assimilate and eradicate. Various degrees of multi-cultural memory thus accompanied processes of migration and stood next to the assimilation of migratory memories into national ones. Memories were often crucial to retaining the migrants' identities who were, after all, frequently threatened with a deep loss of memory after arriving on alien shores. Living in new countries and retaining memories of the old often meant the establishing of hybrid forms of identity among migratory groups. Nostalgic ideas of a lost homeland stood next to the emergence of transcultural memories that incorporated also those who encountered migrants (Welsch 1999).

Secondly, and very much related to the memory of migration is the memory of ethnicity, in particular ethnic minorities. Since the 2000s, studies in public memory, race, and ethnicity have been proliferating in many parts of the world (Reyes 2010). Like memories of migration, memories of ethnic groups are often denying and contradicting constructions of national homogeneity. In many Western societies studies of race often highlighted how dominant cultural memories were inflected with constructions of whiteness that excluded all non-white memorial cultures. In the US, "black critical memory" aims precisely to undermine such dominant whiteness in memorial cultures (Baker Jr. 2001). In Jewish memory, memories of the diaspora loom large over representations of Jewishness in different parts of the world. Often linked to the memory of the Holocaust, Jewish museums have been proliferating in recent decades in many parts of the globe, whilst interestingly in Israel itself the diasporic memory has also been a crucial part of Israeli state-building, with the Palestinian-Arab memory struggling to be heard in Israel (Semi, Miccoli, and Parfitt 2013). In Africa, memories of different ethnicities played a huge role in conflicts surrounding state-building. Thus, for example, in Nigeria an ethnicized state has been struggling with containing multiple social and national conflicts that are often associated with and

FIGURE 0.4: Pierre Nora. Credit: Wikimedia Commons (Public Domain).

influenced by ethnic memories (Anugwom 2019). The Communist Soviet Union was based on the idea of interethnic voluntary association of different peoples. The Soviet state, whilst being at the very least ambiguous about the superiority of Russian culture within the Union, fostered ethnic cultures in those regions outside of Russia proper, the Ukraine and Byelorussia (where Russian culture dominated). Here, Soviet political leaders coming from non-Russian ethnic groups often formed a strong relationship with cultural elites foregrounding their respective non-Russian ethnic cultures—something that contributed to no small extent to the collapse of the Soviet Union after the fall of communism. Vernacular memory cultures rooted strongly in non-Russian civil society associations played a major role in establishing national cultures hostile to any notion of a union of republics under Russian tutelage. In Georgia, for example, a rich memorial counter-culture dating back deep into the Soviet period, played a major role in the conflict between Georgia and Russia in the post-Soviet era (Jones 1994).

Thirdly, there is the memory of ideological conflict in the twentieth century. If the key ideologies of the nineteenth century had been liberalism and socialism, the ideological forces that shaped the twentieth century were communism and fascism. All four ideologies were based on a strong vision of the future and a clear idea of historical developments. All four produced strong memory cultures around particular events and social movements. Thus, liberalism celebrated key constitutional movements and the constitutionalization of politics more generally as well as liberal revolutionary moments, such as 1848 in Europe (see volume 5 in this series). Socialism came in different variants, but one of the most important, the Marxist one, certainly had a clear idea about historical development moving in the direction of the ultimate victory of the idea of the classless society. And socialists, on May 1 and other occasions commemorated key struggles, such as the Paris Commune, the fight against anti-Socialist forces, and the martyrdom of those who fell for the "just cause" of the revolutionary future (Bos 2014). Communism in many ways carried the mantle of this nineteenth-century socialist tradition into the twentieth century. The commemoration of the 1917 revolution in Russia became the key memorial event in the global Communist movement of the twentieth century (Messenger 2020). It was the birthplace of a brighter future for all believers. In the Cold War world of the second half of the twentieth century, memories of communism still inspired many anti-colonial movements in Asia and Africa at a time when communism in the West, at least in those countries where it reigned, had already lost much of its luster (Featherstone 2017). In fact, already in the interwar period communism had produced a violent response to its liberationist agenda in the form of fascism. Its memories were based around nationalist mobilizing moments in the past which served as reminder of the need to raise the nation to new heights in the future (Zamponi 2003). Its hyper-nationalism and its racism (especially in the case of National Socialism) was producing destructive utopias that left much of Europe in ruins in 1945 and produced in the murder of European Jewry one of the paradigmatic memory events of the twentieth century. Whilst the latter is being dealt with extensively in the subsequent pages of this volume, the memory of the key ideologies of the twentieth century could have been explored in greater depth. These are just three examples of fields that are underexplored in what follows, and we are sure that other readers will find more gaps. They are, we would argue, inevitable in a short volume dealing with a century so rich in memory cultures in different parts of the world.

POSSIBLE DIRECTIONS FOR MEMORY STUDIES IN THE TWENTY-FIRST CENTURY

After reviewing the development of memory studies in the twentieth century and trying to point out some of the red lines that connect the contributions in this current volume as well as highlighting some of the gaps and desiderata that are still left, we want to end these introductory notes by highlighting some of the directions which seem to us to be particularly promising in the twenty-first century. First, we would like to underline the importance of progressing the agenda of studying "transnational memory"—ending the obsession with national memory that we identified as being so characteristic for the twentieth century. The predominance of national memory in the twentieth century, including studies on national memory has had much to do with the existence of nationalized public spheres and the absence of transnational public spheres. Even in a space like that of the European Union, no serious integration of public spheres has taken place, so that a space that is in many respects transnationally regulated is still carrying out its public debates in largely nationalized spheres (Walter 2017). Yet within the strongly transnationalized sphere of academia there has been, for some time now, a trend to examine transnational forms of memory, for example with regard to Holocaust memory but also with regard to memory laws and the memory of Communist dictatorships (de Cesari and Rigney 2014). The recognition that most events that generated memory discourses were events that affected more than one nation was vital in fostering analyses that looked at how those memory discourses were nationalized but could rarely be restricted to national containers but instead interacted with other nationalized memory cultures around the same event.

The memory cultures and memory wars surrounding the First World War are a good example of the entangled natures of national memories (Winter 1995). Other examples include the memory cultures around the Second World War, the Holocaust, other genocides, and forms of collective violence against ethnic groups or classes. Of course, transnational memory studies presuppose that memory scholars are familiar with more than one national context and often also with more than one language. The internationalization of academic disciplines has made this possible to a considerable extent, so that we now have the opportunity of making a step change in memory studies—away from national memory and toward pointing out to what extent the very idea of national memory has always been a fiction as it was constructed through processes of adaptation, translation, and borrowing, as memory discourses traveled from particular spaces to others over time.

Secondly, we would like to underline the importance of progressing the agenda of moving beyond the memory of war and genocide that has been so dominant in twentieth-century memory studies. In particular, the strong ties between memory and trauma need to be problematized further (Alexander 2004; Kansteiner 2004a; Edkins 2003), although a growing attention to trauma is noted in a recent survey (see Darian-Smith and Hamilton 2013: 375; and Hamilton 1994: 16).

There is no automatic relationship between traumatic memory and the silencing of the past. After all, many traumatized people cannot stop talking about the events that have been traumatic for them, whilst, indeed, some retreat into silence. Undoubtedly, however, traumatic events, or what Anne Fuchs (2011) has called "impact events" and Dipesh Chakrabarty (2007) has described in terms of "historical wounds" generated vivid memories and in many cases, from the last third of the twentieth century onwards, led to a "politics of regret," in Jeff Olick's (2007) memorable phrase. Traumatic histories become haunting memories, in which the past does not "cool off" but retains a present that calls into question the common-sense notion that history over time turns into memory. Instead, past, present and future as well as memory and history move closer together (Lorenz 2004; Ricoeur 2004).

Whilst we have had an abundance of research on the most traumatic events in the twentieth century, the two world wars, the ethnic cleansings and genocides as well as the Stalinist crimes, including the Gulag, it may be time to explore historical memory in its more everyday connotations. Memory studies can forge important links to a wide variety of other subject areas that have not yet discovered the importance of memory to their themes.

If we take the example of social movement studies, we can observe that it only turned to memory studies relatively recently (Kubal and Becerra 2014: 865; Harris 2006: 19). Notions of "memory activism" (Gluck 2007: 57; Wüstenberg 2017; Gutman 2017) and of "heroes of memory" (Etkind 2013: 172–96) have been introduced quite recently to show how social movements have used memory to foster their particular aims and ambitions.

The cultural turn in social movement studies has undoubtedly contributed to the discovery of the role of memory in the framing of diverse social movements and collective identity, e.g. in relation to the global 1968 movement (Neveu 2014: 277, 295). Nicole Doerr (2014) has asked how social movement activists have constructed collective memories in order to further their activism in wider society and build strong internal collective identities. Priska Daphi has been leading a research project on protest and memory, focusing on the long 1960s in West and East Germany (Merrill, Keightley, and Daphi, forthcoming). Lorenzo Zamponi (2019) has been looking at the role of memory in the construction of media narratives of Spanish and Italian student movements. Priska

Daphi and Lorenzo Zamponi are also currently preparing a special issue of *Mobilization* on the topic of social movements and memory. Donatella della Porta and her collaborators (2018) have looked at the impact of memory on forms of democracy in contemporary southern Europe. These are just some of the examples of how social movement studies has recently turned to memory studies.

And the reverse is true as well—memory studies have been turning to social movement studies. Thus, for example, historians of memory have contributed to the study of the memory of 1968 (Gildea, Mark, and Warring: 2017; Cornils and Waters 2010), and they have looked at the importance of memorializing the civil rights movement in the US (Romano and Raiford: 2006). The study of terrorism in Italy has also been enriched by perspectives from memory studies (Hajek 2013). One of the most canonical works in the field of memory studies unpacks the various ways in which the death of an Italian Communist has been remembered (Portelli 1991). In the future an even stronger focus on social movements and their constructions of the past would arguably contribute further to a better understanding of the political "dynamics of cultural memories" (Erll and Rigney 2009). If we take, for example, the role of social movements in the production of heritage, a rich field for further examination opens up. As memory activism in the form of industrial-heritage movements becomes institutionalized, memory often becomes part of branding campaigns for place identities, touristified and commodified for profit motifs (Wicke, Berger, and Golombek 2018). The touristification of the past, memory activists have argued, may also involve the banalization of remembrance, as for instance the site of

FIGURE 0.5: Berlin's Memorial to the Murdered Jews of Europe. Credit: Wikimedia Commons (Public Domain).

the Berlin Holocaust memorial illustrates, where visitors have frequently behaved disrespectfully. The artist Shahak Shapira recently—and controversially—produced an online artwork juxtaposing the cheerful selfies of visitors to the memorial with disturbing images of Nazi atrocities (Gunter 2017).

If social movements are conscious of their own role in the political process, and if their representatives are highly articulate, they are far more likely to leave memory work that in turn can influence and has to be deconstructed by historians. As Richard Vinen has pointed out in relation to 1968, activists dominate the memory literature on 1968 and they are not shy about securing their special place in history. Vinen has shown that "the leading figures in 68 often had a highly developed sense of themselves as historical actors and as people who would one day be the object of historical research" (2018: 7). This was reinforced by 1968ers subsequently working as historians seeing "politics and historical research as intertwined" (2018: 7). This affected the way we think of 1968. By contrast, Vinen points out, working-class protest in and around 1968 is rarely present through ego-documents of workers: "Students in 68 are portrayed in words, frequently their own words, but workers are often remembered in pictures" (2018: 11). There are currently a range of other projects under way which will bring the history of memory much closer to the history of social movements (Rigney 2018a; Berger, Scalmer, and Wicke 2020). These include the editors and contributors to a handbook on memory activism that is currently being prepared by Yifat Gutman and Jenny Wüstenberg. Of note here also is the European Research Council senior project headed by Ann Rigney who also looks at the interrelationship of social movements and memory (University of Utrecht 2018). And the history of social movements has only served here as an example of how fruitful it is to move beyond the traditional focus on war, genocide, and ethnic conflict to incorporate other fields and subjects in which memory has played a crucial role.

Thirdly, we would like to stress that it has been one of the strengths of memory studies that it has been theoretically diverse and underline that this theoretical diversity is also present in the current volume. We have already referred above to the importance of psychoanalytical and psychological theories for memory studies. In addition, we have Marxist approaches to memory studies, Foucauldian approaches as well as a very wide range of theories associated with deconstruction (Jacques Derrida) and narrativity (Hayden White). Here we would like to plead in favor of methodological and theoretical eclecticism, as different methods and theories have all proven their ability to throw an interesting light on how memory has been used in diverse contexts throughout the centuries. The way in which memory studies has developed has been characterized by a particularly dichotomous way of understanding the relationship between history and memory. Nora, strongly influenced by Halbwachs, saw history as opposed to memory. Whereas memory was unreliable and subjective, history was seen as scientific and objective. Such scientificity has been severely dented over recent years, so that today it may be better to understand historians as just one of several memory groups in society seeking to influence the public memory. For Andreas Huyssen, the critique of historical discourse as a tool of domination, attacks on linear and causal explanations in history, and postcolonialism have all contributed to an increasing mistrust in the objectivity of history and the "hypertrophy of memory" (2003: 3). Contestation over memory has been one of the central characteristics of memory discourses and memory politics is strongly related to struggles over the meaning and significance of particular memories. In 2016, the memory scholars Anna Cento Bull and Hans Lauge Hansen published an insightful article in which they point to the strong political dimension of memory discourses, distinguishing between three types of memory:

antagonistic, cosmopolitan, and agonistic memory (Bull and Hansen 2015). Antagonistic memory discourses are those which operate on the basis of a clear "us" versus "them" distinction. Heroes are constructed from the "us" group and all the villains come from the "them" group. They are mobilizing emotions and passions of belonging on the basis of strengthening the "us" and vilifying the "them." They are not discursive and self-reflective but monologic in the extreme. Typical antagonistic memory discourses are nationalist ones, but also Communist class-based memory courses have been antagonistic.

Bull and Hansen differentiate antagonistic memory discourses from cosmopolitan ones. The latter are also characterized by an "us" versus "them" distinction: here "democracy" is associated with the good "us" whereas totalitarianism is seen as the "bad" "other." As with antagonistic memory, moral categories are vitally important. Cosmopolitan memory also mobilizes passions, in particular compassion with the victims of totalitarianism. A victim-centered perspective in cosmopolitan memory also limits the multi-perspectivity of cosmopolitan memory, which is dialogic but still aimed at achieving, through dialogue, a consensus. Bull and Hansen contrast antagonistic and cosmopolitan forms of memory with a third possibility, agonistic memory. Building on the theories of Chantal Mouffe around "agonistic politics" (Mouffe 2013), they argue that agonistic memory amounts to a form of radical historicization that contextualizes memory without using *a priori* moral categories. Its multi-perspectivity includes perspectives from perpetrators and bystanders in order to understand and engage with a multiplicity of contested memories. In a Bakthinan sense, it is open-enddly dialogic and is not aimed at producing consensus (Todorov 1984). Rather it realizes the deeply political nature of memory and makes memory into a political area in which different memories of the past engage in the present in order to promote different ideas about the future. For them, agonistic memory thus becomes a potential tool of the left to gain voice in political contexts and mobilize the passion of solidarity for policies aimed at greater social justice.

Notions around agonistic memory have of late engendered considerable discussion in memory studies and even led to a three-year Horizon 2020 project of the EU (www.unrest.eu) in which scholars worked with the concept in order to analyze European memory regimes vis-à-vis wars in twentieth-century Europe and promote forms of agonistic memory as a way to fight the rise of anti-European right-wing populisms across the EU (Berger and Kansteiner 2020a). Agonistic memory, the project argued, could well be a means to repoliticize memory for projects of the political left and thus give the political left more of a voice again. Left-wing memory activists could use agonistic memory to promote anti-neoliberal, anti-nationalist, anti-racist policies as well as policies aiming at greater social and gender justice. It would also form a bridge between scientific, academic memory studies and committed and engaged memory activism (Gutman and Wüstenberg 2020). The cultural history of memory in the long twentieth century has been characterized by deeply politicized forms of memory, fighting for nationalist and a broad variety of other right-wing and left-wing social movements, either with or against forms of state power. Its overt politicization has been partly hidden from sight in Europe and the global west by the strength of cosmopolitan memory discourses based on ideas of Habermasian forms of deliberative democracy that have uncannily sought to depoliticize memory discourses (Williams 1998). Powerful global actors, including nation states, the EU and the UN have all adopted forms of cosmopolitan memory regimes as dominant memory regimes by the beginning of the twenty-first century. The debate in future will have to be led around questions of whether we need a repoliticization of memory through forms of agonistic memory.

CHAPTER ONE

Power and Politics

JAY WINTER

The twentieth century saw the birth of collective memory, understood as the memory of collectives, made up of relatively small groups of men and women who do the work of remembrance, not at the behest of the state but alongside it (Halbwachs 1980). There are three special features of the last 100 years which justify this claim. The first is the exponential growth of the power of the state to reach everywhere and everyone. The second is the development of technologies of remembrance, from radio to television, to audio and video recording, to the internet and beyond, which revolutionized the preservation, retrieval, and dissemination of narratives about the past. The third is the robust activities of millions of memory agents, men and women in civil society determined not passively to follow the lead of the state, but to shape and transmit narratives of their particular past, at times totally at odds with state narratives. Thus, the history of the interaction of memory, power and politics in the twentieth century is dialectical in character.

Of central importance in the ways state and civil society worked as narrators of collective memory was the democratization of death in wartime. War dominates the twentieth century in new and monstrous ways, which separated the history of armed conflict from earlier periods. On the one hand, the killing power of weapons of war grew to the point that they could destroy the entire world. On the other hand, armies grew so rapidly from 1914 on that they mobilized most of the able-bodied male populations of combatant countries. Seventy million men served in the First World War; perhaps 90 million served in the Second World War. Of those people, some 10 million died in the First World War and up to 50 million died in the Second.

Casualties on this scale made the memory of war everybody's business. And while all states sought (and still try) to seize the microphone of commemoration and use the sacrifices of war to justify the hold of particular elites on power, they rarely succeeded in strictly imposing their view of the past on their societies. There were exceptions: Stalin virtually destroyed civil society in the interwar years, and made individual remembrance outside of the parameters of the party and the state a crime punishable by death. The Indonesian military and their allies destroyed all traces of their murder of up to 500,000 political enemies in Bali alone in 1966. They have succeeded in drawing a veil of oblivion over their crimes. But virtually everywhere else throughout the world, the memory of the oppressed and the powerless have survived the ruthless effort of the powerful to destroy it.

How the voices and memories of the many defied the attempts of the few in control to orchestrate or homogenize them is one of the most striking features of the history of the twentieth century. Part of the resistance to top-down memory lay in religious institutions, important allies outside of sites of oppression and repression. The example of the Polish

Catholic Church is significant in this context. Other sources of resistance lay in indigenous cultures, which retained their coherence through maintaining a distinctive language and traditions at the village level. The case of mourning practices in Vietnam, encoded in ghost stories, enabled women to tell stories about war below the radar, as it were, of the Communist party (Kwon 2008). Working-class movements survived every attempt of colonial and neo-colonial powers to enforce what Gabriel Garcia Marquez called 100 years of solitude, the isolation of the oppressed and the downtrodden. In Spain after the fall of the Franco dictatorship, the same villages that voted socialist in the 1930s voted socialist in the 1980s, despite millions of deaths and broken lives.

These few instances indicate the argument of this chapter. In most (though by no means all) cases, civil society is more powerful than the state in shaping frameworks of memory over the long term. Only when states present narratives consistent with those of civil society do those states shape memory regimes.

This interpretation varies from a large literature treating memory essentially as the plaything of those in power at the national or imperial level. And there is much force in that interpretation. Historian George Mosse was the foremost spokesman of this school. In a number of important studies, he argued that commemoration in the twentieth century was a moment when the nation worshipped itself. The cult of the fallen was fashioned by many leaders, fascist and non-fascist alike, in order to justify their hold on power and to promote military build-ups and interventions which ultimately led to the Second World War. He admitted that there was no upsurge of national feeling in 1939 as there was in 1914, but nonetheless argues for a functional interpretation of the relationship between memory and politics in twentieth-century Europe. The nationalization of the masses, in his felicitous term, led to the nationalization of commemorative practices, through the sacralization of the state. Memory, in short, was what the state wanted it to be (Mosse 1975; Mosse 1990).

Long after the Second World War, dictators of various colors seized on commemorative narratives to shore up their political projects and personal ambitions. One such example should suffice for many others. Saddam Hussein set in motion a campaign to rewrite history in such a way as to suggest that not only was Saladin an Arab, but that there was a direct line between his rule and that of Ancient Babylon (Baram 1983: 426–55). This ballooning of national pride through the hijacking of the past, or rather of a falsified version of the past, in the interests of the consolidation of a dictator's rule, is a phenomenon used by men in power all over the world.

What I term the Mosse school of the history of memory has provided deep insights into the way narratives of the past serve political visions of the future. But a strictly national interpretation of the way commemorative practices have evolved over the twentieth century and beyond leaves out a substantial part of the history of remembrance practices which develop either independently of the state or in opposition to it. For this reason, this chapter focuses on the dialectic between state and civil society, arguing that commemoration lasts when their visions are braided together. Top-down commemoration, in all too many cases, lacks the social support to enable commemorative practices to survive the passage of time and the move from one political regime to another. In short, the Mosse school suffers from the faults of political determinism, that form of political thinking which treats the history of commemoration like the story of Toscanini at the Mozarteum. The master directs; the people follow. Unsurprisingly, I might add, the place where Mosse's work has left the deepest legacy is Italy (Gentile 1996 and Gentile 2006).

One way of understanding the interaction between elites and masses in the sphere of commemoration is to focus on the complex process of the construction of memory regimes. They are ways groups of people, both in power and far from it, frame their understanding of the past. These regimes are closely related to what Jan and Aleida Assmann term "cultural memory," in that they go beyond direct experience to privilege the symbolic representations of events whose origins lay outside the reach of contemporaries (Assmann 1995: 125–33; Assmann 2011). These ways of putting the past into the present do not only rely on the voices of those who were there. They also extend beyond the generations who sit around the dinner table, and who tell stories about how "I remember when." Even after they pass away, later generations share narratives about what happened in the increasingly distant past. This move is, in Jan and Aleida Assmann's terms, a shift from communicative memory, that of lived experience, to cultural memory, that of imagined experience. That shift from communicative memory to cultural memory happens in all societies.

My central point is that this movement from one kind of memory to another is governed by a dialectic between state and civil society, including families in the latter category. In schools, in the press, in the media, in some coopted churches, state edicts establish a narrative those in power want "the people" to learn. The problem is that states are successful in this mission only when their narratives fit in with stories about the past arising from below. The cultural memory of a society is an alloy, a hybrid, and amalgam between what the powerful want and what the powerless believe. In some places, state leaders do speak for the people when they commemorate important dates in the past; in other places, state figures erect Potemkin villages of memory, stage sets propping up those in power in ways everyone sees but no one dares to disclose. Thus, until the very end of the Soviet regime, the parades to mark the Bolshevik revolution threaded through Red Square in Moscow, oblivious of the fact that the regime had lost its legitimacy and its right to rule. The upshot of this argument is that we can never examine the matrix of memory, power, and politics solely at the level of the state. To do so is to miss the dynamic forces that made collective memory in the twentieth century a living and changing reality.

There were three separate periods in which we can examine the dialectical processes of the forging of collective memory. The first surrounded the two world wars and lasted roughly from 1900 to 1950. The second surrounded wars of decolonization, from China, Korea, India, and Palestine to Cuba and Vietnam, covering the period from 1950 to 1980. The third began roughly in 1980 and extends to our own times. Each of these periods was marked by technological developments in the retention, retrieval, and dissemination of documents and voices of those who lived through war and violence. The first period had radio and television, telephone and telegraphy at its disposal. The second was the time when audio and video recording opened up new pathways of preservation of voices and faces of those who lived through violent times. The third period—our own—has learned to treat the internet and computing as a landscape of great variety providing people the licit and illicit means to tell stories and discover secrets. Digital memory is a term describing gadgets much more powerful than audio cassette recordings, though both are technologies for the preservation and dissemination of traces of the past at risk of penetration and discovery by adversaries. Digital libraries are capable of storing all the archives in the world, though both "hard copies" and digital copies of documents can fade over time. Both can be erased; both can be faked or forged by skilled technicians. Lying about the past is probably easier than ever before, though the impulse to lie among those in power hasn't changed a bit.

THE FIRST MEMORY BOOM

The carnage of the Great War brought bereavement into the households of millions of ordinary families all over the world. And the sheer scale of the losses throughout the Great War overwhelmed conventional forms of remembrance. In the prewar period, some middle-class widows wore black crepe dresses to signify their status; by 1916 there was no more crepe to be had. The churches tried to offer consolation to parents in mourning, but the deluge of loss defeated them. Instead, there was an efflorescence of spiritualism, a belief in the social practice of communicating with the dead through mediums, almost always women. This practice was anathema to the Christian churches; to reach the dead without the intercession of Christ or of his church was blasphemy. Traditional Jewish teaching treated spiritualism as an abomination, but the same wrenching losses forced Jewish families into unconventional practices during and after the war (Winter 1995).

Many churches were established; that is, their ties to the State were long-standing and official. When the war came to an end in 1918 in the West, and the aftershocks of the war especially in eastern Europe and Russia subsided by the mid-1920s, three empires had collapsed, and so had the churches which both served and sacralized the Hohenzollern, the Habsburg, and the Romanov dynasties. In these post-imperial nations, there was neither the inclination nor the money to devote to commemorative projects. Furthermore, how to commemorate those who died in a lost cause was a complex question. In Germany, a private Lutheran organization, the Volksbund Deutsche Kriegsgräberfürsorge (German War Graves Commission) was founded in December 1919 and launched an initiative to look after the war graves and cemeteries of German soldiers who had died in the Great War. Their problems were multiple, and their work was circumscribed by the lingering bitterness engendered by the war. Not surprisingly German war cemeteries were allocated much smaller plots than were the war cemeteries of the victors. This meant that there were more mass graves in the German than in the Allied cemeteries, and over time these German cemeteries were consolidated into a few larger cemeteries, where the remains of German soldiers who died in the war rest today.

The iconography of these German cemeteries varied from those of the Allies. There were more large trees in the German case, suggesting the ambiance of "Heroes' Forests" of German legend (Mosse 1995). Dark stone was used here, in contrast to the white Portland stone of the Imperial (later Commonwealth) War Cemeteries. The choice of stone color varied by cemetery and by architect. In the 1920s, most German war cemeteries were marked by crosses; in the 1930s and after, the crosses were replaced by stone slabs, once again more appropriate for consolidated cemeteries in which six or eight names were listed on one slab, indicating the approximate site of them all (Winter 2017: 14–71).

The contrast with the cemeteries constructed by the Allies is striking. Here too we see the contrast between state and civil society initiatives in the development of commemorative forms. The state had the right to allow parents to claim the bodies of their loved ones who had died in the war. After three years of debate, the French gave permission for such reburials in country graveyards far from the battlefields. The exhumation, transport, and reburial costs were borne by the state. The American army allowed removals to American cemeteries, while leaving substantial numbers buried in a few cemeteries in northern France. The British did not permit the return of bodies to Britain, in part because those running the war graves cemeteries knew all too well that a substantial number of those graves contained either no remains or those of several men; the most respectful way of treating them all was to leave them all where they were.

FIGURE 1.1: Commonwealth War Graves Commission Cemetery, Lone Pine, Gallipoli. Credit: Jay Winter.

FIGURE 1.2: French War Cemetery, Hellespont, Gallipoli. Credit: Jay Winter.

FIGURE 1.3: German War Cemetery, Bayeux, France. Credit: Jay Winter.

One of the innovations of the First World War was the proliferation of tombs of Unknown Soldiers, men whose identity was "known unto God" and to no one else. Here was another form of recognition that the Great War was revolutionary, in turning from being a killing machine, which all wars are, into being a vanishing act. Half of all those who served and who died in the war have no known graves. Consequently, individuals and groups, including the French association Le Souvenir français, during the war gathered support for the symbolic burial of one Unknown Soldier in the nation's capital. This required state approval, secured in London in September 1919. The burial of the Unknown Soldier took place at Westminster Abbey on November 11, 1920, and beneath the Arc de Triomphe in January 1921.

In 1932, a huge monument, designed by the British architect Sir Edwin Lutyens, was unveiled at Thiepval on the Somme. It listed the names of 73,000 British soldiers who had no known grave. This was a reformulation of Lutyens's thinking on the memorialization of the missing. In 1919, he had designed in a few days a cenotaph, or empty tomb, to be constructed of plaster of Paris, and to be erected on Whitehall in London, roughly equidistant from the Prime Minister's residence at Downing Street, the Ministry of War,

FIGURE 1.4: The Cenotaph, London. Credit: Jay Winter.

and the Houses of Parliament. When the victory parade was held in London on July 19, 1919, roughly two million people marched past the Cenotaph. Many left flowers or other objects in memory of the dead of the war. The British people voted with their feet for this site as their national war memorial. An empty tomb, without Christian notation, breathtakingly simply in its design, was the right solution to the difficult problem of how to honor those who died in the war without honoring war itself. "To the glorious dead" is the sole inscription on it. The dead are glorious, not the war, and not the living. In addition, this pre-Christian design of a Greek tomb suited an imperial war, in which men of all faiths and no faith died. Christian notation was absent, much to the distress of British churchmen (Winter 1995: 78–116).

The Unknown Warrior—named as such to include sailors as well—was buried only a few hundred meters away, in Westminster Abbey, the Church of the Royal family. It was striking then, as it is now, that the British people chose the Cenotaph, a statue in public space, rather than Westminster Abbey, a church of the Establishment, as that site for national mourning which has endured throughout the century which has followed the war. Both symbolically brought home the dead and placed them right in the middle of official England. It appears that Lutyens' Cenotaph on the space on Whitehall, the political heart of the nation, resonated more with those in mourning than did the slab at the entrance to the Church of Kings. The British people found in the Cenotaph the symbol of a war in which death was democratized.

Other countries inaugurated Tombs of Unknown Soldiers, and in each case the state played a leading role in the effort (Inglis 1993: 1–12). In the United States, an Unknown Soldier was interred in Arlington Cemetery in Virginia, placed there after the Civil War on land which had belonged to the Commander in Chief of the Confederacy, Robert E. Lee. There is no movement here towards binding together the wounds of the North and the South; a point to which we shall return below. In Italy, an unknown warrior was buried in the Tomb of Vittorio Emanuele II in Rome in 1921. Ten years later, at the invitation of the Prussian government, the architect Heinrich Tessenow designed a memorial to the fallen of the Great War placed in the Neue Wache, the guard house, on Unter den Linden in Berlin. That building, too, has an interesting post-history, to which we return below.

Many other monuments of a similar kind were built in the 1920s and 1930s, and virtually all of them were funded by a partnership between state and civil society. This was emphatically the case with the 60,000 or so local war memorials built in France and Britain between the wars. None was solely the product of the state, and all honored those who died in wars declared and run by states. Even in dictatorships, war memorials still had lives of their own, not simply those rubber-stamped by Hitler or Mussolini. Stalin had no such problem, since the event commemorated in the USSR was not the war, but the 1917 revolution, a state upheaval if there ever was one.

There was no similar wave of commemoration after the Second World War. In part, this was due to the implicit plea in many war memorials of the interwar years that they were the product of those who said "never again war." What do you do when "never" lasts for fifteen years? In addition, the Second World War bankrupted some of the victors to the point that public and private money for commemorative projects was in very short supply. The solution was to add the names of the fallen, much less numerous for the 1939–45 war than for the 1914–18 conflict, to the statues built after the Great War.

It took considerable time before the subject of the Holocaust entered into the public narrative of the Second World War. The post-1945 period was a time in which to honor resistance movements; despite the fact that there were resisters among the Jews murdered in the Holocaust, most were ordinary people who went to their deaths without adding to the heroic story of taking up arms against the Nazis. How could it have been otherwise? Could 1.5 million children murdered in the Holocaust resist? How about the elderly, the sick, mothers and babies? For a time, the prestige of resisters occluded the suffering of the victims of the Holocaust.

THE SECOND MEMORY BOOM 1950–80

This occlusion ended in the 1960s and 1970s. Part of the reason was technological. In these years, there emerged audio cassette recorders and then video cassette recorders which enabled survivors of the Holocaust to speak up. In the Nuremberg trials, the weight of evidence was documentary, but in 1961, the trial of Adolf Eichmann in Jerusalem brought back to life the voices of the victims, at times in terrifying ways. One man, Yihiel Dinur, collapsed during his testimony, speaking for a moment as someone who had returned from Planet Auschwitz, another universe, before the effort defeated him. He vanished not only from the trial but from public life for years.

A few years later, there was a series of trials under the laws of the German Federal Republic in which twenty-two people who ran the Auschwitz concentration camp were brought to justice. Of the 360 witnesses called, 210 were victims. Six of the accused were given life sentences, but probably of greater importance was that the trials, like that of Eichmann in Jerusalem, were seen in public and recorded for posterity.

On one level, the balance between state and civil society had altered when the subject of remembering the Holocaust emerged as an integral part of the history of the Second World War. The Israeli state believed that the Eichmann trial was the best way to educate their younger generation into the subject of the Holocaust, which Prime Minister David Ben Gurion and others posited as a justification not only for the existence of the State of Israel, but for its vigilance in the face of the threat posed by its Arab neighbors. The same educational purpose underlay the Auschwitz trials and others, steps on the way to fortifying the democratic character of the West German state.

But civil society was part of the story of the emergence of the Holocaust as a central subject in contemporary history. An American four-hour television series entitled *Holocaust* was released in the US in 1978 and in West Germany in 1979. Half the adult population of West Germany watched it, and this massive reception helped reinforce the movement in Germany to cancel the statute of limitations on Nazi crimes, due to expire that year.

The abomination of the Holocaust showed in vivid form what the absence of human rights meant. By the 1970s, a popular human rights movement drew from the earlier Universal Declaration of Human Rights a sense that the denial of human rights in one country was a denial of human rights for all. This propelled a number of important initiatives, including Oxfam, the Oxford Committee on Famine Relief, which was founded in 1942, but which came into international prominence in the 1960s. Amnesty International was founded in 1961, as a platform for the defense of prisoners of conscience. Sharing this organization's focus were Nelson Mandela and those in prison with him in South Africa, Soviet prisoners of conscience like Armenian Paruir Airikian and Alexander Dmitrievich Feldman, a Zionist. One of the most outspoken critics of the Soviet policy on dissidents, Andre Sakharov, won the Nobel Peace Prize in 1975, the same year that the Soviet Union and the United States signed the Final Act of the Strategic Arms Limitation Treaty (SALT). In return for Western recognition of the boundaries of the USSR, the Soviets accepted Western monitoring of their treatment of dissidents. This was a fundamental step in the crumbling authority of the Communist party's control of their country.

Human rights movements worked to expose and limit the damage states did to the human rights of their own citizens. Thus, civil society was at the heart of a world-wide movement, which had remembrance of the horrors of the Holocaust and the Gulag in its very core. Soon enough in the late 1970s and 1980s, a vicious wave of repression in South America triggered mass protests all over the world. In Argentina and Chile, mothers protested against the disappearance of their children. They continue to do so today.

In the same year as the Final Act of the SALT treaties were signed, Spanish dictator Francisco Franco died. In the following year the Spanish Cortes legally laid the groundwork for a transition to democracy. In the 1980s, the new regime made it clear that the transition to democracy required an amnesty on pursuing the perpetrators of crimes committed by the Franco regime. The socialists who ran the new government sacrificed justice in the interests of political stability. This meant that the victims of the old regime had to live with the monuments the fascist state had erected to its victory. Here is a case where the state defined the boundaries of remembrance. And yet over time, that diktat has eroded under the pressure of civil society. The final outcome of this memory war is still unclear.

Much more evident is the victory of the Indonesian state over those who would draw attention to the murder of perhaps 500,000 people in 1965–6. The regime said that they were killed because they supported a Communist movement about to seize power. That claim is almost certainly false, but here the regime was able to destroy not only its perceived enemies, but virtually every trace of the massacre. Here is a case of memory erasure at the hands of a military elite in full control of a state. All that remains of the victims is silence, still very hard to penetrate fifty years after. Some initial steps have been taken to disinter this story, but there is a long way to go before the memory and the history of the massacre come to light.

THE THIRD MEMORY BOOM

In the last two decades of the twentieth century, there was a major increase in attendance at museums and historical sites throughout the world. There are many explanations for this shift to the right in the demand curve for public history in general and for representations of war in particular. One source is the massive expansion in university provision in the United States, Continental Europe and Britain, and the Antipodes since the 1960s. More educated people were spending more of their disposable income on travelling to sites of historical importance than ever before.

A second source is the presence within families all over the world of three generations of people. In 1980, for instance, children born during or in the years immediately after the Second World War were in their thirties. They are the so-called baby boomers. Their children were born in the 1970s and 1980s. Given the major increase in life expectation in the post-1945 period, there was every chance that the grandparents of these third generation of children were still alive.

Let us consider what this would mean for a family of Armenian Americans, or Polish American Jews. The grandparents in 1990 were the children who survived the Armenian genocide or the Nazi Holocaust and made it to the United States. They were determined to turn a new page, and to put behind them the horrors of war and genocide. Hence, in the 1960s and 1970s, the two older generations—survivors and their children—tended not to talk about their suffering, but to make new lives.

Then came the third generation, the grandchildren. They turned to their grandparents and asked them questions hidden previously. They stripped away the silence which had enabled families to live without daily interrogations of the horrors they had endured, and created a cohort of memory activists, people determined to have their people's story told and preserved.

In the 1980s and 1990s, they had the affluence and the tools to create the third memory boom. Once more technological change made a major difference. In addition to audio and visual recorders, there was now word-processing and the internet, enabling thousands of people to create and contribute to web sites of memory. There was also what has come to be termed "dark tourism" where the grandchildren of Holocaust survivors retraced their grandparents' (and sometimes their parents') steps. The growth of the European Union as a third force in world affairs and the collapse of the Soviet empire spread the word: the age of the witness was upon us (Wieviorka 2001).

In 1982, the first Holocaust archive was created at Yale University. Its creator, Geoffrey Hartmann, was a child of the Holocaust himself. Subsequently, dozens more of these archives appeared. They dealt with other catastrophes in other parts of the world. Some used the Holocaust as a metaphor for their own suffering; others joined in these sites of remembrance because they felt a responsibility to remember. Some even went so far as to adopt Holocaust memory as part of their own lives, even though they were born long after the Second World War. One scholar has termed this "prosthetic memory," the fusing of the memories of others with one's own (Landsberg 2004).

What tied their identities together with those of many other people was the notion that they were all victims of traumatic memory. Trauma was what happened to people who went through violent, life-threatening experiences, and who were forced (for a variety of reasons) to bury those memories. Victims of sexual abuse found that no one believed them, and that they were subject to breakdowns long after the insult or crime they suffered.

It is at this point that the state gave to these people a kind of legitimation. They were indeed damaged and needed treatment. The reason this happened is that the men who fought in the Vietnam War (and on both sides) came home and, in a sense, became walking time bombs. They could explode with rage for little apparent reason, or when isolated, commit suicide. The violence they performed, sadly against their own families or themselves, finally broke down generations of resistance among soldiers, the military, the medical profession, and the state to admit that war damages surviving soldiers in a host of ways long after the conclusion of hostilities.

In 1980, five years after the end of the Vietnam War, the American Psychiatric Association amended its Manual of diagnoses and treatments to include what we now know as PTSD: post-traumatic stress disorder. This condition differs from shell shock, in that it has a long latency period. The artillery barrages of the Great War created all kinds of psychological states, most of which were never recorded or recognized for purposes of gaining a pension and the help that goes with it. By the early twenty-first century, soldiers themselves helped lead the way into a new domain in the memory boom, one inhabited by fighting men who now could admit that they too were victims of war (Winter 2017: 172–202).

This major change in public recognition of PTSD had repercussions all over the world. Armies are conservative institutions, but even they change with the times. And although the macho, stoical, silent profile of men in uniform still persists, states made room and financed the treatment of those who were damaged while serving in the forces, even though they (in many cases) had not a scratch on them.

In Europe, the extension of victimhood to all soldiers had one consequence which many people regretted. In universalizing victimhood, the distinction between those who suffered under the Nazis and those who fought for them began to blur. This moral equivalence enabled US President Ronald Reagan in 1985 to visit Bitburg cemetery in Germany, where the remains of SS soldiers are interred. Another kind of blurring of distinctions happened eight years later, also in Germany. In the Neue Wache in Berlin, Chancellor Helmut Kohl had installed a sculpture derived from a design of the German artist Käthe Kollwitz. Without the consent of Kollwitz's descendants, he had another artist create a cast of one of Kollwitz's pietàs, substantially bigger than the one she had initially designed. This was done to make the sculpture fit the large space of the Neue Wache. Even worse was the addition of a dedication to the sculpture. It honored all the victims of war and dictatorship, thereby equating the victims of communism with the victims of the Nazis. The fact that Kohl had chosen a pietà, a Christian image to represent (in part) Jewish suffering added insult to injury. None of the storm of criticism stirred up by this crude mobilization of art in the name of conservative politics moved Kohl to change this design. It remains there to this day (Koselleck 1993).

RELIGIOUS TRADITIONS

The third memory boom, from the 1980s to our own times, has been fueled by other traditions too. Many of them are religious in character. A Shinto shrine in Tokyo, the Yasukuni shrine, honors all those who died for the Emperor, including those war criminals executed after the Second World War. Adjacent to it is a museum of the Second World War, with a narrative of the war offensive to those who defeated Japanese imperialism at great cost. Outside the museum is a bronze statue of a Kamikaze pilot, whose bravery cannot be doubted, but whose suicidal intensity could stand for the Japanese war effort as a whole. Here is one place where war is still glorified.

Another kind of glory, also with a religious rhetoric behind it, is commemorated in both Poland and the former Soviet Union. Museums honoring those of the faithful who perished at the hands of the Communist regime before 1991 include beautiful icons. They are made out of the mug shots the KGB took of their prisoners, before shooting or incarcerating them. These photographs are surrounded by gold foil and gilt and create icons of a kind which have attended the lives and deaths of saints in the Orthodox Church for centuries.

In 2015, the Katholicos of the Armenian Apostolic Church in Yerevan canonized all those Armenians who lost their lives in the genocide of 1915–17 (Bogumił and Łukaszewicz 2018). This was a political act, unsurprising in a culture in which the church has played a central unifying role. The timing—the centenary of the beginning of the genocide—can be explained as an act of protest at 100 years of Turkish denial both that the genocide occurred and that they were responsible for it (Winter 2017: 121–42).

Religious language with political implications can be found in a number of countries that honor those who died in defense of their country, or in decolonization struggles. There are martyrs' days in the following countries today (2017): Afghanistan, Azerbaijan, Bangladesh, Burma, India, Lebanon, Libya, Malawi, Pakistan, Panama, Syria, Togo, Tunisia, Vietnam, and Uganda. Similar rhetoric marks Islamic radicalism and Palestinian nationalism as well. Here politics, power, and memory are inextricably braided together.

SLAVERY AND RACIAL CONFLICT

The same is true whenever the subject of slavery and race relations is the focus of sites and acts of remembrance. In South Africa, students at the University of Cape Town led a campaign to remove a statue of Cecil Rhodes, imperial leader and champion of white hegemony in Africa. A more conventional site of memory is that of Robben Island, where Nelson Mandela spent over twenty years of his life. A former lepers' colony, it has been kept just as it was under apartheid. Former inmates guide visitors around the site to this day.

Most recently, there have been a series of confrontations over the fate of memorial statues to honor the leaders or the men who served and who died in the defense of the Confederacy in the US Civil War of 1861–5. As historian David Blight has shown, this conflict started during and after the war itself. Memorial Day, at the end of May, was celebrated first by freed slaves, but not long thereafter, their story of the civil war—the story of emancipation of the slaves—was occluded by two other linked narratives. The first was the story of the Northern struggle for the defense of the Union. The second was the story of the Southern defense of states' rights—a lost but (from their viewpoint) a noble cause. In 1913, fifty years after the Battle of Gettysburg, the turning point in the Civil War, old men who had once been Northern and Southern soldiers came together to shake hands and honor each other's cause. What was not visible at the time was that by taking the hand of friendship, they were whitewashing the history of the war and its consequences for American race relations.

Fifty years after that 1913 reunion at Gettysburg, in 1963, Martin Luther King spoke in the Mall in Washington of his dream of racial harmony and reconciliation. He was assassinated five years later, and his dream remains just that, fifty years later. Nothing shows the deadly mix of politics, power, and memory better than the struggle over flags and monuments to the Confederacy in America today (Blight 2001).

In June 2015, Dylann Roof murdered nine black men and women at a prayer meeting in the Emanuel African Methodist Episcopal Church in Charleston, South Carolina. One of the victims was a state senator. In response, the state legislature agreed to remove the Confederate flag from the grounds of the state capitol. Six months later, the mayor of New Orleans ordered the removal of statues honoring four leaders of the Confederacy. He got an ordnance through the City Council to do so.

These measures triggered a backlash of support for the preservation of what President Trump has called "our beautiful monuments." This opposition depends on maintaining the distinction between the Southern cause, and the bravery of the men who defended it. The first is not defensible, but the second still commands popular respect throughout the United States. That is why a clash between demonstrators defending Confederate monuments and those determined to remove them turned violent. One protestor was killed, and in the aftermath President Trump said there were good people on both sides. During the Civil Rights movement of the 1960s, when a Southerner, Lyndon Johnson, was President, no one would have dared to equate white supremacists and civil rights activists. Now fifty years later, the memory wars take on the colors of the politics of the day (Chotiner 2017).

A similar, though less incendiary, conflict is ongoing in Australia. Aboriginal activists, in their part of the memory boom, engaged in a long and successful legal struggle to establish the fact that their ancestors were residents of Australia and that they resisted British and European conquest of it. In the Mabo decision of 1992, judges accepted the historical research of Henry Reynolds and others which destroyed the contention that the continent was *terra nullus*, empty land, and open to seizure by anyone able to sustain a settlement there. The land had been occupied, and 200 years later, the courts recognized the rights of the descendants of these aboriginal peoples to the product of their land, including uranium.

Here was a judicial earthquake, and its consequences have resembled in form, though not in venom, American quarrels over the legacy of slavery. Aboriginal artists and activists now want to rename statues to Captain James Cook which state that he is the "discoverer" of Australia. One artist put in the National Gallery of Art in Canberra a version of a famous bust of Cook, modified by a balaclava, the facial covering of thugs and thieves.

In both the American and Australian cases, there is a rough consensus that the best way forward is not to destroy monuments, but to add explanations to them which can educate those, especially the young, in how to go beyond ancient hatreds. In a similar manner, Helmut Konrad, the Rektor (Vice-Chancellor) of the Austrian University of Graz, insisted that Nazi frescoes painted on the walls of the university in the 1930s be preserved, and matched by a commentary, reminding all students of the university's Nazi past and of the dangers of racial hatred and intolerance.

This strategy of addition to a site rather than its removal still leaves the question as to who decides what to add. That is still a political question, entailing an ongoing triangulation of memory, politics, and power, which is likely to endure for a considerable time to come.

CHAPTER TWO

Time and Space*

CHRIS LORENZ

INTRODUCTION

Although the study of memory has undoubtedly been booming in the late twentieth and early twenty-first century, memory has remained an essentially contested notion. This is especially true among historians, who have a long tradition and a strong inclination to conceive of memory as the opposite of history (Barash 2016). Most of its reflexive practitioners agree that the field of memory studies has gained a certain maturity and has certainly been blossoming since at least the 1980s. Nevertheless, quite a few of those practitioners also wonder whether—and if so, in which directions—this interdisciplinary field will develop and, if so, whether it will generate more of the same research or produce interesting novelty. As Gavriel Rosenfeld asked in 2009, can memory studies expect a crash or a soft landing in the future (Rosenfeld 2009)? Ironically, the study of memory that developed because the modernist faith in the future and in history was replaced, since the 1980s, by the post-modern experience of crises—as Pierre Nora, François Hartog, and John Torpey famously have argued—appears to be facing the question of progress itself in the twenty-first century (Nora 1989; Hartog 2015; Hartog 2016; Torpey 2006).

This chapter asks how the dimensions of space and time have been framed and discussed in memory studies and how memory has been distinguished from history in the long twentieth century. I will first present a three-part periodization of memory studies in the long twentieth century: the foundational period, identified with the work of Maurice Halbwachs on collective memory, the memory boom period identified with the sites of memory approach of Pierre Nora, and the present-day period of transnational, transcultural and multidirectional memory, identified with the work of memory scholars like Michael Rothberg, Ann Rigney, Astrid Erll, Daniel Levy, and Nathaniel Sznaider and—last but not least—Aleida and Jan Assmann.

I will secondly flesh out the explicit and implicit ideas about space in the work of Halbwachs and Nora. I will argue that they both ultimately frame memorial space in terms of the relatively closed container-space of the nation-state. In the case of Nora this identification is exemplified in the remarkable absence of the French overseas empire from his memorial construction of France.

Thirdly, I will argue that a fundamental break with notions of container-space and container-time are the two major characteristics of the post-Nora, transnational, transcultural, transgenerational, transmedial, and multi-directional period. Memory scholars in this period usually emphasize that all memory is "traveling" in relatively open

---

*I would like to thank Allan Megill, Marek Tamm, and Katie Digan for their critical comments on earlier versions.

multiscalar spaces and in multidirectional times—and thus cannot unambiguously be located in one place or in one time, nor connected to one fixed identity. Michael Rothberg's analysis of the interrelationship between the memory of the Holocaust and of decolonization and Daniel Levy's and Nathaniel Sznaider's analysis of the globalization of Holocaust-memory exemplify these recent approaches.

Fourthly, I will address the framing of time in memory studies by analyzing the influential analyses of François Hartog and Aleida Assmann—the only two book-length analyses concerning the changing experiences of time over time. Both Hartog and Assmann hold that the relationships between past, present, and future have fundamentally changed since the memory boom, but they offer completely different analyses and evaluations of this change. While Hartog—following Nora—interprets the memory boom as a pathogenic symptom of a crisis of—modern—time, Assmann interprets memory studies as a cultural-political achievement of post-Holocaust and postcolonial societies that have learnt the hard way that change does not automatically equal progress.

A PERIODIZATION OF MEMORY STUDIES IN THE TWENTIETH TO THE TWENTIETH-FIRST CENTURY

Before going into issues of place and time in memory studies, a minimal reflection on the object of our analysis and its relationship to history as its presumed contrast seems required because the variety of topics and methods in memory studies is so notoriously elastic that it is sometimes viewed as a proof of its incoherent character (Klein 2011; Algazi 2014). Nevertheless, its proponents have been remarkably inventive in locating a unity behind all this diversity. Geoffrey Cubitt has recently fleshed out the following three assumptions as the largest common denominator of all meanings of memory in this interdisciplinary field: The first assumption is that what is 'made of the past'—meaning both 'making sense' and 'making use'—is a vital element of human culture (Cubitt 2018: 128). For most historians, this assumption is not problematic as long as the monopoly of professional history is acknowledged when it comes to establishing what the past is.

What usually causes historians considerably more headaches is the second assumption, because it implies a direct connection—a direct continuity—between (the experience of) the past and present-day self-understanding, or, ideas about identity:

> The second assumption ties this notion of memory to notions of experience and identity. Memory, in this understanding, does not consist simply of facts or stories or images about a past reality, but of structures of consciousness, binding these things together, that purport to speak, not just of "what happened" but of how what happened was experienced and of the mark this experience leaves in subsequent being and self-understanding, whether of individuals or of societies.
>
> —Cubitt 2018: 129

Because professional history traditionally presupposes a break—a discontinuity and a distance—between the past and the present, many historians are quite suspicious about the grounding of identity-claims in the past (Barash 2016: 60–84). This suspicion grows when the past is used to claim collective identity, as some historians fundamentally doubt that this is an adequate category of analysis (Niethammer 2000; Brubaker & Cooper 2005; Megill 2007; Barash 2016). Similar doubts have been raised concerning collective memory as an analytical category because in a *literal* sense only individuals have the faculty to remember. Collective memory is therefore always based on individual memories and can only be used as a notion in a *metaphorical* sense: as the memories that are transmitted in interpersonal communication and that are shared by several generations (communicative memory in Aleida Assmann's terms). Collective memory is thus always on the move in time—simultaneously expanding and retracting, as individuals are born and die—and is limited to three or four generations (Klein 2011; Algazi 2014; Barash 2016). Halbwachs' idea that memory deals with that which remains the same between the past and the present (identity/continuity) while history deals with what is different (non-identity/discontinuity) has therefore been quite popular among historians—especially because Nora reproduced Halbwachs' idea about the division of labor between history and memory.

The third assumption of memory studies is relatively uncontroversial among historians—especially since historians, under the influence of Freud and Foucault, have come to recognize that much of history consists of telling silences: "The third assumption is that memory processes, both in the individual and in society, are fundamentally selective and reconstructive". "This continuous reprocessing of the past in memory is itself an integral part of the historical process" (Cubitt 2018: 129). Accordingly, in contemporary memory studies remembering is inseparable from forgetting (Ricoeur 2004; Connerton 2009; Rigney 2018b; Assmann 2016).

Starting from these three assumptions, leading memory scholars have proposed a rough—periodization of the development of memory studies in the long twentieth century.

The *first* phase in memory studies is unambiguously identified with the pioneering book on collective memory by Maurice Halbwachs (1877–1945), originally published in 1925, while Aby Warburg and Walter Benjamin are also increasingly seen as founding fathers of "mnemnohistory" (Tamm 2013; Tamm 2015; Robbe 2014). Originally entitled *Les cadres sociaux de la mémoire,* the book was (mis-)translated into English as *The Collective Memory* in 1980, although Halbwachs deals with both individual and group memories while substantiating the Durkheimian thesis that the significant—relative stable—attributes of individual thinking, feeling and experiencing are socially preconfigurated. According to Halbwachs, every individual is a member of various groups—like household and kinship groups, religious groups, economic groups, city- or countryside groups and legal groups. All these groups taken together constitute a society—which in its modern variety is always identified with the nation-state.

There is also little controversy regarding the beginning of the *second* phase of memory studies. Especially for observers in the francophone world, this phase starts with Pierre Nora's famous alternative history of France aka his *Lieux de mémoire* project (7 volumes, 1984–92). This project was organized around the categories of *La Republique, la Nation,* and *les France* (Nora 1998). The sites of memory approach did not focus on *"wie es eigentlich gewesen,"* but on how French national history is told based on a collection of symbolic sites.

For observers outside the francophone world the second phase usually starts with the memorialization of the Second World War in general—and of the fortieth and fiftieth anniversaries of events in the history of the Third Reich in particular. This phase coincides with the increasing international presence of Holocaust-memory, which interacted directly with the growing awareness of the new genocides worldwide (Rwanda, Bosnia, Kosovo), as Andreas Huyssen observed and as Michael Rothberg later on theorized (Huyssen 2000; Rothberg 2009). In this phase, the specific (West-) German discourse and practice of

Vergangenheitsbewältigung developed into the international phenomenon of reparation politics and a politics of regret that was directed at historical injustices in general and at the legacies of slavery and colonialism in particular (Olick 2007; Torpey 2006). This second phase is usually identified with the memory boom—and for good reasons, because only in this phase did memory studies become a booming interdisciplinary field of knowledge in which founders and their precursors could retrospectively be located.

As to the *third* phase of memory studies (Feindt et.al 2014), there is not one generally accepted period-label yet, nor a generally accepted beginning. Nevertheless, the notion of cultural memory has largely replaced social or collective memory. Moreover, Astrid Erll proposed to baptize this phase as one of transcultural memory because transcultural catches "the transnational, diasporic, hybrid, syncretistic, postcolonial, translocal, creolized, global or cosmopolitan" (Assmann 1999; Erll 2011a: 9). Transcultural approaches go beyond the nation and thus beyond the Nora-type of approach. They emphasize the interconnections of national, sub-national (for example, local and regional) and supra–national (for example, European and global) framing, of the national and the trans-national contexts. Quite a few of the sites of memory projects were and are still primarily politically inspired on the national level, though, and meant to construct or strengthen specific collective identities (Niethammer 2000; Majerus 2014: 123–30).

This phase is basically characterized by the insights that memory is not contained by *any* spatial or social unit—no nation, nor a group, nor a culture—and that it is never fixed. No social frame of memory is given and therefore all memory is dynamic, dependent on remembrance alias on memory work. Moreover, memory work is always entangled, mediated, and on the move (Rigney 2018c). "Memory *becomes* collective when it is shared, and for it to be shared it must be mediated. By mediation is meant both the channels of transmission and the very cultural forms that are used to make sense of events," in Ann Rigney's apt phrasing (Rigney 2018c, 243; Barash 2016: 114–68). Memory scholars of the third phase have realized that most contemporary societies are characterized by the phenomenon of mass media and of mass migration and that "mass migration provides a daily challenge to a container thinking that would neatly line up ethnicities, national borders and public cultures of remembrance" (Rigney 2018c, 250). Astrid Erll has proposed the term "travelling memory" in this context, meant as a "metaphorical shorthand, an abbreviation for the fact that in the production of cultural memory, people, media, mnemonic forms, contents, and practices are in a constant, unceasing motion" (Erll 2011a: 12; Erll 2011b). Tentatively one can locate the beginning of the third period somewhere between 2000 and 2010.

MAURICE HALBWACHS AND PIERRE NORA ON SPACE, GROUPS, AND COLLECTIVE MEMORY

The idea that collective memory can be situated in space and that it is connected to material objects was so important to the founder of memory studies that he devoted a special chapter to it in *The Collective Memory*. In Halbwachs' mind, the social frames of memory were also—in various degrees—spatial, temporal, and material frames. As mentioned before, he conceives of society as a collection of groups, so logically he also locates the connection between individuals and space in the group: "The group not only transforms the space into which it has been inserted, but also yields and adapts to its physical surroundings. It becomes enclosed within the framework it has built"; "place and group have each received the imprint of the other" (Halbwachs 1980: 130). So, a "place" is basically the space as experienced by a group.

The connection between group memory and place also pertains to groups without an apparent spatial basis, that are typical for modern societies, like legal, economic, and religious groups, although each of these groups is superimposed on localized groups. So all group memories are connected to specific places—like courts for legal groups, markets for economic groups and holy places for religious groups—and although the spatial aspects of groups and group-memories have become less important in modern times then they were in the Middle Ages, still "every collective memory unfolds within a spatial framework" (Halbwachs 1980: 134–9) and is "topophilic." As a consequence, "there are as many ways of representing space as there are groups" (Halbwachs 1980: 138).

Space, in Halbwachs' view, is thus fundamentally socially constructed along group-boundaries and collective memory is fundamentally spatially constructed (see also Marcel and Muchelli 2008: 145). Although individuals usually belong to many groups and thus participate in various collective memories, for the Durkheimian sociologist Halbwachs the groups and social frames tend to be given and to function as the *explanans*. In Halbwachs' view, the irreducible spatial and temporal character of memory—"each locally defined group has its own memory and its own representation of time" (Halbwachs 1980: 104)—also explains the opposition between memory and history: "history can be represented as the universal memory of the human species. But there is no universal memory. Every memory requires the support of a group delimited in space and time" (Halbwachs 1980: 84). Therefore, Halbwachs does not mix memory and history, as Nora does when he introduces the notion of "history-memory" of the nation for nineteenth and early twentieth century nationalistic history.

Although Nora (occasionally) refers to Halbwachs' ideas and although he usually—though not consistently (see Barash 2016: 80–4)—reproduces his opposition between history and collective memory, it is far from accidental that mostly he uses the term memory without the adjective collective: "memory is blind to all but the group it binds—which is to say, as Maurice Halbwachs has said, that there are as many memories as there are groups, that memory is by nature multiple and yet specific; collective, plural, and yet individual. History, on the other hand, belongs to everyone and to no one, whence its claim to universal authority" (Nora 1989: 9). According to Nora, "at the heart of history is a critical discourse that is antithetical to spontaneous memory. History is perpetually suspicious of memory, and its true mission is to suppress and destroy it" (1989: 9).

In Nora's view, however, (French) society as analyzed by Halbwachs in 1925 as "a group of groups" no longer existed in the 1980s. This more or less traditional type of society had gradually been replaced by one that is fundamentally individualistic due to the "acceleration" of modern history as analyzed by Reinhart Koselleck and others. Because modern individuals have become increasingly mobile in social and geographical spaces, they have literally lost their fixed places in the world. As a consequence, in Nora's traditional and nostalgic view, those lost in space have developed an immediate desire to substitute memories of the world they have lost.

So, Nora's explanation for the memory boom is simple: "We speak so much of memory because there is so little of it left. [. . .] There are *lieux de mémoire,* sites of memory, because there are no longer *milieux de mémoire,* real environments of memory" (Nora 1989: 7). Nora's assumption is therefore the same as Halbwachs': there used to be an authentic—traditional—connection between groups, collective memories, and spaces—a connection that was constitutive for the collective identity of groups. In Nora's view, what is nowadays—in postmodern times—called memory is actually no longer real collective memory. Since "the atomization of a general memory into a private" one, there is only a search for memory that has taken the form of an obsession with the archiving of traces—including self-archiving—and with local and regional histories: "modern memory is, above all, archival [. . .] what we call memory is in fact the gigantic and breathtaking storehouse of a material stock of what it would be impossible for us to remember, an unlimited repertoire of what might need to be recalled" (Nora 1989, 13). The disappearance of authentic collective memory and the obsession with archiving everything are directly connected. Because postmodern individuals no longer know what to remember they try to remember everything in the form of archives: "What we call memory today is therefore not memory but already history. [. . .] The quest for memory is the search for one's history" (Nora 1989: 13,16).

However, because in postmodern times also the future no longer provides any guidance, the present is left as the only category of self-understanding for individuals. This presentist condition is effectively making the writing of national history as usual impossible in Nora's eyes. For Nora, the nation is no longer experienced as the origin of "the group of groups," nor as its *telos* in the future—because in Nora's eyes real French nationalism finally eclipsed with Charles de Gaulle and with him French national politics *as such*. Nora also regards the end of leftist revolutionary politics in France in the 1970s— after a revolutionary tradition of almost two centuries—in terms of the eclipse of the nation as the main actor in politics. In retrospect, 1968 turned out to be the tombstone on this tradition and not the phoenix of the revolution rising from its ashes. Therefore, the history of the French nation can only be written as the history of the sites through which France is remembered (Nora 1992, 27; cf. Hartog 2015). This kind of history is "ni résurrection, ni reconstruction, ni meme représentation but a "remémoration [. . .] une histoire de France, donc, mais au second degré" (Nora 1992: 25).

So, paradoxically, memory nowadays has taken the form of its supposed opposite, history, and history has transformed into a "prosthetic," unreal memory of a nation that actually only lives on as a ghost (Englund 1992). Postmodern individuals are drowning themselves both in archival traces and in heritage, but they are still lost in real memorial space. Unsurprisingly, Nora locates his sites of memory approach exactly at this crossroad of history and memory: "The study of *lieux de mémoires*, then, lies at the intersection of two developments that in France today give it meaning: one a purely historiographical movement, the reflexive turning of history upon itself, the other a movement that is, properly speaking, historical: the end of a tradition of memory" (Nora 1989: 11).

Here—at last!—Nora provides an explanation of his enigmatic notion of "sites of memory":

> Combined, these two movements send us at once to history's most elementary tools and to the most symbolic objects of our memory: to the archives as well as to the tricolor; to the libraries, dictionaries, and museums as well as to commemorations, celebrations, the Pantheon, and the Arc de Triomphe; to the Dictionnaire Larousse as well as to the Wall of the Fédérés, where the last defenders of the Paris commune were massacred in 1870.
>
> —Nora 1989: 12

What these sites have in common in Nora's eyes is that they all—material and symbolic— are *metaphors* for the French nation and a *projection screen* for French identity. Therefore, Nora characterizes his sites of memory both as "Russian dolls" and as a "Pandora's box" (Nora 1992: 23).

Nora's nostalgic diagnosis of French historiography is ultimately based on a group and a space that is missing in Halbwachs' analysis of "intermediate" groups in *On Collective Memory* and that only makes it appearance as an example of "larger groups": the nation. Although Halbwachs refers to the nation regularly, true to the Durkheimian sociological tradition, society remains his ultimate container concept (for a fundamental critique of Durkheim's "groupism" see Brubaker 2002). For Halbwachs in the 1920s and 1930s, society simply coincided with the nation as "the group of groups": "between the individual and the nation lie many other, more restricted groups. Each of these has its own memory" (Halbwachs 1980: 77). And as all groups, the nation also has its collective memory: "the memory of the nation" (Halbwachs 1980, 51, 76–7), but Halbwachs explicitly warns against the identification of national memory and national history: "the collective memory is not the same as formal history, and 'historical memory' is a rather unfortunate expression because it connects two terms opposed in more than one aspect." "General history starts only where tradition ends and the social memory is fading or breaking up" (Halbwachs 1980: 78).

For the historian Nora in the 1980s, however, society and the nation are no longer the same. In Nora's eyes, simultaneously conditioned by the end of the French overseas empire (see below) and by the astonishing international success of the *Annales* conception of history as preached and practiced by Francois Simiand, Marc Bloch, and Fernand Braudel, society represents the core concept of social-economic and geographic/demographic history—for which "history of society" or the "*Annales*-conception of history" became the historiographical shorthand. During the heyday of this *Annales*-type of history writing between 1950 and 1975, the national/political *as such* was seen as the superficial layer of events that contrasted with the deeper—social-economic, demographic, geographic—structures of society. Nora therefore views society as the *successor concept* of the nation-state in history—a change that put an end to the world as historians knew it at the time (long before "culture" succeeded "society" as the hegemonic concept in history). By replacing the nation-state by society, the *Annales*-historians had also destroyed the nation as the undisputed narrative backbone and as the primary *milieu de mémoire* of history accordingly: "No longer a cause, the nation has become a given; history is now a social science, memory a purely private phenomenon" (Nora 1989: 11).

Although practically all elements of Nora's diagnosis and approach have been subjected to fundamental criticism—especially his distinction between authentic and inauthentic memory and his (inconsistent) way of distinguishing between history and memory—this criticism has not hindered the intensive international transfer of his sites of memory approach to other nation-states and the adaptation of his approach to spaces besides national spaces. This successful historiographical export of the sites of memory approach is all the more remarkable because Nora himself initially claimed that it only applied to France (Majerus 2014: 121). And although Nora presents his approach as an alternative for old-fashioned national history, critics have pointed out that Nora's sites of memory approach actually represents France as a closed spatial and apparently homogeneous entity, as traditional national history did: all sites of memory are spatially firmly located within the French hexagon.

The spatial representation of "France" as a hexagon leaves out *la France d'outre mer* and thus the spatial dimension of French colonialism, although formally Algeria had been a department of France between 1840 and 1962 and had been a crucial military pillar of Vichy-France between 1940 and 1943. Nora is also silent about French slavery and the presence of quite a few of the slaves' descendants in present-day France. Unsurprisingly,

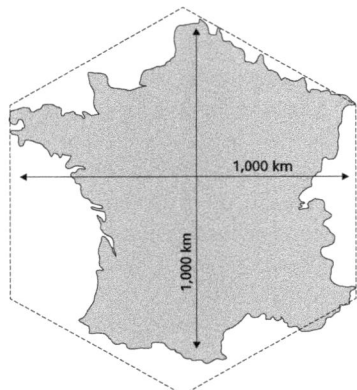

FIGURE 2.1: "France" as hexagon.

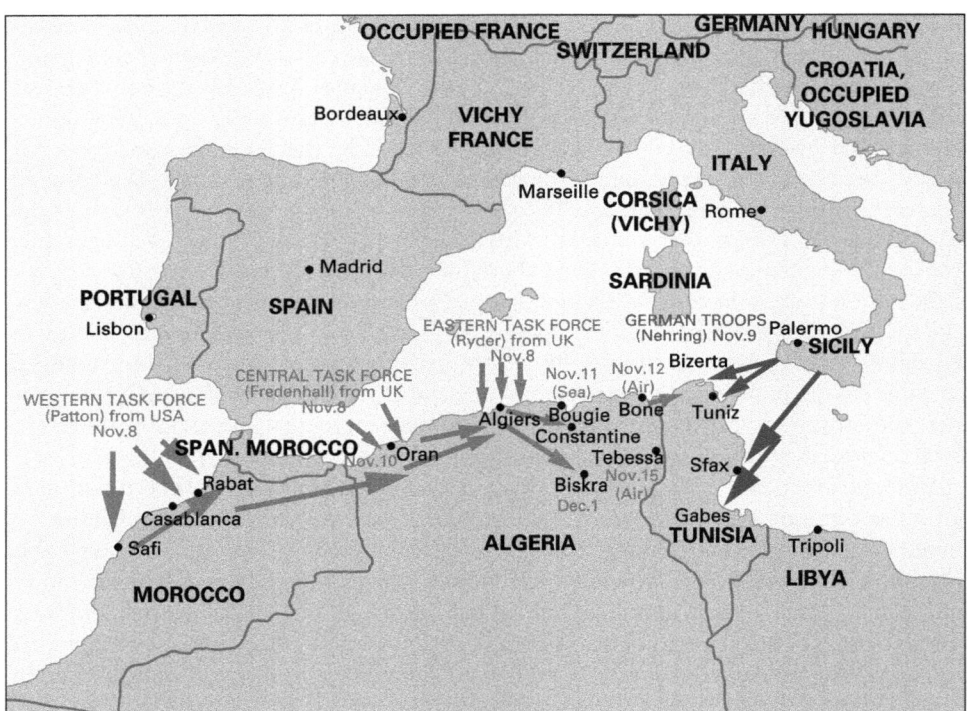

FIGURE 2.2: "France" unlike the hexagon: "Vichy-France" in November 1942 during "Operation Torch."

as Algeria is missing as a part of Nora's France, so is the massive immigration of the pied noirs to France after 1962—and this goes for postwar immigration in general (Shepard 2016). A similar story goes for French Indochina—with the consequence that the crucial French military defeat at Dien Bien Phu by the Vietnamese army in 1954 apparently does not qualify as a site of memory of France (Rothberg 2010; Ho Tai 2001). So, on closer analysis, Nora's France as a spatial container turns out to be remarkably gallocentric because it is freed from its supra-national, colonial/imperial history and from its minoritarian histories. This, of course, does not mean that the historian Nora is unaware of the colonial and minoritarian aspects of French history—as the author of a book on Algeria he surely is (see, for example, Nora 1992). But it does mean that these aspects are not conceptualized as integral parts of his sites of memory project.

FROM THE SOCIAL FRAMING OF COLLECTIVE MEMORY TO TRANSCULTURAL AND MULTIDIRECTIONAL MEMORIES

The fundamental fact that most of the Western nation-states have been colonial empires well into the second half of the twentieth century and the circumstance that colonial memory is not only part of their past, *but also of their present*, has not been ignored by the memory scholars of the third period. On the contrary, much of the work of scholars like Michael Rothberg, Ann Rigney, Aleida Assmann, and Astrid Erll is aimed at recalibrating the basic concepts of memory studies to the postcolonial and the post-Holocaust condition (Confino 2011, 38–40). This condition requires quite different ways of connecting space, memory, and identity than found in Halbwachs and Nora.

In analyzing postcolonial settler societies like the US and Australia, the group and society/the nation can no longer be conceived of as given spatial containers of memory and identity because indigenous first nations enter the picture with completely different conceptions of time, space, the nation and the law. Unsurprisingly, indigenous groups usually have (oral) memories of the past that are in fundamental conflict with the idea of the past as modern national history, as Brian Attwood argued for the aboriginals in present-day Australia (Attwood 2005) and as Brenda Macdougal and John Borrows did for the First Nations in Canada (Macdougal 2017; Borrows 2017). The postcolonial and the settler-condition clarify to what degree forgetting is a precondition for national memory *to exist at all* and to what degree national memory remains *irresolvably* agonistic. In this respect it differs from the forgetting that was needed to forge European, (presumedly) non-settler nations like France according to Ernst Renan (Renan 1887). In short: the recognition of the postcolonial condition changes the group and the nation from an *explanans* into an *explanandum*. On closer scrutiny, the social, temporal and spatial frames of memory are in a flux and need to be explained *themselves* (Cubitt 2018: 141). This kind of approach "avoids tying culture—and by extension cultural memory—to clear-cut territories and social formations" (Erll 2011a: 6). Instead of—static—*places* of memory (*lieux de memoire*) one needs to conceive of—dynamic—*knots* of memory (*noeuds de memoire*) (Rothberg 2010).

The beginning of this post-Halbwachs and post-Nora approach is exemplified by Michael Rothberg's *Multidirectional memory. Remembering the Holocaust in the Age of Decolonization*. Rothberg wanted his book to be paradigm changing. He explicitly locates it "in a Transnational Age" and analyzes, as its subtitle suggests, the interconnections between the memory of the Holocaust and the memory of decolonization in a variety of case studies that "addresses more than a half-century of cultural history in Europe, North America, the Caribbean, and North Africa" (Rothberg 2009, 23). He sums up the distinctive characteristics of his new approach as follows.

The *first* characteristic is the rejection of the idea that collective memories—like those pertaining to the Holocaust, colonialism, and slavery—are necessarily in competition with each other "as a zero sum struggle" over scarce resources for pre-eminence. Instead, Rothberg proposes to see them as multidirectional, that is: "as subject to ongoing negotiation, cross-referencing and borrowing; as productive and not privative" (Rothberg 2009: 3). This means that winners in the competition for memorial recognition do *not* automatically produce losers but that—contra-intuitively—the contrary is true: "the emergence of Holocaust memory on a global scale has contributed to the articulation of other histories—some of them predating the Nazi genocide, such as slavery, and others taking place later, such as the Algerian War of Independence (1954–62) or the genocide in Bosnia during the 1990s." Therefore, multidirectional memory "is meant to draw attention to the dynamic transfer that takes place between diverse places and times during the act of remembrance" (Rothberg 2009: 11). As a consequence, multidirectional memory can only be studied with a comparative approach that avoids the traditional national framing ("methodological nationalism") (Rothberg 2009, 6, 16–21). According to Rothberg, his research shows that memory of the Holocaust and of the struggles for decolonization have consistently broken the frame of the nation-state since 1945. This is also due to the fact that after formal decolonization history was actually "brought home" by the postcolonial migrations to their former colonial motherlands. With these migrations, the legacies of colonialism and slavery moved along into the motherlands, as Gert Oostindie has argued (Oostindie 2009a and 2009b). Multidirectional memory therefore can only be spatially analyzed in terms of *"multiscalarity."* In Ann Rigney's phrasing, "multiscalarity recognizes the existence of multiple, partly overlapping frameworks of memory including the intimate and local as well as the regional and the global" (Rigney 2018c: 250). This observation, of course, is not meant to deny that "the nation has undeniably provided the dominant frame for large-scale *public* acts of remembrance in the last 200 years" (Rigney 2018c: 249).

The *second* characteristic of the new approach is the rejection of the traditional direct connection between groups and identities: "Memories are not owned by groups—nor are groups 'owned' by memories. Rather, the borders of memory and identity are jagged; what looks at first like my own property often turns out to be a borrowing or adaptation from a history that initially might seem foreign or distant" (Rothberg 2009: 5). Therefore, the approach of multidirectionality is "partially disengaged from exclusive versions of cultural identity and acknowledges how remembrance cuts across and binds together diverse spatial, temporal, and cultural sites" (Rothberg 2009: 11). In other words: multidirectional memory has no intrinsic connection to fixed positions in time, nor in space, and is "freed from the (never actually) homogeneous space—time of the nation-state" (Rothberg 2010: 12). Therefore, the multidirectional approach has no problem— as Nora had—dealing with memory in societies in which nativism is no longer the norm because a substantial part of the population has a migration background, as is obviously the case with older and newer settler- and immigrant societies. Seen from a long-term perspective, indeed, *all* societies are immigrant and settler societies because all *homo sapiens sapiens* or *Anatomically Modern Humans* (AMH) emigrated out of Africa between 120.000 and 60.000 years ago although this historical fact is obviously no longer part of human memory. (López, van Dorp, and Hellenthal 2016).

The rejection of exclusive versions of cultural identity connected to groups and places in the third phase of memory studies often directs the gaze at the inherent conflictual and agonistic character of memory work. As Ann Rigney emphasizes, "the desire to assert something in face of its possible denial" is "an important motivator behind acts of

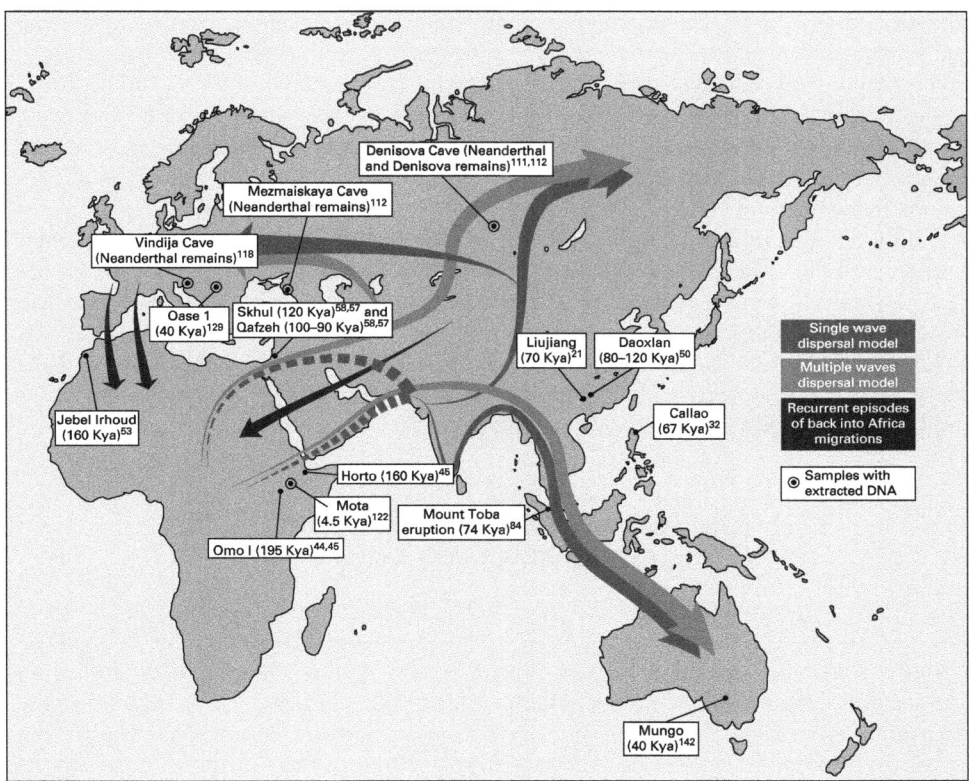

FIGURE 2.3: History beyond memory: the traveling or migrant past of *Homo sapiens sapiens*, 120,000—60,000 BCE (putative migration waves out of Africa and location of some of the most relevant ancient human remains and archaeological sites (López, van Dorp, and Hellenthal 2016).

remembrance." Memory work is as much driven "dissensus by as by consensus" (Rigney 2018c: 244; Bull and Hansen 2015). Memory wars—just like history wars—therefore are a continuation of politics by other means. There is no fixity in this respect either, because "preoccupation with memory is itself historically variable and at some periods in history it has been more important than in others as a key to identity" (Rigney 2018c: 244, 246).

In the transcultural and traveling phase, memory studies has thus become contextualized and historicized to such a degree that its supposed methodological and functional opposition to history has all but vanished. Most memory scholars nowadays formulate the distinction between memory and history in terms of their *complementarity* and no longer in terms of their presumed *opposition*, as Halbwachs (always) and Nora (often) did and as Barash still does. Jay Winter, for example, characterizes their relationship as follows: "History is memory seen through and criticized with the aid of documents of many kinds—written, oral, visual. Memory is history seen through affect. And since affect is subjective, it is difficult to examine the claims of memory in the same way as we examine the claims of history" (Winter 2007: 12). Ann Rigney similarly argues that history provides society "with documented evidence and well-informed judgements on what really happened, while collective memory consists of narratives that provide a sense of collective purpose, value and identity in the present" (Rigney 2018b: 148; Confino 2011: 42–3). Influenced by Holocaust studies, memory has long been identified with traumatic memory, victimhood, and suffering, but this identification is of a historical and not of a conceptual nature. Non-traumatic memory is as legitimate an object of memory studies as traumatic memory.

So, by all appearances, the transcultural memory studies in the twenty-first century have entered the phase of peaceful coexistence with academic history—a process that has been bolstered by a growing number of historians who not only emphasize the memorial, presentist and haunting aspects of historical time (Rousso 2002; Bevernage 2011; Bevernage and Lorenz 2013; Lorenz 2014; Kleinberg 2017) but who also argue that the historical past is characterized by a similar absence of uniformity as the contemporaneous and memorial present (Bevernage 2016; Kleinberg 2017).

THE RISE OF A GLOBAL/COSMOPOLITAN HOLOCAUST MEMORY

One of the pioneering transnational approaches that has been developed in the third phase of memory studies is set out in *The Holocaust and Memory in the Global Age* authored by Daniel Levy and Nathan Sznaider (Levy and Sznaider 2006). Based on a comparison of the memory cultures of Germany, the US, and Israel, they characterize the Holocaust as the force behind the transformation of national memorial cultures into a global or cosmopolitan memory. They distinguish three periods in the memory of the Holocaust: a period of silencing, followed by a period of iconographic formation, and finally a period of cosmopolitization.

The first period of silencing the Holocaust is located roughly between 1945 and 1960. In this phase, the memory of the Holocaust still remained firmly located within the framework of the nation. The—relative—silence, that actually was a very selective way of dealing with the Holocaust, was only broken in the early 1960s following the Eichmann (1961–2) and Auschwitz trials (1963–5) in Israel and in Germany respectively. Levy and Sznaider posit that this was followed by the second period, in which the foundations of the iconographic formation of the Holocaust were established. This situation lasted until approximately the end of the 1980s. During this period, the Holocaust was cut loose from its particular location in the various national pasts and it was mapped onto different present-day political settings. The New Left in Germany, for example, developed strong identifications with the Holocaust-victims and so did Israel's governments in their conflicts with its Arab neighbors—especially after the Six Day War of 1967. In the US, the growing presence of the Holocaust among Jews coincided with the general emergence of ethnic identity politics. So, while the memory of the Holocaust was increasingly historicized, it was also subject to a growing de-contextualization and de-territorialization. This exemplifies the multiscalar and multitemporal character of multidirectional memory.

During this second period, the Holocaust was recast as a catastrophic event with not only a past—historical—meaning, but also with a present and a future—memorial— meaning: the Holocaust developed a "temporal duality" (Levy and Sznaider 2002: 96). Although the Jews in Europe had been the victims of the Holocaust in the Nazi past, in the future Holocaust-like genocides could happen to anyone. Thus, the Holocaust acquired a universal meaning, without losing its national meanings:

> The Holocaust does not become one totalizing signifier containing the same meanings for everyone. Rather its meanings evolve from the encounter of global interpretations and local sensibilities. The cosmopolitanization of Holocaust memories thus involves the formation of nation-specific and nation-transcending commonalities.
>
> —Levy and Sznaider 2002: 92

In our age, John Torpey argues that we have to reckon with "one, two, many Holocausts" (Torpey 2001: 341). In this sense the lesson of "Auschwitz" started to resemble that other universal lesson of the Second World War, the lesson of "Hiroshima and Nagasaki" concerning the permanent and global nuclear threat since 1945. The Holocaust too now had acquired an urgent relevance for both the present and the future, thus exemplifying its temporal stretching.

Levy and Sznaider argue that in the third period, starting in 1990 with the end of the Cold War, the process of universalization of the Holocaust became complete. Only now could the Holocaust acquire a really global significance, because "1990" meant the end of the division of the world in two blocs with two fundamentally different political discourses. The discourse of communism had to disintegrate before the Holocaust could really transform into the universal symbol of evil in cosmopolitan memory and into "the golden standard of reparation politics" (Torpey 2001). After the German reunification in 1990, this process was also pushed forward within the post-national framework of a united Europe.

The European integration actually enabled Germany to *de*-nationalize the Holocaust and to frame it as a *European* event—even as (postwar) Europe's founding event. Germany's participation in the UN intervention in Kosovo (1999) was explicitly justified in terms of preventing "another Holocaust"—the "Kosovocaust." The Intergovernmental Conference on the Holocaust in Stockholm in 2000 codified this process of Europeanization further when it declared "the prevention of another Holocaust to be the civilizational foundation of a new European memory" (Levy and Sznaider 2002: 100).

It would not take long, however, before it became clear that the legacies of communism and *not* the legacy of the Holocaust dominated the memory landscape in most states of Eastern Europe (Himka and Michlic 2013). Charles S. Maier characterized the new borderline between eastern and western Europe in 1993 as based on a "surfeit of memory," as Tony Judt did in 2002:

> If the problem in western Europe has been a shortage of memory [after 1945, CL], in the continent's other half the problem is reversed. Here there is too much memory, too many pasts on which people can draw, usually as a weapon against the past of someone else.
>
> —Judt 2002: 172; Maier 1993

Retrospectively, we can therefore safely argue that the thesis concerning the cosmopolitization of Holocaust-memory is a premature universalizing spatial claim because "cosmopolitization" is as yet predominantly a West European and North American phenomenon. National differences, however, may continue to outweigh transnational commonalities and there is no way of knowing whether in the future the cosmopolitization will replace the present "surfeit of memories" or not.

FRAMING TIME IN MEMORY STUDIES: FRANÇOIS HARTOG AND ALEIDA ASSMANN

This observation leads us to the question which conceptions of time are implicit in the experience that the past remains stuck in the present—the experience often held responsible for the "memory boom." John Torpey locates a fundamental change of temporal experience around 1990:

> Since roughly the end of the Cold War [. . .] the distance that normally separates us from the past has been strongly challenged in favour of an insistence that the past is constantly, urgently present as part of our everyday experience.
>
> —Torpey 2001:19

According to Torpey, this development directly relates to a "collapse of the future," or a growing inability to create progressive political visions. This inability has been replaced by the assumption that "the road to the future runs through the disasters of the past." As he formulates it in a bold metaphor: "When the future collapses, the past rushes in" (Torpey 2001: 6, 23).

Aleida Assmann seems to be arguing along similar lines when she characterizes the memory boom as a reflection of a "general desire to reclaim the past as an indispensable part of the present" and as the acknowledgement of "the multiple and diverse impact of the past, and in particular a traumatic past, on its citizens" (Assmann 2001 and 2013a). Assmann, however, disagrees with Torpey's claim that memory *only* looks back in time and agrees with Olick about the forward-looking dimension of memory, as we will see below.

In traumatic memory, the arrow of time is not irreversibly progressive and pointing forward, as was the case in modern linear time. The implied time conception of a traumatic past is reversible and non-progressivist and thus "multidirectional." This also holds for the concept of time in the human rights discourse—the "last utopia" as Sam Moyn famously called it—that represents the theoretical backbone of "the politics of regret," according to Jeffrey Olick:

> The discourse of universal human rights is tied directly to a politics of regret because its advocates believe that only gestures of reparation, apology, and acknowledgement can restore the dignity of history's victims and can deter new outbreaks of inhumanity. The retrospective gaze of this discourse is thus part of an anticipation of the future.
>
> —Olick 2007: 12

Eelco Runia has suggested that a multidirectional, non-linear, and reversible conception of time has replaced the linear and irreversible idea of time since the 1980s (Runia 2006 and 2015). Multidirectional time implies a pluralization of times because the past, present, and future are no longer conceived of as chronological, that is as sequential and as discrete points on a straight line. Rather, past, present, and future are conceived as a three-dimensional complex of intersecting, non-linear timelines, that according to Bruno Latour can better be visualized as a plate full of spaghetti than as the modern arrow of time. Moreover, because multidirectional time is not fleeting, like chronological linear time is, it is no longer inevitably erasive: multidirectional time can also be conceived as durational. As Gabrielle Spiegel phrases it, while "chronological time is the 'normal' flowing, passing time of 'normal' history, durational time resists precisely the closure—the putting an end to the past—that chronological time necessarily effects; durational time persists as a past that will not pass, hence as a past is always present" (Spiegel 2002: 159).

Now although most memory scholars *presuppose* durational time and thus a break with modern, linear and irreversible time, there have been surprisingly few systematic attempts to analyze this break and the new temporal condition. I will now analyze the two most influential book-length attempts so far: the theory of "regimes of historicity" by François Hartog and the theory of cultural time by Aleida Assmann. While Hartog is fundamentally critical of memory and of memory studies, Assmann—as we saw—belongs to the most well-known representatives of present-day memory studies.

François Hartog's book *Regimes of Historicity. Presentism and experiences of time* (2015; original in French in 2003) presents an analysis of "our" present temporal experience that directly builds on Nora's *lieux de mémoire*-project and on Reinhart Koselleck's thesis of "increasing acceleration" of modern history. Hartog shares Nora's (and Torpey's) view that the future no longer offers an orientation in politics and in self-understanding since the 1980s, as it typically did in modern societies since the French Revolution. Hartog also agrees with Koselleck that an orientation towards the past was the dominant feature of pre-modern, traditional or classical societies. Since the 1980s, however, the *present* has eclipsed both the future and the past and has become the dominant horizon of thinking, acting, and self-understanding. This present takes the shape of a pathological longing for a past *of its own making* which expresses itself in an insatiable thirst for memory (Hartog 2015 and 2016; Lorenz 2019).

Based on the epochal caesura of "1789" and "1989" and the implied tri-partite periodization, Hartog distinguishes three regimes of historicity alias three orders of time. He defines a regime of historicity as a particular view on and experience of the relationship between past, present and future, in which one of them is supposed to be dominant.

The first regime of historicity is the classical one that reigned supreme before "1789" and in which the orientation toward the past was dominant (as formulated in the *historia magistra vitae* maxim). Histories only existed in their plural form because History as a "*Kollektivsingular*"—history as Progress and as process—had not yet been invented, as Koselleck famously argued. The dual notions of History and Progress only developed beginning with the Enlightenment.

The second regime of historicity is the modern one that dominated between "1789" and "1989" and in which the orientation towards the (always radiant) future was characteristic. Modern histories were characterized by a progressive development because History was seen as a process with a direction, alias as Progress. The past in the light of the future then became the modern key category of self-understanding. During the modern regime of historicity, the present was always imagined as a temporary transit-station between the past and the future-in-the-making:

> The future illuminating the past and giving it meaning constituted a *telos*, called, by turns, "the Nation", "the People", "the Republic", "Society", or "the Proletariat", each time dressed in the garb of science. If history dispensed a lesson, it came from the future, not the past. It resided in a future that was to be realized as a rupture with the past, or at least as a differentiation from it.
>
> —Hartog 2015: 102

History's *telos* was always represented as some version of the Promised Land.

FIGURE 2.4: *Moses and the Promised Land*. The Judeo-Christian—eschatological—prototype of the modern regime of historicity: the—sacred—future orients the present and the past. Credit: Culture Club/Hulton Archive/Getty Images.

FIGURE 2.5: "Beloved Stalin is the People's Happiness" (1949)—secularized, Communist version of the modern regime of historicity (Koretzky 1949). Credit: Patrick Lorette/Bridgeman Images.

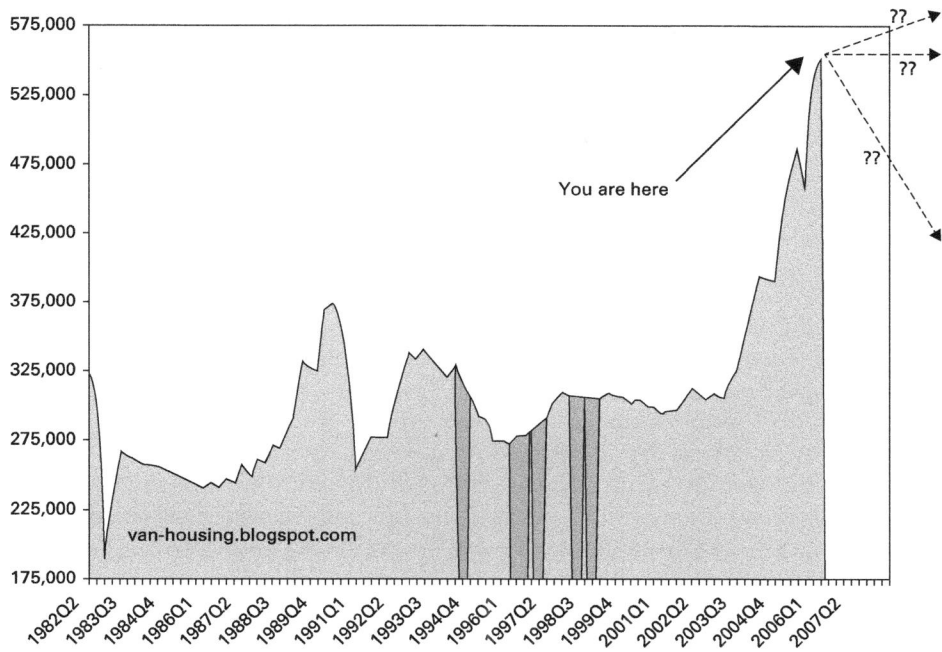

FIGURE 2.6: Vancouver Westside condo prices. Secularized, capitalist version of the modern regime of historicity.

The third regime of historicity is the presentist one, which developed somewhere in the 1980s and in which the orientation toward the present is dominant. In presentism, the present itself has become the key category of thinking and of self-understanding. The past and the future have become mere extensions of the present—which according to Hartog explains why presentism is characterized by an obsession with memory, commemoration, heritage and identity and why the interest in the "alterity" of the real past—and therefore the interest in real history—has vanished. This extended present—in which everybody basically has become contemporaneous!—lacks both the openness and the sense of progressive direction that were so typical of modern history.

As far as there is a sense of the past and of future direction in presentism, it is a sense of trauma due to historical injustices like the Holocaust, slavery, or colonialism, or other irreversible, man-made catastrophes—like global warming and environmental pollution. So, as far as there is any experience of direction in presentism, it is the sense of Progress in reverse. In Hartog's phrasing: "The past is knocking at the door, the future at the window and the present discovers that it has no floor to stand on" (Hartog 1996: 110).

In Hartog's view, the omnipresence of the discourse of—universal—human rights is the clearest manifestation of our present general "unhistorical condition" in which the presentist *memoria magistra vitae* has replaced the classical *historia magistra vitae* topos (Hartog 2016, 107). Since there are no statutes of limitation in human rights, its proponents have created a truly post-modern world, freed from temporality and thus of history.

Aleida Assmann's theory of cultural memory also departs from the thesis that "time has been out of joint" since the 1980s because the relationship between past, present and future is no longer experienced and conceived of as progressive. The modern regime of historicity thus clearly has lost its hegemony—at least outside the domain of science and technology. Assmann, however, rejects Hartog's thesis that the post-1980 temporal condition is therefore unhistorical, inauthentic, or pathological. Apparently, Hartog—like Nora—presupposes that the modern regime of historicity with its clear-cut differentiation between the past, present and future is somehow the normal temporal condition, even though this order of time only became hegemonous after "1789." It also appears that Hartog—like Nora—is turning a blind eye to the basic fact that not just memory, but *all* history—and not just contemporary history—is irreducibly presentist. The same goes for the fundamental fact that time is not automatically experienced by all as fleeting and erasive—as the memory of the Holocaust and of slavery seem to testify, although the memory of slavery is no longer part of (three to four generation) "communicative memory."

In contrast to Hartog, Assmann proposes to accept the present "multidirectionality" of times as a fact of present-day life instead of viewing it as a pathology caused by the heritage industry and the "memory craze." She also emphasizes that the past was *never* a given object and has always been a construction in a present with both cognitive and normative/affective aspects and functions—just like the future (Assmann 2013: 267–76). In this sense Assmann is also a presentist.

Last but not least, Assmann rejects Hartog's modernist presupposition that dealing with the past is or should be the exclusive territory of historians for several reasons. First of all, there is the basic fact that the temporal width of "communicative memory" completely overlaps with that of contemporary history. Therefore, the recent or contemporary past (say the last eighty to one hundred years) are inevitably shared by both specialists in memory and in history. Second, there is the basic fact that every individual and collective that describes its distinguishing characteristics—that is: describes its individual and collective identity—is harking back to its past and is anticipating its future. Individuals and collectives do so by tapping into what Aleida and Jan Assmann have coined cultural memory, consisting of symbolic and material "things": "Cultural memory is a kind of institution. It is exteriorized, objectified, and stored away in symbolic forms that, unlike the sounds of words or the sight of gestures, are stable and situation-transcendent. They may be transferred from one situation to another and transmitted from one generation to another" (Assmann 2008, 110–11).

In line with Marcel Proust, Aleida and Jan Assmann argue that human memory as a faculty does not only depend on communication with other individuals with memories, but also on the interaction with things that *trigger* or *store* memories, such as "artifacts, objects, anniversaries, feasts, icons, symbols, or landscapes" and other "*lieux de memoire.*" On the level of groups "the role of external symbols becomes even more important, because groups which do not 'have' a memory tend to 'make' themselves one by means of things meant as reminders such as monuments, museums, libraries, archives, and other mnemonic institutions. This is what we call cultural memory" (Assmann 2008, 111; cf. Barash 2016, 172–5).

In this way cultural memory conveys to people a collective, that is, cultural identity, because "memory is knowledge with an identity-index, it is knowledge about oneself, that is, one's own diachronic identity, be it as an individual or as a member of a family, a generation , a community, a nation, or a cultural and religious tradition" (Assmann 2008, 114). So collectives construct their cultural identities based on the knowledge stored in cultural memory and these may hark further back than communicative memory (as is, for example, the case with those descendants who at present hark back to the legacies of slavery and of the Armenian genocide) because cultural memory is stored in symbolic, institutional, and material forms that can transcend the boundary line of three or four generations.

Now when one recognizes that time is basically "multidirectional" and may be durational, as Aleida Assmann does, then reflexive societies—like reflexive individuals—do not simply face their past as a distant, historical past—antiquarian in Nietzsche's sense, aka as the historians' "foreign country"—but also as a practical past with a normative/affective, present-day and future relevance. As Nietzsche also clarified, this practical relevance may be of monumental character—nowadays better known under the label of heritage—or of a critical nature—presently better known under the label of historical injustices. Since the increasing recognition of human rights after 1945 and since the increasingly experienced need of a politics of regret, "forgive and forget" is decreasingly seen as a defensible practical option vis à vis historical wounds (Chakrabarty 2007). So, with Chakrabarty, Aleida Assmann argues that it is the task of responsible and reflexive political communities to address the "historical injustices" in their past not only in a historical but also in a practical way (Assmann 2013a, 296–304; De Baets 2019).

According to Assmann dealing with the past therefore always requires *both* historical inquiry—in order to establish "what really happened" based on critically processed evidence, including oral evidence (Assmann 2001; Assmann 2013a: 298, 307–8)—*and* a politics of memory. The latter consists of a variable mix of politics of regret and politics of self-affirmation alias identity (Assmann 2013a: 307). All in all, Assmann proposes to use the recent implosion of the modern regime of historicity as the *zeitgemässe* occasion to embrace the "culturalization of time" in the open, that is to accept the present entanglement of past, present, and future as the normal temporal condition *and* to accept the practical implication of this condition: that politics is not only a matter of taking responsibility for the present and the future, but also for the "historical injustices" in the past (Assmann 2013a: 269–75). In the same vein memory is not conceived of only oriented towards the past, but towards the present and the future as well (Assmann 2013a: 318).

Assmann's plea to de-modernize the present view of time also implies a plea to de-modernize the present view of space. This boils down to "provincializing Europe" and embracing global perspectives—a plea formulated earlier by Dipesh Chakrabarty (2000) and Bruno Latour (1993). Assmann thus consciously builds her theory of cultural memory, centered around the core concepts of culture, identity, and memory, on the ruins of the theories of modernization (2013a: 288–312). The hope that memory studies will keep on flourishing in the future therefore remains connected to the rejection of the modern idea of progress.

CHAPTER THREE

Media and Technology

WULF KANSTEINER

INTRODUCTION: THREE MODERNITIES

On October 19, 2019 the Nigerian newspaper *Daily Trust* reported of "mixed feelings about oil discovery in the north" of the country. That headline would prompt many European readers to expect an article contrasting the commercial opportunities of oil discovery with its environmental risks. But the news story does not deliver on those expectations. Environmental concerns are only mentioned in passing. Instead, the author Daniel Adugbo caters to the regional and national memory cultures of Nigeria and its underlying political and economic priorities. In this case, oil exploration is remembered in terms of commercial viability. Consequently, Adugbo recalls the failures and triumphs of the history of oil prospecting in the North of Nigeria where multinationals like Shell and Chevron tried their luck without much success in the 1990s. Now, the wells in question are in public hands, administered by the Nigerian National Petroleum Corporation which struck "hydrocarbon" because it was willing to drill much deeper than the multinationals two decades previously. Alone, the question remains how viable the find will turn out to be and Adugbo returns to this topic incessantly, relating a lot of technical information about gravity ranges, drill stem tests, and 3D seismic data, and assuming that his readers remember what these terms mean, living, as they do, in a society dependent on oil exports. Finally, at the end of the article the new successful drilling in the North is related to the established oil industry in the South of the country in the Niger delta. In this context Adugbo refers to the "trauma of having crude in the Niger delta." However, the phrase is again not the large-scale destruction of the delta region due to decades of oil spills and other abusive practices. Rather, Adugbo highlights the injustices of Nigeria's first oil rush which "left no visible impact in terms of real difference in the lives of the people." Here emerges an alternative set of values and memories differentiating between just and unjust exploitation of Nigeria's natural resources (Adugbo 2019).

A North-Westerner without ties to Nigeria is not likely to read the *Daily Trust* but there are other, more entertaining media products readily available through upload platforms and streaming services that cater to North-Western perceptions of Africa and inform about the environmental sins committed in Nigeria. Consider, for example, the 2015 Nollywood-USA movie *Black November* by Nigerian director Jeta Amata featuring such well-known actors as Mickey Rourke and Kim Basinger. *Black November* tells the story of a group of militant Nigerian activists who abduct an oil executive to fight corruption and pollution. The movie is generally considered a cinematic failure due to its stereotypical characters, preachy tone, and amateurish editing although it does advance a third set of values prioritizing environmental protection above export profits (Tsai 2015; Lodge 2015). Incidentally, the movie is available for streaming in Nigeria on Amazon Prime and

FIGURE 3.1: *Black November* poster. Credit: TCD/Prod. DB/Alamy Stock Photo.

despite the fact that Nigeria ranks number 106 in the world in terms of internet speed, a significant share of the country's 122 million internet users should be able to watch *Black November* if they are so inclined and can afford it (Speedtest 2019; BBC 2019).

Between the *Daily Trust* and *Black November* spans a complex media landscape that I would like to conceptualize in three overlapping layers of memory. The focus on the effective exploitation of Nigeria's oil wealth, fueled by confidence in the technological mastery of nature for the purpose of national enrichment, mobilizes memories of Nigerian nationalism which has been a decisive component of Nigeria's oil bonanza since its beginnings in the 1970s (Apter 2005). Nigerian nationalism has a complicated history because different national projects have been implicated in colonial rule, anti-colonial resistance, and pan-African initiatives (Oduntan 2018). Nigerian nationalism anchored in state institutions including the oil industry competes with important ethnic, tribal, and religious authorities in the multiethnic and multireligious country (Ajayi 2018). Nevertheless, on a structural level, the project of Nigerian national memory shares important traits with European memory cultures of the first modernity which have existed since the nineteenth century (Nora 1996–8). The nationalisms give rise to similar stories of progress, heroism, industrialization and material affluence, national unification, and national exclusion, in Nigeria for instance directed at the legacy of Biafran secession and militant Islamist struggle (Nwakanma 2019).

Adugbo's reference to the trauma of the Niger delta constitutes a different memory gesture. Adugbo focusses the reader's attention on the victims of multinational economic exploitation and Nigerian corruption arguing for the need to get the next oil boom right and distribute the spoils evenly among the population. The concern for past victims and the plea for a fundamental sense of justice in a globalized world is reminiscent of Europe's memory culture of the second modernity. After the traumas of the Second World War and Nazi genocide, Europe slowly developed a special respect for the victims and survivors of the Holocaust and embraced a new code of ethics anchored in the concept of universal human rights (Levy and Sznaider 2005). The cosmopolitan memory paradigm of the second modernity shared with its precursor of the first modernity a sense of optimism and progress but cast its inclusive story of justice for all on a transnational rather than a national level. Cosmopolitan memory, conceived in an era of accelerated globalization, individualization, environmental crisis, and gender revolution projected a sense of material affluence and intellectual control despite the recognition that its globalized economy carried the risk of human self-destruction (Sørensen and Christensen 2013). While the national memory culture of the first modernity thrived in the mass media of the late nineteenth and early twentieth century, especially print, architecture, political ritual, and film, the cosmopolitan memory of the second modernity was propagated particularly successfully in the visual media of photography, cinema, and television. It is based on "stories that are relatively simple, graphically compelling and easily photographable" (Balabanova 2015: 32).

The globally distributed Amazon Prime product *Black November*, available to consumers in 200 countries, premediates yet another layer of memory that I call the memory of the third modernity. The memory of the third modernity follows a radically different, counterfactual logic of time based on the prefigurative dynamics of anthropocenic memory. Humankind has to remember future ecological disasters in compelling detail in order to prevent the occurrence of these disasters through decisive political action in the here and now (Crownshaw 2017; Craps 2017). The memory of the third modernity with its counter-intuitive succession of memory before history thrives in increasingly globalized digital cultural infrastructures that are transforming the basic parameters of social memory (Reading 2016). This globalized digital memory, of short global, memory features an increasingly non-chronological experience of time, an unpredictable dynamic reshuffling of private and public spheres, and new transhuman memory actors shaped by the fusion of humans with their algorithmically controlled digital devices (Hoskins 2018). Moreover, global memory is implicated in new forms of surveillance capitalism. The large-scale harvesting of behavioral data and the large-scale digital manipulation of human behavior toward the most profitable outcomes constitutes yet another prefigurative memory of life choices and consumer decisions that have not even been made yet (Zuboff 2019). Surveillance capitalism, based on the aggregation and precise deployment of digital data on a vast scale, is incompatible with the concept of individual human rights, as a closer look at any terms-of-service agreement with a digital service provider indicates. Thus, two key components of globital memory, the surveillance memory of transhuman consumers and the anthropocenic memory of climate death, channel visions of abundance *and* scarcity; equality, occasionally even solidarity *and* relentless competition for survival. In the third modernity, any vision of progress has given way to a state of pronounced memory perplexity. As a result, trust in the power of cosmopolitan self-reflexivity and empathy has eroded.

Ulrich Beck, the key theorist of the second modernity, was convinced that "the tears we guiltily wipe from our eyes before the television or in the cinema are no doubt consciously produced by Hollywood trickery and by how the news is stage-managed. But that in no way alters the fact that the spaces of our emotional imagination have expanded in a transnational sense. When civilians and children in Israel, Palestine, Iraq, or Africa suffer and die and this suffering is presented in compelling images in the mass media, this produces cosmopolitan pity *which forces us to act*" (Beck 2006: 6, my emphasis). Beck's invocation of the forces of television and cinema was already an anachronism in 2006. In the meantime, humankind has relearned, or had never unlearned, its ability to watch others being violated without feeling much of a compulsion to intervene, not least of all because that ability is an integral element of our lives as consumers.

The history of memory in the twentieth century is the story of the interdependence of visual media, economic transformations, and the rise and fall of cosmopolitan memory politics—or of the illusion of their temporary existence. Despite its global ambitions and reach, the story remains a Western-centered narrative reflecting the exceptional affluence and power of Western societies, cultures, and elites. That story will be explored here as a tragedy in three case studies, focused respectively on the construction of cinema as a powerful site of memory independent of academic history, the invention and limits of cosmopolitan television, and the challenges of digital Holocaust remembrance (Kansteiner 2017b; Kansteiner 2018a; Kansteiner 2019). The first case study relates how film revolutionizes the construction of social memories through increasingly transnational practices of communal visual immersion. The second reports how TV, channeling fantasies of historical innocence and vicarious memory activism, helped popularize the moral foundations of cosmopolitan memory through immersive explorations of the Nazi past in the private setting of the postwar living room. Finally, the third case study explores new opportunities of self-critical history education in the wildly popular terrain of video gaming and serious gaming encouraging game developers to craft interactive immersive settings that address the topic of social violence in a decisively self-critical key.

Clearly, immersive experience of the past through visual culture is the pivot point of twentieth and twenty-first century memory culture. The business of making sense of the past relies on many media, genres, and institutions including literature, professional history, art, architecture, memorials, museums, and many others but in terms of reach and immersion none of them rival film, TV, and gaming's ability to turn encounters with the past into a deeply moving emotional experience. From the first silent film of the Lumière brothers to the latest instalment of *Assassin's Creed*, visual culture has excelled at unframing mediated experience and transposing audiences into a mental state of heightened affective involvement, increased cognitive absorption, and captivating interactive identification (Dogramaci and Liptay 2016).

FIGURE 3.2: Promotional Material for *Assassin's Creed Odyssey* (2018). Credit: Ubisoft

FILM: FROM HISTORY TO MEMORY

For lack of imagination and conceptual alternatives, discussions about film and history and historical film have often invoked the world of academic scholarship. That intellectual habit does a serious disservice to both sides of the equation (Rosenstone 1995). With hindsight and the benefit of a memory studies vantage point (Olick et al. 2011; Erll 2011b), the traditions and tools of academic history stand in stark contrast to film culture based on mechanical/digital recording devices that owe their tremendous success to their uncanny ability to recall the past as visual performance. Today, academic history is a non-visual, non-immersive, and for many people unattractive technique for representing the past. That has not always been the case. As a narrative practice for capturing national history, professional historical writing had a decisive influence on the politicization of nineteenth century memory cultures (Berger, Donovan, and Passmore 2002). But in the twentieth century, professional history and popular culture have parted ways. Some historians have tried to influence society as public intellectuals while most members of the discipline have embraced a professional ethos defined in opposition to visual culture and its ability to sustain powerful fantasies of shared pasts (Berger 2019a). Hence, memory studies, not history, is the appropriate academic framework for discussing filmic renditions of the past (Guynn 2006: 165–78).

Film and TV mark an intriguing layer of media technology involved in intense intermediation with both print culture and digital interactive culture (Rippl 2015). Film and TV were the key media platforms shaping everyday lives across the globe for most of the twentieth century before they had to yield that role to digital media. The media events of film and television history have provided the rhythm of autobiographical memory and represent the cultural kernels around which generational, national, and transnational collective memories and identities have been constituted (Dayan and Katz 1992). Throughout the long and eventful twentieth century, from the decades before the First World War all the way to 9/11, film and television established entertaining and highly centralized regimes of memory and forgetting, sorting the visible and unforgettable from the invisible and negligible. Despite providing plenty of opportunities for experimental film and television, the celluloid and broadcasting media ecologies of the first and the second modernity gave rise to highly integrated media dispositifs with specific patterns of memory aggregation and forgetting. Babelsberg, Hollywood, Bollywood, and commercial and public television have crafted such cohesive visions of society and history that the fascinated critic might be forgiven for conflating homogeneity in terms of content and aesthetics with homogeneity in terms of reception. In fact, modern mass media spawned memory studies in the sense that the concepts of collective, social, and cultural memory are based on the experience of modern media events and the notion that said media events delineate powerful national and transnational scripts of memorability. The many aspects of the past that these media ignored, one is tempted to conclude, might as well never have happened. With hindsight that homogeneity never existed; audiences have always been creative and recalcitrant and crafted diverse and fluid vernacular memories (Keightley 2013). In this sense collective memory is only a useful academic fiction. Yet none of these arguments render film less relevant for the history of memory. Hollywood, to take the most extensively studied example, has always been both self-fulfilling prophecy and machinery of forgetting (Klein 1997).

Consequently, film and television represent humanity's memory of the first and second modernity which we can better appreciate from the perspective of 2020 since the political projects of the first and the second modernity and the media technologies of film and television appear dated today. As sophisticated interactive digital games and social media platforms come to dominate memory cultures in a rapidly expanding cross section of the globe, film and television continue to offer great opportunities for exploring the origins of modernity and its past mediascapes featuring film in a starring role as (1) an icon of modernity like the train, the car, and the factory; (2) the arena which shaped and distributed the dynamic culture of modernity and its iconography; (3) the communicative space which taught people how to be and act modern; (4) and, last but not least, the cultural resource permitting us to immerse ourselves in the culture of the first and second modernity from an already slightly detached vantage point. Nevertheless, film/TV technology continues to offer fabulous opportunities for remediating digitized participatory formats and content. Moreover, TV remains the key visual mass medium for about 30 percent of the world's population. Film and TV culture thus perpetuate an imperial gaze—yet another key legacy of modernity—and facilitate the gaze's purposeful or inadvertent deconstruction (Kaplan 1997; Melgosa 2012).

Popular film culture began on the fair grounds and in vaudeville theaters of European capital cities of the 1890s. The cinema of attraction, as it has been called, featured a wide variety of visual wonders, including technological marvels of industrialization, the unfamiliar flora, fauna, and indigenous cultures of Europe's far-flung empires, scenes of contemporary European everyday life with an emphasis on the surprising and grotesque, and short clips of fiction with little narrative depth (Gunning 1986; Gaudreault 2011). Audiences were enthralled with the new moving images although reports about intense immersive incidents, for instance, of film spectators stampeding out of movie theaters when confronted head on with a moving train on the screen, seem to be more urban legend than historical fact (Loiperdinger 2004). Put differently, the sense of pleasurable unease with which today's audiences might react to violent movie and TV fare contains more than faint repercussions of the anxiety felt by early movie audiences. Moreover, and more important, the twitch of empathetic unsettlement past and present contains the potential for emotional bonding and future remembrance. It takes exposure to moving images to explore self-reflexively how moving images have shaped our sense of self and our attachment to prosthetic memories. As Alison Landsberg argues, due to its special mimetic, immersive capabilities "cinema is the archetype of the new technologies of memory created in the twentieth century" (Landsberg 2004: 14).

A decisive break-through in the history of filmic immersion was the invention of the Hollywood paradigm in the 1920s which has shaped codes and rituals of visual narration for a century (Gaines 1992). Hollywood has elicited very different intellectual responses over the decades. For many film critics of the 1970s who adopted a Marxist point of view Hollywood fostered rather than critically engaged with the fundamental social contradictions of capitalist modernity (McCabe 1974). Their one-dimensional assessment of Hollywood as a purveyor of false consciousness was fundamentally revised in the 1980s when a new generation of critics concluded that a productive tension between critical and instrumental reason was inscribed into the technical apparatus of film. If the notion of an all-powerful culture industry was a key concept of the intellectuals of the first modernity (Adorno 1991), the invention of the active audience became a guiding principle of media studies in the age of the second modernity. Consequently, critics now appreciated Hollywood as a complex, contradictory cultural institution shaped by forces of commerce *and* enlightenment (Bordwell et al. 1985). The progressive effects of Hollywood cinema stand out more clearly if one focuses on questions of reception. Only few Hollywood productions boast decidedly self-reflexive implied audiences, but many mainstream feature films have nevertheless been implicated in critical social practices and memory regimes. Due to its complex visual language and global commercial reach, Hollywood helped underprivileged groups including women, migrants, and workers develop non-hegemonic transnational identities. In this way, blockbusters have had all kinds of social consequences including spawning alternative public spheres (Hansen 1991). The cultural behemoth Hollywood has clearly never been a monolithic site of memory. It can be sliced and formed into all kinds of layers, vectors, and genre formations, especially with hindsight. Consider for instance the concept of film noir as one of many strategies of making sense of film history. The bewildering narrative worlds of film noir created in the 1940s and 1950s reflect and helped render memorable an era of rapid technological innovations, postwar consumerism, and social fragmentation leading up to the political confrontations of the 1960s and 1970s. Moreover, the concept of film noir crafted after the fact in the 1970s for a series of highly stylized Hollywood crime-dramas oozes mourning and nostalgia especially once the films became a successful liberal site of memory conveying a profound sense of sadness about the unfulfilled political promises of Western modernity (Dimendberg 2004).

The field of cinema studies offers other useful frames of interpretation and remembrance. Film historians and theorists have paid a lot of attention to experimental film, both the classical Avant-garde of the 1920s and their post-1960s successors (Turvey 2011). Experimental films undercut the narrative and perspectival conventions of popular

FIGURE 3.3: Movie poster of the film noir *T-Men*. Credit: Wikimedia Commons (Public Domain).

cinema and thus constitute a visual counter-memory of Western modernity (Landy 2015). Similar motives of resistance are attributed to the critically acclaimed yet often popularly ignored European tradition of auteur filmmaking which flourished from the 1940s to the 1970s in Italian Neo-Realism, the French New Wave, and New German Cinema. For the enthused critics, sound film modernists like Rossellini, Bergman, Truffaut, and Kluge managed to develop decelerated visual semantics which capture subjective psychological states of mind and experiences of time in ways that had previously simply not existed in visual media (Deleuze 1992; De Baecque 2011). The filmmakers used their unusual degree of cultural autonomy courtesy of the European welfare states to cast intellectual perceptions of life in fascist and post-fascist Europe into sensuous and self-reflexive film languages and elite memories. Put differently, the auteur film scene tried and sometimes succeeded in creating anti-fascistically structured memories of fascism for elite audiences which amounted to fully developed cosmopolitan memories *avant la lettre* (Kaes 1989). But these self-critical, anti-immersive, or perhaps rather intellectually immersive explorations of humanity's penchant for self-destruction remained exceptions and lacked popular appeal. The film industry after the First World War for instance never used its hold over people's historical imagination for a concerted promotion of pacifism in the same way that television advanced a critical memory of the Holocaust after World War Two (see below).

The use of film theory to mold and lift to consciousness self-critical frames of remembrance embedded in cultural practices thus still has great media archaeological potential. That applies first and foremost to the postcolonial turn in visual studies which appears ideally suited for the creation of self-reflexive memory cultures in affluent countries struggling with long traditions of racism in conjunction with large-scale migration.

Postcolonial perspectives on film had a tough time taking hold in Western academia. Non-Western filmmakers had already in the 1960s identified their work as belonging to a Third Cinema in provocative distinction to the First Cinema, i.e., Hollywood, and the Second Cinema, i.e., the postwar European auteur film tradition (Gabriel 1995). But a postcolonial perspective was only gradually integrated into the cinema studies canon in the 1990s—with important intellectual consequences. In addition to confirming that film had played a decisive role in maintaining European colonial empires at home and abroad, the postcolonial turn firmly established non-Western traditions and actors in the history of film and called into question many of the traditional, Western-centric narrative trajectories of cinema and cinema studies (Ponzanesi and Waller 2012). In essence, film was rescued from the nostalgic intellectual space demarcated by the engagement with early cinema, Hollywood, experimental film and European auteur cinema and reestablished as a vibrant cultural platform for the discussion of key contemporary global challenges.

As a result of this recalibration of the history of cinema, the medium of film can be better deployed as a tool for crafting progressive memory strategies in response to pressing global problems like pollution and migration. Both challenges are fraught with collective memory problems. When it comes to the movements of people around the globe, Western societies systematically misremember past migrations with dire consequences for today's political decision-making processes. Some movements of people are deemed troublesome and challenging. They are remembered as migrations and cast in racist visual stereotypes as for example the movements of so-called guest-workers in Europe since the 1950s and of war refugees today (Nail 2015). Other movements of people might have constituted severe challenges when they occurred but are (mis)remembered as homecomings, expulsions, or liberations, as for instance the large-scale population transfers in the immediate post-Second World War years. The point here is not that these movements cannot or should not be remembered as homecomings, expulsions or liberations but that they also should be remembered as migrations plain and simple. By constructing different registers for the memory of people on the move in contrast to each other, i.e., migration vs. homecomings, expulsions, and liberations, contemporary Western societies cast self-images of settled stability against perceptions of alien migratory threats and fail to develop lasting perspectives of cosmopolitan solidarity with war and climate refugees. Western societies need new memories of themselves as people on the move receiving other people with similar experiences, desires, and objectives (Kleist and Glynn 2012).

While film and prime-time TV play a decisive role in reproducing dangerous stereotypes, they also offer opportunities for crafting new collective symbols and self-reflexive memories. Consider in this context the topic of pollution which has been subject to repeated waves of forgetfulness since it first garnered sustained international media coverage in the 1970s. Today, the topic attracts a lot of global attention in digital media which, in a process of remediation, might help penetrate existing layers of amnesia and passivity. In 2015, the media event *Under the Dome*, a documentary about environmental pollution in China, attracted 300 million viewers within one week before its online distribution site was shut down by Chinese authorities. In the best of all media worlds, digitally remediated film and TV formats help craft collective memories of future environmental and demographic challenges in a concerted effort to avoid the most catastrophic climate and mass migration scenarios. In a similar way in which collective memories of war and genocide invented after the Second World War have possibly helped parts of the world avoid warfare in the second half of the twentieth century, we now need the digitally enhanced narrative resources of the memory machines of film, TV, and video games to craft memories of climate change in the hope that such dystopian memories of the future can still be turned into counterfactual memories. But there is one decisive difference. Twentieth century memory culture perceived of Auschwitz as a catastrophe of the Holocene. The numerous genocides of the long twentieth century, from Armenia to Syria, might have changed humankind's perspective on the value and grievability of human life (Butler 2004) but cultural responses to these man-made catastrophes worked on the assumption that it was not too late to safeguard humanity, as well as enlightenment concepts of humanity, through collective memory work *after* the catastrophes had occurred. In contrast, comprehensive nuclear war and climate death are clearly catastrophes of the Anthropocene requiring a new type of anticipatory memory culture (Craps et al. 2017). Once the tipping point of global warming has been reached, memory culture as we know it might cease to be a useful political tool because anthropocenic catastrophes require nothing short of a reversal of the relationship between history and memory. We require compelling, self-reflexive, entertaining, and popular memories of climate death *before* the catastrophe takes place in order to have a chance to prevent its occurrence. Collective memory in the Anthropocene needs to adopt a new anti-intuitive memory-before-history logic.

Film scholars remain optimistic about the global reach and emancipatory potential of cinema. They see promising film cultures, also outside of the North-West, for example in Latin America and Asia where actually existing cosmopolitanisms (Robbins 1998) offer visions of global conviviality (Navitski and Poppe 2017; Chan 2017). Considered from a more skeptical vantage point, however, it seems that film and TV dispositifs face serious structural obstacles in turning anthropocenic or re-invigorated cosmopolitan memories into politically decisive cultural interventions. Film and television have been better at facilitating, explaining, and remembering violence than at preventing it, as a closer look at TV memory culture indicates.

COSMOPOLITAN TELEVISION: FROM HERO TO SURVIVOR

The memory cultures sustained by television since the second half of the twentieth century have been as variegated as the societies that embraced the new technology. Television is a mainstream, centralized medium in search of a mass audience. Its inherently conservative aesthetic and political tendencies are counterbalanced by the need for entertaining innovations and, in some settings, the progressive leanings of its creative personnel. Consequently, a great deal of television reflects the political objectives of social elites and the assumed parameters of popular taste. In this way, nationalistic and sexist TV fare has played a decisive role in propping up repressive regimes around the globe, for instance in China and Russia (Wijermars 2019; Hutchings and Tolz 2015; Bai and Song 2015; Zhu 2008). Mass media at their worst can play an important role in the mobilization for genocidal action as was the case with radio before and during the genocide in Rwanda (Thompson 2007). Television has also shaped problematic collective self-images in the democratic West (Gray and Bell 2013). One is tempted to assume, for instance, that phenomenon like Trump and Brexit would not have succeeded as political projects had they not been able to tap into robust narrative worlds of white male resistance against globalization and cosmopolitanism that existed as well-integrated mass media memories before they became political realities. Could one imagine Brexit without the kind of nostalgia channeled by *Downton Abbey* and Trump without the excess of righteous violence featured in *24*?

But television can also be a force of progressive innovation notwithstanding the fact that said innovations are subject to TV's structural limitations. Since the 1970s, television has been the key platform for the creation and popularization of transnational cosmopolitan memory. The construction of a moralizing, victim-centered memory culture, focused on the Holocaust and advocating for the rule of human rights, represents the single most important memory accomplishment of the last century—despite the fact that cosmopolitan Holocaust memory has often diminished the visibility of other crimes and victim groups, helped the perpetrators dodge public attention and appropriate punishment, and contributed to the de-politicization of collective memory processes and thus indirectly and inadvertently furthered the rise of neo-fascist movements replete with their own type of vociferous anti-cosmopolitan memories.

In the second half of the twentieth century, the swastika reigned supreme in the TV culture of the West reflecting a collective fascination with the violence of war and genocide and a concerted didactic effort to supply consumers of the second modernity with a stable, self-reflexive historical consciousness (Gedziorowski 2014). In part, the affinities on display between television and Nazi memory result from simple timing. Television became a key theater of cultural reflection at the very moment when European societies belatedly engaged in discussions about their communicative memories of the Second World War and shortly thereafter began crafting enduring transnational cultural memories of the war for future generations (Bignell and Fickers 2008). In addition, there were other, more sinister affinities at work that explain the intimate relationship between TV culture and the memory of National Socialism (NS). Television and swastika enjoyed a close, symbiotic relationship based on compatible strategies of making sense of the world. Throughout formerly occupied Europe and Germany, viewers fascinated by the violent histories unfolding on their TV screens eerily resembled the citizens of a Nazi dominated continent similarly enthralled by the violence erupting outside their homes. Television technology was an extraordinarily suitable communicative apparatus for addressing memories of Nazism, because the little screen in the living room offered similar imaginary vantage points of non-involvement as the living room window during the Nazi era. Window and screen neatly separated private from public sphere, "normal" citizens from Nazis and Jews and thus fostered seemingly clear-cut categories of belonging that rendered violence manageable. Television worked beautifully for the process of coming to terms with the past because it doubled and helped side-step the key moral challenge of the Nazi years providing, yet again, a position of comfortable voyeurism and propagating a myth of Heimat as a safe and non-political space. With critical distance, the problem of the bystander of mass violence thus emerges as a key problem of televisual remembrance equipped with an uncanny ability to naturalize and validate the bystanders' point of view after the fact through specific routines of television consumption. The apologetic structures of televisual and filmic entertainment were further enhanced by the fact that many creative minds in the postwar TV and cinema business had previously supported Nazi entertainment, propaganda, and occupation efforts across Europe.

Key memory events in postwar Europe served the strategic objectives of first generously extending the exculpatory category of "fellow travelers" and "resistance fighter" to include almost the entire population of the continent. Then, in later decades, memory disputes exposed former NS perpetrators and collaborators who had been enjoying postwar prosperity seemingly safely tucked away in the memory comfort zone of NS bystanding. In this fashion, the memory politics of the 1940s and 1950s championed large-scale amnesties whereas the social movements of the 1960s and 1970s targeted specific individuals and issued sweeping indictments against entire generations (Niethammer 1972, Frei 1996, Wernecke 2015). Exposing the fascist leanings and collaborationist exploits of the contemporaries of the Third Reich and turning them into present-day political liabilities worked wonders as a political weapon precisely because the vast majority of Germans and Europeans of the World War era considered themselves passive spectators of the war catastrophe. The generational rebranding efforts called into question self-serving fantasies of communal resistance and non-involvement across Europe (Lebow et al. 2006).

The intense negotiations about where to draw the line between historical valor, innocence, shame, and guilt fueled political battles across a diversified print media landscape and, in less explicit and incendiary terms also set the agenda for historical coverage in the elite-controlled, consensus-driven media environment of public television. Decades of historical programming provided viewers with an opportunity to investigate repeatedly and at times obsessively the four central, regularly readjusted historical subject positions of Nazi era perpetrator/collaborator, bystander, victim, and hero. These four emblematic figures constitute a robust narrative machine reminiscent of Greimas' semiotic square (Greimas 1983), spewing forth a seemingly endless series of documentaries, docudramas, TV plays, and feature films.

The few available quantitative analyses and a more extensive set of case studies suggest that the Second World War and Holocaust memory on Western television developed in four overlapping phases: first, in the 1960s and 1970s broadcasts mentioning the history of the "Final Solution" for the most part lacked conceptual focus and relied on well-worn narrative stereotypes and aesthetics of detachment. In the TV cultures of the victorious Allies, these explorations of the moral depravity of Nazi anti-Jewish policies complemented Second World War memorial pride. In West Germany, the programs acknowledged the fact of genocide but often contained them within apologetically structured narratives and only occasionally developed a decidedly self-critical edge especially when they pursued a memory angle, i.e., when they focused on postwar efforts of coming to terms with the past (Classen 1999; Feil 1974).

The second wave of broadcasting in the 1970s and 1980s consisted of a string of emotionally engaging and highly entertaining American and European productions constructing and conveying the enormity of the Holocaust often by focusing on everyday life and persecution during Nazism (Keilbach 2008; Geisler 1992; Kansteiner 2006a); The programs had decidedly self-critical effects in West Germany and became the blueprint for future EU memory highlighting the need for self-critical memory politics and also raised questions about Allied heroism since the world had apparently not reacted appropriately to the absolute evil that was the Holocaust.

The third phase of Holocaust and Second World War memory featured an even more extensive, less self-reflexive succession of professionally produced documentaries and docudramas transnationally screened around the turn of the century and conveying intriguing, ambivalent, highly entertaining, and immersive visions of Nazi culture often highlighting themes of civilian victimhood (Bangert 2014; Ebbrecht-Hartmann 2016; Keilbach 2006; Kansteiner 2006a; Lersch and Viehoff 2007).

A possible fourth phase, as yet insufficiently documented and analyzed, featuring narratively and ethically complex and ambitious inquiries into the experiences of the "normal" perpetrators of the Third Reich and memorializing the heroes of postwar efforts of coming to terms with the past. The last phase is even more subject to re- and pre-mediation processes than the previous phases (Graff 2015; Classen 2013).

In the course of these four phases and five decades, a process of professionalization changed the way in which TV communicated with its viewers about the past. In the first decades of its existence, television addressed questions that also dominated other spheres of historical culture in the West. Like many intellectuals, academics, and artists, TV journalists and producers tried to grasp why the Nazis had come to power and wreaked havoc across Europe. Since the second phase, TV professionals shifted gradually to a different set of guiding questions trying to figure out how it felt like to suffer from Nazi persecution or partake in Nazi crimes. The shift from why to how, from causality to re-enactment, corresponded to a shift from primarily discursively to primarily visually constituted programming and probably resulted in different kinds of collective memories of the Nazi past. Over the decades, television constructed and conveyed different feelings about the Nazi past moving from a concern with a sense of intellectual control supported by discursive aesthetics of why to a persistent curiosity about sensing facets of trauma through simulative aesthetics of how. The shift towards new modes of perception and entertainment also aimed at enhancing the bystander experience because TV focused now specifically on offering viewers an opportunity to experience vicariously the Nazi past and acquire a sense of memory advocacy (Highmore 2017; Bruzzi 2015; Elsaesser 2014). By feeling their way into narrative worlds of the war years, second generation viewers assumed the comfortable role of secondary witnesses combining tantalizing experiences of moral ambivalence with the firm belief of always already having been on the right side of history. Television had to learn what film already practiced for many decades. By sidestepping academic-intellectual historiographical concerns, TV became a well-integrated and extraordinarily successful memory machine marshaling images, sound, and language for immersive experiences of the past. But in the North-West, TV executives and creative staff did not have much time to enjoy the days of televisual supremacy. In the decades after 2000, TV entered in an increasingly competitive relation to social media and videogame culture. That process of intense cross-mediation has invigorated TV culture but will also end TV's hold over popular historical imaginations.

When collective memory shifted decisively in 1978/1979 after the broadcast of the NBC miniseries *Holocaust*, cultural elites found themselves in a tricky situation. They had to explain to the public why they had paid relatively little attention to the history of the Holocaust now unequivocally considered a key event of modern history. From today's perspective, that criticism seems both reasonable and problematic. Reasonable because Holocaust memory remains a key anchoring point for collective identities in the West and, judged by its standards, postwar European memory culture appears to have lacked moral integrity for failing to recognize the extraordinary historical and ethical-

FIGURE 3.4: Cover of the German magazine *Der Spiegel*, January 29, 1979. Credit: Der Spiegel.

political relevance of Nazi genocide. But the ex post factum indictment of postwar memory culture also seems problematic from today's perspective because over seventy years after the collapse of the Third Reich and over thirty-five years after the conception of popular Holocaust memory the potential ethical shortcomings of Holocaust memory, including its ethnocentrism and political opportunism, are more vigorously discussed than ever (Fogu et al. 2016). As a result, the invention of the Holocaust paradigm in the 1970s no longer qualifies as unequivocal memory progress and the pre-Holocaust memory culture of the 1950s and 1960s no longer appears as a bleak memory-scape of denial (see also Rothberg 2009).

Notwithstanding the different conceptual perspectives for the assessment of postwar memory culture, *Holocaust* remains a pivot point in the history of modern memory. *Holocaust* was a scandal before it became a cause célèbre. Many critics on both sides of the Atlantic initially vigorously rejected its fast-cut, relentlessly entertaining, emotionally manipulative, profit-mongering aesthetics (Shandler 1999; Wilke 2004). In an exceptional feat of mass communication, *Holocaust* nevertheless succeeded in solidifying a specific moral perspective that previously had only limited social-political reach. Once established as a moral certainty, that perspective proved highly efficient for the purpose of criticizing postwar Nazi apologetics and turning Nazi genocide into a popular site of memory. The media event *Holocaust* was both a reflection and an important catalyst of the popular turn to memory that swept Western societies a quarter century after the Second World War (Erll 2011b). The series helped usher in the kind of cultural externalization of memory in memorials, museums, and visual culture whose existence is largely taken for granted today. *Holocaust* thus represents a first highlight of the politics of regret that became official (West) German and European memory in the 1980s and 1990s (Olick 2016). Moreover, the turn to victim-centered, self-critical memory changed the academic landscape. Academics responded to shifting memory priorities by developing new research fields such as Holocaust historiography and cultural trauma studies in an effort to grasp the origins of the "Final Solution" and honor the survivors. The rise of memory studies as we know it was also directly related to the fundamental shift from national-heroic to transnational-cosmopolitan memory politics as advanced and exemplified by *Holocaust*.

Holocaust set an unprecedented and never again reached benchmark for self-critical memory politics. Before *Holocaust*, prime time historical programming that elicited 100 to 150 viewer responses counted as successful history television. Therefore, nobody was prepared for tens of thousands of Germans pouring out their hearts in phone calls and letters expressing deep felt regret, confusion, and resentment (Jordan 2008). A combination of emotion-centered, innovative, and expensive color TV aesthetics (especially innovative in the German context), excellent script writing and acting featuring attractive victim and non-stereotypical perpetrator figures, unparalleled PR efforts, and an affluent historical culture already sensitized to self-reflexive Nazi memory (especially through television)—all these factors combined turned *Holocaust* into a perfect storm of a media event. Thirty-four years after the liberation of Auschwitz, significant segments of the society that had launched genocide understood the scale of their crimes, felt empathy for the victims, and a sense of loss at their own moral depravity. *Holocaust* thus inadvertently set a high bar for history culture past and present. A mass media product could apparently play a decisive role in crafting new paradigms of historical self-criticism. Ever since, the representation of historical violence in popular culture can be held to higher standards. Television, films, and video games dealing with past crimes may entertain and make money, but they should ideally also serve an ethical function. Writers and producers can and should ask the question of what ethical-political purpose media violence serves and how a production can trigger self-critical reflections about past and present human rights violations. Put bluntly, mediations of trauma should contribute to the important task of preventing people from becoming perpetrators (again). The Holocaust memory paradigm ushered in by *Holocaust* might be dated but the high expectations directed at mass culture that the TV series raised are worth retaining (Rosenfeld 1997; Novick 1999).

After *Holocaust*, visual culture in the West has continued to produce consciously crafted responses to the NBC miniseries including such memorable media events as *Shoah* (1985), *Heimat* (1984), *Schindler's List* (1993), *Holokaust* (2000), and *Generation War* (2013). In a testament to the relative diversity of emerging Holocaust memory, cultural elites, ever skeptical of popular TV in general and *Holocaust* in particular, chose their own sites of Holocaust memory, most prominently Claude Lanzmann's over nine-hour-long documentary *Shoah* (1985). To this date, *Shoah* remains an important reference point for academic memory culture enthralled by a narrative universe in which the narrator figure of Lanzmann pulls the strings alternately duplicitously cuddling up to real Nazis in an undercover sting operation, relentlessly seducing survivors into restaging their humiliating past, or obsessing about alleged Polish callousness and merriment in the face of judeocide. *Shoah* lacks self-critical depth and amounts to Western academic memory kitsch exploring the abyss of genocide from the superior point of view of a peculiar anti-intellectual intellectualism, which takes great pride in unflinchingly confronting victims, perpetrators, and bystanders of genocide without realizing that this attitude of cold aloofness is implicated in the crimes (LaCapra 1998).

Like *Holocaust*, *Heimat*, *Shoah*, and *Schindler's List* are transnational sites of memory that played an important role in the evolution of NS memory. However, in terms of popular resonance the auteur films have been overshadowed by a series of stunningly successful and morally disappointing documentaries and docudramas originally broadcast by public television in Germany, the UK, and the US since the turn of the century and screened on cable channels around the globe. The programs elegantly circumnavigated, at times even subverted the Holocaust paradigm by paying lip service to pacifism and Holocaust memory but embracing the bystanders of war and genocide as the true measure of normal behavior in times of crisis. The docudramas and documentaries—in Germany linked to the name of the ZDF TV executive Guido Knopp—amounted to a third wave of history TV. They lacked the self-consciousness of auteur cinema and settled on predictable transformations of bystanders into victims (Fischer and Wirtz 2008; Ebbrecht-Hartmann 2016; Keilbach 2008; Kansteiner 2006a). The hitherto last response to *Holocaust*, *Generation War*, deserves credit as a high-profile program focusing squarely on average NS perpetrators. The series belongs to a sustained, internationally traded wave of entertaining, high quality docudramas dealing with historical topics and settings (Ebbrecht-Hartmann and Paget 2016). *Generation War* also seems to be part of a more extensive, belated televisual inquiry into "normal" Nazi perpetrators (Browning 1992)—one which includes, for instance, Stefan Ruzowitzky's *Radical Evil* (2014)—although we lack comprehensive TV data to assess the volume and the social relevance of these programs.

The narrative square seems to have come full circle. Before and after *Holocaust*, television only sporadically confronted its viewers with the most painful legacy of genocide, i.e. the deeds and continued presence of hundreds of thousands of perpetrators and many more bystanders in the midst of post-genocidal societies. Belatedly the networks acknowledged the crimes and the suffering of the victims with impressive detail, candor, and frequency but they also often let average perpetrators and bystanders linger in the shadows—nameless, faceless stereotypes devoid of stories worth exploring. The aesthetic construction of these lacunae changed substantially over time. In the 1960s and 1970s, the perpetrators and bystanders of the "final solution" did not become primetime protagonists because television culture had not yet conceived of Nazi genocide as the primary focus of its efforts at coming to terms with the past. In the 1980s, a consciousness of the extraordinary characteristics of the Holocaust quickly permeated all layers of historical cultures in the North-West but now the perpetrators and bystanders took a backseat, visually and narratively, to the survivors of the "Final Solution" who came to play a decisive role in the narrative worlds of television. Finally, since the 1990s, the average perpetrators were overshadowed by the figures of the Führer and his henchmen who conveniently absorbed all responsibility for the Holocaust. At the same time, TV embraced the aged figure of the bystander as the measure of appropriate moral conduct in times of war and genocide. Television only seems to have developed a more persistent curiosity about ordinary men's complicity in genocide over six decades after the crimes at a point in time when the vast majority of murderers and bystanders were already dead and when historical coverage had lost social relevance and thematic focus in a highly diversified TV market. It seems unlikely that the exploration of genocidal narrative worlds will pick up speed any time soon in the dated setting of television. The next narrative history frontiers are video games and AI settings whose immersive, simulative, and counterfactual environments offer fabulous opportunities to explore the moral conundrum of genocide by-standing and complicity—if genocide memory institutions can muster the courage to develop truly interactive digital memory-scapes.

With the Holocaust paradigm television made a decisive contribution to the transformation of memory cultures in the North-West. Given its popular appeal it is not surprising that the iconography and narrative infrastructure of the paradigm have been deployed for the representation of many other genocidal events, including the Armenian genocide, the Nanking Massacre, the genocides in Rwanda and Cambodia, apartheid, human rights violations in Latin America, the civil wars in the former Yugoslavia, and, more recently, the genocides committed against the Yazidi in Iraq and the Rohingya in Myanmar (Jinks 2016; Avedin 2019). For the most part, however, the films and programs about these events can be sorted in two overarching categories. They either constitute an effort by cosmopolitan memory proponents in the North-West to look outward into the world and cast human-on-human violence into the robust and time-tested framework of Holocaust remembrance or they attest to victims' efforts to receive recognition and help to alleviate their suffering. The cultural products generally lack the self-critical edge that *Holocaust* inadvertently assumed in the late 1970s. The Holocaust paradigm has thus triumphed as a form of cosmopolitanism-lite, i.e., as a narrative template permitting victim groups to stress their suffering and the North-West to showcase its allegedly civilized anti-genocidal convictions. In this fashion, even in Germany, Holocaust and Holocaust-type stories are routinely deployed for purposes of non-self-critical identity affirmation (Assmann 2013b). Apparently, we urgently require new cultural products and formats to think and feel (again) more self-critically about the making of perpetrators and the complicity of bystanders. In principle, gaming and AI environments offer fabulous new opportunities for self-critical immersion into violent historical settings but in practice those options have not yet been implemented.

VIDEO GAMES: FROM WATCHING VIOLENCE TO WATCHING ONESELF BEING VIOLENT

Video games and social media are the most important media shaping cultural memories in the twenty-first century and they are certainly not shying away from violent content matter. But in 2020 the video game industry is still avoiding the topic of genocide. A few serious and independent games initiatives have tried to address Holocaust history but had to desist due to lack of funding or opposition from Holocaust memory institutions. The large media franchises, aware of this opposition, have carefully danced around the Holocaust and explored it in game appendices and epilogues that suspend normal game rules and cast gamers into the unusual role of television viewers.

Reservations about the compatibility of the medium video game with serious historical subject matter are not limited to Holocaust themes and extend to other topics including 9/11 (Robertson 2015) and slavery (Wainwright 2019). At the same time, video games have conquered the historical imagination of many players as games with historical themes proliferate (Kappell and Elliott 2014; Kline 2014; Winnerling and Kerschbaumer 2014; Huntemann and Payne 2010). Moreover, as a result of the development of serious gaming during the last fifteen years, video games now play a decisive role in government and corporate training, education, health care, and public policy (Loh et al. 2015; Dörner et al. 2016; Ritterfeld et al. 2009). The gaming community is very aware of the disconnect and some game critics have already concluded that the status quo in digital Holocaust memory is untenable. Given the cultural prominence of video games in general and games with historical themes in particular it amounts to a strange case of Holocaust denial in reverse that no sophisticated game about the topic yet exists (Day 2014). That way, the field is left wide open to dubious right-wing concoctions like KZ Manager ("KZ Manager" 2016) and, even more important, the medium's extraordinary didactic potential remains untapped. As prominent history game designer Brenda Romero has emphasized, due to their interactive nature "games convey complicity like no other medium can" (Romero in Waddell 2016; see also Harrigan et al. 2016). Therefore, they are in principle particularly well suited for having gamers intimately explore the experiences and decisions of people living in foreign worlds, including historical narrative worlds. And that intimate knowledge of past actors, may they be victims, perpetrators or bystanders, offers great potential for self-reflexive memory politics (Chapman 2016).

The disconnect between a burgeoning historical gaming culture one the one hand and the lack of state-of-the-art Holocaust gaming on the other hand turns video games into an important cultural arena illustrating par excellence Andrew Hoskins' perceptive remarks about the bifurcation of memory culture in an age of digitization. Hoskins identifies a clear division of "two media/memory cultures: one formalized, institutionalized, regimented (including online); the other more emergent, confrontational, yet fragmented" (Hoskins 2014: 60). Obviously, both spheres of social memory are closely intertwined and influence each other with the second, more fluid and emergent culture featuring a "virality that undermines attempts to sanitise history" (Hoskins 2014: 60; see also Hoskins 2009). For Hoskins the "immediacy, mobility, flexibility and interactivity" of the new emergent memory is the result of digital hyperconnectivity and particularly pronounced in social networks and file sharing platforms (Hoskins 2014: 55; see also van Dijck 2013). Due to its scale and speed the new memory problematizes the relationship between the hitherto stable cultural constructs of "past" and "present," raises anxieties about people's ability to actively shape social memory and prompts a rush to judgment that disrupts time-tested rituals for containing and forgetting potentially unsettling pasts. The gaming industry, focused on a few particularly profitable markets and dominated by two dozen companies, clearly belongs to the regimented memory culture. In the world of Tencent, Sony, and Microsoft, the formal regimes of oblivion and containment, translated into effective processes of self-censorship, are clearly (still) functioning. One factor in the mix is the nontransparent censorship process at transnational commercial institutions like Google and Facebook which relies on search engines, user input, and professional content screeners to craft the lowest common denominator in questions of historical taste in an effort to prevent offending any constituency of commercial relevance. The efforts at what is euphemistically called "commercial content moderation" occasionally produce disturbing results. In June 2016, Google for instance, suddenly and without previous communication with the author removed the DC-Blog of punk-artist Dennis Cooper and thus wiped out fourteen years of creative work (Gay 2016).

The proponents of the emerging field of digital memory studies highlight historical developments that cannot be successfully studied by existing scholarly strategies—namely the digital revolution with the instruments of traditional memory studies—and showcase a new set of intellectual tools better suited for the job at hand (Worcman and Garde-Hansen 2016; Rutten et al. 2013). On the deconstructive side, all essential binaries of memory studies become subject to critical review because digital memory requires nothing less than radically "changing the parameters of the who, what, when, and why of remembering" (Hoskins 2017b: 88). Digital memory no longer evolves along the individual-collective axis. In the post-broadcast era, there is no collective to speak of, at least not in the way in which television used to aggregate consumers into audiences through narratives and media events. For the same reason, there are also no clearly identifiable private or public spheres. Participatory digital culture features active individuals constantly posting, editing, liking, and linking in pursuit of fluid we's and for the purpose of crafting and exhibiting an attractive self. That job requires an intimate, affective, and symbiotic relationship to digital technology, and it is often the machine that dictates the rhythm of communication (Parikka 2017; Parikka 2015). As a result, transhuman entities do the remembering, requiring digital memory studies to leave behind the comfortable human-non-human divide (Lagerkvist 2019). Since transhuman selves are immersed in expansive networks always in the state of becoming, digital memory also obliterates the conventional differentiation between archives and lived historical culture with serious consequences for the social construction of time (Ernst 2013). In fluid networks, audiovisuals of the present rub elbows with audiovisuals from the past rendering impossible any collectively organized, self-reflexive process of balanced remembering and forgetting. In fact, the very distinction between past and present becomes very flexible with transhumans living in an "extended now" (Pogacar 2017), being unable to leave behind the ghosts of past humiliations, and battling the dystopias of eternal memory, on the one hand, and technological obsolescence and memory death, on the other hand (Pogacar 2016).

Cosmopolitan memory was invented in the era of analog and electronic media. It is first and foremost a creature of television and film—as well as radio, architecture, and conventional museum aesthetics—and was fully developed before the rise of digital culture. Despite its long analog history, the cosmopolitan memory of the twenty-first century is synonymous with digital technology. On a few occasions, Holocaust culture has even produced path-breaking digital advances as in the case of the Shoah Foundation's database of 53,000 survivor testimonies which are turned into superior research and teaching tools through highly innovative search engines (Presner 2016). But the rigid interpretive frame and carefully moderated distribution systems of cosmopolitan memory render it incompatible with central elements of our digitized everyday life. Official cosmopolitan memory is professionally managed for the purpose of safeguarding the mission and long-term interests of the respective memory institutions may they be museums or other public agencies. In its current format, official cosmopolitan memory culture therefore represents an antithesis to the nimble, decentralized exchanges of opinions driving social media communication. Moreover, with its fear of counterfactual historical representations linked to concerns about genocide denial, official Holocaust culture is a particular hostile environment for cutting edge simulative and immersive virtual reality technologies. There is a significant degree of Holocaust-denial-phobia in Holocaust culture, some of it instrumentalized for fund-raising purposes.

The problems lie elsewhere and should be more clearly and honestly addressed. Cosmopolitan Holocaust memory and emergent digital Holocaust culture (to the degree that the latter exists) represent different, competing types of history edutainment with the emergent culture featuring a wider spectrum of narrative scripts and much more dynamic, at times unpredictable vectors of interpretive power than its well-established predecessor. Fast-paced and un-scripted discussions about the politics of memory in social media facilitate multi-directional, volatile confrontations about important problems of interpretation that defy cosmopolitan culture. These kinds of discussions have significant politicizing potential but are generally systematically sidestepped by risk-averse memory institutions eager to avoid political exposure. The discussions thus highlight a central dilemma of cosmopolitan culture: One cannot successfully pursue the political objective of genocide prevention while strenuously trying to avoid political risk-taking. Genocide prevention requires political courage and that is in short supply in cosmopolitan memory institutions.

For related reasons, official cosmopolitan memory keeps a careful distance from the captivating virtual environment of video game culture observing helplessly from the sidelines the rise of a paradigm of popular entertainment that threatens its business model and allegedly also its ethical raison d'être. Video games facilitate a new quality of absorbing, shared immersion in narrative cultural worlds, including realistically shaped historical worlds, based on rapid multi-sensory input, ludic pleasure, and a significant degree of narrative and especially spatial control. It is now technologically completely realistic to recreate virtually Nazi society according to our (scholarly) ideas of how that society functioned. Or, to put a finer point to it, we can bring to virtual, interactive life our interpretations of the extreme social universe of Auschwitz, any of the 42,500 other Nazi camps that covered the continent of Europe (Lichtblau 2013), or any other site of human rights abuses. The virtual camp scenario constitutes a central representational taboo of contemporary memory culture. That taboo has a lot to do with taste, power, and the history of Holocaust memory—and it represents perfectly legitimate concerns about the political and ethical purposes that could possibly be served by breathing a second, virtual life into the hell that was Auschwitz. These concerns do not represent any absolute limits of representation but reflect the limits of our present-day didactic-ludic imagination. We simply do not yet know what lines of historical interpretation and corresponding game rules a virtual Auschwitz should embody so that the gamers immersed in that truthfully recreated and therefore extremely violent world would emerge from the game with a self-reflexive democratic historical consciousness. How can the act of releasing into the world algorithms for a virtual Auschwitz support a human rights agenda of inter-cultural respect and non-violence? However, putting those legitimate concerns into writing immediately holds up a critical mirror to our familiar, comfortable cosmopolitan Holocaust memory experiences. How did we ever assume that a historical culture that incessantly and compulsively circles around the dark holes of torture, mass death, and extreme moral depravity serves those very same objectives? Does spelling out the dark holes in virtual detail really makes all that much of an ethical difference?

While we might not yet be able to design a good Auschwitz game that problem does not apply to other didactically valuable, ludically viable, and historically realistic game ideas about war and genocide. What would be wrong with designing the virtual world of Nazi occupied Poland, France, the Netherlands, or Denmark, having players assume the perspectives of Jews caught in the maelstrom, seeking out the few existing loopholes to safety, and learning in the process that the vast majority of Jews were increasingly faced with choiceless choices and no hope for rescue? Such a game should be at least as capable of inducing empathy with the victims as the Holocaust movies of past decades which are probably becoming increasingly ineffective as a didactic tool for younger audiences steeped in digital culture. And why stop there? Why not work on a spin-off Aleppo 2016 game which follows the trial and tribulations of Syrian refugees on their way to Europe as they try to escape from Assad, rebel troops, Isis, and Russian air strikes and try to overcome global disinterest and prejudice in very much the same way as German Jewry in the summer of 1939. If scripted intelligently, such an Aleppo-game would go a long way to expose the depravity of Europe's political elites of 2016 as they tried to shed their Geneva Convention, UN Human Rights Charter, and EU Convention on Human Rights obligations. It is difficult to imagine any video game about the topic that would be in such poor taste as the "game" that said politicians have been playing with the lives of millions of refugees whom they have denigrated and sought to contain in overcrowded camps outside the EU and the US. In fact, one successful and ethically valuable game that follows the suggested trajectory already exists. *This War of Mine*, released by a Polish developer in 2014, lets players experience the struggle for survival of a group of civilians in a fictional

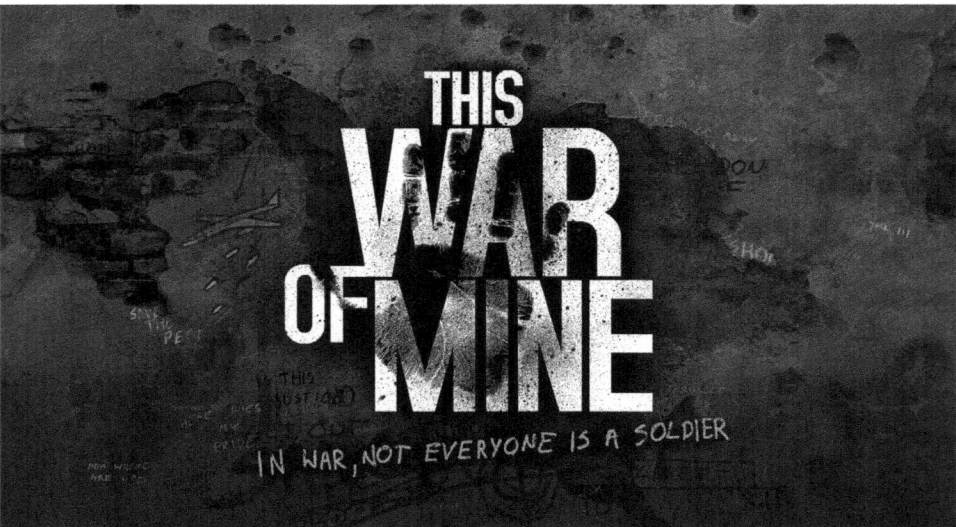

FIGURE 3.5: Promotional material for *This War of Mine* (2014). Credit: 11bits Studios.

besieged Eastern European city. Loosely based on the 1992–6 siege of Sarajevo the game goes a long way in creating empathy with war victims (De Smale 2019).

Simulative interactive narrative worlds exploring past and present crimes against humanity could offer new, decidedly self-critical perspectives on perpetrator and bystander biographies. Digital game formats seem to be very well suited to have players experience in their own virtual life the slippery slope of conformism, prejudice, and fanaticism that precedes genocide. In this fashion, genocide gaming could assume a radical self-reflexive quality and teach players, reflecting on their own virtual ethical failures and virtual crimes, how to recognize and counteract the early warning signs of radicalization and indifference. Since gaming with its extraordinary immersive potential offers the ambivalent (and for "analogers" very troublesome) experience of being simultaneously inside and outside a given simulative world, a Holocaust game could help overcome a didactic impasse that cosmopolitan Holocaust culture has thus far never been able to solve: it could complicate and possibly undermine the troublesome structural parallels between the bystanders of the Holocaust of the 1940s and the consumers of TV Holocaust culture of the last four decades, a culture that taught consumers the virtues of remembering the victims (never again genocide without memory) but provided little meaningful guidance in preventing large scale victimization in the first place (never again genocide).

CONCLUSION: THE COSMOPOLITAN DILEMMA

In 2015, two countries tried to live up to the tenets of cosmopolitan memory. Both failed. Government and civil society in Germany and Sweden made noteworthy efforts to accommodate refugees from Africa and the Middle East but politicians pulled the emergency break when significant segments of the voting public opposed accepting asylum seekers (Dahlstedt and Neergaard 2019; Ostrand 2015). The majority of elected officials in both countries now recall the decision to welcome refugees as a serious political mistake. As a result, the EU's failure is complete (Anderson 2017). An extremely wealthy political and economic union comprising 510 million people and steeped in human rights rhetoric proved unable and unwilling to craft a new home to a small number of 2.6 million newcomers (Pruitt 2019). Nobody in his right mind can attribute the failure to lack of resources (Khiabany 2016). The dubious political decisions about migration were caused by bad politics, bad values, and xenophobic culture raising disturbing questions about the precise role of memory in the dysfunctional mix. Has memory simply no influence on policy? Or is there something specifically wrong with cosmopolitan memory that might explain its political impotence? Does the memory of "never again" live in a realm of its own far removed from the levers of political power? Has cosmopolitan memory always been a comfortable elite memory serving the needs of specific carrier groups and covering up a plethora of far less appealing vernacular memories? Probably all of the above although many of the questions are now moot. The era of cosmopolitan memory appears to be over.

In election after election before and after 2015, the topic of migration has played a key role across the West and has provided well organized and social media savvy right-wing parties with a string of electoral triumphs, a stable voter base, and long-term financial resources. The right-wingers have relentlessly exposed the glaring contradiction between cosmopolitan theory and nativist practice and put on display for everybody to see the hypocrisy of the political establishment and the exclusion of the figure of the migrant from mainstream, liberal cosmopolitanism (Lochocki 2018; Vieten 2018). Hollow rituals of cosmopolitan memory will survive. Holocaust memory is well institutionalized across the continent. But the set of values allegedly supported by these rituals will probably never play an important role in shaping migration policies. Official values, affluence, demography, and economic interests all point in the same direction: Europe has benefited from immigration and should welcome it (Portes 2019; Goldin et al. 2011). But cosmopolitan veneer and instrumental reason run up against a more powerful memory regime: racism.

Racism and resistance against racism are feats of memory (Winfield 2007; Stevens et al. 2013). Racism is learned and remembered and thus perpetuated. The cultural labor required for that purpose takes place in plain sight. The postcolonial societies of Europe have lost their colonies in Africa and Eastern Europe but, over decades, fondly recalled fuzzy yet powerful visions of racial supremacy. Any systematic look at the structure of political discourse, news coverage, film and TV fictions, and digital media reveals plenty of well-intended attempts at teaching tolerance and a devastating continuity of understated narrative and visual templates of racial othering (Van Dijck 1991; Poole 2002; Saha 2012; Kansteiner 2018b). However, the failure of cosmopolitan memory and the perpetuation of racism also results from the peculiar history and communicative processes of modern media ecologies.

When it comes to historicizing media memories, the model of three modernities, three media ecologies, three versions of capitalism, and three corresponding memory paradigms is best conceptualized as consisting of increasingly complex and variegated layers of technologies, platforms, and genres that do not replace each other but shape each other in intense complementary and competitive relations. Modern memories have always been a messy affair of pre- and remediations. Contemporary memory culture is thus characterized by media ecologies that transculturally share formats and contents, including non-concurrently, but differ drastically from each other in terms of material wealth, technological resources, and ideological orientation. For about half of the world's population, classic media dispositifs such as radio, film, and TV continue to play a decisive role in the construction of cultural memories. Plus, the digitized interactive memory culture of the North-West contributes to global inequality because it monopolizes scarce raw materials to maintain its expensive multi-media ensembles (Reading 2016).

The media technologies and ecologies implicated in these networks of extreme power differentials have faced one decisive moral challenge in the exceedingly violent twentieth century: how can media which are politically and aesthetically implicated in the reproduction of mass violence, including the structural violence of extreme inequality, develop modes of self-critical remembrance capable of curbing human self-destruction? Modern media ecologies have often failed at this task which is linked to the fact that media are not neutral containers of historical content. Each ecology has particular strengths, blind spots, and biases, and shapes memory accordingly. One key hypothesis remains worth testing in this context. It might have been a fateful coincidence that cosmopolitan memory developed in the media ecology of film and television because the latter seems to be particularly adept at offering experiences of immersion in combination with the active construction of pleasurable fantasies of social non-involvement. The voyeur, the bystander, the TV viewer, the film connoisseur, the eyewitness, the historical witness, the survivor—these are all popular media figures channeling memories of innocence and non-implication (Rothberg 2019). Put differently, the media ecology of film/television inadvertently gave cosmopolitan memory an anti-political twist that might explain its very success but also turns cosmopolitan memory into a blunt tool when it comes to practicing and protecting human rights in the present. Now we can just hope that transhumans, operating in interactive settings that provide the opportunity to experience complicity first-hand and counterfactually, are much better at learning and implementing in concrete political terms the lessons of anthropocenic memory.

With hindsight it appears questionable how cosmopolitan the West has really ever been. Was Holocaust memory in Israel not always a very useful fig leaf for an increasingly racist state (MacDonald 2013)? Did the US ever decide to abandon one of its ill-fated and illegal military adventures mindful of the cosmopolitan lessons learned from the Second World War and enshrined in memory institutions across the country? And did Germany after unification not quickly manage to leave behind a state of cultural trauma and don the mantel of global memory champion thus turning disturbing self-critical memory yet again into comfortable self-reflexive memory (Assmann 2013b)? It seems that for many of its proponents, cosmopolitan memory has always been an identity comfort zone regardless of the brutality of the events recalled. And yet, cosmopolitan memory did bestow recognition on historical victims, championed human rights, invoked high standards of discursive conduct towards others, and, last but not least, held at bay some explicit expressions of xenophobia and racism – its temporary hegemony will be dearly missed.

CHAPTER FOUR

Knowledge: Science and Education

NICK TOSH

A one-chapter survey of twentieth-century memory science would be a high-altitude operation indeed. I shall not attempt it. Instead, I will pick a few interesting examples and zoom in. Topics covered here include Freud's psychoanalysis, Ebbinghaus's repurposing of the methods of psychophysics, Bartlett's notion of constructive remembering, post-war efforts to assimilate human memory to computer memory, and the present connectionist paradigm. Some unifying themes will, of course, emerge. One is the striking role of metaphor and simile in scientific memory discourse. In this respect, the twentieth century resembles the nineteenth; indeed, it resembles classical antiquity.

One omission is worth flagging: I do not discuss the taxonomy of memory "kinds"—declarative vs. non-declarative; episodic vs. semantic—that is taken for granted in modern scientific work on memory (Schacter (1996) is a good introduction). Sketching the history of this taxonomy would mean paying close attention to clinical neurology cases and to the gross anatomy of the nervous system. My focuses will be elsewhere.

BEGINNINGS

Between 1879 and 1884, philosopher Hermann Ebbinghaus spent much of his time reading, memorizing, and reciting—to the steady beat of a metronome—strings of nonsense syllables. Expressed qualitatively, his conclusions were unsurprising: long strings take longer to learn than short ones; study breaks are helpful; forgetting is a gradual process. But Ebbinghaus's project was a methodological proof-of-concept. He had brought the techniques of the nineteenth-century laboratory to bear on human memory, and the techniques had not failed.

That, at any rate, is the retrospective verdict. Ebbinghaus's 1885 report is directly ancestral to the twentieth-century tradition of laboratory-based memory research, and therefore (arguably) to the modern science of memory *tout court*. I do not wish to challenge this verdict. However, for the purposes of this volume we shall need to look a little further afield. Consider the case of Sigmund Freud. Modern scientists rarely present themselves as Freud's intellectual heirs, but a cultural history of memory science cannot possibly ignore psychoanalysis. I shall begin there.

PSYCHOANALYTIC MEMORY SCIENCE

Freud's scientific reports look nothing like Ebbinghaus's. They range with novelistic freedom over the life stories of individual patients. They contain no quantitative data. They contain few detailed descriptions of methods. Nothing remotely resembling a controlled trial—let alone a trial as austere as Ebbinghaus's—is ever alluded to. Still, psychoanalytic approaches to memory were widely regarded as scientific in the early years of the twentieth century. (Psychoanalysis was mentioned favorably at the formal opening of the Cambridge Psychological Laboratory in 1913 (Forrester 2008: 38–9). From 1914, it was taught at Johns Hopkins University Medical School (Schwartz 2003: 149).) It helped that Freud was a physician, and that he could frame so many of his works as medical case histories. It helped also that the characteristically Freudian coup—reconstructing a repressed memory from scattered and superficially insignificant clues—marked psychoanalysis out as a "retrospectively prophetic" activity: fit, perhaps, to be classed alongside geology and paleontology.

The broader intellectual backdrop is important here. Historians of science sometimes speak of a "laboratory revolution" in the nineteenth century. The phenomenon was real enough: Ebbinghaus and the other founders of experimental psychology rode its coattails. Nevertheless, some of the century's most admired scientific achievements owed little to laboratory work; they emerged instead from the natural historical tradition of collecting, classifying, and systematizing. Geologists' refutation of biblical chronology and Darwin's theory of evolution are stand-out examples. By 1880, T.H. Huxley could, with some justification, present geology and paleontology as paradigms of scientific rationality. Researchers in those fields, Huxley wrote, "strive towards the reconstruction in human imagination of events which have vanished and ceased to be." They succeed because "they perceive endless minute differences," present-day traces of the past, "where untrained eyes discern nothing" (Huxley 1882: 142). Huxley and his colleagues inferred evolutionary trees from present-day taxonomies and the fossil record. "In no very distant future," he thought, it would be possible "to reconstruct the scheme of life from its beginning" (Huxley 1882: 155). But the human sciences had their retrospective prophets too. Philologists had recently reconstructed Proto Indo European (using methods rather similar to those of Huxley et al.); historians were placing greater and greater emphasis on primary-source-based sleuthing; and Schliemann was sifting through the ruins of Troy. The idea that a future science of human memory would aspire to something like an archaeology of the mind would probably not have struck Huxley as implausible.

This was Freud's project from the very first. "Hysterics suffer mainly from reminiscences," he wrote with Josef Breuer in *Studies on Hysteria* (1895), but they "are not at the patients' disposal" (Freud 1966, vol. 2: 7, 9). The therapist's task is to reconstruct them. The "procedure was one of clearing away the pathogenic psychical material layer by layer, and we liked to compare it with the technique of excavating a buried city" (Freud 1966, vol. 2: 139). Interpretation was a challenge, but he and Breuer felt they had cracked the code. They "often compared the symptomatology of hysteria with a pictographic script which has become intelligible after the discovery of a few bilingual inscriptions" (Freud 1966, vol. 2: 129). Freud drew freely on archaeological language throughout his career. Behind the extended similes was a serious argument: the inferential leaps made by psychoanalysts resembled those made by archaeologists; *ergo*, readers who trusted the latter should trust the former too. Perhaps more importantly, psychoanalysis itself seemed to offer a window into the deep past—to be, in a sense, a branch of archaeology in its own right. The enabling principle here was a commonplace of fin de siècle biology known as the biogenetic law. It ruled that every animal's developmental trajectory from egg to adult was a high-speed replay (a "recapitulation") of its ancestors' evolutionary history; it thereby encouraged the notion that scientists might learn about the psychology of prehistoric humans by studying the psychology of children. Backed by this "law," Freud could offer a two-level science of memory. At the individual level, psychoanalytic therapy would help patients recover repressed childhood memories. At the species level, a general theory of psychological development (grounded in psychoanalytic case history data) would enable humanity to recover collective memories of its prehistory (Gould 1977: 155–64).

"Memories of prehistory" is no metaphor. Freud was not just a recapitulationist: he was also a Lamarckian. He believed that acquired characteristics could be passed on in biological inheritance. (This view was close to orthodoxy when Freud trained as a physician and remained respectable for at least the first decade of the twentieth century.) Memories are acquired characteristics of the nervous system. Thus, Lamarckism invites the hypothesis that memories might sometimes be inherited. To find the invitation tempting, one must already be committed to unconscious mentality—no one *consciously* remembers what his ancestors did—but of course Freud was so committed. By 1913, he was arguing that the Oedipus complex memorialized an actual parricide: one committed, in the very distant past, by the subjugated sons of a tribal patriarch (Freud 1966, vol. 13: 161). Archaeologists and anthropologists were, it is fair to say, unpersuaded, but their complaint was that Freud had provided insufficient evidence for his specific hypothesis, not that the Lamarckian foundations of his project were unsound (Kroeber 1920). As the long nineteenth century drew to a close, psychoanalysis seemed set to play a significant role in shaping the modern science of memory. The psychoanalytic movement was small but growing. Case history data would, presumably, continue to accumulate; therapeutic and interpretative techniques would continue to improve; and it was a safe bet that enterprising writers would continue to probe humanity's shared psychic inheritance by (as it were) putting the species as a whole on the couch. The psychoanalytic movement did indeed continue to grow strongly throughout the first half of the twentieth century, but the prospects for a psychoanalytic science of memory did not.

Freud himself had a crisis of confidence—though a strictly private one—in 1897. "I no longer believe in my *neurotica*," he wrote to his friend and confidante Wilhelm Fliess (Masson 1985: 264). He was referring to a theory he had publicly presented eighteen months earlier in a lecture to the Vienna Society for Psychiatry and Neurology. There he had maintained that the origin of hysteria was, always, sexual abuse in early childhood. As evidence, he had pointed to the eighteen hysterics he had so far treated: in every one of these cases he had discovered repressed memories of abuse. So he had told the Society, and so he had then believed. They had not believed him—"it sounds like scientific fairy tale," the sexologist Richard von Krafft-Ebbing had remarked—and now he was giving up on the idea himself (Masson 1985: 184). Why? This is not the place for a detailed account of Freud's abandonment of the seduction theory. The details are, in any case, controversial, but the basic source of Freud's difficulties is clear enough. The "memories" he had "discovered" were, in fact, reconstructions. Patients did not volunteer them. Instead, Freud made suggestions, which patients vehemently rejected—at least initially (Freud 1966, vol. 3: 204). Freud talked some of them round in time, but that did not prove much. He was, after all, a persuasive man. The reconstruction process was guided and justified by psychoanalytic theory. Psychoanalytic theory was, in turn, justified by the accumulated stock of case history material, past reconstructions very much included. Circularity of this sort is not automatically vicious. However, a virtuous circle should have brought Freud to a *stable* understanding of both the cases (in light of the theory) and the theory (in light of the cases). Freud's understanding was far from stable. In early 1896, the adult abusers in his theory had been "nursemaids, governesses and domestic servants" (Freud 1966, vol. 3: 164). In the Vienna Society lecture, the cast of villains remained broad, but "all too often" the abuser was "a close relative." By the summer of 1897, it was simply fathers. Freud reported to Fliess his "surprise that in all cases, the father, not excluding my own, had to be accused of being perverse" (Masson 1985: 264). Had Freud forgotten his earlier cases? No: he had simply reinterpreted them. But his heart was no longer in it. Many authors have proposed discreditable explanations: cowardice (Masson 1984); filial piety (Robinson 1993: 154–5); a desire to uphold the patriarchy (Rush 1996). The fact is, though, that by September 1897 the objective grounds for skepticism were overwhelming. Freud could not keep his story straight, and he knew it.

For several years, Freud dialed down the repressed memory talk. He could not unwrite his seduction theory papers, but he could, and did, avoid mentioning them in print. By 1906, his reputation was secure. Well-received books on dreams (1900), parapraxes (1904), and jokes (1905) had diversified the psychoanalytic brand, and Freud felt confident enough to revisit the awkward episode of 1896–7. It was a scab at which he would pick, on and off, for the rest of his life. Allen Esterson has mercilessly chronicled the various iterations of Freud's story; I will just note a few highlights (Esterson 2001). In 1906, Freud wrote that he "was at that period [mid 1890s] unable to distinguish with certainty between falsifications made by hysterics in their memories of childhood and traces of real events" (1966, vol. 7: 274). The implicit hint that he was *now* able to "distinguish with certainty" between veridical and non-veridical memories was disingenuous, but it was also a one-off: Freud would often admit to uncertainty on this point in future. More important was the suggestion that "falsifications" (when they did occur) should be attributed to the patients rather than to the psychoanalytic process. Non-veridical reconstructions would no longer be embarrassments. Quite the reverse: they revealed patients' fantasies, and fantasies were—like dreams and slips of the tongue—grist to Freud's mill. In his later work, Freud would still occasionally claim to have reconstructed "certain external happenings, certain impressive events of [patients'] childhood years" (1966, vol. 20: 216). However, he was increasingly inclined to downplay their clinical significance. Fantasies, he argued in 1917, "possess psychical as contrasted with material reality, and [. . .] in the world of the neuroses it is psychical reality which is the decisive kind" (1966, vol. 16: 368). The *locus classicus* for this shift is the "Wolf Man" case history. In the first draft, written in 1914, Freud reconstructed a "primal scene" of parental intercourse allegedly witnessed by the patient at the age of eighteen months. By 1917, he had decided that the scene might just as easily have been a fantasy, but that this was "not in fact a matter of very great importance" (Freud 1966, vol. 17: 97). Freud had retreated on the memories-of-childhood front. However, when it came to *inherited* memories—memories of prehistory—he doubled down. His new claim was that children commonly fantasized scenes of parental intercourse, seduction, castration threat, and so on. But where did these scenes come from? To Freud the answer was clear. They were "unquestionably an inherited endowment, a phylogenetic heritage." We needn't worry too much about what the Wolf Man himself actually saw, because "a child catches hold of this phylogenetic experience where his own experience fails him. He fills in the gaps in individual truth with prehistoric truth; he replaces occurrences in his own life by

FIGURE 4.1: Sigmund Freud, *c.* 1921. Credit: Wikimedia Commons (Public Domain).

occurrences in the life of his ancestors" (Freud 1966, vol. 17: 97). Again, it is important to stress that all this was meant literally. The Freudian science of memory, in its mature form most of all, was fully committed to Lamarckism.

Lamarckism was already a dicey prospect in 1917. By 1939, the final year of Freud's life, it was worse than dicey. The scientific consensus had shifted dramatically, and Freud was left defending biological claims that lay so far outside the mainstream that they could no longer be called controversial. He was unrepentant: "My position, no doubt, is made more difficult by the present attitude of biological science, which refuses to hear of the inheritance of acquired characters by succeeding generations. I must, however, in all modesty confess that nevertheless I cannot do without this factor in biological evolution" (Freud 1966, vol. 23: 98). Freud wrote those words as a world-famous intellectual whose scientific credentials had, only months before, been put beyond challenge by the Royal Society of London (Edmundson 2007: 176–7). He could afford to buck an orthodoxy or two. Since his death, psychoanalysts have rarely hazarded the claim that childhood fantasies are ancestral memories. ("Biological science" remains inhospitable to the idea.) Nor, on the whole, have they tried to resuscitate Freud's original brand of retrospective prophecy. The history of psychotherapeutic attempts to reconstruct repressed memories does not come to an end in 1939, but it does, arguably, cease to be part of the history of science (Schacter 1996: 248–79).

In one of his final extended treatments of the supposed parallels between psychoanalytic and archaeological reconstruction, Freud insisted that the former was in most respects easier than the latter. But he was prepared to admit two facts that "weigh against the extraordinary advantage" enjoyed by psychoanalysts: first, "that psychical objects are incomparably more complicated than the excavator's material ones," and second "that we have insufficient knowledge of what we may expect to find, since their finer structure contains so much that is still mysterious" (Freud 1966, vol. 23: 260). Throughout his long career, Freud told complicated stories about complicated psychical objects. By their very nature, complicated stories have many degrees of freedom: they can be bent and tweaked in many places and in many different ways. That becomes problematic when "we have insufficient knowledge of what we may expect to find." Freud did not intend the remarks I just quoted to be a repudiation of his whole approach to memory, but it is nevertheless tempting to read them that way. Retrospective prophecy does not work when wildly different visions of the past can be made to account, equally compellingly, for present-day traces. Natural scientists have a standard prescription for dealing with complexity-overload: the artificial simplicity of the laboratory. Psychological narratives with the novelistic depth of a Freudian case history will never emerge from experimental trials. On the other hand, even the earliest experimental work on memory produced results that modern researchers can still defend. It is time to return to Ebbinghaus.

EBBINGHAUS: NONSENSE SYLLABLES AND THE INSCRIPTION METAPHOR

Ebbinghaus was not the first to study mental phenomena in the laboratory. In the 1830s, Ernst Weber had investigated how the perceived intensity of a stimulus (e.g. brightness or weight) varied with its objective physical intensity. Gustav Fechner built on this work in the 1860s, coining the word "psychophysics" to describe it. Psychophysical investigators aspired to conduct controlled experiments, to make quantitative measurements, and to discover mathematical regularities in their data. Ebbinghaus's innovation was to extend this approach to the study of "higher" mental processes: specifically, those involved in learning, remembering and forgetting. The schoolroom connotations of "learning" are appropriate here, for Ebbinghaus focused on the kind of memory we (and he) would associate with reading and academic study. He made no attempt to probe personal autobiographical memory. Still, Ebbinghaus expected his readers to be skeptical (Ebbinghaus 1913: v). What, after all, was he supposed to measure? What would he manipulate? And how could he hope to control all the other variables that might be relevant? Finding appropriate raw material—content to be memorized—was especially tricky. Poetry and prose lay "nearest at hand," but Ebbinghaus judged both unsuitable. A reader of ordinary literature is subject to "a multiplicity of influences which change without regularity." The text "is now narrative in style, now descriptive, or now reflective; it contains now a phrase that is pathetic, now one that is humorous; its metaphors are sometimes beautiful, sometimes harsh" (Ebbinghaus 1913: 23). Ebbinghaus wanted to eliminate these sources of variation. The solution he hit upon was to work with *meaningless* texts: strings of nonsense syllables generated, as needed, by drawing from an enormous pack of cards (one card per syllable). Given this crude apparatus, the variables most obviously suitable for manipulation and measurement were length of string, time spent learning, time since learning, and a binary measure of success: could he recite a given sequence from memory or not? In his most famous study, Ebbinghaus memorized some thirteen-syllable strings by reading them aloud until he could confidently recite them unaided. He noted the time required to do this. Then, after a rest interval during which he did not look at or rehearse the strings—a period of time during which his memory would gradually fade—he *re*learned the strings, again noting the study time required. Given an original study time t_0 and a relearning time t_1, the quantity $100\ (t_0 - t_1)/t_0$ represented Ebbinghaus's retention, expressed as a percentage. Thus, a relearning time of zero would correspond to 100 percent retention (no relearning needed), while a relearning time equal to the original study time would correspond to 0 percent retention. Ebbinghaus investigated the relationship between retention and the duration of the rest interval. To nobody's surprise, he found that retention declined as the duration of the rest interval increased. However, Ebbinghaus's method allowed him to pin down the mathematical form of this decline. He found that retention declined quickly at first, falling to 50 percent after only an hour, but then declined more and more slowly, so that a full month after the original learning retention was still roughly 20 percent. Plots of Ebbinghaus's "forgetting curve" remain a staple of experimental psychology textbooks to this day.

It is worth stressing one aspect of Ebbinghaus's work on forgetting. After rest intervals of more than a few minutes, Ebbinghaus lacked *conscious* memories of the originally learned strings. The proof of this was that he was unable to reproduce them. He nevertheless took for granted that a "subliminal" sort of memory existed—one which admitted of "graded differences" (Ebbinghaus 1913: 8). He operationalized those graded differences through his relearning method. Like Freud, then, Ebbinghaus claimed to have discovered a way to uncover and appraise memories that are not available to introspection. Unlike Freud, he had a tightly controlled experimental protocol, and reliable records of the original stimuli. He faced no analogue of the veridicality worry. Moreover, the uniform meaninglessness of his raw material all but eliminated the temptation to engage in case-by-case interpretation.

Ebbinghaus investigated several other relationships too: study time required for initial memorization vs. length of string, retention vs. original study time, retention vs. number of relearnings, and so on. Within the confines imposed by his basic technique, the work was impressively thorough (William James (1950: 676) called it "heroic"). Still, those confines were narrow. Humans do not usually waste their time attempting to memorize nonsense. We prefer to memorize texts we can understand. The fact that we find the latter task *easier*—and not just more appealing—suggests that understanding plays an important role in memorization. But it played no role at all in the scenario Ebbinghaus studied. Had he hit upon a clever method for isolating a single psychological faculty? Or was his nonsense-memorization protocol too artificial to tell us anything interesting about human memory? Ebbinghaus's many imitators in Germany and the United States naturally favored the first hypothesis (Danziger 2008: 131–3). Meanwhile, Wilhelm Dilthey led pleas for a "descriptive" psychology, founded upon the hermeneutic method, and centrally concerned with questions of meaning. Ebbinghaus wrote a bad-tempered response in 1896 (Teo 2005: 72–3). By this time, he could afford to treat Dilthey as a minor irritant. On both sides of the Atlantic, psychology laboratories were churning out studies inspired more or less directly by his own work; and they were citing each other, not Dilthey. The first major rival *within* experimental psychology to the Ebbinghausian memory paradigm would not appear until the 1930s. (We discuss it in the next section.)

Ebbinghaus's laboratory manipulations were novel, but his conception of memory as a distinct mental faculty separable, in principle, from the understanding was not. Millennia earlier, Plato had invited his readers to think of memory as a block of wax in the mind: "we hold this wax under the perceptions or ideas and imprint them on it as we might stamp the impression of a seal ring" (Hamilton and Cairns 1963: Thaetetus 191d). Ebbinghaus used an essentially identical metaphor:

> These relations can be described figuratively by speaking of the series as being more or less deeply engraved in some mental substratum. To carry out this figure: as the number of repetitions increases, the series are engraved more and more deeply and indelibly; if the number of repetitions is small, the inscription is but surface deep and only fleeting glimpses of the tracery can be caught; with a somewhat greater number the inscription can, for a time at least, be read at will; as the number of repetitions is still further increased, the deeply cut picture of the series fades out only after ever longer intervals.
>
> —Ebbinghaus 1913: 52–3

Inscription metaphors encourage the notion that human memory might usefully be probed by the method of nonsense syllables. After all, a block of wax will preserve meaningless marks just as efficiently as meaningful ones.

We have hinted at the worry that Ebbinghaus's protocol was excessively artificial. In fairness, we should note that one common human predicament does bear some resemblance to the predicament of the Ebbinghausian test subject: rote learning. Here, plausibly, memory metaphors and pedagogy interact. Teachers who think of memory as a wax tablet may more readily believe that information can be "inscribed" in the minds of uncomprehending students. Conversely, those who associate education with rote learning may be more inclined to embrace Plato's (or Ebbinghaus's) metaphor. Ebbinghaus himself worked briefly as a schoolteacher in his youth. As a professor, he lectured on the history of pedagogy. Unfortunately, the lectures do not survive, and we have no direct evidence that he was an advocate of rote learning in the classroom. We do know that when the Breslau school board invited him, in 1897, to investigate the (presumed) decline of students' mental freshness over the course of the school day, he included a digit-memorization task in the suite of tests he administered (Dahlstrom 2014: 69). We also know that his work inspired educational psychologists in Germany and the United States; Danziger (2008: 129–31) describes this short-lived movement. Ultimately, however, the Ebbinghausian laboratory tradition persisted "not because of any practical applications but because it developed a set of procedures that promised to yield scientific knowledge about memory in the form of quantitative 'laws'" (Danziger 2008: 131). The procedures could be tweaked in countless minor ways. Researchers who bought into the paradigm knew that they would be able to plan and run "small-scale studies of modest theoretical scope, easily packaged as journal articles or doctoral dissertations" (Danziger 2008: 257). The results might not be Earth-shattering, but they would be quantitative, replicable, and publishable.

CONSTRUCTUVE REMEMBERING

There are two acknowledged classics in the psychology of memory. Ebbinghaus's 1885 report is one. The other is Frederick Bartlett's *Remembering: A Study in Experimental and Social Psychology*. This appeared in 1932, but the long series of experiments it describes were begun in 1913, when the Laboratory of Experimental Psychology opened in Cambridge. Bartlett began his investigations by following Ebbinghaus, but he quickly became dissatisfied with the method of nonsense syllables (Roediger 2003: 319; Bartlett 1932: v). That method was motivated, he thought, by the idea that psychological experiments should target "recall uncontaminated by any of the related functions with which it is contaminated in everyday life" (Bartlett 1932: 5). Bartlett, who had come to memory via the study of perception, doubted that "uncontaminated" memory was worth investigating: "Remembering is not a completely independent function, entirely distinct from perceiving, imaging, or even from constructive thinking, but it has intimate relations with them all" (Bartlett 1932: 13). Relatedly, Bartlett rejected the inscription picture: "Remembering is not the re-excitation of innumerable fixed, lifeless and fragmentary traces. It is [rather] an imaginative reconstruction, or construction," driven by the remembering subject's "effort after meaning" (Bartlett 1932: 213, 20). Since nonsense-syllable protocols tended to frustrate that effort, they were precisely the wrong tool for Bartlett's purposes. He was determined to employ "as nearly as possible the sort of material [. . .] commonly dealt with in real life" (1932: 12). How, though, was this to be done? Bartlett had some kind words for psychoanalysis: it had "brought psychological science into closer touch than has ever been achieved before with life as it is lived day by day" (1932: 15). But he had little patience for the elaborate psychical mechanisms postulated by Freud. Moreover, for all his disagreements with Ebbinghaus, Bartlett had trained as an experimental psychologist, and was from 1917 the director of the Cambridge Laboratory. He was "determined to try to retain the advantages of an experimental method of approach, with its relatively controlled situations" (Bartlett 1932: v). The general method Bartlett adopted was therefore a compromise. Like the Ebbinghausians, he assigned well-defined memory tasks to his test subjects. They were shown a stimulus, and asked, after a given interval of time, to recall it. Unlike the Ebbinghausians, Bartlett used meaningful stimuli, and he recorded his results qualitatively. His data, then, like Freud's, could be described as a connected corpus of anecdotes. But while Freud's anecdotes connected in series—one leading into another, in the context of a freewheeling exploration of a patient's psyche—Bartlett's connected in parallel. He assigned the *same* stylized task to dozens of different subjects. He compared the results. The comparison was discursive rather than statistical, but Bartlett (with his relatively homogenous raw material) had less room for interpretative maneuver than Freud.

Bartlett's most famous experiment involved a stimulus that his subjects were intended to struggle with: a Chinook folk tale, lightly adapted from a translation by Franz Boas (Boas 1901: 182–6). It is worth quoting in full.

The War of the Ghosts
One night two young men from Egulac went down to the river to hunt seals, and while they were there it became foggy and calm. Then they heard war-cries, and they thought: "Maybe this is a war-party." They escaped to the shore and hid behind a log. Now canoes came up, and they heard the noise of paddles, and saw one canoe coming up to them. There were five men in the canoe, and they said:
"What do you think? We wish to take you along. We are going up the river to make war on the people."
One of the young men said: "I have no arrows."
"Arrows are in the canoe," they said.
"I will not go along. I might be killed. My relatives do not know where I have gone. But you," he said, turning to the other, "may go with them."
So, one of the young men went, but the other returned home.

And the warriors went on up the river to a town on the other side of Kalama. The people came down to the water, and they began to fight, and many were killed. But presently the young man heard one of the warriors say: "Quick, let us go home: that Indian has been hit." Now he thought: "Oh, they are ghosts." He did not feel sick, but they said he had been shot.

So, the canoes went back to Egulac, and the young man went ashore to his house, and made a fire. And he told everybody and said: "Behold I accompanied the ghosts, and we went to fight. Many of our fellows were killed, and many of those who attacked us were killed. They said I was hit, and I did not feel sick."

He told it all, and then he became quiet. When the sun rose he fell down. Something black came out of his mouth. His face became contorted. The people jumped up and cried.

He was dead."

—Bartlett 1932: 65

For modern European readers, "The War of the Ghosts" is a confusing story. Its cultural setting is unfamiliar, and the connections between the events it describes are not always clear. ("Now he thought: 'Oh, they are ghosts.' Why?") But that is precisely the point. Given such a text as a stimulus, a modern test subject's "effort after meaning" might be expected to introduce tell-tale distortions. It was these distortions Bartlett wished to study.

Bartlett asked his subjects to read the story through twice, at their normal reading rates, and then to attempt to reproduce it fifteen minutes later. He sought further reproductions at longer intervals "as opportunity offered" (Bartlett 1932: 65). (The longer intervals might be hours, months, or even years.) Over repeated reproductions, "The War of the Ghosts" tended to become progressively less alien, less "jerky" (Bartlett's word), and more coherent—all judged, needless to say, by twentieth-century English standards. Bartlett did not attempt to measure these changes quantitatively, but there is a faint echo of Ebbinghaus's forgetting curve all the same: the process of transformation was well under way after fifteen minutes, but proceeded more slowly after that. Unsurprisingly, proper names ("Egulac," "Kalama") were mangled or eliminated. Exotic activities and objects were replaced by more familiar ones: "to hunt seals" became "to fish"; "canoe" became "boat," and so on. More interestingly, subjects tended to insert connecting elements—"and so," "as," "nevertheless." They also tended to minimize, or explain away, the apparently supernatural elements. "The net result," Bartlett wrote, "is that before long the story tends to be robbed of all its surprising, jerky and apparently inconsequential form, and reduced to an orderly narration. It is denuded of all the elements that left the reader puzzled and uneasy, or it has been given specific associative links which, in the original form, were assumed as immediately understood." He called this process "rationalization" (Bartlett 1932: 86). Bartlett's anecdotes about "long-distance remembering"—that is, cases in which subjects attempted to reproduce "The War of the Ghosts" several years after reading it—are especially suggestive. Some subjects offered only a couple of isolated details. Others offered joined-up stories, but only after considerable effort. For example, one began his account like this:

1. Brothers.
2. Canoe.
3. Something black from mouth.

4. Totem.
5. One of the brothers died.
6. Cannot remember whether one slew the other or was helping the other.
7. Were going on a journey, but why I cannot remember.
8. Party in war canoe.
9. Was the journey a pilgrimage for filial or religious reasons?
10. Am now *sure* it was a pilgrimage. (Bartlett 1932: 77)

After racking his brain a little further, the subject produced a tolerably coherent narrative: "While on their pilgrimage they met a hostile party of Indians in a war canoe. In the fight one brother was slain, and something black came from his mouth. [. . .] The cause of the journey had *both* something to do with a totem, and with filial piety" (Bartlett 1932: 77). As Bartlett noted, in cases like this the "memory process is strongly and evidently constructive" (Bartlett 1932: 93). The subject just quoted did not in any literal sense retrieve or reproduce the pilgrimage story; rather, he generated it on the fly. This is not to deny the obvious points: that *something* was preserved in the subject's brain from his original reading of "The War of the Ghosts," and that it played a role in the genesis of the pilgrimage story. What Bartlett wished to insist upon was that the remembering process involved a good deal else besides: imagination, general knowledge, and conscious and unconscious inference. These "constructive" aspects of remembering were most obvious in cases where test subjects made mistakes. However, Bartlett's view was *not* that people resort to construction when their normal memory fails. Rather, his view was that remembering is, generically, a constructive process. It is constructive even when its deliverances are accurate, and even when the original stimulus has none of the puzzling jerkiness of "The War of the Ghosts." Indeed, Bartlett's general hypothesis is biologically plausible precisely because constructive remembering would tend to work best when people are dealing with ecologically realistic material.

In the 1940s and 1950s, there were various attempts to replicate Bartlett's empirical results. Opinions differ as to whether they were successful (Johnston 2001: 348–51; Danziger 2008: 140–1). One problem was that it was difficult to say what, precisely, would *constitute* a successful replication. Bartlett had never aspired to the "rigidity of control" of "the Ebbinghaus school" (Bartlett 1932: 6). In fact, he thought it positively undesirable. What the experimentalist needed, Bartlett believed, was "stability of response"; and to get that, he must be prepared to accommodate the idiosyncrasies of his test subjects. "I have not hesitated to [. . .] adapt the conditions of [the material's] presentation, if it appeared to me that by doing so I could best get comparable conditions on the subjective side" (Bartlett 1932: 11–12). Bartlett did not document his case-by-case accommodations in any detail. He was, in effect, asking readers to trust his judgement. Even for a well-connected Cambridge professor, this was a stretch. For junior scientists hoping to establish their professional reputations, similar complacency was out of the question. Bartlett's methodology did not catch on. Why, then, has *Remembering* been "consistently referred to as a classic in the one- to two-page descriptions provided in the majority of introductory and cognitive psychology texts, from the time of its publication to the present day" (Johnston 2001: 341)? A simple answer is that it is a rich book full of quotable snippets, which different authors have mined for different purposes. (One important purpose is the assessment of eyewitness testimony: see e.g. Lacy and Stark (2013).) A more illuminating answer is that it owes its canonical status to the "cognitive revolution" of the 1950s and 1960s. In the decades following *Remembering*'s publication, developments in computing technology, information theory and neuroscience persuaded many psychologists of two things. First, that the human brain was an information processing system *par excellence*. Second, that its internal operations could usefully be analogized to those of electronic computers. While there was no difficulty casting inscriptional models of memory in computational terms—a computer can write data to a tape and read it back later—these models weren't computationally *interesting*. Bartlett's dynamic picture of remembering was. Psychologists who wanted to argue that remembering involved transformations performed on data structures could, with only a little poetic license, cite Bartlett as a distinguished antecedent. For example, Ulric Neisser, author of *Cognitive Psychology* (1967) and a central figure in the cognitive revolution, stated that his approach was "more closely related to that of Bartlett than to any other contemporary psychologist [. . .] The central assertion is that seeing, hearing, and remembering are all acts of construction" (Neisser 2014: 9–10). A few pages earlier in the same work, he had written the following: "The task of a psychologist trying to understand human cognition is analogous to that of a man trying to discover how a computer has been programmed. In particular, if the program seems to store and reuse information, he would like to know by what 'routines' or 'procedures' this is done" (Neisser 2014: 6). There is a superficial appearance of tension here. If remembering is the reuse of previously stored information, can it also be "constructive" in anything like Bartlett's sense? Neisser insisted that it could be. After all, "the metaphor of construction implies some raw material." Information is the raw material. Even if it is *stored* passively, its subsequent reuse may involve very elaborate computations. Neisser's choice of image would have delighted Freud: "out of a few stored bone chips, we remember a dinosaur" (Neisser 2014: 270–1). But while Freud would have imagined an analyst and his patient toiling together for weeks, the process envisaged by Neisser was fast, automatic, and internal to the remembering subject's brain.

How many bone chips does it take to reconstruct a dinosaur? That depends on the paleontologist: cleverer ones will get by with fewer. The "bone chips" model of remembering, then, hints at the possibility that brains might economize on storage space by maxing out on processing power. British psychologist R.C. Oldfield had pitched something like this idea as early as 1954. He invited readers to imagine:

> a "black box" capable of taking in messages in the form of sequences of 0's and 1's, and storing them. At some future time, on receipt of an appropriate stimulus, the box is to redeliver the original message. [. . .] It seems fairly clear that unless the various messages received by the box incorporate *some* detectable elements of common pattern, there is no possibility of economy in their storage. If, however, *any* common patterns run through them, there arises the possibility of re-coding them in briefer form, and so of storing more messages in a given storage space.
>
> —Oldfield 1954: 18

Oldfield saw that a system that learned commonly occurring patterns would be able to "remember" constructively. ("[S]uch a system would have some of the properties of schemata as postulated by Bartlett" (Oldfield 1954: 23).) It would encode a stimulus as a set of pattern-generating instructions. Decoding, i.e. remembering, would then be a matter of executing the instructions. Distortions akin to those observed by Bartlett would occur when the system attempted to encode atypical stimuli in terms of familiar patterns. All this would require considerable processing power, of course. Oldfield's insight was that the system's information *storage* requirements might well be less demanding than those of a cruder recording device that made no attempt to spot or exploit patterns.

Throughout the computer age, brain scientists have had a relatively easy time identifying biological analogues of active processing elements, and a much harder time identifying biological analogues of passive storage elements. (We will look at the early decades of that story in the next section.) Bartlett's model of memory did not abolish the need for information storage: the bone chips had to be kept somewhere. But, *per* Oldfield, it did diminish it; and it gave cognitive psychologists interested in memory an excuse to cut along, rather than against, the neuroscientific grain, by focusing their attention on active processing. Ebbinghaus's talk of a "mental substratum" in which stimuli were "engraved" offered no similar excuse.

NEUROPHYSIOLOGY, COMPUTERS, AND VON NEUMANN

One of the liveliest biological controversies of the 1880s and 1890s concerned the basic structure of the nervous system. Many anatomists believed that it was a continuous network of tissue. They knew that nerve cells existed, but they maintained that the

FIGURE 4.2: Santiago Ramón y Cajal in 1899. Credit: Wikimedia Commons (Public Domain).

branching fibers growing from those cells eventually fused together to form a fine mesh—a "reticulum"—that filled the brain. Reticularists such as Camillo Golgi believed that the nervous system's functioning would therefore need to be understood holistically (Shepherd 2016: 98–9). Proponents of the *neuron doctrine* denied that the reticulum existed. Every bit of nerve fiber belonged, they claimed, to a specific, anatomically bounded cell; inter-cellular connections were a matter of contiguity, not continuity. By the turn of the century the reticularists were in full retreat. Spanish pathologist Santiago Ramón y Cajal had persuaded most observers not only that the nervous system was composed of discrete cells, but also that the cells were polarized: signals came in through one kind of fiber and left though another (Shepherd 1954: 127–215).

The way was now open to *reductive* explanations of nervous system functioning, in terms of the input-output characteristics of individual neurons. Pinning down those characteristics experimentally was not straightforward, however. One problem was that the electrical signals transmitted by nerve fibers were very small, and therefore difficult to measure. "[P]rogress in this branch of physiology has always been governed by the progress of physical technique," British electrophysiologist Edgar Adrian remarked in his 1932 Nobel lecture (Adrian 1932). The key "physical technique" in the 1920s turned out to be the use of the triode valve amplifier. This device was already revolutionizing radio and telephone communications, and it would soon power the first generation of digital computers. Adrian used it to listen in on individual nerve fibres. Building on earlier work by his mentor Keith Lucas, he established that: "[t]he impulses which make up a nervous

FIGURE 4.3: ENIAC, *c.* 1950. Credit: Wikimedia Commons (Public Domain).

message are of fixed size in each nerve fibre. Each is a brief explosive wave involving the entire resources of the nerve fibre and all the nervous signalling which takes place in the body is carried out by such unvarying units" (Adrian 1934 in Hodgkin 1979: 11).

Some years before the outbreak of the Second World War, the rough outlines of a scientific consensus were taking shape. The nervous system, brain included, was a collection of billions of functional subunits—neurons—wired together in complicated ways. Neurons communicated by exchanging electrical pulses. One pulse was intrinsically much like another, but *patterns* of pulse activity (across nerve fibers and through time) varied. Different sensory experiences, and different behaviors, corresponded to different patterns.

For logicians, the physiological principle that a neuron either fired a standard-sized pulse or did not fire at all had an irresistible resonance. Propositions were, after all, either true or false. The algebra of their logical relations—Boolean algebra, developed in the 1850s—dealt with binary variables. George Boole himself had thought his work pregnant with "intimations concerning the nature and constitution of the human mind" (Boole 1845: 1). Had the experimentalists now proven him right, at the *cellular* level? American researchers Warren McCulloch (a neurophysiologist) and Walter Pitts (a logician) made the case for something like that thesis in 1943: "Because of the 'all-or-none' character of nervous activity, neural events and the relations among them can be treated by means of propositional logic" (McCulloch and Pitts 1943: 115). What was certainly true was that Boolean algebra could describe the basic operations of digital computing devices; and these, like brains, were assemblies of functional subunits that cooperated by exchanging electrical signals. Computing technology progressed rapidly during the 1940s thanks to vast wartime investments by the United States and Britain. In the popular press, systems such as the US Army's ENIAC were brain-like because they excelled at tasks (e.g. arithmetic) that humans found intellectually demanding (Haigh et al. 2016: 141). But for John von Neumann, a founding figure of the computer age, the more revealing brain-computer parallels were at the level of mechanism. The nervous system's "functioning is *prima facie* digital," he wrote in *The Computer and the Brain* (published posthumously in 1958, but mostly written in 1955). "The nervous pulses can clearly be viewed as (two-valued) markers," in the sense that "the absence of a pulse [. . .] represents one value (say, the binary digit 0), and the presence of one represents the other (say, the binary digit 1)." Moreover, the neuron is "comparable to the typical basic, digital, active organ," because it can function as a logic gate, computing Boolean functions of its inputs (von Neumann 1958: 39–40, 43, 53). There was a problem with von Neumann's vision. If the nervous system is a network of logic gates—a Boolean reasoning machine—then it would appear to resemble the *processing* unit of an electronic computer. But what about memory? Does the brain also contain a separate system, distinct from the neuron network but somehow hooked up to it, that resembles computer memory? This was a speculative hypothesis for which there was not a shred of biological evidence, but von Neumann took it seriously:

> We know the basic active organs of the nervous system (the nerve cells). There is every reason to believe that a very large-capacity memory is associated with this system. We do most emphatically not know what type of physical entities are the basic components for the memory in question.
>
> —von Neumann 1958: 68

Why could the neuron network not do the information-storage job itself? Every electronic engineer knew that logic gates could be used to build flip-flops (devices that toggle between two stable states and hence store one bit each). Unfortunately, such memories were "in every sense that matters, extremely expensive." Using groups of mutually-stimulating neurons to store individual bits—one bit per group—was no way to build a big biological memory: there simply weren't enough neurons to go round. Hence von Neumann's hunch that memory resided in a distinct system. It was "a priori unlikely" that nerve cells alone could do the trick (von Neumann 1958: 66–7).

That hunch did not age well. Indeed, to twenty-first century eyes, there is a hint of cognitive dissonance in *The Computer and the Brain*. At the very beginning of his discussion of "possible physical embodiments of the memory," von Neumann mentioned the hypothesis that "the thresholds—or, more broadly stated, the stimulation criteria—for various nerve cells change with time as functions of the previous history of that cell." "If this were true," he granted, then "the memory would reside in the variability of the stimulation criteria" (von Neumann 1958: 64). It was hardly a left-field idea. Cajal himself had hinted at something like it as early as 1894 (1894: 466–7). More recently, the Canadian psychologist Donald Hebb had offered a fully-fledged (if rather speculative) theory along these lines ([1949] 2002). Hebb's vision was analogue rather than digital: the propensity of neuron A to fire in response to pulses received from neuron B was, he supposed, a matter of degree, and hence not something one could model with Boolean

FIGURE 4.4: John von Neumann in 1956. Credit: Wikimedia Commons (Public Domain).

logic. Nor was he tempted to see pulse trains as strings of binary digits. Following the electrophysiologists, he instead emphasized the signaling role of *frequency* (pulses per second: another analogue quantity). Von Neumann knew the electrophysiological evidence as well as Hebb did; indeed, he summarized it (von Neumann 1958: 76–7, 22–3). But he stuck with his view that the nervous system "probably is primarily digital" (von Neumann 1958: 59). What was wrong with the theory that inter-neuron connection strengths were graded and malleable? Nothing, apparently, except that von Neumann did not want to talk about it: "It is certainly a possibility, but I will not attempt to discuss it here" (von Neumann 1958: 64). He preferred to assume that neurons worked like logic gates; and on that assumption, "[w]e are as ignorant of [memory's] nature and position as were the Greeks" (von Neumann 1958: 61).

The hypothesis that biological memory resided in the connections between neurons did not threaten the conceptual distinction between information processing and information storage. (The former was an activity—neurons actually had to fire—while the latter was a matter of neurons' dispositions.) But it did imply that the *architectural* distinction between the processing and storage components of electronic computers had no biological parallel. Von Neumann, after whom the basic architecture of modern computers is named, was unwilling seriously to countenance so radical a divergence. It would be uncharitable to attribute this to ego. Technological metaphors have dominated memory discourse since antiquity: Plato had his wax tablet, medievals their book of memory (Carruthers 2008). The electronic information storage technologies of von Neumann's day were in every respect more promising metaphors than these, for they were integrated into functioning "organisms"—computer systems—that seemed poised to emulate an ever-widening range of human competences. Separating memory from processing was a roaringly successful engineering strategy. If human scientists had hit upon it, perhaps evolution had too. True, there was no direct neurophysiological evidence that this was the case, but then there was (*c.* 1955) no direct neurophysiological evidence for Hebb's proposal either. Going only on what *was* then known about neurons, it was fair to say that they looked more like processors—"active organs," in von Neumann's parlance—than like memory elements. Perhaps Ebbinghaus's mental substratum would turn up elsewhere.

CONNECTIONISM ASCENDANT

When you write information on a wax tablet or in a notebook, you write at a specific location. If you hope to cram in a lot of information, you write small. Similar principles hold for computer memory. Strings of bits are stored at specific physical sites (on a tape or disk or chip); the smaller the sites, the higher the information density. One way or another, the mammalian brain stores a lot of information. So—one might think—if there is an Ebbinghausian substratum whose functioning is in any way analogous to that of a wax tablet or a computer memory, its records ought to be rather sharply localized.

In a series of experiments extending over thirty years, Hebb's mentor Karl Lashley trained rats to run mazes, and then destroyed portions of their cerebral cortices. He found that eliminating 5 percent to 10 percent of the cortex barely affected a rat's maze-running performance, irrespective of the precise anatomical location of the lesions (he tried many). Larger lesions did degrade performance, but again their location appeared to be irrelevant: all that mattered was their size (Lashley [1950] 1966: 19). Surveying his own work and a good deal of other literature in 1950, he concluded that it "is not possible to demonstrate the isolated localization of a memory trace anywhere within the nervous system" (Lashley [1950] 1966: 27). Memory traces, Lashley thought, were distributed entities, with each one associated with a large portion of brain. His case was far from watertight. It was obvious that maze-running involved a wide range of motor and sensory functions. Perhaps *these* functions were implemented in cortex in a distributed and partially redundant fashion, while localized memory traces were stored in deeper, non-cortical regions of the brain (Kandel 2006: 124–5). Still, Lashley's was an influential voice. Among psychologists, his survey shifted the conventional wisdom in favor of the distributed-memories view. It is therefore ironic that this same survey popularized the term "engram" for the physical brain change underpinning a memory: "en" for *within* and "gramma" for *thing written*, hence *inner writing*—a thoroughly Platonic/Ebbinghausian metaphor. Lashley's jargon was at odds with his thesis. Nevertheless, the jargon stuck. "[E]very instance of recall requires the activity of literally millions of neurons," Lashley guessed (1966: 28). If that was true, then the detailed neurophysiology of "recall" was going to be forbiddingly difficult to pin down. Lashley probably had conscious processes in mind, but memory in the broadest sense had to include simpler phenomena. After all, even creatures with very small nervous systems had the capacity to learn. *Their* engrams could hardly involve millions of cells. Nevertheless, it was possible that the most basic mechanisms of learning had been conserved by evolution—in which case researchers might learn something about human memory by studying creatures as simple as slugs.

FIGURE 4.5: *Aplysia californica*. Credit: Wikimedia Commons (Public Domain).

The neuroscientist most closely associated with the "slugs first" approach is the Austrian-American Nobel laureate Eric Kandel. Throughout much of his early career, Kandel's long-term goal was to become a psychoanalyst. The prospect of locating Freud's ego, id, and superego within the human brain drew him to neurophysiology in 1955 (Kandel 2006: 44, 53). Three years later, he was working on the cat's hippocampus, but with the aim of learning how "long-term memory for people, places and things"—the raw material of psychoanalysis—was stored in the brain (Kandel 2006: 136, 143). This too proved over-ambitious, and in 1962 he passed to invertebrates: specifically, the sea snail *Aplysia californica*. *Aplysia*'s neurons are unusually large, which makes them easy to manipulate in the laboratory; and it doesn't have too many of them, so the wiring networks are relatively simple. Kandel and his colleagues spent twenty years mapping and probing the neural circuits responsible for three simple forms of learning in *Aplysia*'s gill withdrawal reflex: habituation, sensitization, and classical conditioning. They demonstrated that "learning [in *Aplysia*] leads to a change in the strength of synaptic connections [. . .] between specific cells in the neural circuit that mediates the behaviour." Importantly, "memory is distributed and stored throughout the circuit, not at a single specialised site" (Kandel 2006: 200, 204). The possibility von Neumann had not wanted to discuss—that malleable inter-neuron connection strengths are the physical embodiment of memory—had been confirmed in an invertebrate. Later work (by many teams) would show that similar mechanisms are responsible for at least some forms of memory in rodents and monkeys (Holtmaat and Svoboda 2009).

The connectionist view of memory is now dominant in neuroscience and in psychology. Global media hype about "deep learning," an artificial intelligence paradigm loosely inspired by connectionism, has increased the latter's cultural salience (LeCun et al. 2015). As in the 1940s, tools are praised for resembling brains, and theories of brain function are signal-boosted when they chime with the latest technology. It is worth emphasizing what is *not* known. Neuroscientists still know little about what is going on at the cellular level when a human being reminisces, or, for that matter, recalls an item of propositional knowledge. But reminiscence and propositional recall are the *central* cases of memory in the ordinary sense: they are what most people think about when they think about memory. What do connectionists have to say about them? In his Nobel lecture, Kandel distinguished between memory *storage* and memory *systems*, and claimed to have shed considerable light on the former (2001: 1038). Memories—of every sort—are stored in the brain's wiring pattern. Laying down a new memory is a matter of adding, deleting, or modifying synaptic connections between neurons. "How exactly?" is a question that can be answered re habituation in *Aplysia*. It cannot yet be answered re, say, autobiographical memory in humans, but few modern scientists doubt that synaptic weights are the substrate here too. The problem is that no one knows what the coding principles are. Relatedly, no one knows how an autobiographical engram gets "read" by the brain when somebody relives a past experience, though it is clear that multiple brain regions are involved (Jin and Maren 2015). (The neuroscience of memory here blurs into the neuroscience of consciousness.) Kandel classified questions about declarative memory recall as memory *systems* questions. Answering them, he predicted, would "require the top-down approach of cognitive psychology," and not just the "bottoms-up approach" he had pioneered (Kandel 2001: 1038). In other words, moving forward would require understanding how the brain processes meaning. Both Sigmund Freud and Frederick Bartlett would have agreed. It is striking that at the beginning of the twenty-first century, Kandel could still present this as a task for the future.

CONCLUDING REMARKS

Twentieth-century memory science is a vast subject. It is so vast that the material I have covered cannot sensibly be called representative: it is merely (and appropriately) heterogeneous. For all that, some recurring themes are discernible. One is the challenge of bringing scientific methods to bear on meaningful human thought—and the consequent temptation to bring them to bear on something else (nonsense syllables, computers, slugs). Another is the conceptual distinction between passive storage and active remembering. Bartlett, Oldfield, and Neisser all argued that the latter has a strongly inferential character. If that is true, then we should hesitate to draw simple lessons from the twentieth century's memory-recovery fiascos. Fiascos there surely were, beginning (though not ending) with Freud's. However, the idea that a patient and therapist working together might *infer* more effectively than a patient working alone is not absurd on its face. Collaborative inference is the engine of science. Perhaps collaborative remembering will fare better in the present century.

A third recurring theme is metaphor and simile in scientific memory discourse. We have seen archaeological, paleontological, inscriptional, and computational examples. The last category is admittedly a borderline case, because some cognitive scientists think the brain is *literally* a computer (Rescorla 2017). But many who do not endorse that thesis are nevertheless happy to use computational language ("encoding," "decoding," "retrieval," "processing") when discussing memory. What should a historian make of this? Fans of the *longue durée* will say it is but the most recent manifestation of a very ancient habit. Plato had information technology; the medievals had information technology; we have information technology. The engineering details change from time to time, but—apparently—the impulse to frame human memory in its image does not. This may be right, but it is important not to exaggerate the significance of the alleged continuity. Memory metaphors inspired by wax and parchment are theoretically loaded in a very straightforward way: they suggest that understanding plays no role in remembering. (Wax and parchment are, after all, passive media.) Computational metaphors are potentially much more flexible. Consider talk of "decoding" engrams. Decoding is an activity, but little else is baked into the jargon. One could, without linguistic strain, say that understanding, imagination, and general knowledge all play important roles in engram-decoding; or (with equally little strain) that some engrams are decoded by specialized brain modules. It is natural to wonder whether important intellectual possibilities are being closed off when we speak of "decoding" in the brain, but much harder to say, even roughly, what those possibilities might be.

CHAPTER FIVE

Ideas: Philosophy, Religion, and History

STEFAN BERGER

INTRODUCTION

The relationship between ideas and memory is a dialectical one: ideas frame memory and out of memory emerge ideas. The people who produce ideas and collective memory are a very wide range of people, and many chapters in this volume focus on particular groups of people engaged in knowledge production that is related to memorial practices. Thus, Wulf Kansteiner's chapter talks about people working in the media. Nick Tosh is concerned with people in the psychological sciences. Jay Winter deals mainly with people in positions of power, i.e. in politics. Patrick Finney tells the story of people working in the cultural industries. Here we are dealing with a group of people working in key historical sciences, mainly in history itself, but occasionally also in fields that have a historical orientation but a different disciplinary identity, such as sociology, political sciences, philosophy and religious studies.

As my own work has been mainly on the history of historiography and on social movements, this chapter shows a bias towards historians as memory activists. It should be added that when I refer to the historical sciences below, I have not necessarily only professional historians or representatives of related academic disciplines in mind. It is important to take into account wider historical cultures, in which non-professional historians, who work as publicists, journalists, or are engaged in history-from-below type activities, can play an influential role. The historical sciences in this broad understanding has been one influential memory community among others, as Wulf Kansteiner has argued (Kansteiner 2004b: 123). In the tradition of Maurice Halbwachs, who was so influential on Pierre Nora and a whole host of other memory historians following in the wake of Nora, the historical sciences have been seen as mirror opposite and corrective to collective memory (Halbwachs 1925; Nora 1984–92). Yet, as Chris Lorenz has shown, this is an expectation that the historical sciences cannot fulfill (Lorenz 2008). They remain deeply implicated in the production of memory and are, as we shall see, in some cases extremely influential on what kind of collective memory is present in the public sphere. Scientificity and the making of memory are tightly interrelated processes.

In the following pages I have selected six broad themes where the historical sciences have had a deep impact on the broader memorial landscape. These are the two world wars and the Holocaust, the history of civil wars, the history of revolutions, the histories of decolonization in the context of the Cold War, and the histories of deindustrialization that are deeply interconnected with the themes of class, race, and gender. None of the memory cultures developing around the knowledge produced by the historical sciences in these fields can be discussed in depth in a short survey chapter like this, but I hope that I will succeed in demonstrating the fruitfulness of examining the historical sciences and memory debates together and in encouraging others to do more work in this direction.

THE HISTORICAL SCIENCES AND THE MEMORY OF THE FIRST WORLD WAR

The First World War is often constructed by representatives of the historical sciences as *Urkatastrophe* (primary disaster) of the twentieth century. In their memory discourse it becomes the beginning of a twentieth century whose first half was disastrous. The short twentieth century, lasting from 1914 to the end of the Cold War in 1989/1992 has become a powerful memory framework for the interpretation of the most recent century (Hobsbawm 1994). In the memory wars surrounding the First World War that started almost immediately after the last bullet was fired, the historical sciences played a crucial role. Central to those debates was the question of war guilt, because the Versailles Peace

FIGURE 5.1: Hans Draeger, *Anklage und Widerlegung*, book cover. Credit: Wikimedia Commons (Public Domain).

Treaty imposed a harsh peace settlement on Germany—justifying it by reference to Germany's sole guilt in the outbreak of war in 1914 (article 231) (Mombauer 2002). German politicians and wider public opinion contested this particular memory of what happened in August 1914 in the interwar period, not least by mobilizing the archives as institutional repositories of memory. Those who stood accused and who had lost the war produced the most impressive archival evidence against the idea that it alone was to blame for the outbreak of war in 1914. The historical sciences played a major role in this process. Historians let themselves be recruited by the German Foreign Office to help not only in the production of forty volumes of documents, but also in scientific publications and in publications meant for a wider national and international audience. They became memory activists with one single purpose: to help Germany fight the Versailles Treaty by proving that its central rationale was wrong (Herwig 2003).

The Western allies awoke to this challenge too late: the British and French documentary undertakings looked flimsy by comparison, although in those countries the historical sciences also rushed to the help of their respective governments to deliver historical interpretations that would bolster the idea that Germany was the only guilty party in the outbreak of war. The memory debates about the outbreak of the First World War had, on the one hand, a strong national inflection. They were played out in front of national audiences and the historical sciences addressed those national audiences in their writings. Yet they also had a strong transnational character: British and American historians liaised closely over the publication of their respective series in order to avoid publishing things that could be embarrassing to one or the other side. German historians cooperated closely with their Soviet counterparts in the hope that the Russian archives would deliver powerful argument in favor of their interpretation of August 1914. And there was an intense search for reciprocal agreements to allow archival access in "foreign" archives (Wilson 1996). Ultimately, the memory activism of the German historical sciences contributed to appeasement policies of British politicians and other Western statesmen in the 1930s, as they had come to believe that Germany was indeed treated unfairly at the end of the First World War (Ziino 2015).

The memory activism of the historical sciences in relation to the First World War continued in the 1960s, when German historian Fritz Fischer provoked a major controversy with his publications on the outbreak of the First World War. He argued that the Imperial German elites had indeed planned for and worked towards war in the years leading up to 1914. And he topped that by suggesting that the First and the Second World War stood in a continuity of imperialist ambitions for world rule that Germany hankered after from the Wilhelmine era to 1945. In Germany, the majority of established liberal-conservative historians opposed Fischer vigorously, whereas a cohort of younger, often left liberal historians came to be among Fischer's strongest supporters (Moses 1975). The German Foreign Office cancelled its financial support for a lecture tour of Fischer through the US, but US universities stepped in and funded the German professor's triumphant tour through key American universities. The transatlantic support for Fischer was both immense and influential. German historians who had been exiled by the National Socialists and who had been able to make careers in North America had not only intellectually prepared the way for Fischer, they now also belonged to his firmest supporters (Stelzel 2019).

The controversy was so intense, arguably because it did not only focus on the memory of the outbreak of the First World War, but because it was essentially about a redefinition of the German historical national master narrative and national collective memory. Even after the Second World War the dominant view among the German historical sciences was that National Socialism had its roots in the advances of Western mass society and in Italian fascism, not in any home-made developments or movements. The National Socialists had been a terrible aberration in an otherwise proud German national history. But in the long 1960s, a younger generation of German historians, less interested in political history and more closely aligned to social history, searched for continuities in German history that might help explain the victory of National Socialism in their country. Fischer's arguments chimed well with ideas of a negative German Sonderweg that resulted in the three major catastrophes of the first half of the twentieth century: the two world wars and the holocaust. The German memorial landscape of the twentieth century was to be deeply influenced by this historical interpretation. And it also was to dominate internationally from the 1970s onwards (Berger 2003).

It was challenged occasionally, in the historians' controversy in 1986/7, after reunification in 1990 and again with the rise of right-wing populism in the 2010s. A major reinterpretation of the outbreak of the First World War from within the historical sciences was provided by the Australian historian of Germany and Europe, Christopher Clark, in 2012 (Clark 2012). He argued that all major powers had practically sleep-walked into war, but if there was a villain in his story, it was not Germany, but rather Serbia and also some of the Austro-Hungarian imperial elites. His interpretation was widely criticized as revisionist, but his book was also widely praised for it had indeed researched in all major and many minor European archives to return to what looked like an older interpretation of the outbreak of war. *Sleepwalkers* certainly did not provide a similarly intense controversy to the Fischer controversy fifty years earlier. Why was this? In my view this had much to do with the fact that in Germany, the liberal elites had achieved a consensus around the idea that the positively accentuated history of the Federal Republic after 1949 was the key anchor of the new Germany's positive identity, whereas the period between 1871 and 1945 was viewed with great skepticism. This was also not changed by Clark's book.

And elsewhere? Well, for a start, Europe and the world has become much less obsessed with the dangers of Germany and instead often perceived the country as a guarantor of European stability, peace, and human rights as well as a model of economic development. After almost seven decades the memorial landscape of "nasty Germans" is giving way to a new memorial landscape of the "second chance Germans" who seem determined to do things better than in the first half of the twentieth century (Fritz Stern famously argued that Germans, through unification in 1990, had gotten a second chance to have a more benign influence on European and world politics than between 1900 and 1945 (Stern 2006)). In Britain, the memory of the First World War caused much more public debate than in Germany, where interest in the First World War literally had to be uncovered by the historical sciences in 2014. The spat between the Regius Professor of History at Cambridge, Richard J. Evans and the then education minister Michael Gove in 2014 centered on the centrality of First World War memorialization in Britain. Whereas Gove, on behalf of the Conservative government, had confirmed his intentions to make the war central to school curricula and to provide funds to allow every British schoolchild to visit Flanders fields, where Britain had allegedly defended Europe's liberty, Evans deplored what he saw as British jingoism that had anti-German and anti-European roots (Evans 2014). The memorial landscape of English Euroscepticism is steeped in a particular view of the past underwritten by an admittedly small section of the historical sciences (Wellings and Gifford 2018). Further afield, hardly any nation committed such large funds to the

First World War commemorations than Australia did in 2014 indicating to what extent the Anzac myths are still at the very heart of Australian national identity today (Sumartojo and Wellings 2014). The debates in Britain and the commemorative razzmatazz in Australia are an indication that the First World War still occupies a major role in the memory landscape of the twentieth century and that the historical sciences continue to be an important interpreter of that landscape, albeit one that is heart to a different extent in different parts of the world.

THE HISTORICAL SCIENCES AND THE MEMORY OF THE SECOND WORLD WAR AND THE HOLOCAUST

The war to end all wars led to a new, even more terrifying world war just about twenty years after the Armistice of November 1918. After six years, much of Europe lay in ruins. The continent had witnessed the Shoah (see the chapters by Winter, Kansteiner, and Niven), and in Japan the atom bombs raised the specter of an even more horrifying war then the one that they had helped to end more quickly than it would otherwise have ended. The legacy of the war left multiple traumas around which memory discourses were constructed after 1945. Once again, the historical sciences were prominently represented in contributing to these discourses (Echternkamp and Martens 2010; Levy and Sznaider 2006; Kim 2015). As after the First World War, the memory discourses were strongly nationally inflected but at the same time had transnational dimensions. In Japan, the memory of victimhood, connected to the atom bombs, contributed to the forgetfulness about Japanese perpetratorship in the war (Seaton 2007). In post-1945 Austria, we detect a similar pattern: memories of having been the first victims of Hitler's expansionism in Europe were meant to harness the forgetfulness about Austrians' perpetratorship as an integral part of the German Reich in the Second World War (Uhl 1997).

Indeed, the war became the most important vector of memory in many European countries after 1945 (Wood 1999). In those countries occupied by the Axis countries, the historical sciences used the history of the Resistance to contribute to a memory culture of resistance that tended to be rather forgetful about collaboration with the occupiers (Lagrou 2000; Yoshida 2006).

Even in those countries which started the war, such as Germany, the historical sciences after 1945 put a strong focus on the Resistance movement as representing an allegedly "good Germany" versus the "bad" National Socialists. When, from the 1970s onwards, a more self-critical historical national master narrative contributed to a different memory culture in Germany, the idea of "working through the past" (*Vergangenheitsbewältigung*) became the guiding idea of historical education, infused with the enlightened belief that such historical education would produce a national memory community that was immune to the lure of right-wing anti-democratic forces in the future (Kansteiner 2006b). Germany has often been praised internationally as a global model for these attempts, in which the historical sciences played such a prominent role. The German example is routinely contrasted with that of Japan, where the historical culture has not been successful to a similar degree in influencing a wider public memory culture to work through the past. Instead, historical revisionism surrounding the atrocities committed by Japan in the Second World War has been much stronger than in Germany (Berger 2012). Hence, the anniversary cultures in the Far East surrounding the memory of the Second World War tend to be far more antagonistic then in Europe (Yang and Mochizuki 2018). There is, in

FIGURE 5.2: Resistance Memorial in Dachau. Credit: Wikimedia Commons (Public Domain).

the Far East, no equivalent to the Europeanization of historical memory culture that is characteristic of the European Union (Sierp 2014: chapter 3).

The historical sciences did not only contribute to national and transnational memory cultures around the histories of the Second World War, they also paved the way for new transnational institutions meant to provide a safer world order after 1945. International historians attempted to underpin the foundation of the United Nations and, together with philosophers helped to construct a human rights tradition which was to be a safeguard against future collapses of civilization (Neier 2012). In Western Europe, the historical sciences were influential in providing the nascent European Union with a historical foundational narrative—it was to replace the dark first half of the century with a brighter second half by overcoming nationalism, antagonism, and violence and replacing it with cooperation, peace, and mutual understanding (Wagstaff 2012). And in Communist Eastern Europe, the historical sciences also constructed a historical narrative with a Communist telos that justified the building of socialist societies and provided a frame for a Communist memory culture that was again at the same time deeply national in orientation but contained transnational element (Antohi, Trencscényi, and Apor 2007).

MEMORY OF REVOLUTIONS

Memories of international communism had their foundational story in the Bolshevik revolution in Russia in 1917. Indeed, for the historical sciences revolutions were often foundational narratives on which they could hang not only class narratives but also national narratives. The "Great" French Revolution of 1789, the Central European revolutions of 1848, the Young Turk revolution in 1908, the Iranian Constitutional Revolution of 1911, the Xinhai revolution in China in the same year, the German revolution of 1918, the velvet revolutions in Central and Eastern Europe of 1989—everywhere these revolutions became central ingredients in national storylines underwritten by the historical sciences (Deneckere and Welskopp 2008). Like with the memory of the two world wars, the memory of revolutions had on the one hand a deeply national trajectory and on the other a transnational one. The 1917 Bolshevik revolution had a worldwide reception: coming out of a strong revolutionary Marxist tradition of the nineteenth century, it was perceived as the first successful proletarian revolution in the world and noticed as such (Pons 2014). The perception in the global world of revolutionary Marxism was that it would be the beginning of proletarian revolutions everywhere. The memory of the Russian October was to spurn the working classes into action in different parts of the world.

And at first it looked as though this might be the case, with revolutions in Germany that had one of the strongest Marxist parties in the world, in Hungary, and Italy. Japanese socialists, keenly observing developments in Europe, were predicting that the world revolution would also have to come to Japan (Schmidt 2013).

FIGURE 5.3: Boris Kustodiev, *The Bolshevik*. Credit: Wikimedia Commons (Public Domain).

When proletarian Communist revolutions were defeated everywhere except in Russia, the memorial landscape of that revolution changed. In some respect, it became a more intensely national event having to justify the build-up of "socialism in one country," in Stalin's famous formula (Corney 2004). But in the global memory-scape of Marxist revolutionaries it always remained the central event promising eventual success and victory also to their respective movements. Communist histories everywhere would forever refer to the model character and inspiration of the Bolshevik revolution. It became the "mother" of all twentieth-century revolutions (Klymenko 2018). As such it replaced the key memorial event for revolutionaries of the nineteenth century, the Paris Commune which continued to have an important memory legacy but was now often seen through the lens of 1917 (Bos 2014). Between the 1870s and the 1890s the Commune was effectively being transnationalized. A work of history was central in this process—Prosper-Olivier Lissagarray's *Histoire de la Commune de 1871* (History of the Paris Commune of 1871). Translated into English by none other than Eleanor Marx and subsequently translated into many other languages, it was crucial for the transnational reception of the Commune and its memory in different parts of Europe and the wider world. March 18, the date on which the revolutionary government in Paris came into being, became a central fixture on the international socialist calendar, and the Commune became a key symbol for the imagined community of a world proletariat.

In fact, all of the revolutions that happened with amazing frequency in different parts of the world between the Russian revolution of 1905 and the Asturian revolution of 1934 were being fought with reference to memories of nineteenth-century revolutionary traditions (Berger and Weinhauer 2020b). The revolutions of the nineteenth century had developed three horizons of expectation: political freedom, national sovereignty, and social equality. At the beginning of the twentieth century, those horizons of expectation exploded into a formidable three decades of revolution that was to end in a massive crisis of liberal democracy, a fascist backlash and after the Second World War a bipolar world order in which the three above-mentioned horizons of expectation still informed many of the conflicts taking place mainly in the decolonizing and developing world. The historical sciences belonged to the key interpreters of those revolutionary moments and movements. Those interested in the study of social movements have also recently turned to questions of memory—asking questions about how particular memories of previous movements, events, and personalities have influenced the course of social movements, from the women's movement in India to the environmental movement in Germany and the peace movement in Australia (Berger, Scalmer, and Wicke 2020).

Social movements were, of course, often at the heart of revolutions, which were violent events creating powerful memorial landscapes informed by the writings of the historical sciences whose representatives gave meaning to revolutions and influenced the wider public memory of revolutions. But a whole variety of non-violent struggles also produced forms of cultural memory that informed the actions of social movements in the twentieth century, and the historical sciences, in giving attention to those struggles, were one of the key constructors of this memory (Reading and Katriel 2015). The memory of non-violent struggles in India harked back to Gandhi's salt march. British feminism recalled the memory of the suffragettes. If the legacy of a social movement is deeply contested, memory struggles become politicized, as can be seen in the contemporary memory debates surrounding the legacy of Solidarnosc in Poland. In all three cases, histories of Gandhism, feminism and Solidarnosc contributed vitally to shaping the memory discourses and memory debates.

Memories of social movements can also be willfully destroyed and silenced. In West Germany, for example, anti-communism was so strong in the early 1950s that the memory of communism's role in the fight against National Socialism was effectively silenced and omitted from all official celebrations of that resistance. The key historians on the German Resistance, such as Gerhard Ritter or Hans Rothfels, would omit the Communist Resistance from their accounts (Berger 2003: 42). The memory of communism had to be recovered in the 1960s when the left-wing student movement took a renewed interest in communism. The writings of the historian Hans Mommsen were influential in recovering the Communist Resistance to National Socialism and problematizing the heroic portrayal of the Conservative Resistance to Hitler that dominated public memory of the Resistance in West Germany in the 1950s.

THE HISTORICAL SCIENCES AND THE MEMORY OF CIVIL WARS—SPAIN AND YUGOSLAVIA

The memories of the Russian revolution of 1917 and of communism loomed large in the memory landscapes of civil wars in the twentieth century. Civil wars were, of course, a global phenomenon, but as a historian predominantly of Europe I shall give two examples from the European continent, i.e. the Spanish and Yugoslav civil wars. They both left a whole host of contested memories which were all underpinned by the historical sciences. After the victory of Francoism in the civil war, the historical sciences inside Spain constructed a story of that war as crusade against international communism, separatists, Jews, masons, and moors. The "good Spain" and its core values, Catholicism and unity, had to be protected against the "evil Spain." The Francoist memory discourses celebrated the greatness of the Spanish nation and put itself in a long line of a proud national(ist) history (Pasamar 2010). But the historical sciences in exile, especially in France and North America, established different historical narratives which became the foundations for a post-Francoist memorial landscape of the new Spanish democracy. Especially the Centre for Research on Spain at the University of Pau in southern France is a good example of how the historical sciences in exile provided a counter-narrative to the Spanish one on which a different memory of the civil war could be built after 1976 (Caussimont 1980).

The transition in the memorial landscape from a Francoist Spain to a democratic Spain was, however, far from straightforward. It is, in fact, an ongoing process more than forty years after Franco's death. When the socialist government of Spain announced in July 2018 that Franco's tomb was to be removed from the Valley of the Fallen, a fascist memorial erected to the memory of the civil war, it still caused major controversy (Jones 2018; Hepworth 2016). The historical sciences produced different narratives underpinning both the actions of the socialist government and the opposition from the Partido Popular and others. The difficulties of coming to terms with the Francoist past in Spain has much to do with the nature of the transition to democracy in the 1970s. Virtually the entire Francoist elite remained untouched and often in positions of power, because of fears that anything else might lead to another civil war. At the center of the Spanish academia, CISC, under Franco a stronghold of the right-wing Opus Dei movement, nothing much changed either under the transition. Hence the historical sciences were never purged, and those returning from exile after 1976 and a younger generation they helped to train co-exist uneasily with more traditionalist representatives and their pupils. The academy in

Spain remains deeply divided today in terms of its politics, and the directorship of the CISC regularly changes hand when the government changes.

Under such conditions it is surprising that the memory of the anti-fascist struggle in Spain was one that took a long time to re-emerge after the transition. Most of the early initiatives to recover that memory inside of Spain came from grassroots movements, in which history-from-below-type groups were prominently represented. Novelists and journalists were to the fore in the 1990s to problematize what many perceived as the forgotten memory of Spanish Republicanism. More official attempts, from within the historical sciences and beyond, to pick up the thread and establish a firm memory of anti-fascism had to wait almost for a generation (Soro 2016). It also did not help that the memory of the transnational antifascist struggle in Spain, i.e. the history of the International Brigades, was dominated by Communist memory, underpinned by Communist narratives, both of which was in deep crisis after the fall of communism in the Soviet Union and Eastern Europe in the early 1990s (Morgan 2010). The historical sciences have only seriously begun to build the foundations for a more democratic memory of Spain from the 1990s onwards—almost a generation after the transition to democracy. An important role here has been played, amongst other disciplines, by anthropology—accompanying the processes of mourning and remembering that went alongside the opening of war-related graves which began in the early 2000s. The exhumations were a powerful trigger to Republican memory and often the beginning of debates about collective memory in Spain. Whereas the political right has accused those in favor of the exhumations of endangering the alleged spirit of reconciliation that had accompanied the transition process to democracy, on the left there has been a continuous search for meaning and

FIGURE 5.4: Mass exhumation of the bodies of those killed in the Spanish Civil War. Credit: Wikimedia Commons (Public Domain).

representation of those exhumations. Especially the extent to which these exhumations and reburials were to be politicized by the left in search of a new collective remembrance of Spain became a major bone of contention between the socialists (PSOE) and Podemos, a new popular party to the left of the socialists. The anthropological sciences have played an influential role in the knowledge-production surrounding the memorial practices connected to the exhumation sites (Ferrándiz 2017).

In Bosnia, anthropologists are also, like in Spain, participating in the sense making around the opening of civil war graves from the 1990s (Jugo and Wagner 2017). The historical sciences in the former Yugoslavia played a major role in laying the foundations for a memorial landscape that prepared the civil war long before its outbreak. By focusing strongly on the histories of their respective federal republics, they contributed to a national discourse that encouraged national memorial landscapes in the individual federal republics (Brunnbauer 2004). After the death of Tito, the specific political conditions of the fall of communism produced tensions that could build on those nascent memorial landscapes that went back to the 1980s. Several representatives of the memory community of historians played an influential role in providing all warring factions in the Yugoslav civil wars of the 1990s with narratives of collective remembrance that underpinned demands for separation, or, as in the Serb case, unity. One of the most famous cases was the president of Croatia, Franjo Tudjman. He had fought with Tito in the Second World War and rose to the position of general in the Yugoslav People's Army. Turning to history, he headed an Institute for Labor History in Zagreb, before falling out with the Communists, who even imprisoned him as a dissident. In 1990, he published a book that attempted to rehabilitate the Croatian fascist Ustasha movement and his writings centered on the establishment of a new national master narrative for Croatia. His historical work paved the way for a nationalist memorial landscape in Croatia that underpinned Croatia's position in the civil war and was eventually to lead Tudjman to the presidency of the new Croatian republic (Hayden 1994).

The civil wars in Yugoslavia left the successor states with strongly antagonistic nationalist memory cultures, often underpinned by the historical sciences. But it also left the memorial landscape of Europe in shock. After all, it ran counter to one of the most influential memory discourses within the EU—namely that it had been the guarantor for peace in post-Second World War Europe. War, in the very same place where the First World War had broken out, the mass slaughtering of innocent civilians at Srebrenica and elsewhere, the eventual bombing of the Serbian capital Belgrade by NATO, all this seemed to belie one of the central tenets of the EU's memorial landscape. The historical sciences responded to this challenge by re-assessing the importance of the nation state and the acceptance of Europeanisation in the post-Cold War world (Berger with Conrad 2015). The goal of the European Union to work toward ever closer political union, as formulated in the Maastricht Treaty of 1992, was now seen more skeptically. Globalization and Europeanisation underestimated the power of the nation state to mobilize emotions around issues of national identity (Gerrits 2016: 100–13). The historical sciences had in the past underestimated the power of those emotions because their members belonged to a transnational elite who had distanced themselves from feelings of national belonging. Within the specific memory community of the historical sciences, it had been possible to imagine the primacy of European and transnational forms of identity vis-à-vis the older and, in the eyes of many representatives of the historical sciences, discredited older forms of national identity. The Yugoslav civil wars were an important step on the road to reconsidering those assumptions.

The violence in Yugoslavia also triggered a wave of refugees to other parts of Europe, which was a powerful reminder, at the end of the twentieth century, that this century had been a century of ethnic cleansings and migratory movements. In some respects, of course, the history of refugees and migrants accompanies human history from its very beginnings. Refugees and migrants also often form powerful communities of memory. Yet, as Gerard Noiriel observed for France, the memory of refugees and migrants rarely enters the mainstream of national memory cultures. Hence, in his contribution to Pierre Nora's seven-volume memory history of France, Noiriel pointed out that migrant memory was not part of national memory (Noiriel 1996). The editors of the German equivalent to the French *lieux de mémoire*, similarly argued in their introduction that migrant memory has failed to enter German collective memory which is why they have also excluded it from their collection (François and Schulze 2001: 22). Overall, the othering of refugees and migrants led to their exclusion from national collective memory and it is only more recently that the historical sciences have been in the forefront of integrating migrant memory into locally, nationally and transnationally constituted forms of collective memory (Glynn and Kleist 2012).

Amongst other things, the Yugoslav civil wars were also a stark reminder of the power of religion over memory discourses: Catholicism in Croatia, Orthodoxy in Serbia, and Islam in Bosnia-Herzegovina underwrote the clash of nations which was also a clash of religions (Sells 1996). At the other end of Europe, in Ireland, Catholicism and Protestantism had been fueling the civil war in Northern Ireland between 1969 and 1994, somewhat euphemistically described as "the troubles." In the peace process after 1994, historians played a powerful role in underpinning, through their historical work, a new public memory culture of reconciliation (Madigan 2018).

FIGURE 5.5: May Day, Belfast, 1984. Credit: Wikimedia Commons (Public Domain).

The power of religion over politics had in the nineteenth century been paralleled by the power of religion over the historical sciences—many historians had trained as priests or descended from families where fathers and grandfathers had been theologians (Hermann and Metzger 2012). Yet, over the course of the twentieth century, the historical profession became more secular. In the Catholic world they often distanced themselves from Catholicism and wrote forms of history that were skeptical of the influence of the Catholic Church in the past. In the Protestant world, the historical community for a long time retained a kind of cultural Protestantism but their representatives grew increasingly distant from the church. With this growing gap between the historical sciences and organized religion, the former also contributed to the notion of the twentieth century as a century of secularization. Whilst undoubtedly, especially from the 1960s onwards, traditional churches lost much influence over society and its moral codes, it was only towards the end of the twentieth century that the historical sciences awoke to the idea that forms of secularization could be paralleled by religious revivals (Hartney 2014). Moving away from a western-centric idea of history, a more global look at the idea of secularization increased the skepticism. Not only did the last third of the twentieth century witness the phenomenal rise of Islamism, in many parts of the world, e.g. Africa and Latin America, but also parts of Asia, Protestantism and Catholicism were vibrant movements, growing in size and importance. And a virulent conservative Protestantism in the USA also became politically important in the Republican Party from the 1980s onwards. The rethinking of the secularization thesis by the historical sciences led to a flurry of research indicating the lasting importance of religion over society and state, which, in turn, both problematized and strengthened the public memory of religion in many parts of the world (Kaschuba 2010).

MEMORY OF DECOLONIZATION IN THE COLD WAR AND THE HISTORICAL SCIENCES

The rise of political Islam that came to world-wide attention with the Iranian revolution of 1979, was a response to failed decolonialization. In the decades after the Second World War, the anti-colonial struggle, often reaching back to the late nineteenth century, was successful in establishing a great number of independent new nation states around the world. Their governments, in which the anti-colonial movements were often prominently represented, developed a discourse and practice of modernization which ultimately aimed at catching up with and overtaking the West. Practically everywhere these modernization projects failed, and the memory of those failures haunted the politics of those postcolonial states. In the Islamic world the ghosts of failed modernization strengthened political Islam. The historical sciences in the West began to pay new attention to Islamic movements in order to understand the rise of these new memory communities, whilst in the Islamic world itself the battle between a secular wing and a religious wing in the historical sciences produced resources for both pro- and anti-Islamic memory communities (Choueiri 2003).

The wider histories of decolonization were intricately bound up in memory cultures of anti-imperialism and anti-colonialism and in attempts to justify at least partially projects of Western colonialism and imperialism (Rothermund 2015). The huge influence of Edward Said's ideas on Orientalism over the historical sciences and also the manifold criticism of Said demonstrates the power of the postcolonial imagination over the historical sciences and, in turn, their influence over memory practices to do with the memory of colonialism and imperialism (Majumdar 2011). Niall Ferguson's hugely popular histories of the British and American empires have been criticized as apologies for imperialism (Hall and Rose 2014: 14). The attempt to recover a colonial memory of the Mau Mau rebellion against British colonial rule out of oral history and a critical reading of the imperial archives, prompted much debate and soul-searching not just among the community of historians (Elkins 2005). On the other hand, an imperial memory of Britain, or perhaps, to be more precise, England, prompted some historians to lament the decline of England. Its contemporary position as a middling power within the European Union could be contrasted, for example, by David Starkey, to the former imperial glory and the Commonwealth (Starkey 2001). The memory of the latter was also mobilized by the Brexiteers in their successful campaign to achieve a British exit from the European Union (Gust 2016).

But the historical sciences and public memory about colonialism and imperialism were not only strongly interconnected in Britain. The memory of Algeria and the Algerian war came to haunt the French historical sciences, and in turn Benjamin Stora, among others, through their historical work, influenced public forms of commemoration about the Algerian war in France (McCormack 2007). The rediscovery of German colonial history by German historians at the end of the twentieth century prompted a public memorial culture surrounding Germany's colonial legacy that found expression, for example, over the debate surrounding the return of human remains from the Berlin Charité hospital to African countries (Mühlhahn 2017).

And in the postcolonial world itself there have been manifold attempts to harness the historical sciences in the cause of underpinning particular memorial cultures of post-

FIGURE 5.6: Brexit campaign. Credit: Wikimedia Commons (Public Domain).

independence nationalism and transnationalism. Thus, for example, Cheik Anta Diop and the Dakar school of historical writing have contributed to the memory of a Black high culture in ancient Africa that could proudly be presented as preceding and equaling ancient European high cultures. The history of the transatlantic slave trade was also used to establish a pan-African historical memory culture (Thioub 2007). And on the Indian sub-continent parts of the historical sciences aligned themselves closely with the Congress party and wrote a history of India bolstering a nationalist memorial culture endorsing the modernizing strategies of the Congress Party in the post-independent period (Chandra 1986). It is currently engaged in a veritable memory war with the governing Hindu Nationalist Party and its supporters among the historical sciences over public memory and the direction of contemporary politics in India. In the meantime, the century-old connection between Muslim and Hindu hostility rooted both in memory and a communalist historiography continues to cost lives on the Indian sub-continent (Brass 2003: 34–7).

In their contributions to public memory debates the historical sciences are often prompted by representatives from the cultural sphere, like novelists or filmmakers. The huge interest in the history of collaboration with National Socialism in France among the historical sciences that had such a deep impact on memorial practices and collective remembrance in France was prompted by the film *The Sorrow and the Pity* by Marcel Ophüls (Hewitt 2008). Similarly, the long-repressed history of the anti-Communist massacres in Indonesia in the 1960s was first made into a major topic by the documentary film maker Joshua Oppenheimer and his *The Act of Killing* (2012). It prompted major historical interest in these massacres by the historical community outside of Indonesia, as the repressive political regime of Indonesia is still preventing any public memory of those events or is continuing to distort them as necessary prevention of an imminent Communist coup in the country (McGregor, Melvin, and Pohlman 2018).

Events in Indonesia in the 1960s were representative of a wider global trend related to Cold War struggles. Anti-communism was a vital aspect of Western historical culture during the hot phase of the Cold War in the 1950s and 1960s, just as anti-capitalism and support for liberation movements against imperialism was an integral part of global Communist historical cultures in the same period. In sum, they fueled and supported many bloody civil wars in colonial and postcolonial states around the world, of which Indonesia was one (of several) gruesome examples. Yet from the 1960s onwards, the historical sciences in the West were increasingly divided over the merits of anti-communism and an anti-anti-Communist school emerged that attempted to restore a certain three-dimensionality to the picture of "the Communist" in the West. This section of the historical sciences subsequently supported détente and a public historical culture of remembrance that sought to overcome the Cold War through dialogue with Communist representatives. At the same time an older anti-Communist tradition continued in the West—among the historical sciences and the wider public memory culture. In Communist regimes there were also signs of division between a more hawkish faction clinging to rigid anti-capitalist, anti-fascist, and anti-imperialist memorial cultures and historical interpretations and reform Communist wings seeking to enter into dialogue with the capitalist West (Jarausch, Osterman, and Etges 2017).

The dictatorial regimes of communism allowed for far less plurality of opinion than was characteristic of the capitalist West, yet we also encounter representatives of the historical sciences questioning the road of communism to build socialist societies and achieve social equality and working-class emancipation. Such questioning under communism could easily lead to loss of jobs, incarceration, and sometimes, in particularly critical situations, even loss of life (Kovács and Labov 2012). The questioning of the dominant historical narratives and the dominant public memorial cultures in the West tended to be less dangerous, but the desire to overcome the binaries of the Cold War was also accompanied in the West with a more self-critical approach to the achievements of capitalism and liberal democracy. The greater ability of the West to allow for more divergent views among the historical sciences and the public memory cultures gave the Western capitalist regimes more stability, whereas the increasing disconnect between the memory of civil society and the memory of state communism in Communist regimes ultimately contributed to the fall of communism in Eastern Europe and a massive crisis of communism in China that could only be prevented to turn into communism's demise through the use of massive violence against protesting students in Beijing in the summer of 1989. Overall, the stories of the Cold War and the interrelated stories of decolonization provide ample evidence of the close relationship between the historical science and the public memory cultures characteristic of the Cold War and decolonization.

MEMORIES OF CLASS, RACE, AND GENDER IN DEINDUSTRIALIZATION AND THE HISTORICAL SCIENCES

So far, much of our discussion of the interrelationship of the historical sciences with wider collective practices of remembrance have focused on national and transnational memories, associated with wars, civil wars, revolutions, and decolonization. With memories of revolutions, of social movements, and of the Cold War we have, however, also touched on memories of social class. The latter are very much to the fore when we turn to the impact of the historical sciences on memories of industrialization and deindustrialization. Deindustrialization has profoundly transformed industrial regions in many parts of the world from the 1960s onwards. It devastated industrial communities and brought unemployment and poverty to sections of a previously well-to-do industrial working class. It ended the short-lived post-Second World War illusion that workers had stable jobs for life in factories operating according to Fordist and Taylorist principles that seemed immune to economic crisis. The histories of deindustrialization triggered reflection among the historical sciences about the meaning of such processes and the means to come to forms of structural change that would prevent whole regions from becoming depopulated and devastated by deindustrialization (High 2003).

In many parts of the deindustrializing world, the historical sciences contributed to public memorial cultures around the material and immaterial remnants of the industrial past that fulfilled diverse functions. Industrial heritage could help bolster regional identity (Wicke, Berger, and Golombek 2018) and it could also underpin class identities (Smith, Shackel, and Campbell 2011). This was, of course, by no means an either/or situation. The historical sciences helped to underpin a more self-reflexive memory practice of memory activists in deindustrializing regions. If we take the example of the Ruhr region of West Germany, the historical sciences were instrumental in underpinning an urban social movement in the 1960s and 1970s seeking to protect the industrial heritage of the region against attempts to get rid of that heritage as soon as industrial plants had shut. When that social movement from below was adopted by the corporatist political culture of the Ruhr in the 1980s and 1900s, powerful political, industrial, and trade union interests ensured not only the survival of entire industrial heritage landscapes, but they also encouraged the historical sciences to underwrite memorial practices that strengthened regional identities and the belief in the success of the structural transformation of the region from a successful industrial to a still successful postindustrial region. Nowhere else in the world has the industrial landscape of yesteryear been so immaculately preserved than in the Ruhr; nowhere else is it so strongly underpinned by a vibrant historical culture (Berger 2019b). Elsewhere the stories are different, but the relationship between the historical sciences and the shape of a specific memorial culture surrounding industrialization and deindustrialization remain important. In the rust belt of North America, for example, we find much less support from above for industrial heritage. Instead there are manifold local initiatives for the retention of working-class ideals that are threatened with extinction by deindustrialization (High, MacKinnon, and Perchard 2017). In Britain the story of deindustrialization is intricately connected with the brutal assault of the governments of Margaret Thatcher on the British unions, as symbolized in the miners' strike between 1984 and 1985 which was reminiscent of a civil war in certain times and places. Parts of the historical sciences in South Wales were instrumental in bolstering local political attempts to retain at least a few sites of mining heritage and produce a memorial counter-culture that was to preserve the memory of working-class culture in South Wales (Berger 2008). In post-Communist Eastern Europe, deindustrialization took place in a post-Cold War world, in which heavy industry was closely associated with the previous Communist dictatorship. In the historical sciences and in the wider memorial culture of post-Communist Europe, there was little support for industrial heritage. The stories of class were too much bound up with the legitimation strategies of discredited Communist regimes (Valuch 2019). Whilst the story of deindustrialization is overwhelmingly a story of the global North, it is not restricted to it. Many parts of China, for example, have experienced forms of deindustrialization, whilst others have been rapidly industrializing. Where the memories and deindustrialization can be successfully linked to a heroic memory of the Communist past, there heritage efforts have been blossoming (Lam 2019). But where those memories are more connected to the histories of Russian and Japanese imperialist, like in the North East of China, there the historical sciences have been struggling to inspire a memorial culture around industrial heritage (Qu and Zhao 2019). Overall, the memorial cultures of deindustrialization are linked to what stories can be told about the pride in industrialization and the socio-economic impact of deindustrialization. Here, the historical sciences have an important role to play—in presenting success stories or stories of failure on which different memorial practices can then be founded. The role which class plays in those narratives differs widely across different de-industrializing regions in the world (Berger and Pickering 2018).

The same is true for the role of race. Processes of industrialization everywhere have been intimately connected to processes of migration of different ethnicities and nationalities. In the US, millions of black workers moved from the south to the industrial centers of the north in the twentieth century which led to complex racial relations in the factories and neighborhoods of those cities. When deindustrialization hit the rust belt, racial issues were very much to the fore. The historical sciences have contributed to an examination of those racial issues (Sugrue 1996) which in turn have informed memorial practices of black working-class communities. Of course, the memories of race and the historical sciences that underpinned them cannot be restricted to deindustrialization. The examination of race in the historical sciences have made major contributions to memorial cultures surrounding the civil rights movements against apartheid regimes in the US and in South Africa (Romano and Raiford 2006; Coombes 2003). Issues of race have also been central in the history and memory wars surrounding first nations in different parts of the world. If we take the example of Australia, the historical work on aboriginal culture and society that has blossomed over the last thirty years has been instrumental in underpinning a powerful memorial culture of the first nations in Australia, which has changed the cultural landscape of the country significantly, even if the political and socio-economic discrimination against Aborigines continues in contemporary Australia (Peters-Little, Curthoys, and Docker 2010).

Issues of class and race have been tightly related to gender in a range of memorial practices in which the historical sciences again played a prominent role. This is true for the memory of industrialization and deindustrialization that was, for many decades, an almost exclusively male memory, especially if we look at typically male industries, such as mining and steelmaking (Clarke 2015). However, women's and gender historians have, over the past decades, provided us with a wealth of information on how work practices and social relations in the neighborhoods were gendered and what role women played in those societies. This work has also influenced public memorial practices in many former regions of industry (Tamboukou 2016).

And if we look at the wider women's movement, we find a similarly close relationship between the historical sciences and the wider memory culture of the movement (Reading 2016). Women writing women's history also contributed to the memorialization of women's struggles in the search for greater liberty and emancipation. The public memory of the suffragettes in Britain, for example, is strongly connected to the historical sciences providing firm knowledge about the movement (Chidgey 2015). Women and gender historians have often been memory activists. The British sociologist and feminist Sheila Rowbotham, for example, was both an eminent historian of the transatlantic English-speaking women's movement and an activist feminist fighting for the rights of women. As a socialist and a peace campaigner involved in the Campaign for Nuclear Disarmament, she is a typical example of a multi-activists involved in diverse progressive social movements underpinned by knowledge derived from the historical science (Winslow, Kaplan, and Palmer 1995).

CONCLUSION

We have traced the memory activism of the historical sciences in a wide variety of different fields in different parts of the world over the entire period of the twentieth century. As the historical sciences were deeply nationalized in the nineteenth century it is not surprising to observe that much of their impact on memory is on national memory. Of particular importance within national collective memories are often wars, civil wars, and revolutions, and we have given a range of examples of how the historical sciences have underpinned public memorial cultures related to those events. Yet, since the 1980s the historical sciences have become far less oriented towards national frameworks and this opening up towards transnational themes has had also a significant impact on the memorial landscapes supported by the historical sciences (De Cesari and Rigney 2014; Assmann and Conrad 2010). Thus, for example, histories of deindustrialization have been able to underpin industrial heritage and other practices of remembrance surrounding deindustrialization processes. Furthermore, histories of race, gender, and religion have supported particular forms of public memory in social movements that are connected to those issues. They can have a national bias, demonstrating the persistence of national memory cultures even in an age where the historical sciences are increasingly moving away from the national framework, or they can be deliberately transnational in orientation. Overall, as this all-too-brief chapter has intended to show, the historical sciences have had a crucial role to play in framing the memory of key events and developments over the course of the twentieth century in many different parts of the world. Much work still remains to be done to shed light on the importance of historical knowledge production for specific memory cultures. In particular, the interaction with other memory activists from politics, from other sciences, from the media and from the cultural sphere has often been absolutely vital and the intersectionality of all disciplines and spheres with each other is worth greater exploration in years to come (May 2015).

CHAPTER SIX

High Culture and Popular Culture

PATRICK FINNEY

In 1960, the Soviet author Vasily Grossman completed the manuscript of his epic novel *Life and Fate*, now regarded as one of the finest literary depictions of the Second World War. This panoramic story tracked the intertwined fortunes of a diverse cast of characters across the sprawling landscape of the Soviet Great Patriotic War, from the desperate street-fighting of Stalingrad through dank interrogation cells in Moscow's Lubyanka prison to the killing grounds of the Holocaust in the Ukraine and Auschwitz-Birkenau. Grossman's evocation of the war fused grim realism, compassionate empathy, and a fierce moral vision. Yet his account was significantly at odds with the official mythological rendering of the Great Patriotic War that was emerging as the key legitimating mechanism for the postwar Soviet system. Grossman lionized the heady yearning for freedom induced by the deprivation and suffering of war and the dreams of alternative futures which were subsequently snuffed out by the postwar reassertion of Stalinist oppression; he also posited numerous affinities between the totalitarianisms of the Soviet Union and Nazi Germany. Both these moves militated against the instrumentalization of the Soviet victory as a proof of pristine moral virtue and ineluctable political superiority (Finney 2013). In February 1961, the Soviet secret police confiscated all known copies of the manuscript and Grossman was compelled to petition the authorities for its "release." In July 1962, Mikhail Suslov, chief ideological enforcer of the Communist party, granted Grossman a personal interview but bluntly dashed his hopes. "It is impossible to publish your book, and it will not be published," he stated. At a time of acute Cold War tension, *Life and Fate* "would bring comfort to the enemy": "why should we add your book to the atomic bombs that our enemies are preparing to launch against us?" (Garrard and Garrard 2012: 357–8).

Across a twentieth century scarred by ideological strife, totalitarianism, and war, Suslov was far from alone in recognizing the transformative potential—for insidious or noble ends—of cultural representations of the past. (*Life and Fate* itself was only published in 1980, with Grossman long dead, after a manuscript copy he had successfully concealed was smuggled out of the Soviet Union.) Not surprisingly, therefore, tracking the mnemonic work performed by high and popular culture texts has also been a key preoccupation in memory studies. In 1975, for example, Paul Fussell's *The Great War and Modern Memory* explored how the experience of the Western Front had been "remembered, conventionalized, and mythologized" in British literature (Fussell 2000: ix). The war, Fussell argued, "was more ironic than any before or since": "it was a hideous

FIGURE 6.1: A Soviet postage stamp from 1961 featuring Hero of the Soviet Union, Dmitry Karbyshev. Captured by the Nazis in summer 1941, Karbyshev organized resistance activities in a succession of POW camps before being murdered in Mauthausen in February 1945. The official myth of the Great Patriotic War was constructed in myriad cultural discourses and with increasing intensity as the 1960s wore on. Credit: Wikimedia Commons (Public Domain).

embarrassment to the prevailing Meliorist myth which had dominated the public consciousness for a century. It reversed the Idea of Progress" (Fussell 2000: 8). Although the book was in some ways a rather narrow study of a slice of British high-brow war memoir and fiction, Fussell nonetheless essayed profound conclusions about the "rupture in cultural expression," even in modern consciousness, that the war engendered (Smith 2001: 246). In his landmark study of *The Vichy Syndrome*, Henry Rousso gave a prominent place to film as a medium for the transmission of memory and the negotiation of French experiences of Second World War occupation. Film, Rousso argued, "played a particularly important role" because it was a mass medium; moreover, it "sometimes proved better than other media at capturing the repressed and the ineffable" (Rousso 1991: 226–7). That said, for Rousso film had to be contextualized alongside other intertwined "vectors" of memory—such as political rhetoric, commemorations, museums and memorials, academic historiography, literature, and television—in order to map the whole landscape of French remembering.

There is now a substantial body of scholarship addressing the contribution of this kind of cultural production. This includes detailed studies of individual media, either in general or in specific geographical and temporal contexts; studies of memory domains in which these cultural media sit alongside other "vectors," as with Rousso, and general collections exploring the particular dynamics of remembering through high and popular culture collectively (for example, Keren and Herwig 2009; Hall and Jones 2011). This work certainly demonstrates the significance of these "vectors" within what Jan and Aleida Assmann have termed "cultural memory," namely "that body of reusable texts, images, and rituals specific to each society in each epoch, whose 'cultivation' serves to stabilize and convey that society's self-image" (Assmann 2011: 215). Historical visions conjured in artistic representations possess enormous intellectual and affective power and may be all the more influential for being consumed primarily as leisure or entertainment activity. They can generate sentiments of identification and connection, offer consolation and inspire repugnance, resentment or shame. Sometimes imagined pasts are propagated with specific didactic or political intent, at other times they may be shaped primarily by commercial considerations. At yet others, their witting motivation may simply be creative and artistic, though even then, of course, they cannot escape entanglement with prevailing cultural and ideological norms.

A persistent criticism of older scholarship in this area held that it was too preoccupied simply with cataloguing representations and reading out their putative ideological import, to the neglect of considering how they were actually received. This mattered because the latter is vital to determining whether potential collective memories actually become successfully established as such (Kansteiner 2002). Meanings are only really established through consumption by different audiences who are, consciously or not, co-producers of subsequent historical understandings and the social identities that they ground. This point has been amplified by recent work on mass cultural representation which is also at the conceptual cutting edge of memory studies. Alison Landsberg, for example, coined the term "prosthetic memory" to connote how mass cultural technologies can enable an individual—"at an experiential site such as a movie theater or museum"—to take on a "deeply felt memory of a past event through which he or she did not live"; this "new form of public cultural memory" has progressive political potential as it can ground new subjectivities, solidarities and modes of empathy (Landsberg 2004: 2; see also Landsberg 2015). Similar questions about how memories of particular events can be incited through cultural texts amongst generations who did not directly experience them are explored in Marianne Hirsch's work on "postmemory" (Hirsch 2012). Relatedly, much conceptual emphasis is now placed on the mobility of memory. On this view texts are much less "privileged containers of mnemonic meaning" and more "points around and through which different, often interconnecting, kinds of practice are organized": culture here becomes "the medium of mnemonic exchanges," the site of endless mediation and remediation (Cubitt 2018: 139). Yet even in work resolutely committed to the notion of "memory unbound," individual films, novels, and digital texts still remain important focuses for analysis (Bond, Craps, and Vermeulen 2017).

This survey of the role of high and popular culture in the twentieth century history of memory locates itself within this broad historiographical context. It explores the changing contribution of cultural texts as "vectors" of memory, conscious that they sit alongside and continuously interact with other modes of remembering, even if constraints of space dictate that these interactions can sometimes only be adumbrated. It sets out how the past has been represented across the whole period since the First World War and attempts as broad a coverage of cultural memory production as possible in geographic and generic terms; this means that issues of consumption—and of exchange and remediation—are, again of necessity, somewhat bracketed off. Focusing primarily on textual representations of history as a medium of memory is perhaps a rather conventional or literal approach to take. After all, even Fussell in his otherwise restricted literary study noted how "the whole texture of British daily life could be said to commemorate the war still," from "odd pub-closing hours" through British Summer Time to the popularity of "eggs and chips" (Fussell 2000: 315–16). Such concrete or indirect forms of memory—and, indeed, other performative mnemonic practices—are also hugely important, and it would have been pleasing to explore them in more detail. However, given the strategic purpose of this volume and limitations of space, providing an overview of the most overt ways in which the past was kept visibly present takes priority.

Further definitional issues arise from considering the relationship between high and popular culture. Here these are treated as related realms, with permeable and unstable boundaries between them. The high-brow arts can insert resonant and durable ideas into cultural circulation, their power lying in the fact that they are produced and consumed predominantly by social elites who possess significant cultural authority. Consider, for example, the part played by the officer war poets Rupert Brooke, Wilfred Owen, and Siegfried Sassoon in forming the British view of the First World War as a muddy bloodbath of epic absurdity. It is tempting to contrast this with more demotic cultural media that exert their force through their consumption by a mass audience. Thus, across the globe young people (in particular) avidly play historically-themed video games like *Call of Duty* which represent twentieth century conflicts from the Second World War through to the War on Terror. According to their publisher, given their phenomenal sales and the repetitive nature of gaming, the *Call of Duty* titles are "likely to be one of the most viewed of all entertainment experiences in modern history" (Ingham 2009).

While there is certainly some mileage in distinguishing between high culture as the domain of elites and popular culture as that of the masses, it is ultimately misleadingly simplistic, since the two are multiply intertwined. Thus it was only really in the 1960s that the voices of the British war poets gained widespread cultural purchase, as a new generation rewrote the dominant meaning of the First World War, rendering it in more negative terms than ever before as "an example of official stupidity, futility and slaughter" (Todman 2005: 221). The publication of new anthologies of war poetry to mark the fiftieth anniversary of 1914 was crucial here, but even more important was "the arrival of First World War poetry on the O and A level examination syllabus" which meant that many subsequent generations of school children were immersed in it (Todman 2005: 157). There was also an intertextual dimension to this phenomenon, as the core tropes proffered by the war poets were recycled in other popular media through the 1960s, such as the satirical theatrical production – and later high-profile film—*Oh! What a Lovely War*, and the landmark British Broadcasting Corporation (BBC) documentary series *The Great War*. Cross-fertilization between high and popular culture forms, and their imbrication, is crucial to their power as conduits of memory.

The issue of consumption also militates against any stark differentiation between high and popular culture forms. Consider, for example, the Memorial to the Murdered Jews of Europe which was dedicated in Berlin in 2005, intended as a profound statement of the centrality of contrition for the Holocaust in the political culture of unified Germany. The opening of the memorial marked the culmination of many years of agonized debate over the political, ethical, and architectural dilemmas entailed in constructing a memorial to victims of genocide at the heart of the capital of the perpetrators. Although the public was widely engaged in these discussions, the abstract form of the final memorial—an undulating field of concrete stelae—made it unarguably a high-brow artistic statement (Foundation for the Memorial to the Murdered Jews of Europe 2007). Over the years, however, the openly accessible site has become a popular tourist destination and troubling questions have been raised about how visitors relate to the memorial, as they appropriate it through sunbathing, picnicking, and parkour. To many, such activities are clearly at odds with the architect's intention to create a space for unsettling reflection on murderous criminality. Moreover, this apparent debasement of the memorial by the mass public has in turn inspired further artistic interrogation. In 2017, Shahak Shapira, an Israeli-German author, harvested irreverent selfies taken by visitors at the memorial from social media sites and superimposed them onto historic images from death camps and other Holocaust murder locations, publishing the pictures on a website called "Yolocaust" to provoke a public debate (Gunter 2017).

This essay offers a necessarily selective overview of how high and popular culture representations have powerfully contributed to the history of memory across the decades since the First World War. It treats them as interdependent forms which combine together, contributing to contestation around understandings of the past within societies, and it draws examples from across the globe. Reflecting my own areas of interest and expertise, the texts discussed predominantly though not exclusively relate to the representation of modern wars and related traumas. There are two key emphases. First, the essay stresses the crucial significance of technological change in producing new modes and media for representing the past, from cinema, through television, to the late twentieth century emergence of digital and networked technologies. Second, it focuses on the interconnections between high and popular culture representations of the past and the larger political currents that have shaped the age, from the inter-war crisis, through the Cold War, to the War on Terror.

THE INTER-WAR YEARS AND THE SECOND WORLD WAR

Several developments intersected during the inter-war period to usher in a new age of mass communication, with significant implications for the history of memory. First, the invention and development of new media transformed popular culture and created novel ways of representing the past. Radio was very important here: the BBC began to operate in 1922 and there were over two million license holders in the UK by 1927 (Street 2002: 27, 39). While listeners may have been chiefly attracted by escapist music and sports programs, news, drama, and feature content had considerable capacity to shape popular memories; indeed, the new—and predominantly state-controlled—broadcasting organizations explicitly aimed to edify the population. In 1933, the Nazi minister for propaganda Josef Goebbels pronounced radio to be "the most modern instrument in existence for influencing the masses" (Welch 2006: 129). Cinema was another medium with pre-1914 roots that came of age in the 1920s and 1930s and developed apace, as silent films gave way to "talkies" and black and white yielded to color. Writing on England, A.J.P. Taylor emphasized how cinema, as a novel mode of communal entertainment with unprecedented affective force, transformed patterns of life and remolded traditional values. With cinema-going becoming "the essential social habit of the age," film "was the greatest educative force of the early twentieth century" (Taylor 1975: 392, 237).

Far-reaching socio-economic change was a second component of this new era. The expansion of the middle class and increased spending power of the urban working class created larger audiences for popular culture products, just as the emergence of new entertainment industries and modes of dissemination made it easier to deliver them in affordable ways. Thus "the 1920s and 1930s formed a key moment in the development of mass culture" (even though audiences nonetheless remained fragmented by age, class, region, and gender) (Crone 2013: 254–5). The third element shaping the new era was political transformation. The inter-war years saw the birth of mass democracy as postwar legislation extended the franchise to many more working men and to women. This created new anxieties amongst democratic governments about the management of public opinion, just as technological change opened up new possibilities for achieving it. These concerns manifested themselves in analogous if more intense ways in the dictatorial regimes that emerged after the First World War. Here, controlling public opinion entailed not only the repression or pre-emption of dissent through censorship and persecution but also propagandistic mobilization in support of state-building and war-making projects. At their most ambitious, totalitarian regimes sought to engineer a "New Man"—"an improved edition of mankind" in Leon Trotsky's formulation—and molding memories—an "intense engagement with history"—was integral to this (Fritzsche and Hellbeck 2009: 313–4).

The founders of the Soviet Union quickly grasped the potential of new technologies to inculcate Communist ideology among the masses, especially given problematic levels of literacy. Vladimir Lenin famously decreed in 1922 that "of all the arts for us the most important is cinema"; he urged in particular that mobile cinemas should be sent into the countryside "where they are novelties and where, therefore, our propaganda will be particularly successful" (Taylor and Christie 1994: 56–7). Historical films were central to this propaganda because Marxism-Leninism rested on a particular interpretation of human history, including an over-arching theory of how change occurred (through class struggle) and a teleology (the realization of human freedom under communism). A striking example of how the regime sought to script its own history within this framework was Sergei Eisenstein's epic *October*, commissioned to mark the tenth anniversary of the Bolshevik revolution. Eisenstein's dramatic rendering of the events of 1917 very clearly delineated positive and negative characters, with the heroic masses of workers and soldiers valiantly battling the evils of Tsarism, the church, and the bourgeoisie. (In one notable scene, a worker is brutally murdered by a group of bourgeois women wielding parasols; one of them also rends a Bolshevik banner with her teeth.) *October* also drove home the regime's self-understanding of its own birth, presenting it as a law-governed inevitability and product of mass popular will. Moreover, whilst the film's overall message is generically Soviet, it also strikes some notes which reflect the particular moment of its creation, as Joseph Stalin was consolidating his power against his rivals after Lenin's death: allegedly, Stalin personally directed Eisenstein to remove the character of Trotsky from the film (Taylor 2002).

Prima facie, *October* seems like a textbook case of official memory-making in a dictatorial state, with new technology providing a potent means for ideological indoctrination. Yet there are complexities here. The film underlines the perennial difficulties in differentiating between high and popular culture, which in this instance had particular consequences for consumption. Manifestly *October* was intended to reach a mass audience and some scenes were highly praised for their documentary verisimilitude and authenticity (indeed, the shots of the storming of the Winter Palace are still routinely mistaken for actual footage from 1917). Yet Eisenstein also deployed a barrage of experimental and avant-garde techniques—collage, montage, intense use of symbolism—that rendered much of the film inaccessible to large swathes of its intended audience. One party official in 1928 argued that propaganda units might have to carry out preliminary "explanatory work" to enable workers and peasants to understand it (Taylor 2002: 22). So, while the film has long been lauded by Western intellectuals as a classic, one contemporary Soviet critic summarized the "unanimous reaction" of the disappointed masses: "admiration for the details of the film and a bewildered coolness towards the film as a whole" (Taylor and Christie 1994: 216). Yet the acknowledged difficulties inherent in effectively transmitting ideologically-inflected understandings of the past even through

FIGURE 6.2: A German language poster for Sergei Eisenstein's first full-length feature film, *Strike*, made in 1925. The film depicted the struggles of workers oppressed by Tsarism in the early years of the twentieth century; at its close the striking workers are murdered, their deaths inter-cut with scenes of cows being slaughtered. Credit: Wikimedia Commons (Public Domain).

powerful new affective media were not viewed as insuperable. Under Stalin, the Soviet Union continued to use historical films in its propaganda work, representing not just the recent past but also more distant eras where suitable heroic forebears and uplifting lessons might be located. Eisenstein's later films, for example, included *Alexander Nevsky*, released in 1938, which revisited the struggles of the thirteenth century titular prince against the Teutonic Knights. "The film was intended to arouse patriotic sentiment against the Nazi threat by emphasising the despicable nature of the enemy," who are shown committing atrocious murders of innocent children. Equally, "Nevsky symbolised the spirit of Russia and its historical resistance to foreign invaders" – as well as Stalin himself (Welch 2013: 169).

The issue of which past to prioritize, and how to do so, could often become an issue of contestation even within putatively totalitarian states. In mid-1930s Nazi Germany, fierce debate erupted over how the new regime should orientate itself in relation to the eighth-century struggles between Widukind and the pagan Saxons on the one hand and, on the other, the Frankish Charlemagne who subjugated them. At stake were politically highly-charged questions about legitimacy and identity. "Were Germans in the Third Reich to model theirs on an original, pre-Carolingian Germanic culture, and immerse themselves in the Edda and Sagas? Or should they embrace the heritage of classical civilisation, and continue to celebrate Roman influence?" (Lambert 2017: 184). The former line was forcefully advocated by key Nazi ideologue Alfred Rosenberg: according to his "originary myth," the "spirit of Nazism was closer to that of Widukind and pagan Saxons than to that of the whole period from 804 (when the last Saxon revolt against Charlemagne was crushed) to 1933." Nazism "not only completed the work of a string of 'rebels against the [First] Reich' but, by extension, also forged an intimate connection with a pure Germanic past before 'oriental' (for which read Jewish) and 'southern' (i.e. Roman) influence had contaminated it" (Lambert 2017: 186–7).

Rosenberg's "Saxonist" view was vociferously contested by the German churches and many conservatives who preferred to position the Third Reich as a successor to the Holy Roman Empire; Charlemagne on this view had laid the foundations for modern Germany by unifying diverse Germanic tribes within his polity. The debate was conducted through a dizzying array of high- and low-brow media, seamlessly entwined, including the press, theater productions, popular and academic histories, pulp novels, epic poems, museums, commemorative pageants and memorials (including a massive stone henge built at the site of an alleged massacre of 4500 Saxons) (Lambert 2014, 2017). Overall, the episode demonstrated the importance of mnemonic grounding for the Nazi movement, but also how difficult it could be to impose an orthodox ideological viewpoint about the past even in a highly repressive state. That said, it was not insignificant here that views on the Widukind question were divided even within the Nazi hierarchy, up to its very apex. Rosenberg and his allies toned down their "Saxonist" agitation after a speech by Adolf Hitler in Nuremberg in 1935 asserted that force had been necessary to transform disparate Germanic tribes into a unified *Volk*. Yet even then debate was not decisively stilled until circumstances changed further. As the Third Reich embarked on expansionism and war, "the Carolingian Reich could function as 'model' and legitimation for the Nazis' 'New Order in Europe'" (Lambert 2017: 185). Consequently, official commemorations in 1942 of the 1200th anniversary of Charlemagne's birth enacted a comprehensive rehabilitation (Lambert 2014: 152–5).

The terms of contestation over public opinion were obviously different in democratic states like Great Britain. State ambitions for the management of opinion were more modest but not negligible. There was censorship: theatrical productions still required a license from the Lord Chamberlain's Office before they could be publicly performed and script changes were often demanded on political or moral grounds. Equally, governments invested considerable effort in influencing news coverage: so, for example, in the later 1930s the press and newsreel producers were successfully persuaded to refrain from stridently canvasing alternatives to Prime Minister Neville Chamberlain's policy of appeasing Nazi Germany (Cockett 1989). In response to the developing external propaganda operations of the totalitarian states, the British also worked to influence opinion abroad. In the mid-1930s the British Council was founded to conduct cultural diplomacy promoting British values and in 1938 the BBC World Service was inaugurated (Taylor 1981). Yet in general government initiatives sought to restrict the dissemination of representations deemed controversial rather than to actively propagate particular interpretations of their own (something which also fitted with the relatively more diverse commercial ecology of the entertainment industries). Film censorship, for example, operated through the British Board of Film Censors (BBFC), which was an independent body organized by the film industry; yet the Board was dominated by Establishment figures and manifestly worked to uphold respectable bourgeois morality, marginalize radical political critiques, and prevent the production of films that might offend important foreign powers. This work was certainly aligned with government priorities, constituting a form of "social control" aiming "powerfully for the maintenance of the *status quo* and all that that entailed" (Richards 1981: 99). Moreover, censorship here was considerably tighter than that over the theatre as the stakes were higher: "the cinema was *the* mass medium, regularly patronized by the working classes, and the potential of films for influencing, even inflaming, this huge audience was fully appreciated by the Establishment" (Richards 1981: 95).

Films on historical topics—revisited with varying degrees of fictionalization—were among those that fell foul of the censors. In 1938, a script on the Relief of Lucknow in 1857 was banned on the grounds that it might inflame relations with India at a delicate time by reviving memories of past conflicts (Richards 1981: 97–8). The Board also labored assiduously to prevent the production of films about Nazi Germany that were too overtly anti-fascist and which might therefore irritate Berlin to the detriment of Anglo-German amity. Several proposed treatments about Nazi persecution of the Jews were rejected, though films which broached the same issue more indirectly, through historical allusion and analogy, might be permitted: witness the Gaumont British 1934 production of *Jew Süss,* set in eighteenth-century Wurttemberg. The outbreak of war in 1939 changed the landscape significantly and numerous films depicting Nazi oppression in the 1930s were hurried into production. The censors were almost as wary of approving films which critiqued the Soviet regime, including depictions of secret police persecution and of the revolution itself; yet even-handedly the screening of Soviet classics celebrating the revolution—such as Eisenstein's 1925 *Battleship Potemkin*—was also prohibited (Richards 1982). The Board, it seemed, wished to steer clear of "any comment on the Soviet state," viewing it as simply too contentious a subject (Richards 1982: 44). The overall strategic goal of the censors was "the avoidance of offence by the elimination of any hostile depiction" of foreign countries; objectively this certainly worked to buttress the government's pursuit of appeasement (Richards 1982: 40).

While the censorship apparatus thus circumscribed explicit engagement with contemporary political issues, there remained considerable scope for more indirect meditation upon them through historical films. British historical cinema in the inter-war years insistently worked through ideas about national identity, staging interrogation of the politics of the present through representations of the past—though it is important to note that this is not all that these period films did and nor is the lens of national identity the only fruitful one that can be employed to read them (Monk and Sargeant 2002). One early example was Maurice Elvey's *Nelson: The Story of England's Immortal Naval Hero*, made in 1918. This biographical treatment presented Nelson as an exemplary national hero, but also drew explicit parallels—through montage and intertitle text—between his victories and those the British had recently won over the Germans. It therefore reinscribed a narrative of continuous national history, in which the British were triumphant, resilient, and honorable (Sargeant 2002). A contrasting but complementary vision of Britishness was presented in Alexander Korda's hugely-successful 1933 rendering of *The Private Life of Henry VIII*, a landmark in British cinema history as "the first major historical film since the advent of talking pictures" (Chapman 2005: 13). Korda offered a comforting "Merrie England" vision of the British past, laden with "bawdy humour and irreverence" redolent of a "provincial music hall" (Chapman 2005: 23, 33). In this it was very much aligned with "the consensual social politics that were supported by the BBFC," presenting "Henry and his subjects [. . .] united by a set of common values and a shared outlook": Henry was "responsive to the needs and opinions" of the common folk, and they in turn staunchly supported the monarchy (for example, sharing Henry's yearning for a male heir) (Chapman 2005: 31).

If Korda's film was thus concerned to promote a sense of national solidarity, as war loomed historical films began to interrogate potentially more divisive foreign policy issues. Despite government efforts to manage opinion, there was a public debate on the wisdom of appeasement which became sharper as the decade wore on and skeptical voices multiplied. The pro-appeasement position was well represented in Michael Balcon's *The Iron Duke* in 1935. This told the story of the Duke of Wellington, Waterloo, and the Congress of Vienna in a way that drew clear parallels with the Versailles settlement and, implicitly, prescribed a moderate policy toward Germany in the 1930s. Wellington is depicted arguing against a punitive settlement, explicitly pleading that fair treatment of the defeated enemy is the only possible foundation for lasting peace. In context, this coded critique of Versailles supported the contention that Germany had justified grievances which should be addressed in the interests of reconciliation; this position reflected the dominant pacific sentiment of British public opinion at this point, as well as government policy (Chapman 2005: 45–63). In contrast, *Sixty Glorious Years*, released in 1938, used another iconic British figure, Queen Victoria, to critique appeasement. The film was co-written by Sir Robert Vansittart, a senior Foreign Office official well-known for his hostility to Nazism, and it was released shortly after the Munich crisis when anxieties about German expansionism were mounting. In presenting various war crises that Victoria confronted, the film preached the virtues of national preparedness and prompt energetic action—including the use of military force—to face down threats to national security (Chapman 2005: 64–90). Once war came, of course, equivocation on this point evaporated. Historical films became more overtly propagandistic, first invoking a grim sense of defiance and national unity in the face of adversity as in 1941's episodic epic *This England*, then a more triumphalist, martial patriotism, most notably in the 1944 adaptation of Shakespeare's *Henry V* (Chapman 2005: 91–142).

The individual production histories of these various films reveal considerable differences in the degree of witting authorial intent evident in their ideological messages. Equally, there is room to debate how far they simply reflected and reinscribed pre-existing sentiments or rather sought to mold feelings anew. But regardless, historical cinema was clearly an important medium for a national conversation about politics and identity. That said, it was never a purely national endeavor. On the one hand, the films were profoundly shaped by transnational influences: Korda, for example, was a Hungarian émigré and many other directors, technical artists, and actors were continental immigrants and exiles. On the other hand, films were objects of transnational exchange. Korda's *Henry VIII* was a landmark partly because of its massive success in the United States where, of course, its depiction of the British past was consumed by audiences with very different preconceptions. By the same token, Hollywood films were avidly devoured in Britain, giving rise to Establishment anxieties about the exposure of British audiences to debasing American mores. For this reason, and to protect the domestic film industry, the government (in common with many European counterparts) legislated to limit the proportion of foreign films that cinemas could screen (Chapman 2005). The transnational nature of film production and reception is well illustrated by the Oscar-winning 1930 film *All Quiet on the Western Front*. This was a Hollywood adaptation of a 1928 novel by the German

Erich Maria Remarque, a dramatization of life amongst German troops in the trenches which eloquently thematized the futility of the First World War, and war in general. The film was rapturously received by American, British, and French audiences, but was banned in fascist Italy where its pacifism jarred with Benito Mussolini's lionization of violence. In Germany, nationalist and Nazi thugs rioted at early screenings and the government soon banned the film on the grounds that it was part of an American-inspired propaganda campaign to blacken Germany's name (Eksteins 1980).

Once the Second World War broke out, representations of the past were vitally important in the propaganda efforts of all combatants. Diverse audiences were targeted as propaganda aimed to mobilize domestic populations, undermine enemy morale and also to woo the inhabitants of occupied territories or neutral countries. Moreover, diverse histories were invoked, including not only the recent wartime past and the war's direct antecedents but also much more distant periods. Imperial Japan offers an excellent demonstration of the utility of cinema here: the Japanese film industry was prolific, rivaling Hollywood in output by 1937, and film was an integral element in Japan's pursuit of imperialism from 1895 right through to the Second World War (Baskett 2008: 3).

FIGURE 6.3: Japanese child's propaganda kimono depicting the martial exploits of the Imperial armed forces, made either in the late 1930s or the 1940s. Credit: Wikimedia Commons (Public Domain).

During the war, Japan's propaganda effort was extremely sophisticated, conceived as part of a larger "thought war," a term coined "to describe the fight for ideological supremacy in Asia and later against the West" (Kushner 2006: 15). Japanese film propaganda spanned many genres. There were combat films such as 1944's *Fire on that Flag!* which recounted the American defeat in the Philippines, highlighting the Americans' "insincerity and natural cowardice" and their "broken promise to the Filipinos" (Baskett 2008: 100); there were action dramas such as 1943's *Tiger of Malay*, which recounted the underground resistance of Japanese against the British colonial authorities and their Chinese Communist allies (Baskett 2008: 97–100); and there were historical epics such as 1943's *Genghis Khan* which valorized "resistance to foreign (non-Asian) aggressors and encourage[d] cooperation among Asians to defeat Western interference" (Baskett 2008: 70). The war also prompted the first full-length Japanese animated film, offering instructive tales of the adventures of Momotaro, the "Peach Boy" of Japanese folklore. He banded together with a disparate group of animals—in a stylized rendering of pan-Asian solidarity—to defeat Western forces in a re-running of Pearl Harbor and the conquest of various Pacific territories (Baskett 2008: 50–1). Thus, new technology was again harnessed to engineer memories in the service of contemporary politics.

THE COLD WAR ERA

After the conclusion of hostilities radio and cinema continued to be hugely influential, but they were increasingly challenged by the new medium of television. Television broadcasting had begun on a limited scale before the war, but it was in the 1950s that it began to become established as a central element in social and cultural life. In Britain, one important moment was the live broadcast of the coronation of Elizabeth II in June 1953 which was watched by 20 million viewers (56 percent of the population), demonstrating television's potential as a "national medium" and a forger of national identity (Jacobs 2003: 71). Naturally, the development of television moved at different speeds in different locations: across most of Europe and the United States broadcasting began (or resumed) in the later 1940s and 1950s, while through the 1950s and 1960s it was established in large swathes of Asia, Africa, and Latin America; "by the mid-1970s virtually every country of the Third World with a population of over 10 million had introduced television" (Berwanger 1998: 190). Despite regional variations, the global trend was clear: over the decades television reached ever larger audiences in greater numbers of homes and businesses; channels proliferated, often as state-run broadcasters came to be challenged by commercial competitors; technological developments improved services, with the introduction of color and higher definition pictures; and the potential geographic reach of broadcasts increased, especially with the growth of satellite technology.

The potency of television in fashioning opinion and sensibilities was well-recognized and caused considerable alarm amongst politicians and commentators anxious about moral decline. The 1962 report of the Pilkington Committee, established in Britain to consider the future development of television, observed that viewers were more vulnerable to pernicious influences than cinema-goers: "sitting at home, people are relaxed, less consciously critical and, therefore, more exposed" (Vincent 2013: 171). Of course, as with radio, television programming ran the gamut from popular to high culture, with sport, game shows, serials, and soap operas at one end of the spectrum and high-brow dramas and documentaries at the other; yet both in part entailed the representation of real or imagined pasts with potential impact on cultural memories.

This growth of television, of course, occurred against a background of profound postwar political, social, and economic change. This was, not least, because of the context of the global Cold War between Western liberal capitalism and Soviet communism. Western Europe and the United States enjoyed three decades of unprecedented economic prosperity: the growth of television ownership and viewing was integral to a larger consumer boom. In the Eastern Bloc, postwar reconstruction proceeded according to a quite different model of modernization but from around the mid-1950s there was an effort here too to meet demand for consumer goods: so, for example, the Bulgarian Communist Party's 1963 blueprint for creating a "new socialist person" encompassed attention to "elevated spiritual and material needs" and the provision of refrigerators, radios, and televisions (Stone 2014: 152–3). The Cold War played out on a global scale, of course, as the two blocs competed for influence in the Third World, especially as decolonization created myriad newly independent nation states across Asia and Africa. This was "a war about two different *Weltanschauungen*, two ways to organize cultural life, two possibilities of defining modernity . . ." Hence, "cultural life and cultural institutions moved from the sidelines to the center of the political confrontation" (Gienow-Hecht 2010: 399, 401). In the context of this global battle for hearts and minds, cultural representations of the past that might help build consensus at home or propagandize abroad were heavily implicated.

The intersections of Cold War concerns with television programing are well illustrated by the profusion of television westerns in the United States in the later 1950s. American culture had long romanticized the myth of the frontier, the notion that the experience of westward expansion, especially in the nineteenth-century era of Manifest Destiny, had forged an exceptional and righteous nation. On this view, the process of battling a hostile environment and racial others—including the indigenous populations—had endowed Americans with a particular rugged individualism and entrepreneurial, can-do spirit; it had also persuaded them of the redemptive and restorative potential of violence as a means of instantiating civilization. It is easy to see how this myth came to serve as "an apology for American expansionism and aggressiveness" (Anderson 2007: 40), permitting relentless imperialism on a continental and then global scale to be recast as defensive, moral and even altruistic. (Indeed, this has been dubbed the quintessential "myth of America" (Hixson 2008).) The enduring appeal of this particular brand of exceptionalist thinking was demonstrated when John F. Kennedy successfully campaigned for the presidency in 1960 using the slogan of "the new frontier" "to summon the nation as a whole to undertake (or at least support) a heroic engagement in the 'long twilight struggle' against communism and the social and economic injustices that foster it" (Slotkin 1992: 3). Although the tropes of the frontier myth were deployed across myriad genres, actual western stories—in the form of novels and then films—had not surprisingly played a key role in its reinscription and renegotiation since the nineteenth century (McVeigh 2007).

The volume of adult westerns in the scheduling of all three major American networks in the second half of the 1950s was remarkable. There were "twenty-eight in the 1958–9 season, when they represented 26 per cent of total network prime time" and nine of them were in the top eleven shows overall (Boddy 1998: 119). These were classic tales of gunslingers, lawmen, cattle ranchers, and saloon-keepers, of frontier communities threatened from within by moral weakness and corruption or from without by minatory aliens. They were also prized for their unprecedented "realism," which was often simply a euphemism for violence. *Gunsmoke* was one landmark production: having begun as a radio show in 1952 it transferred to television in 1955 and ran for a record-breaking

FIGURE 6.4: Scene from the US television western *Gunsmoke*, with lead actor James Arness playing the lawman Matt Dillon on the right. This still is from 1974 when the series was winding down after its phenomenally successful run. Credit: Wikimedia Commons (Public Domain).

twenty seasons. It centered on Matt Dillon, the Marshal of 1870s Dodge City, Kansas, offering "a harsh look at life out west at a time when lawlessness prevailed" until men like Dillon "risked their lives to establish a system of law and order" (Terrace 2011: 423). Dillon was not trigger-happy and, indeed, he reflected the official self-image of the United States in the early Cold War: a "strong man," staunchly committed to defending his community and its values, "reluctant to use violence unless given no choice by his enemies" but ruthless if pushed to the "last resort" (Mills 2011). The cultural work which these westerns performed in the Cold War context was recognized at the time. Some liberal commentators worried that the violence of the shows would harm the United States' image abroad, especially in the Third World. Yet conservatives argued that the toughness and unreconstructed masculinity of the lead characters might be instructive for American policy makers: "Would Wyatt Earp stop at the 38th Parallel, Korea," one such wrote in 1959, "when the rustlers were escaping with his herd? Ridiculous!" Collectively this western boom tapped into conservative yearnings for "a less complex moral universe" and traditional values (Boddy 1998: 133–4).

With the public appetite surfeited, the number of television westerns declined rapidly in the 1960s. (Although arguably the frontier myth template was simply transferred onto other genres of adventure series.) Nonetheless, many of these classic shows retained their influence as they were continuously recycled in the syndicated television market. In the 1980s, their enduring popularity was linked to the conservative ideological resurgence of the Ronald Reagan era: the "return to simpler times without tricky moral complications" that one critic noted they offered seemed now well fitted to cure the United States of its post-Vietnam malaise (Boddy 1998: 136–7). It should be noted, however, that the western as a genre was not monolithic or necessarily incompatible with more progressive messages. There were significant differences in tone between the myriad 1950s television westerns and one of the most famous Hollywood westerns of the period, 1952's *High Noon*, which was widely regarded as an attack on the McCarthyite atmosphere of the contemporary United States. The genre of "law-and-order westerns" which *High Noon* begat subsequently tracked the shifts in American popular culture through to the end of the 1960s, and critically interrogated the Cold War consensus and its conformist norms (Costello 2005). *Firecreek*, released in 1968, was the last film in this line, offering a bleak vision of a frontier community devoid of any certainty, "a moral morass, with nothing but survival as a goal": "the lack of a moral vision and the failure to see any defenders (or potential defenders) of morality imply a loss of faith in America's mission" (Costello 2005: 194). Part of the reason for the longevity of *Gunsmoke* was its malleability: during the 1960s it "adapted to the desires of its viewing audience, becoming increasingly aware of and sympathetic to ethnic minorities, in tune with the national mood during the civil rights era" (Lule 2016: 387). Televisual representations of the past could thus serve to mediate social changes and anxieties in the present.

The cultural Cold War was fought on various fronts and with varying degrees of intentionality. Both sides established formal external propaganda agencies to conduct public diplomacy, presenting positive images of their own system and its achievements not only to citizens of the other bloc but also to those of their own allies and potential allies. In 1953, the United States Information Agency (USIA) was created to oversee all overt American information work around the globe; its activities included the production of documentaries on historical topics and the recent news which were distributed "to new and content-hungry TV stations in developing countries." The USIA also worked to influence the commercial media which were exporting images of America according to their own independent imperatives (Cull 2010: 442–3). The Soviet public diplomacy apparatus was bureaucratically complex but nonetheless energetic: signature initiatives included "the mass production of cheap editions of classic Russian literature" and "the export of prestige motion pictures" such as *The Cranes are Flying*, a 1957 epic about the personal damage inflicted on Russians by the Great Patriotic War (Cull 2010: 440). In the West, these efforts to massage external opinion went hand in hand with the more subtle cultural mediation of the past at home; in the East the guiding hand of the state was more in evidence, though it certainly left room for some dissent from orthodoxy.

In cultural production on both sides of the Iron Curtain, certain key themes were in evidence: "destruction (and especially nuclear destruction), espionage, and epic renderings of history and fantasy." This last meant "stories depicting the past or future in real or imagined worlds told on an immense canvas, frequently with a strong dose of morality and self-righteousness." These initially "helped to sustain wartime cohesion and cement loyalties and identities"; later on, they "allowed vicarious participation in events and mobilized people behind their leaders' projects through grand narratives of good versus evil and tales of national destiny." As far as history was concerned, important here on the Western side were film and television productions of various biblical and classical epics, such as Cecil B. DeMille's *The Ten Commandments* of 1956: these demonstrated "the cultural power of the society capable of mounting such a spectacle and showcase[d] America's religiosity in contrast to Soviet hostility to faith." War films—especially those located in the Second World War and analogizing that "good war" to the contemporary Cold War—were also hugely popular, highlighting "the 'need' for military preparedness" and the necessity of doing one's patriotic duty (Cull 2010: 451–5).

On the Soviet side, war films also loomed large, especially from the 1960s when the legitimating cult of the Great Patriotic War fully bloomed. The first ever Soviet television miniseries was a popular war treatment *We Draw Fire on Ourselves*, screened in 1963–4. This reinforced the virtue of the Soviet war-effort against Nazis depicted not only as evil but as "idiotically inept"; in fact, it marked a notable retreat from the honest humanism and authenticity of war films made during the earlier post-Stalin thaw (Youngblood 2007: 139–40). With the Great Patriotic War cemented as the key foundational moment of the modern Soviet Union, films on that subject were freighted with particular and serious representational responsibility. Other historical conflicts could be presented in more escapist, light-hearted, or even comical terms, as was evident during the fiftieth anniversary of the post-revolutionary Civil War between 1967–70. A seven-hour-long television miniseries from 1969, *His Excellency's Adjutant*, regaled the audience with the swashbuckling and romantic exploits of a glamorous Soviet intelligence agent operating in the Ukraine against the counter-revolutionary Whites. This demonstrated that "the state regarded the Civil War as an aspect of Soviet history that was best forgotten, unless treated humorously or sensationally" (Youngblood 2007: 150–2).

Cultural representations of the past flowed transnationally in multiple directions, raising interesting questions about consumption and memory-making. In particular, it was certainly not the case that the imperial capitals of Moscow and Washington simply transposed their history and values onto their satellites. On the one hand, the flow could sometimes be in reverse. For example, state television in the German Democratic Republic (GDR) was staunchly committed to the building of socialism and went through an extremely creative period in the late 1950s and early 1960s. In 1961, it broadcast an historical miniseries, *Revolt of the Conscience*, which tracked the life of a former Nazi soldier who was captured by the Soviets in 1945 and who, upon his release, became a champion of postwar German unity; this led to his arrest and persecution by American intelligence officers prior to his "ideological conversion and decision to settle in the GDR." The show was subsequently broadcast widely across Eastern Europe and in Cuba, Austria, and Sweden; in 1962 it was shown in the Soviet Union and very much influenced Soviet television producers, inclining them toward producing similar historical miniseries blending entertainment with edifying ideological messages (Gumbert 2014: 135–6).

On the other hand, the assumption that foreign cultural products were simply consumed wholesale elsewhere is not persuasive. Inter-war anxieties about "Americanization" continued into the postwar period, with frequent laments across Western Europe about American "cultural imperialism" that intensified within the leftist political movements that engendered "1968." However, the fear that American values were simply being imposed onto Europe belied the actual mixture of admiration and resentment with which American films, music, and consumer goods were regarded there; moreover, their consumption involved a complex process of negotiation, appropriation, and adaptation. American visions of the past were always remade by European consumers (Gienow-Hecht 2000). Equally, the potentially productive influence of American culture should not be disregarded. So, the broadcast in the Federal Republic of Germany in 1979 of the American television miniseries *Holocaust* "raised public awareness for the Nazi genocide like no event before or since"

(Kansteiner 2006a: 42). Some Holocaust survivors like Elie Wiesel found the program aesthetically offensive and argued that it was trivializing to transform "an ontological event into soap-opera" (Wiesel 1978); yet the broadcast triggered an unprecedented searching public debate about German responsibility for this murderous atrocity.

Historical television programs that might shape memories and mold identities became ubiquitous across the globe during this period. Their potential role in consolidating particular configurations of national identity was evident as decolonization proceeded apace: former colonial countries generally required particular historical narratives to ground their new independent identities. In 1984, Singaporean television broadcast a four-part miniseries entitled *The Awakening* to mark the twentieth anniversary of independence; this narrated the growth of modern Singapore through the eyes of its majority Chinese inhabitants, tracing their fates from early twentieth-century immigration through the Japanese occupation in the Second World War to the achievement of independence from the British colonial state and to the (then) present day. (The show has achieved iconic status and was remade in 2018.) In a similar way, in 1983 Iranian television broadcast an epic miniseries *Sarbedaran*, "based on the revolt against the Mongolians in 1357"; this represented an effort to endow the new Islamic regime with a legitimating lineage rooted deep in Iranian history. Of course, these programs varied substantially in their aesthetic qualities and artistic ambitions. In Nicolae Ceaușescu's Romania, historical dramas intended to shore up his particular brand of national communism were plentiful: witness, for example, *Independence War*, shown in 1976–7 which celebrated the centenary of Romania's independence from the Ottoman Empire. Unfortunately, they tended to be "dull and unchallenging." Much more satisfying was the work of Hungarian auteur Miklós Jancsó whose nine-part 1984 miniseries *Faustus Faustus Faustus* chronicled the history of postwar Hungary, allegorically critiquing communism and Soviet imperialism. In parts of Latin America, the unique genre of the telenovela has a particular historical sub-genre, with programs located against particular key episodes in national history: in Mexico *The Carriage*, shown in 1971–2, focused on "the struggles of President Benito Juárez to maintain an authentic Mexican government between 1864 and 1867". Quite what memories viewers might derive from these programs is problematic to discern: while they can contain potentially powerful political statements they are also shaped by genre conventions and are above all intended to entertain (Paterson 1998: 62).

AFTER THE COLD WAR

Infiltration by Western cultural products purveying corrosive images of material abundance contributed to the collapse of communism in Eastern Europe at the end of the 1980s, and the concomitant end of the Cold War. So too did the pace of technological development in the west, especially in relation to computing: creaking state socialist economies were ill-equipped to cope with the challenges of the information age. Over the three decades since communism's collapse, the exponential increase in computer processing power and connectivity has transformed everyday life across the globe. The flowering of a digital and networked era has had huge implications for cultural representations of the past: indeed, this technological change is one of the key precipitant factors behind a veritable "memory boom" in recent times (Winter 2006: 17–51). Digitization and the internet have allowed for the unprecedented production and accumulation of traces and representations of the past, and for their instantaneous consumption and exchange on a global scale. (This is true even as "information overload" has fostered "new modes of reading, such as skimming and scanning, that sacrifice depth for speed" (Rosenfeld 2015: 295).) Moreover, beyond the creation of digital archives of documents, photographs, and videos, the web has also facilitated the emergence of entirely new forms of representation such as "virtual memorials," blogs, social media, and other web 2.0 applications. In many ways this information revolution is democratizing, as it undermines established hierarchies and empowers individuals and groups to participate in shaping public consciousness (though one might sometimes regret the accompanying voiding of traditional quality controls). Yet the web consequently presents as "a babel of contending narratives" (Morris-Suzuki 2005: 210), in which it is difficult to discern which voices in a conversation have greater authority or to gauge which representations might gain purchase and become established as powerful memories (Hoskins 2017a).

The growth of this new landscape of technology and memory was intimately intertwined with the complexities of post-Cold War politics. For some time in the 1990s, it seemed as if superpower confrontation had given way to an age of American unipolarity; in the new century this complacency was shattered by the terrorist attacks of 9/11 and the beginnings of an apparently interminable "war on terror." The 2008 economic crash exacerbated the woes of the global liberal order, ushering in an age of austerity and eventually the rise of a new authoritarian populism. The "memory boom" was both backdrop to these epochal political shifts and constitutive of them. Conflicts played out and identities were consolidated and contested through clashing representations of the past. These involved traditional and new media, high-brow and low-brow forms, and the intermingled agency of state authorities and diverse other memory entrepreneurs, both in traditional forums and across the anarchy of cyberspace. New norms around human rights, justice, and apology, and the emergence of myriad new non-state actors changed the terms of debate over past conflicts and traumas. Increasingly, memories have become more mobile and flow unbounded (Bond, Craps, and Vermeulen 2017), acquiring an intensified transnational character as they play out within a global public sphere (Assmann and Conrad 2010).

The increased visibility of the Second World War across politics and popular culture from the 1990s testified to the burgeoning "memory boom." The Yugoslav wars were fought out with a blizzard of competing rhetoric from Serbs and Croats dredging up wartime antagonisms suppressed during the Communist era of "brotherhood and unity"; Western debates about intervention were saturated with the memory of appeasement (MacDonald 2002). As commemorations of key Second World War anniversaries became ever more lavish, a veritable secular religion developed in the United States honoring the achievements of the "greatest generation" of veterans that had fought it to victory (Bodnar 2010: 200–34). "Good war" nostalgia was so entrenched by the turn of the century that it was almost inevitable that the terrorist attacks of 9/11 would be dubbed a new "Pearl Harbor" by the American president, and the subsequent "war on terror" be presented as reprising the earlier global war against fascism (Noon 2004). Often, the media of memory in play here were quite traditional: Steven Spielberg's 1998 film *Saving Private Ryan* and the 2001 television miniseries *Band of Brothers* were key texts spurring the "greatest generation" movement and there was, in one sense, little novel in politicians invoking past wars rhetorically to legitimate contemporary ones, and having these words disseminated through the broadcast and print media. Yet increasingly, even conventional representations of the past—including also the war museums and memorials that began to proliferate—were acquiring a parallel web presence, and in the new century virtual engagement with the wartime past increased exponentially.

FIGURE 6.5: Warrior armored personnel carriers of the Irish Guards are cheered on as they pass refugees from Brazda camp on the Macedonian-Kosovar border on their advance towards Pristina, June 1999. The conflict between NATO forces and Serbia over Kosovo was saturated with references to the Second World War, as Western politicians and media presented the Serbs as akin to Nazis enacting a Holocaust against Muslim Kosovars. Credit: Wikimedia Commons (Public Domain).

It has aptly been observed that "paradoxically, the further from the war we get, the more its impact is being felt and the more its meanings are being fought over" (Stone 2014: viii). New media are central to this contestation, as is evident from the way in which war-related topics, especially those that speak to sensitive issues of national identity, are intemperately fought over on Facebook, Twitter, and other social media. More soberly, these platforms also serve as hosts to myriad memorial projects: witness the Facebook memorial page of Henio Zytomirski, a six-year-old boy murdered in the Holocaust (Scislowska and Gera 2010), or diverse projects that live-tweet the war on a day by day basis (such as @RealTimeWWII). Relatedly, in the early twenty-first century, the BBC created the "People's War" website to solicit and then serve as a repository for the wartime experiences of viewers and listeners: almost 50,000 stories were eventually uploaded (Noakes 2014). This level of public participation in the shaping of national war memory seems laudable, even if the project's framing left very little space for testimony to seriously unsettle pre-existing national myths. Elsewhere, the untamed profusion of representations of the war on the web has generated more profound anxieties: for example, the ubiquity of Hitler memes—combining "cheeky satire, puerile parody, and freakish kitsch" (Rosenfeld 2015: 293)—has been interpreted as an element of a wider pernicious condition whereby the unique evil of Nazism is being trivialized, normalized, and relativized. The field of war representation across our culture is certainly extremely diverse, spanning a range from Prix Goncourt-winning novels like Laurent Binet's 2012

HHhH through to pulpy schlock like the 2009 Norwegian Nazi-zombie horror film *Dead Snow*. The frenzied pace of cultural production and the intense concerns about authenticity that animate and surround it are also related to the imminent end of living memory: as the participant generation passes away, the yearning to secure "true" memories of the war has intensified (Finney 2017).

Technological developments have created forms of affective and embodied experience that generate new kinds of memories. One obvious example here is the rise of immersive experience in war museums. The Imperial War Museum in London was a pioneer here with its "Blitz Experience," which opened in 1989 (Noakes 1997); in the years since such experiences have become commonplace and infinitely more sophisticated. The phenomenon of historical video games representing twentieth-century conflicts is also important here. Digital games represent the past in sophisticated ways, freighted both with enormous possibilities and significant limitations (Chapman 2016). Although historical games generally vaunt their "realism," there are often grounds to critique the accuracy or completeness of their depictions of the past: certain kinds of violence—for example against civilians—tend, somewhat ironically, to be heavily sanitized in First Person Shooters. But by the same token, analysis of how these games function as media of memory needs to take seriously how they are consumed by players who are as interested in the ludic experience as in historical narrative (Kingsepp 2017).

Manifestly, video games can convey political messages: the "war on terror" is a popular setting for many, and these tend both to promote the militarization of society in general (Robinson 2012) and the myths of American exceptionalism—with the United States the innocent victim responding legitimately to external aggression—in particular (Robinson 2015). The intimacy between the ideology of these games and the purposes of the American state bespeaks participation in a shared cultural discourse as much as direct government influence, yet it is undoubtedly true that game developers have built up complex interdependent relationships with military establishments in the United States and elsewhere. The kind of controls that existed with, for example, film censorship in the inter-war period may be absent now (and of course the state was never omnipotent over culture), but governments are not without considerable direct and indirect influence in this realm of cultural production. Over the last thirty years, the People's Republic of China has consciously instrumentalized memories of the so-called "Anti-Japanese War of Resistance" as part of a nation-building project, stoking nationalist anger over Japanese war crimes and contemporary lack of contrition. This work has included the development and promotion of numerous video games, such as *Anti-Japan War Online,* in which heroic Chinese characters do battle with Japanese troops (Nie 2013); a 2014 game *Shoot the Devils* allowed Chinese players to enjoy executing Japanese Class A war criminals (Sarkar 2014).

Enhanced consciousness of the Holocaust as the defining atrocity of the war, if not of the modern age, was central to the broader phenomenon of expanding war remembrance—indeed, in key respects it propelled it. Landmark developments in the early 1990s testifying to the burgeoning profile of the Holocaust included the release of Spielberg's blockbuster film *Schindler's List* and the opening of the United States Holocaust Memorial Museum in 1993. Thereafter, the Holocaust's visibility accelerated dramatically in film, fiction, historiography, memorials, political rhetoric, and across the web. Increasingly, Holocaust memory gained a universal and cosmopolitan character, responding to "the need for a moral touchstone in an age of uncertainty and the absence of ideological master narratives." This in turn was closely tied to the emergence of more expansive

FIGURE 6.6: Exhibition in the Tallinn Museum of Occupations and Freedom, Estonia, 2012. The pairing of a Nazi deportation train with a Soviet one is evidently intended to suggest similarities between the oppression inflicted successively by the two totalitarian regimes, in line with the "double genocide" discourse which has flourished in post-Communist Eastern Europe. Credit: Wikimedia Commons (Public Domain).

norms of apology, restitution, and regret, with a concomitant focus on victimhood: "Holocaust memory and the new rights culture have been mutually constitutive" (Levy and Sznaider 2006: 18, 5). Within Europe, Holocaust recognition became enshrined as a normative expectation through political instruments such as the Stockholm Declaration of 2000. As the European Union (EU) expanded eastwards in the subsequent decade, acknowledgement of the Holocaust's special character and unique lessons was embedded as a *sine qua non* for prospective members: as Tony Judt famously wrote "Holocaust recognition is our contemporary European entry ticket" (Judt 2005: 803). Many East European countries bristled at this expectation, not only because it raised sensitive questions about their wartime collaboration with Nazism but also because it threatened to obscure the wrongs inflicted on them during decades of Soviet rule: on their view the crimes of communism deserved an equally prominent place within the broader European story (Mälksoo 2009). The 2008 Prague Declaration on European Conscience and Communism, organized by prominent politicians and intellectuals, was a riposte to Stockholm to this effect, and the EU eventually responded to the pressure by establishing a memorial day for all victims of totalitarianism and educational projects on Communist oppression (Neumayer 2018).

The dynamic process whereby the Holocaust was simultaneously sacralized and relativized played out across countless cultural media. For example, Polish film played an important role in mediating the ongoing debate about how to contextualize the Holocaust in the national past: Andrzej Wadja's 2007 *Katyń* thematized Polish victimhood at the hands of the Soviets while Władysław Pasikowski's 2012 *Aftermath* dramatized the uncomfortable contemporary uncovering of Polish collaboration in the wartime murder of Jews. Again, high and low culture forms were mutually implicated: compare, for example, Jonathan Littell's mammoth, brutal, and ostentatiously high-brow 2006 novel of Holocaust perpetration, *The Kindly Ones*, and the mawkish 2008 film adaptation of John Boyne's *The Boy in the Striped Pyjamas*. Yet the online sphere was also crucial, and not only as a forum for heated social media debates or the mounting of virtual exhibitions and memorials. It has long been recognized that the web opened up new possibilities for interaction with traces of the Holocaust, both in terms of archiving and retrieval of material for historical research and in terms of artistic representation (Zelizer 2001); this has only become more evident in the world of "big data" and immersive experience, which facilitate new modes of narrativization (Fogu, Kansteiner, and Presner 2016). For some decades, diverse organizations and institutions have been video-recording testimony from Holocaust survivors about their experiences, and many of the resultant archives—such as the University of Southern California's Shoah Foundation Visual History Archive—have now been digitized and made viewable and searchable online: these resources are seen as especially important for perpetuating Holocaust memories for future generations as the era of living memory comes to a close (Shandler 2017). Conversely, the web has also facilitated the activities of those who would not merely relativize the significance of the Holocaust but actively traduce and deny it. While Holocaust denial has a long history, the internet's "democratic character" allowed "previously marginal material to gain mainstream status" and neo-Nazi hate sites now flourish online (Rosenfeld 2015: 301). The age of "fake news," conspiracy theories and racist populism is, unfortunately, one in which Holocaust denial has "found new momentum" (Doward 2017).

The potential of the web in relation to artistic innovation in Holocaust representation was demonstrated in 2010 by Melbourne-based artist Jane Korman. Korman visited Europe with her Holocaust-survivor father, four children, and niece, and engaged like many others in commemorative tourism around Holocaust sites. However, unusually, Korman filmed the whole family dancing—with affecting maladroitness—to the Gloria Gaynor disco anthem "I Will Survive" at various locations including Auschwitz-Birkenau and Dachau. Once uploaded to YouTube, Korman's various videos became a viral sensation, and provoked fierce debate. Was this trivializing and profane or, as Korman claimed, an exuberant affirmation of survival that would help galvanize Holocaust memory for the future? (Flower 2010). Either way, this was an intriguing fusion of popular culture and high concept performance art and the transnational and global mass memory event that Korman precipitated would not have been possible without digital recording technologies and the web. It may also be, however, that much more extensive formal inventiveness will be required if Holocaust memory is to exploit the full potential of the digital age: anxieties about the sanctity and pristinity of the Holocaust have so far inhibited the full embrace of "the immersive and interactive" and the "simulative" (Kansteiner 2017b: 311).

There is infinitely more to the post-Cold War "memory boom" than the rise of Second World War and Holocaust remembrance. Recent decades have witnessed an upsurge in a whole range of historical practices that have made the past absolutely ubiquitous in contemporary culture, not just as an object for consumption but as a field for popular participation and creativity. A by no means exhaustive list of such practices might include the reading of popular history books and magazines (at all levels—witness the *Horrible Histories* children's books); metal detecting and treasure hunting; antiques dealing; genealogy and family history (greatly facilitated by commercial online archives); historical re-enactment; popular music nostalgia tours; the fad for vintage clothing and lifestyle products (in Britain, notably, austerity chic harking back to the Second World War); and the production and viewing of a whole gamut of historical television programs ranging from documentaries through reality shows to costume dramas (De Groot 2009). Collectively, these phenomena testify to the emergence of a dense and vastly complicated landscape for the making of memories, facilitated in significant part by technological change but with other drivers too. This development is certainly vulnerable to a range of political critiques. The desire to wallow in real or imagined pasts might well be seen as a refusal to engage with the urgent political problems of the present. In a British context, "austerity chic" has rightly been characterized in this way: "from the marketing of a 'make do and mend' aesthetic to the growing nostalgia for a utopian past that never existed, a cultural distraction scam prevents people grasping the truth of their condition" (Hatherley 2016: inside jacket cover).

It would be wrong, however, to utterly despair of contemporary memory making. One of the many other pasts made insistently visible during the "memory boom" has been the First World War, the centenary of which has been elaborately marked in myriad ways in many of the former combatant countries from 2014 through to 2018. Perhaps inevitably in the era of Brexit, in Britain this has encouraged the venting of hackneyed nationalist views about German responsibility for the conflict and attacks on the supposed left-wing

FIGURE 6.7: Performance art event "We're here because we're here . . ." under way in London, July 1, 2016, marking the centenary of the beginning of the Battle of the Somme. Credit: Wikimedia Commons (Public Domain).

myth peddled by academics and the media—witness the 1989 BBC comic television series *Blackadder Goes Forth*—that the war was a "misbegotten shambles" (Perry 2014). Yet the commemorations have also included much thoughtful, sensitive, and creative reflection upon the tragedy of war and the experiences of those that fought it; equally, hitherto under-emphasized topics—such as the imperial character of the war and the contribution of non-Europeans to it—have been productively foregrounded.

On July 1, 2016—the anniversary of the first day of the Battle of the Somme—one of the most moving art projects in modern British history unfolded. Under the creative direction of Jeremy Deller, "We're Here Because We're Here" saw 1,400 professional actors and volunteers, dressed as soldiers who had lost their lives on July 1, populate cities and towns across Britain in small groups. The memorial was unannounced and early morning commuters were astonished to see First World War soldiers walking the streets like ghostly apparitions. The soldiers were silent if approached, simply distributing cards with details of the individual they represented, and only occasionally burst into the signature sung refrain of "We're here because . . ." before moving on to another location. Social media exploded with reported sightings of the soldiers and admiration for the moving tribute they were paying to the fallen. Over two million Britons were estimated to have witnessed this piece of national memorial theatre personally (14–18–Now: 2016). Here high art concept, re-enactment and mass popular performance, charged by the "memory boom," came together to create a truly stunning immersive experience that instilled fresh memories of a terrible conflict.

CHAPTER SEVEN

The Social: Rituals, Faith, Practices, and the Everyday

JEFFREY K. OLICK

Though it is my task in the pages that follow to write about "the social" in the cultural history of twentieth century memory, and thereby to enable comparison with "the social" and "social memory" in earlier epochs, doing so is, in many ways, to put the cart before the horse. "The social," after all, is not a trans-historical category, but the product of transformations in social organization itself, not least those of the most recent centuries. Indeed, theorizing these transformations was the goal of numerous writers in the late nineteenth and earlier twentieth centuries in particular—the centuries in which "the social" may be said to have come into its own as both a phenomenon and a category of analysis (though in some ways, as we will see, it fragmented just as quickly). Before turning more directly to "the social" in the cultural history of memory, then, it will be helpful to lay some background, especially since not all readers will come to the topic from the point of view of the "social" sciences or know more about their foundations.

SOCIOLOGY AND THE SOCIAL

Some of the writers who began addressing "the social" in new ways—or at all—in the nineteenth century saw themselves as practicing something called "sociology," adapting a term first used by the French political writer Emmanuel-Joseph Sieyès in 1780, but more commonly attributed to the philosopher August Comte, who coined it independently in 1838; "socio-logy" combined the Latin "socius" with the Greek "logos" to create a new term for seeing partly old and partly new phenomena in a new way, however old—though discordant— the pieces of the name. "Sociology" as a distinctive field of inquiry devoted to the study of society or "the social" was, in turn, institutionalized as an academic discipline by the French "sociologist" (the first to call himself this) Émile Durkheim in the early twentieth century, partly in debate with his British counterpoint, Herbert Spencer, among many others, who himself had published a three-volume *Principles of Sociology* in 1898. Indeed, sociology and the social might be said to have called each other into existence: the former by giving a name to a new way of being, the latter demanding a new way of thinking about it.

"The Social" and those who studied it as such were indeed in many ways emblematic of the thought—and organization—of the age, an age in which, as Karl Marx had put it in 1848, "All that is solid melts into air, all that is holy is profaned, and man is at last compelled to face with sober senses his real conditions of life, and his relations with

FIGURE 7.1: Herbert Spencer. Credit: Wikimedia Commons (Public Domain).

his kind." In this vein, the goal of the new "sociologists" of the late nineteenth and early twentieth centuries was to explain the rapid transformations they observed taking place around them in Western Europe and the United States—not least, the emergence of "the social" as a distinct realm from the economy or the state (in a slightly different tradition, political philosophers from Marx to Jürgen Habermas have traced alterations in "civil society" and the "public sphere," analogous concepts to that of "the social").

The processes of change—urbanization, industrialization, rationalization, etc. that led to the rise of the social—were multifarious, and different theorists emphasized different elements, and asserted different causes for them. But most agreed that the changes were profound, and that, despite a widespread faith in progress and "enlightenment," the shape of the new order was troubling. As Walter Benjamin wrote in the years after the First World War, and commenting on it, "a generation that had gone to school on a horse-drawn streetcar now stood under the open sky in a countryside in which nothing remained unchanged but the clouds . . ." (Benjamin 1968: 84). At the same time, for Benjamin and many others, "beneath these clouds, in a force field of destructive torrents and explosions, was the tiny, fragile human body . . ." hardly a positive image of what the massive social changes they observed had wrought. All that is solid had not just melted into air; it was being blown to smithereens.

For his part, Durkheim (1893)—who like Comte before him asserted sociology's preeminence over other modes of inquiry because he saw "the social" as primary—characterized the "modernization" of society as stemming from long-term developments in social organization, in particular the rise of a complex division of labor. Like many others (perhaps most prominently Ferdinand Tönnies, whose 1887 book *Gemeinschaft und Gesellschaft* (Community and Society) gave sociology an enduring slogan), Durkheim theorized a fundamental distinction between earlier social forms and contemporary ones. For Durkheim, the main difference resided in the forms of solidarity—the sense of commonality that binds a group together—in the two main formations. Before the industrial era, when the division of labor was low, solidarity was "mechanical": people had similar experiences and bases of knowledge to their neighbors; they felt themselves part of a group because their commonality was obvious. With the radical increase in the division of labor, with the conglomeration of people with different backgrounds, beliefs, and customs in large cities, with the formation of occupational and sectoral differences (the hallmarks of "modernization"), however, there arose a strong sense of individuality and difference, and it was no longer obvious what these different people with their different experiences and commitments owed to each other. The new formation would require a new form of solidarity—an "organic" one based on individuality and difference rather than similarity—and Durkheim was uncertain whether this new form would emerge; the First World War and the fractures it left as much in the fabric of societies as in the souls of their members certainly did not lead to optimism.

Since our topic here is "memory," it is worth mentioning one further difference between the worlds of community and society, namely their supposedly different understandings of time, in particular of the relationship between past and present. The time of community is, according to yet another overdrawn dichotomy (itself a tendency of the epoch), cyclical and repetitive, and in it change is gradual; communal time generates customs, ways of doing that flow smoothly from one generation to the next without need of explicit conceptualization. In contrast, the time of society is supposedly progressive and developmental, and change is rapid (it is no mere coincidence that the term for modernity in German, *Neuzeit*, is literally "new time"): generations have different experiences from one another and different attitudes based on those experiences, and the distances between them become greater and greater; connection to the past in society therefore requires explicit commitment, which takes the form of traditionalism and orthodoxy when it appears at all, and these flow less smoothly—when at all, and that is the point—than custom (Koselleck, 1985; Hobsbawm and Ranger, 1983).

According to Pierre Nora (1989), perhaps the most influential latter-day theorist of memory (writing in the 1980s), we have moved from living in *"milieux"* of memory (in communities)—in which the past is the very air we breathe—to consecrating *"lieux"* (places or realms) of memory (in societies)—in which we segregate contemplation of and attachment to the past as special topics, not part of everyday life. In one of the best-known characterizations of the history of memory, Nora claimed—not uncontroversially—that we now "speak so much of memory because there is so little of it left." As L.P. Hartley wrote in 1953, and many others have quoted since then, the past has become "a foreign country" (Lowenthal, 1985). The fate of solidarity, we will see shortly, however, depends on the ability to connect to that foreign country, literally and figuratively. It was the apparent difficulties of doing so that led Nora, along with many others, to his characterization of contemporary society as having so little memory left, or at least of having a very difficult relationship to the past indeed, despite being overwhelmed by its fragmentary remains.

COLLECTIVE MEMORY

The forms and places of memory *in* society thus changed with the reconfigurations *of* society and of the place of "the social" within it, not least the very emergence of the social as a category of analysis. And "the social" clearly raises numerous questions for a cultural history of memory, not least what is "social" about memory in the first place. Conventionally, of course, we think of memory as an individual phenomenon, something that we do privately and that depends on substrata and capacities that belong to each of us alone (i.e. brains and cognition). Yet Durkheim's contribution (developed in contradistinction, again, to Spencer, whose view was shaped by liberal notions of the individual) was to recognize that the social, not the individual, is primary, and hence that sociology surpasses individual psychology as a frame of reference. Where individualists like Spencer saw "the social" as the aggregation of individual-level phenomena, Durkheim saw individual-level phenomena as the products rather than sources of social patterns. To make his case, he identified what he called "social facts": "A social fact" he wrote in his *Rules of Sociological Method* from 1895, "is every way of acting, fixed or not, capable of exercising on the individual an external constraint; or again, every way of acting which is general throughout a given society, while at the same time existing in its own right independent of its individual manifestations" (Durkheim, 1982: 147). "Social facts," Durkheim—or at least Durkheimians—intoned like a mantra, are *"sui generis."* Because of this, "sociology is [. . .] not an auxiliary of any other science; it is itself a distinct and autonomous science" (145).

FIGURE 7.2: Bust of Emile Durkheim in Paris. Credit: Wikimedia Commons (Public Domain).

Among the social facts "sui generis" that sociology brings into relief—indeed foremost among them—are categories of time and space that shape the way individuals think, act, and, especially, interact, the "*a priori*" from Immanuel Kant that Durkheim reconceived as socially, rather than philosophically, transcendental. The very thought processes of individuals take place in and through what Durkheim called "collective representations," which include these basic categories of time and space, but also other social facts ranging from language and concepts to images, beliefs, and practices. In his late work from 1912, *The Elementary Forms of Religious Life*, Durkheim wrote with special eloquence of the sacred and of ritual, in particular emphasizing funerary and other mnemonic practices, as, and as shaped by, collective representations. These representations undergird society rather than, as in transcendental philosophy, existing outside of it. But they do exist outside of, or at least prior to, the individual.

Yet it remained for Durkheim's student and follower, Maurice Halbwachs, to show what Durkheim's sociological approach meant for memory (and vice versa). For Halbwachs (1992), memory is fundamentally "social" or "collective," and "collective memory" is clearly a fundamental "social fact" working in, through, and as collective representations. Halbwachs of course was not the only theorist in the late nineteenth or early twentieth century to emphasize "social" memory—or indeed to see memory as preeminently social. Following the success of Charles Darwin's theories of biological inheritance, Richard Semon (1921) hypothesized a cultural equivalent to genes—what he called "mnemes"—as mechanisms of transmission of meanings and symbols across time. The art historian Aby Warburg drew on Semon when he developed his concept of "social memory" as the residues of past images in the form of iconological accumulation and layering (Gombrich, 1986). Sigmund Freud, for his part, rejected Semon's approach, yet still sought, especially in his last book, *Moses and Monotheism* (Freud, 1939), a mechanism of cultural inheritance; Carl Jung's concept of a "collective unconscious," in contrast, cited Semon quite positively (Jung, 1976). Taken together, despite their differences, these works, among many others, demonstrate the numerous ways in which leading figures in Western European science and letters at the dawn of the new century were discovering both the importance of memory and its social nature.

Yet it is the work of the Durkheimian Halbwachs in the 1920s and 1930s that has given us the common term "collective memory," and that has best articulated the social nature of even the most individual sense of the past. His insight is in many ways central to understanding memory as having a cultural history, as well as memory being an essential feature of social organization in the twentieth century, to say nothing of earlier ones; to see memory as social, cultural, or collective, and to see social, cultural, or collective memory as essential parts of the reconfiguration of "the social" is, in many ways, a quite significant (though also incomplete) revolution in contemporary thought, itself the product of changes—including the ones theorized by Durkheim and his contemporaries at the start of the century—that enabled this recognition.

For Halbwachs, individual memory was directly connected to the groups and other "social frameworks" that generated it. In contrast to the intuitionist philosopher Henri Bergson (with whom Halbwachs had studied in high school), who emphasized memory's role as the thread out of which the subjective sense of temporal continuity is sewn (Bergson 2004), Halbwachs argued that "What makes recent memories hang together is not that they are continuous in time: it is rather than they are part of a totality of thoughts common to a group, the group of people with whom we have a relation at this moment" (Halbwachs 1992: 54). As a result, the "various modes by which memories become associated result from the various ways in which people can become associated": in other words, the forms of the social. "We can understand each memory as it occurs in individual thought," Halbwachs argues, "only if we locate each within the thought of the corresponding group" (Halbwachs, 1992: 53). The question, then, is what the corresponding groups might be, how (and whether) they hold together (Durkheim's question of solidarity writ small), how they change, and the forces that affect our membership in them.

At the heart of Habwachs' analysis of collective memory in his 1925 book *The Social Frameworks of Memory* was attention to at least three main institutions of late nineteenth and early twentieth French society: the family, religion, and social classes. Taken together, these three discussions make a variety of points. In the first place, family works extremely well as an example of the social frameworks of memory because it is the primary site of socialization and personal identity. It is here that one acquires one's most fundamental memories and in this group that one shares them most often; and it is in reference to landmarks of family life that one organizes one's other memories. The association with family is indeed one of, if not the, most important identities, conferring a common name on its members, controlling reproduction, and organizing daily life.

Yet Halbwachs also wanted to demonstrate that the family not only organizes the memories of its members but generates a group memory of its own. "Even when they live near each other, but all the more so when life keeps them distant, each family member recollects in his own manner the common familial past" (Halbwachs, 1992: 54). So far so good: the social frameworks of individual memory are now broadened out to a collective topic, the family group, though not yet fully to collective memory, the memory *of* the group. Even though it would be ontologically untenable to ascribe action to the family separate from the individuals who comprise it, however, Halbwachs also argues that "it is only natural that we consider the group itself as having the capacity to remember, and that we can attribute memory to the family, for example as much as to any other collective group" (54). Indeed, the family's collective memory is, more than anything, what binds it together, the source of its solidarity, and what generates its sometimes extraordinary commitment. But this collective memory—its various collective representations, the family itself being one of them—is socially *a priori* to the individuals who comprise it.

This is because families, just like "the family," are "institutions," which Durkheimians take to be made out of collective representations. For instance, a family may gain or lose a member, and certainly does so over the long term, yet remains in some way or another continuous and whole. This is true of other social forms as well: universities or museums or publishing houses, to say nothing of nation-states, remain themselves (though of course changed) as their incumbents (for instance, we) enter and leave their collective lives. The institutions themselves maintain memories of their collective existence, stories of their pasts and present, that transcend the individuals who comprise them, shape the memories of those individuals (both individual memories that are framed by their memberships, and individual memories of the group's past), generate occasions for remembering together, include a memory of their own, and thus preserve and maintain the group as a group (and the identities of the individuals who pass through them). It is not difficult to see how recognizing the emergent rather than just aggregate qualities of social institutions over time depends on the new forms of social organization that emerged in the course of the nineteenth century, for instance historical and other record keeping about institutions in a complex web of others.

Particularly important mechanisms for the maintenance of family memory, and thus of the family as a group, include the kinds of things that, as already mentioned, interested Durkheim (1912), for instance the cult of the dead, funerary practices, feasts, and genealogy. Each of these regenerates a sense of belonging, reaffirms collective representations of the family, and provides yet further materials for memory of it. Families also exist in spaces—perhaps a home or territory—and loss of those places can be a significant challenge to the continuity of the family, not only because it decreases the likelihood of continued co-presence, but even more because it eliminates a common reference point—a familial collective representation—though that place can remain a powerful collective representation for the family even after the place is gone; in some ways, a lost home can be even more powerful in its absence as an object of representation than in its presence as a reality, for instance through nostalgic longing. Families also possess objects, languages, symbols, and meanings, the origins of which might be obscured, but the maintenance of which is essential—in jokes, shared sentiments, tacit knowledge, etc. A family remains a family because of its continuous memory, just as other basic institutions of society do. The group is thus not merely an interactive unit, but an interactive unit constituted by its collective representations, including its collective memories.

The family, however, is not an isolated institution, nor the only institution or group of which its members are members, and it is thus particularly important to understand the place of the family in the life of its incumbents, how it is cross-cut by other affiliations through its members, how it is situated in the ecology of other families, and how the ecology of families is situated in other institutions. Indeed, recognizing this led Halbwachs to his second major institution, namely religion, which in many ways infuses and defines the life of families (or at least did in Halbwachs' time and place). But religions work in, on, and through memory in different ways as well.

In the first place, according to Halbwachs, religions are great repositories of deep memories, especially since the most significant ones are quite ancient. Though Halbwachs does not use the term, all religions are also, to greater and lesser extents, syncretic—they combine elements of older and neighboring traditions, and thereby preserve them in coded form (here there are perhaps more similarities between Halbwachs' analysis and that of Aby Warburg than usually acknowledged—multiple layerings accumulated in a tradition). Additionally, according to Halbwachs, religions work to solidify their institutional power by transfiguring a story in time—e.g. the lives of founding figures—into a doctrine or dogma that seems out of time; this "story," or memory, is reenacted across epochs with strong continuities, thereby sustaining the religious community as a community of shared memory through practice. These ritual practices are at least as important as the explicit tradition of doctrine.

Taken together, these different practices and beliefs give those who reproduce them a sense of being able "to resist the assault of societies that came and went in the world around them" (Halbwachs, 1992: 96). Of course, as Halbwachs concludes, this is misleading, for "although religious memory attempts to isolate itself from temporal society, it obeys the same laws as every collective memory: it does not preserve the past but reconstructs it with the aid of the material traces, rites, texts, and traditions left behind by the past" (1992: 119). And, again, just as families interact with religious institutions, religious institutions interact with families, as well as other forces like the state. For Halbwachs, though, groups have collective memories, and frame the individual memories of those who exist in them, individuals always exist at the intersection of their multiple group memberships; at the same time, groups, constituted by their memories, also always exists at the intersection of their members. Unlike many others writing after him about particular groups in isolation, Halbwachs always emphasized the complex ecology (or, in Durkheimian language "social morphology") of groups and collective representations.

Finally, Halbwachs addresses social classes and their traditions. This topic stems from earlier work Halbwachs did on the consumption habits of different classes (Halbwachs 1959). Namely, Halbwachs had demonstrated that even when their incomes and means were the same, families from different classes spent their money in very different ways and valued their possessions very differently. For Halbwachs, this was a way of extending Durkheim's critique of Spencer: complex societies are not made of individuals and their rationality, but of groups with distinctive habits, preferences, and routines.

In his 1925 book, Halbwachs provided a fascinating discussion of the ways social classes change in relation to each other, even if their incumbents do not understand the origins of their own preferences. Many years later, the sociologist Pierre Bourdieu's analysis of the ways in which classes are defined by what he called "cultural capital" became a bestseller in France (Bourdieu 1984). Yet, in re-reading Halbwachs, it is clear how much of a debt Bourdieu's analysis owed to that of his forebear (yet another form of collective memory, this time forgotten). As Halbwachs showed, presaging his more famous progeny, "every activity that has as its goal the production of commodities, their sale, and more generally, the valorization of wealth, also shows a twofold aspect. It is a technique but, on the other hand, those who practice it must take their inspiration from the needs, customs and traditions of a society" (1992: 166).

For Halbwachs, it was of particular interest how different classes appropriated elements of each other's techniques and authority in an ever-shifting dance of power and position. Yet the functioning of this dance always entailed reference to the past—the authority (rather than just effectiveness) of a technique. Working people appear legitimate because they wear the appropriate garb, just as does the judge or the doctor, even if academics only don their robes once a year, and even if none of this has anything to do with their skills. Halbwachs quotes Pascal, who said that "It is dangerous to tell people that the laws are unjust, for they obey them only because they think they are just" (Halbwachs 1992: 166). According to Halbwachs, "to locate the law within the tradition of a social life that is both old and strongly organized is to strengthen the latter with all the authority of the spirit; it is to reveal society behind the technical apparatus" (1992: 164). In reaction to Spencer, Durkheim had argued that contracts are not the results of rational negotiation between partners, but require "non-contractual elements" to support them, namely trust and the threat of superior disinterested enforcement by third parties (in modern societies, the state). Here Halbwachs shows how all professions and technical tasks involve such institutional elements, and in particular that memory and tradition are essential parts of these. Not even the most technical of tasks in modern industrial society take place without reference to and use of traditional authority, much as the authority of authority itself may have declined since Halbwachs' time.

To be sure, family, religion, and class do not exhaust the institutions of contemporary society, nor the loci of collective memory. Perhaps surprising in re-reading Halbwachs, for instance, is how little he writes of the nation. In some ways, Halbwachs' predecessor Ernest Renan (1882) had already made similar arguments about the nation to Habwachs' understanding of social classes and of religion. For Renan, a "community of interest" does not "suffice to make a nation [. . .] Community of interest brings about trade agreements, but nationality has a sentimental side to it" (Renan 1990: 18). An important part of this sentiment, for Renan, was "the possession in common of a rich legacy of memories [. . .]

FIGURE 7.3: Portrait of Ernest Renan (before 1875). Credit: Wikimedia Commons (Public Domain).

The nation, like the individual, is the culmination of a long past of endeavors, sacrifice, devotion. Of all cults, that of the ancestors is the most legitimate, for the ancestors have made us what we are" (Renan 1990: 19). In re-introducing Renan and his ideas on the nation in the 1980s, the Irish political scientist Benedict Anderson famously wrote that nations are "imagined communities," that is, communities that understand themselves as such. The nation "always conceived as a deep, horizontal comradeship" always depends crucially on a "subjective antiquity" (Anderson 1991: 6–7). For his part, Pierre Nora emphasized a nexus between memory and the nation that marked the apogee of the nation-state in the late nineteenth century (Englund 1992: 315). While much of the history of memory in the twentieth century has been written in terms of the memory-nation nexus, however, Halbwachs was much more interested in the smaller groups that exist in what other theorists (e.g. Husserl, 1936) would call the "life-world," the world of everyday interaction, rather than broadest abstraction. But the ways in which groupness is established and maintained in groups small and large can be analogous: interest and interaction do not suffice; imagination, indeed mnemonic imagination, is crucial.

In his 1925 book, but also in a series of later works, Halbwachs thus argued vigorously against the individualist understanding of memory, and for the role of memory in constituting groups, if not society per se: For Halbwachs, it is impossible for individuals to remember outside of their group contexts, which provide social frameworks for individual memories and without which they would be impossible. Overstating the case, which he later (1950) modified, he argued that "there is no point in seeking where [. . .] [memories] are preserved in my brain or in some nook of my mind to which I alone have access: for they are recalled by me externally, and the groups of which I am a part at any given time give me the means to reconstruct them" (Halbwachs, 1992: 38). Groups, he argued, provide us the stimulus or opportunity to recall, they shape the ways we do so, and they provide the materials. "It is in society," he wrote, "that people normally acquire their memories. It is also in society that they recall, recognize, and localize their memories." This framework in many ways is the apotheosis of "the social" (Halbwachs 1992: 38).

THE HISTORY OF SOCIAL MEMORY IN THE TWENTIETH CENTURY

Halbwachs' work on collective memory was clearly not merely an application of Durkheim's collectivist ideas to a particular, or particularly interesting, domain. As already discussed, the changed understanding of time in modernity is a crucial, rather than derivative, dimension of life in the contemporary period. Nora's (1989) distinction between *"milieux"* and *"lieux"* of memory, for instance, descended from Halbwachs' own sense that the premodern world was a world of memory whereas the modern world had become a world of history, which itself is a form of "dead memory," memory to which we no longer have an organic connection. The question then is what the forms or mechanisms of that connection might be, and especially how they have changed over time. And the history of social or collective memory in the twentieth century is indeed a dark one, one of multiple disruptions, reconfigurations, and fragmentations, the kind that left Benjamin's individual alone in a field of destructive torrents. The question is what role memory plays in processes of solidarity that can maintain social order in the face of such disruptions, or, as is sometimes the case, itself serve as a force of disruption and change.

As a starting point, we might look at the profound changes in the institutions already discussed. It is, of course, foolish to generalize too much about institutions that have appeared in so many different forms in so many different times and places, and that have different meanings to different people. For instance, in a well-known work on "the family" in the United States, historian Stephanie Coontz (1992) points out that contemporary discussions of the "decline" of the family are caught in a "nostalgia trap," and that we recall "The Way Things Never Were," as the title of her famous book puts it; whatever we have to say about "the family" in the twentieth century, we must remember that there are many kinds of families and many understandings of the term's meaning. With regard to religion, the so-called "secularization" thesis has been proven, disproven, modified, and remodified countless times. And who now speaks of "the working class," or of classes at all, when we are all in the 99 percent? And just as often as we declare the nation-state superseded by the transnational or cross cut by borderlands and melting pots, we witness a wave of nationalist sentiment. Furthermore, these four institutions don't even begin to scratch the surface of the groups and identities constituting and constituted by memory over the vast twentieth century (if the cliché about the nineteenth century is that it was long, what can we say about the twentieth?!). Nevertheless, a brief discussion of each of these will illustrate the broadest contours of mnemonic change across the twentieth century, before underwriting a general characterization.

Family memory

As already indicated, discussions of family change have been beset by the temptations of nostalgia, a false memory of a family structure that never existed. In the US context, one has spoken of the "nuclear family," an expression itself shot through with the mnemonic resonance of its time, the 1950s. Halbwachs' discussion of family memory, for instance, while sometimes referring to the primary group of mother, father, and child, more often spoke of a multigenerational and complex family structure, and made frequent reference to broader notions of kinship. What were the conditions of family life in the 1920s when Halbwachs was writing and how do they differ from contemporary conditions? And how do these changes affect "family memory"?

In the West, perhaps the most salient change has been the dramatic decline in marriage rates (Cherlin, 2009). A concomitant element of this is the rise in cohabitation, an arrangement that tends to be less stable over time. Marriage itself used to be for many primarily an economic arrangement, a mechanism of preserving property, and still is for some; yet marriage and other romantic entanglements have in many places become much more expressive rather than institutional arrangements. Partly as a result, so-called "complex" families are now commonplace, and with them the solidaristic and solidarizing memories of family life may be more fractured. At the same time, however, new technologies of memory—e.g. photographs, home videos, social media, etc.—can serve to intensify family contact and thus family memory across time and space, in the absence of physical co-presence, instantaneously, and durably (e.g. through infinite storage and search functions). The biologization of genealogy, through DNA testing, has also changed the conditions for family memory, perhaps establishing hidden connections or disrupting established ones. Like many other basic social institutions in the twentieth century, families, and family memory, have also been reconfigured through changed patterns of migration. Where the past used to literally be a foreign country, now the foreign country can be visited regularly, either physically or virtually. Family networks can thus be maintained and activated across previously unbridgeable distances. By the same token, new patterns of migration, especially the vast new category of refugee, has often meant the destruction of families and the loss of their memories in numerous and novel ways.

Religious memory

As already mentioned, the operation of religious memory—and of religions as what one of Halbwachs' major contemporary legatees, the sociologist Danièle Hervieu-Léger (2000), has called "chains of memory"—has been reconfigured by vast changes in its social context, often summed up as "secularization." There is no question that the institutional authority, political power, and attractiveness of many longstanding religious organizations has declined in the West in the twentieth century. Where religious organizations were one the primary repositories of records and arbiters of disputes, the state has now taken over most of these (in part mnemonic) functions. At the same time, religious membership and practice has declined, and with it the continuities in the chain of memory. Where once practitioners performed liturgies, now they pick and choose and recombine elements, often from very different traditions; it is no longer just the religions that are syncretic, it is also their practitioners, who now recombine pieces of sacred practice into new rituals, some steady but most not. Moreover, the main criteria of their value is less adherence to a tradition than the sense of momentary personal fulfillment those practices and ideas provide. Indeed, reconfigurations of family life combine with reconfiguration of religious life, and it is reasonable to expect increasing mnemonic deficits it both. The question, as always, is what takes the place of these more mnemonically robust and powerful institutions of the past.

FIGURE 7.4: Memorial to Karl Marx in Frankfurt. Credit: Wikimedia Commons (Public Domain).

FIGURE 7.5: Theodor Adorno. Credit: Wikimedia Commons (Public Domain).

Social class memory

As for class, as already stated, who now speaks of it? The modern world Durkheim and others describe as having developed in the wake of the old regimes of Europe was one that was already moving away from the rigidities of caste, or at least the clear divisions among the estates. As the middle classes grew and diversified, and as movement within them became more fluid (or at least the perception became widespread that such movement was possible), we *all* became middle class. When Halbwachs wrote of the working class in particular (Halbwachs, 1959; 1992), part of his goal was to describe what Marx had discussed in terms of class consciousness in the Durkheimian language of collective representations—in this case, collective class memories. In particular, the working class, and particular groups and organizations that constituted it, shared memories of struggle that underwrote their solidarity and endowed them with future goals. But the unimaginable reconfigurations of capitalist economies, particularly in the last decades of the twentieth century, took Marx's melting into air to extremes even he had been incapable of imagining: if the commodity took on the appearance of a thing with real value even though its value consisted only in its capacity for exchange, what can one say of the fully financialized world which, to adapt a phrase from Max Horkheimer and Theodor Adorno (1944), radiates disaster triumphant? More mundanely, there is little left in the contemporary West of labor movements and the class identities that went along with them (Hall and Joyce 1997). We can hardly remember what a world of lifetime employment and local production looks like, just as the world can no longer be divided into workers and owners, bourgeoisie and proletariat.

The Nation and memory

Finally, even though a great deal of the social memory scholarship that takes Halbwachs as one of its founders has focused on the nation-state as the primary container of memory, and as the primary object of reminiscence, numerous recent theorists have demonstrated how memory now "overflows" the "container of the nation-state" (e.g. Levy and Sznaider, 2006; De Cesari and Rigney, 2016). Where the rise of national media cultures enabled through the spread of what Benedict Anderson (1991) called "print capitalism" helped solidify nation-states of the nineteenth century, contemporary media cultures and what might be thought of as electronic capitalism has created not Marshall McLuhan's utopian global village, but a transnational cultural ecosystem in and through which cultural contagion breeds and spreads with little chance of being checked. Older media theorists initially calmed their fears about radio working like a "hypodermic needle" to manipulate the masses by hypothesizing a "two step flow" through which propagandistic messages might be hindered (Gitlin 1978). But with the decline of "old media" institutions, themselves constituted by shared memories and safe-guarding them, everyone has become his own opinion leader, which means no one is really anyone's anymore. Through these media, and the other more tangible migrations, memory has become "multidirectional" (Rothberg 2009) and flows through unpredictable pathways back and forth across borders that were never really as solid as our representations of them suggested.

To be sure, family, religion, class, and nation do not begin to exhaust the major institutions of the "the social" that contemporary sociologists identify as key to their (our) analysis of contemporary societies. In the US context, this list does not even include two of the "big three": race, gender, and class. Indeed, the rise of a so-called new "identity politics" has raised questions of collective memory in remarkable new ways. Ethnicity, for instance, used to be understood as a mainly biological phenomenon. In earlier discourses (e.g. Jung 1976) for instance, one wrote of "racial" memory, meaning the memory of family and ethnic groups. Under the dramatic conditions of complex migration already discussed, however, we have seen older "ethnic" identities reconfigured in sometimes baffling ways—for instance, in the United States, when Japanese, Chinese, and Koreans are grouped together as "Asian-Americans" despite centuries of antipathy. Similarly, ethnic identities that used to be quite significant in determining life chances—for instance being Irish-American or Italian-American—have now become what sociologists (Waters 1990) have labelled "symbolic ethnicities," varieties of whiteness that can be adopted at will and inconsistently almost as a form of entertainment. The groups activated by such collective memories are very different, just as are the collective memories activated by them: recalling the flight of one's parents from starvation in a famine and the discrimination they faced on arrival in their new country is rather different than the memory contained in the "Kiss me, I'm Irish!" of St. Patrick's Day celebrations in the US.

UNENDING CONCLUSION

It would, of course, be very strange to conclude a discussion of "the social" in twentieth century memory without an explicit discussion of the unprecedented mass violence and destruction that characterizes the epoch, though it is true (and an issue of not insignificant intellectual-historical debate) that Halbwachs himself articulated his theories of collective memory in the decade following the First World War with barely an explicit mention of it (Becker 2005). For indeed one of the most significant cultural products of the twentieth century has been both the concept and experience of trauma. And here it is once again helpful to return to Walter Benjamin, who somehow captured the essence of the century even before its most destructive torrents—Buchenwald, Dresden, Hiroshima, ethnic cleansing, the dark web, climate change, terrorism, refugee crisis after refugee crisis, etc. (the first of which consumed Halbwachs himself)—had destroyed our faith in "man's emergence from self-imposed immaturity," as Immanuel Kant defined enlightenment in 1776, the year of the US Declaration of Independence.

In many ways, unfortunately, we must take Benjamin more as a prophet than as an historian or sociologist when he described the fate of the generation that had gone to school on a horse-drawn streetcar and whose tiny bodies stood in the field in this way: "Never has experience been contradicted more thoroughly that strategic experience by tactical warfare, economic experience by inflation, bodily experience by mechanical warfare, moral experience by those in power." Benjamin—who himself committed suicide in face of possible capture by Nazis as he attempted to flee—might not have been at all surprised by what was to come, no matter how unimaginable. Famously, in his "Theses on the Philosophy of History" from shortly before his death in 1940, Benjamin discussed a painting by the expressionist painter Paul Klee, *Angelus Novus*, which Benjamin described as showing "an angel looking as though he is about to move away from something he is fixedly contemplating. His eyes are staring, his mouth is open, his wings are spread. This is," Benjamin says, "how one pictures the angel of history. His face is turned toward the past. Where we perceive a chain of events, he sees one single catastrophe which keeps piling wreckage and hurls it in front of his feet." Benjamin wrote these lines in 1940, before the construction of crematoria at Auschwitz or the first use of atomic weapons on human beings.

Benjamin's aphorism, however, captures the dialectic between the century's endless generation of destruction and trauma with its repeated injunction to "Never forget!" "The angel would like to stay," Benjamin writes, "awaken the dead, and make whole what has been smashed. But a storm is blowing in from Paradise; it has got caught in his wings with such a violence that the angel can no longer close them. The storm irresistibly propels him into the future to which his back is turned, while the pile of debris before him grows skyward. This storm is what we call progress." Yet perhaps it is we ourselves, with individual desires unmoored from robust conditions of memory, who constitute the storm in the first place. Severed from old traditions, interested only in the new, we have paradoxically built an anamnestic society—one that records every thought permanently in unfathomable databases—on top of an amnesiac culture, for we have much to forget indeed.

Is there a new "social"—if not organic solidarity, at least a way of talking with each other—that will give us shelter from the storm that we ourselves are generating and recording in high definition? The changes in the institutional conditions of memory surveyed above leave the question open, just as it was for Durkheim at the beginning of the century.

CHAPTER EIGHT

Remembering and Forgetting

BILL NIVEN

INTRODUCTION

This chapter considers the history of forgetting in the twentieth century. It argues, essentially, that the history of memory in that, or indeed any other century cannot be understood without taking into account the dialectical relationship between remembering and forgetting—a relationship, admittedly, that we will never completely understand, given that it is much easier to know what we remember, than it is to know what we have forgotten, so that any appreciation of the connections behind the two processes is inevitably inhibited. But that connection is perhaps less difficult to explore on a social than on a personal level: there is always someone else who will remember, and want to remember, what we, or others, forget or would prefer to forget. In the following, I understand the political and social history of memory in the twentieth century as a continual struggle against forgetting, a struggle in which memory – or, better, "recall," as forgotten or neglected events were forcefully retrieved and given public attention— gradually seems to have asserted itself. The memories retrieved, often, are memories of violence, injustice, and discrimination. Their retrieval has often been made possible by, and contributed to, processes of democratization, processes reinforced by the human rights' discourse which informs the articulation of repressed memories of victimhood. Of particular importance is memory of the Holocaust, which has become a European, perhaps even global reference point when remembering the atrocities of which the human race is capable. In a world where we have perhaps taken leave of faith in the inevitability of progress, we tend more and more to look back, rather than forwards, in the hope that our future might be assured if we approach it critically in the light of our past. For all that, there are voices to be heard which warn of an inflation of memory toward the end of the twentieth century, and point out the benefits of a degree of forgetting.

THEORIES OF FORGETTING

The twentieth century, perhaps, is the century of memory. In the aftermath of the First World War, the laying out of mass memorial graves to those who had been killed emphasized the importance of recalling their sacrifice: never before had the deaths of soldiers been remembered with such intensity, indeed vehemence. In Germany, the supposed ignominy of defeat in The First World War, and of the Treaty of Versailles imposed afterwards, provided an important reference point for the aggressive policies of the National Socialists. The deaths of German soldiers were not only to be mourned, but to be understood as a call to renewed arms at a future date. The Versailles Treaty was not just a thorn in the side of nationalists in Germany, it was remembered by several countries which felt disadvantaged by its terms as a "scandal" which needed to be reversed. Six weeks after the Soviet invasion of Poland on September 17, 1939, for instance, Soviet Foreign Minister Molotov described Poland as "this ugly creature of the Treaty of Versailles" (Moynihan 1990: 93), whose destruction by Hitler and Stalin he clearly rejoiced in. If in the first half of the century memory was the motor of resentment, after 1945—if haltingly, only gradually and inconsistently—it became a kind of ethical elixir. By the time of writing, the Holocaust has established itself around the world as central to a more positive form of memory: by remembering what may have been the worst crime in history, we recall what human beings are capable of, and that recollection animates us to prevent future violence; that, at least, is the idea.

Perhaps in reaction to assertions of the triumph of what we might call "progressive memory," some cultural historians and others are turning their hand to the question of what we *forget*, as well as remember. Often, memory seems to come with the stigmatization of forgetting. *Lest we forget*, is a frequent invocation, expressing a deep fear of forgetfulness, on the premise that progress depends on continued memory of deeds and people from the past. Yet a degree of forgetting may be quite healthy. Plato believed that it was necessary to forget things—certainly the less important things—if one wanted, in the process of anamnesis, to retrieve memory that was innate to us (Gross 2000: 51–2). Well-known is Nietzsche's comparison between sheep and humans: sheep appear happy because they are blessed with the inability to remember; humans, by contrast, less so because they are so immersed in the past (Nietzsche 1999: 248–9). In Jorge Luis Borges' classic short story "Funes el memorioso," first published in 1942, the main protagonist Funes is possessed of a prodigious memory. But it does not do him any good: he dies of pulmonary congestion at the age of twenty-one—memory kills him at the very moment he comes of age (Borges 2000).

The last two decades have seen a remarkable rise in neurological and psychological studies of memory, many of which pay due attention to the relationship between what we remember and what we forget: the former, after all, is constituted by the residue which escapes obliteration (Shaw 2016; Baddeley, Eysenck and Anderson 2015; Kandel 2006; Tulving and Craik 2005; Henderson 1999). It may be true that there are ever more semi-popular books giving supposedly surefire tips on what we can do to perfect our memories, as if forgetting is something we might learn to overcome (O'Brien 2005; Buzan 2009). As a result of developments in digital technology, we have become obsessed with the ideal of the perfectibility of memory. At the same time, the rise worldwide in the number of those suffering from Alzheimer's disease has been accompanied by an increased fascination with the neurogenerative process of memory loss, its effects, and the possibilities of prevention (Sherzai and Sherzai 2017; Shenk 2001). At the turn of the twenty-first century, psychologist Daniel Schacter put forgetting firmly on the scholarly map with his groundbreaking study of the ways in which individuals forget or misremember, identifying seven "sins of memory" (Schacter 2003). These he divided into "sins of commission" (misattribution, suggestibility, bias, and persistence) and "sins of omission" (transience, absent-mindedness, and blocking). What is striking about Schacter's categorization is that it does not always understand forgetting as negative: absent-mindedness can be explained, for instance, by the fact that our mind is focused on more important things. Rather than seeing the "seven sins" as "design flaws," Schacter believes them to be "by-products of otherwise adaptive features of memory, a price we pay for processes and functions that serve us well in many respects" (Schacter 2003: 173).

Perhaps taking his numerical cue from Schacter, social anthropologist Paul Connerton also came up with a scheme which separates forgetting into seven types: repressive erasure, prescriptive forgetting, forgetting that is constitutive in the formation of a new identity, structural amnesia, forgetting as annulment, forgetting as planned obsolescence, and forgetting as humiliated silence (Connerton 2008). In contrast to Schacter, however, Connerton's interest here is mainly in forgetting at a collective, social and political, rather than an individual level: not only, then, is there a collective memory (Halbwachs [1925] 1992), there can also be a collective amnesia. Repressive erasure involves the forced eradication of traces of an undesirable past, as when the French Revolution sought to remove "all elements of the ancien régime" (Connerton 2008: 60–1). Prescriptive forgetting also implies deliberate forgetting, but one which is publicly acknowledged as it is believed to be in the interest of all, for instance after civil conflict, to forget and move on (Connerton 2008: 61–3). That forgetting can be a gain is clearly demonstrated by the third type, according to which memories that have ceased to serve any practical use in a changing society are discarded as identity is reconstituted (Connerton 2008: 62–4). According to the fourth element in Connerton's typology, structural amnesia, memories that are no longer systematically passed down, for whatever reason, are forgotten (Connerton 2008: 64). Forgetting by annulment happens when, overburdened by a surfeit of information, we discard knowledge that is no longer relevant, or banish it to the archive (Connerton 2008: 65–6). Planned obsolescence, the sixth form of forgetting, is built into the "capitalist system of consumption" (Connerton 2008: 66–7), as product life cycles become shorter. Finally, forgetting as humiliated silence happens when a nation averts its gaze from a collective trauma. Connerton cites the example of postwar Germany's silence on the subject of the bombing of German cities—not the best of examples, given that references to the bombings abound in postwar German culture, as the numerous "rubble films" and literary reactions testify (Hage 2003). In fact, it was a collective sense of victimhood, not shame, which typified postwar Germany (Margalit 2010).

Aleida Assmann provides us with yet another septuple typology of forgetting which shares features in common with previous models. First, she claims, there is automatic forgetting, which might be understood in some of its aspects as the equivalent of Schacter's notion of transience or Connerton's of structural amnesia (Assmann 2016: 30–6). Forgetting by keeping (*Verwahrensvergessen*), her second type, differentiates between functional memory, which operates with the knowledge we need for our everyday lives at any given stage in our social evolution, and storage memory, where knowledge not immediately needed is held until it is activated or reactivated. She describes the difference between these forms of knowledge in terms of "canon" and "archive," recalling Connerton's theory of forgetting by annulment (Assmann 2016: 36–42). The third type, selective forgetting, relates both to the tendency of individuals to remember as it suits them, and to the social frameworks which shape rules of communication, rules that determine what we recall and what we forget (Assmann 2016: 42–8). Assmann's fourth type, repressive forgetting or *damnatio memoriae*—condemning to oblivion—mirrors Connerton's repressive erasure (Assmann 2016: 49–53), while her fifth category, defensive and complicit forgetting in the interest of protecting perpetrators, contrasts rather with Connerton's forgetting as humiliated silence: you can want to forget what you did, and you can also want to forget what was done to you (Assmann 2016: 53–7). Assmann's concept of constructive forgetting brings us close again to Connerton, this time to his idea of forgetting that is constitutive of a new identity (Assmann 2016: 57–64). Finally, Assmann draws our attention to therapeutic forgetting, when the past can be left behind us through conciliation, acknowledgement and regret (Assmann 2016: 64–6). Assmann endorses Avishai Margalit's definition of successful forgiveness as depending not on forgetting the wrong done ("blotting-out") but on overcoming "the resentment that accompanies it" ("covering-up") (Margalit 2002: 208).

Schacter, Connerton, and Assmann repeatedly stress that forgetting is not really the opposite of remembering. It exists in a constantly shifting relationship to it. What we remember today may be forgotten tomorrow; what is forgotten today may return to mind the day after tomorrow (and so on). Yet to date we have few empirical studies of social and political memory which examine the dynamic shifts between remembering and forgetting, and the causes for these. This is certainly a deficit. Not only do remembering and forgetting alternate diachronically, they also coexist synchronically. Thus, a state which seeks to repress memory of the past, usually in order to prevent an unwanted identification with alternative political ideals, is never going to succeed entirely, because it is simply not possible to remove memories from people's heads by decree. Prescribing certain memories at the cost of others is not going to work completely for the same reason. Remembering and forgetting exist in tension; the lived memory of individuals, the residue of their experience, cannot simply be substituted by state memory, though it will certainly interact with it in numerous ways that remain to be explored. Furthermore, while the theories outlined above most certainly can be and need to be deployed to understand the flow between memory and forgetting in the twentieth or indeed any other century, they are not without their problems. The elaborate typologies have the effect of implying that forgetting proceeds in one of seven different ways, whereas in fact all these types (and indeed any others) are too closely connected to be truly separated. Imagine a case where a new political order strives to extirpate memory of certain individuals and events ("memorycide"). Surely this is a form of selective remembering, albeit for invidious purposes. The result of such a restriction on memory would be that some memories would struggle to survive, leading, effectively, to structural amnesia. And of course, erasing unwanted memories would partly be achieved by foregrounding wanted ones, the constant emphasis upon which would serve to dictate to citizens how they should remember in a manner considered appropriate for identity formation.

THE INTERACTION OF MEMORY AND FORGETTING

State-mandated views of the past can be as much about seeking to silence memory (for instance, through censorship) as fostering it, given that such views are often very one-sided or even false and cannot be effectively sustained unless alternative memories are suppressed. Ordained remembering is thus also ordained forgetting. But it rarely achieves what it sets out to achieve. Alternative memories are pushed to the margins, or "go under ground," but they do not disappear. In South Korea, anti-Communist state memory of the Korean Civil War operated according to the "June 25" narrative, which dated the beginning of the war from the day the Soviet-backed People's Army invaded South Korea in 1950, rather than from the time of the conflict within South Korea itself following the US-backed decision to support separate elections there (Wright 2018: 113). Communism, in other words, was made responsible for all the conflict and violence of the war, as well as being dismissed as an international conspiracy without any national credibility. Yet as Brendan Wright has recently shown, in South Korean culture (e.g. literature), this dominant narrative was occasionally challenged through humanizing those who fought on the Communist side, and there were campaigns for compensation by the descendants of those leftists executed by government forces during the war (Wright 2018: 117–18). To a degree incipient signs of liberalization in authoritarian societies enable such non-mandated memories to emerge. This was the case with the Soviet Union following de-Stalinization under Khrushchev, and in the course of glasnost under Gorbachev. There developed, however, an uneasy relationship between a Communist regime only prepared to go so far in admitting to past purges and repression lest a too critical memory of Stalinism trigger revolutionary impulses, and grassroots groups insisting on a full confrontation with the Soviet past as a prerequisite for true democratization (Smith 1996).

However fluid and ambivalent the relationship between state-ordained memory and alternative memories—in the USSR, there was a degree of interpenetration at times—it is often with the collapse of the political system that the "forgotten" memories begin to truly assert themselves. The end of twentieth-century dictatorships, Fascist or Communist, was usually accompanied by iconoclasm. The destruction or removal of memorials was motivated not just by protest against imposed images of history, but also by anger at the long-standing suppression of different and more critical views. The most well-publicized case is that of *The Bronze Soldier* statue in Tallinn (Kattago 2016: 86–90). Erected in honor of the Red Army in 1947, it remembered the sacrifices of Soviet soldiers, and also served to justify the occupation of Estonia as a "liberation." For many Estonians, however, the memorial told a lie, or at least symbolized the denial of the truth: namely that Soviet

FIGURE 8.1: *The Bronze Soldier*, Tallinn, Estonia before its removal to another site. Credit: Wikimedia Commons (Public Domain).

liberation meant invasion and the imposition of communism. After the "Singing Revolution" in 1991, in newly independent Estonia, anger at this history of oppression focused on the memorial, and the Estonian government opted to remove it. One should be wary, however, of always seeing official memory as absolutely distortive, and the memory suppressed by this memory—the memory "to be forgotten"—as always representing "the truth." Of course, Estonians suffered under the imposition of the Soviet regime, but many also collaborated with it, and the Red Army did indeed make enormous sacrifices to end fascism. Besides, the forgotten memory, as it emerged, quickly calcified into another kind of official memory, this time an Estonian one. Casting Estonians as purely victims (of Nazism and communism) underscored the right to independence, helped with nation-building and served to create distance to Putin's Russia. Interestingly, too, at the turn of the millennium, many of Estonia's 300,000 Russians came to identify with the *Bronze Soldier* in the same measure as the Estonians rejected it. Feeling discriminated against in independent Estonia, Russians viewed the treatment of the statue as symbolic of the way they themselves felt they were being treated: as outsiders with diminishing rights.

In the twentieth century, then, the emergence of officially suppressed memories usually accompanied and strengthened developments towards enlightenment and democratization, but there was always a danger that the repressed memory could, once set free, itself take on assertively one-sided traits. When the GDR began to crumble, in January 1990, an angry crowd stormed the Stasi (State Security Service) headquarters in Berlin to try to put a stop to the destruction of files which contained information on the spying on East German citizens. They were seeking to uncover a hidden history of surveillance and suppression, to prevent it being forgotten before its true extent was really known. The later opening of the Stasi files to the public (Miller 2004), the memorialization of the Soviet Special camps at Buchenwald and Sachsenhausen (Niven 2001: 39–59), and the installation of various memorial sites recalling the GDR's inhumane border regime and its treatment of dissidents have ensured that the memories of Communist violence—illicit memories in the GDR—have found wide expression in united Germany and played their part in exposing state violence and reinforcing the importance of open democracy (Clarke and Wölfel 2011). Nevertheless, focusing exclusively on GDR state criminality does play into the hands of those who wish to delegitimize East German antifascism as totalitarian in all its elements and trumpet the supposed superiority of West Germany's confrontation with Nazism. When the Sabrow Commission set up by Germany's Social Democrat-Green government in 2005 to reconsider the presentation of the GDR in museums came up with the suggestion that any such presentation should also consider the relationship between politics and society in the GDR, and between everyday life and resistance, it was accused in some conservative quarters of trivializing East Germany (see the assessment by Horst Möller in Sabrow 2007: 51–9, 325–9). Memory of injustice, when it can be articulated, can help to shape democratic renewal, but to make of that memory the only yardstick by which to judge lived experience is to overlook the complexity of that experience (Sabrow 2009).

Forgotten or repressed memories surface clearly at moments of historical transition, but such moments are not always determined by revolutions or other forms of radical political change. In June 2015, twenty-one-year-old Dylann Roof murdered nine African Americans in a church in Charleston. On his website, Roof had posed with photos of the Confederate battle flag. That the southern states had never truly confronted the racism behind the confederate cause during the American Civil War (1861–5) was hardly

FIGURE 8.2: Berlin Wall, Border Crossing Oberbaumbrücke in 1987. Credit: Wikimedia Commons (Public Domain).

a new concern (Cook 2017). But Roof's explicit linking of that cause with his own murderous campaign gave that concern a new intensity, and that intensity found expression above all in calls across the southern states for statues to confederate heroes such as Robert E. Lee to be removed. Some of these were indeed removed, or subjected to vandalism, or at least to what could be termed "guerilla memorialisation" (Rice 2010), where protestors used paint or banners to turn the confederate memorials into warnings against white supremacism. Many of these memorials had been built during the Jim Crow period (1877–1954) or the time of the Civil Rights Movement (1954–68), their purpose being to shore up anti-black feeling and intimidate African Americans. Confederate memorials have long legitimated the historical cause of the southern states, and continuing practices of discrimination. Traumatic memories of suffering and injustice at the hands of such discrimination were, in this way, officially discredited and silenced. But after mid-2015, as the connection between memorial traditions which glorified confederate ideals and present-day violence became glaringly obvious, these traumatic memories could no longer be suppressed. Admittedly, however, far from all memorials have been removed.

Forgotten memories appear in many forms, such as protest against the "lies" of existing memorials; eye-witness accounts of atrocities published in sympathetic media; reports by new governments, or testimony given in trials against former perpetrators or during other hearings associated with transitional justice (see below). But it is worth stressing the importance of the recovery of material traces, either in the form of bodies, or of the reconstitution of ruined lives through photographs and artifacts. The twentieth century found radical ways of destroying human lives so as to make the bodies well-nigh

FIGURE 8.3: Robert E. Lee Memorial, Richmond, Virginia. Credit: Wikimedia Commons (Public Domain).

unrecoverable. The main example of this, of course, is the Holocaust. Recovering the names of as many as possible of those killed, as the memorial site at Yad Vashem in Israel has done (Yad Vashem 2018), restores to them post hoc their individuality, and counteracts the oblivion to which Nazism sought to condemn their victims. During Argentina's so-called "Dirty War" (1976–83), under the ruling military junta, between 20,000 and 30,000 Argentine civilians were taken from their homes, never to be seen again: they simply "disappeared" ("*los desaparecidos*"). The junta found perverse ways of disposing of their victims: during "death flights," they were dropped, sometimes drugged, into rivers or the sea. Following the democratic election of Raúl Alfonsín in 1983, a commission into the fate of the Disappeared was established, under the name of CONADEP (Crenzel 2011). For all its efforts, however, the commission was unable to trace the whereabouts of the vast majority of victims. In recent years, memorial initiatives such as the Memory Park along the riverbank of the Rio de la Plata in Buenos Aires (inaugurated in 2007) have helped to recall the fate of the citizens "disappeared" by the military junta by listing the names of the victims. Online memorials, which have the advantage that they can be constantly updated, also provide names and photographs: "memory will succeed," declares the website Desaparecidos.

FIGURE 8.4: Pictures and newspaper clips of *desaparecidos* (victims of forced disappearance) in a former illegal detention center in Rosario, Argentina. Credit: Wikimedia Commons (Public Domain).

A key technique involved in forgetting, then, is the eradication of traces, an eradication, in the twentieth and twenty-first centuries, often built into the process of murder. Argentina is not the only country that has experienced "disappearances." Other examples include Lebanon, from where some 17,000 people vanished between 1975 and 1990 (Young 2000), as well as Chile during the Pinochet regime. In some respects, the Holocaust served here as a precedent: those identified as enemies were murdered far away from their place of origin, in ways that were hidden, and their bodies were never meant to be found. In other words, not only was there to be murder, there was to be no memory of murder. When entire communities were murdered, there was to be no memory of disappearance either. After the First World War, memorials around Europe reproduced the names of the dead. Tombs were constructed for the Unknown Soldier, or, as in the case of the Thiepval Memorial to the Missing of the Somme, to servicemen with no known grave (Stamp 2006). Here already there was the impulse to counteract the anonymizing effects of increasingly industrialized forms of killing, but this was all done to honor sacrifices made on behalf of the nation; state memory aligned with regional, local and individual memory (see the chapter by Winter in this volume). Since then, states have often turned violence on minorities and their own citizens (as supposed "inner enemies"). Memory of ever more obliterative and clandestine forms of killing has endured *despite* the state. The recuperation of victims' names or their bodies—witness the recent exhumation of some of those killed in the Spanish Civil War (Aragüete-Toribio 2017)—reinscribes the very history of their destruction.

TRANSITIONAL JUSTICE

The above paragraphs have demonstrated the struggle of memory against forgetting in the twentieth century. In recent years, the term "transitional justice" has come into use to define the various ways in which post-conflict societies seek to come to terms with recent histories of state violence, war and human rights' abuses: methods used include war crime tribunals, various forms of corrective and distributive justice, truth commissions, and lustration (Kritz 1995; Teitel 2000; Simić 2017). This at times elaborate system of confrontation with the past is also characterized by a high degree of flexibility and pragmatics, but underpinning it is a quite extraordinary faith in the transformative power of *articulated* memory, and of making memory *work*. This can be set in contrast to the theory of "communicative silence" provocatively put forward by Hermann Lübbe in 1983 (Lübbe 2007; 11–38). According to Lübbe, staying silent about the past in the postwar period was a prerequisite to the acceptance and development of democracy in West Germany. The same idea, at least officially, informed the "Pact of Forgetting" ("*Pacto del olvido*") in Spain after the death of Francisco Franco in 1975. The pact was designed to stop those who identified with either the nationalist or republican position during the Spanish Civil War bickering over the past, in support of the shift from dictatorship to democracy (Aguilar 2002; Jimeno 2018). For the supporters of transitional justice, however, only *talking* about the past, openly confronting its problems, can truly contribute to the consolidation of democracy, whether this be in Chile, South Africa, Rwanda, or elsewhere. The example of Spain might seem to prove that talking is better than not talking. The 1977 Spanish Amnesty Law provided the legal basis for the "Pact of Forgetting." Arguably, this pact merely served to protect the interests of the Francoists, many of whom benefited from the Amnesty, and to slow down rather than accelerate the pace of democracy in the so-called "Spanish transition" (Encarnacion 2014). Only when the Pact was called into question by Spain's new socialist government in 2004, which passed the Historical Memory Law and challenged laws passed by the Francoist regime, did a true reckoning with Francoism begin, signaling Spain's emergence from the shadows of the Spanish Civil War.

The rich and diverse forms of transitional justice, as practiced in the late twentieth and twenty-first centuries, would seem to signal the triumph of memory over forgetting. In post-genocide Rwanda, the past was confronted through the work of national courts (special chambers), the international Criminal Tribunal for Rwanda (ICTR), local tribunals, and the inkiko gacaca courts, whose proceedings "were public and took place in individual communities encouraging public confession of crimes, truth telling, and community service in exchange for reduced punishments" (Loyle 2018: 668). By the time the gacaca courts had stopped their proceedings in 2014, some 1.5 million cases had been heard (Loyle 2018: 668). There is no doubt the use of gacaca courts was hugely ambitious (Chakravarty 2016: 7; Clark 2010: 3): the aim was to involve almost the whole population—victims, bystanders, and perpetrators—in a collective addressing of the past that was simultaneously an act of civic reparation and repair. Public memory work, semi-ritualized, formal or informal, is one key hallmark of transitional justice. South Africa's Truth and Reconciliation Commission, which also worked with public hearings, gave victims and perpetrators the chance to talk about their experiences and actions during the apartheid period (Du Bois and Du Bois-Pedain 2008; Sitze 2016). In contrast to Rwanda, the commission was entitled to offer amnesty to those who had violated human rights. But this was not amnesty on behalf of a campaign of silence. Rather, it was granted only to those who had fully and publicly owned to their crimes, and shown remorse. There are many other examples of the use of public hearings in transitional justice systems, such as in Peru, where a Truth and Reconciliation Commission was established in 2001 to confront human rights' abuses committed—including "forced disappearances"—during the 1980s and 1990s (Friedman 2017).

Transitional justice has not been without its critics. In Rwanda, for instance, the focus has been on calling the Hutu to account for their crimes against the Tutsi, but little effort has been made to confront Tutsi crimes against the Hutu, including the abuses committed by the Rwandan Patriotic Front (Loyle 2018: 664). The work of truth commissions, specifically, has been criticized for being overburdened with unrealistic expectations, used as a platform for self-exculpation, instrumentalized by governments for their own ends rather than for creating social justice and harmony, and too much influenced in some cases by members of the regime whose crimes they are supposed to investigate (see, for instance, Chapman and Van der Merwe 2008: 1–22). In other cases, truth commissions were limited in the way they operated, with little public participation. This was sometimes the case in Eastern Europe, with Romania providing a good example. Here, a Presidential Commission for the Analysis of the Communist Dictatorship in Romania was created in 2006. For a start, this commission had a clearly politicized function: it was designed to smooth Romania's passage into the EU by condemning communism. It only had six months to complete its work and had no subpoena powers enabling it to compel former perpetrators to appear before it (Stan 2013: 125). Its membership, moreover, was drawn "primarily from among anti-Communist intellectuals" (Stan 2013: 126), and the commission did not interact with the general public. As a result, despite the publication of a 700-page report in November 2006, the Commission's findings did next to nothing to increase the knowledge of Romanian citizens of Communist crimes (Stan 2013: 130). The report, rather than helping to bring about reconciliation in post-Communist Romania appeared to have done little to overcome nostalgia for communism or make a significant contribution to political progress (Hogea 2010). A distinction could be made between historical truth commissions, like the Romanian one and the German Enquete Commissions, and the more public ones such as in South Africa, but neither system is free of problems.

It should be reiterated that transitional justice does not consist just of the work of truth commissions, in whatever shape or form, but also, for instance, of processes of formal legal prosecution, punishment, and redress, as well as lustration mechanisms. Nevertheless, it is the endeavors of the commissions to find what Bishop Desmond Tutu has called a "third way" between, as he calls it, "Nuremberg or National Amnesia" (Tutu 1999: 10), that has made them the focus of so much public interest and scholarly research. For Tutu, this "third way" consists in the "granting of amnesty to individuals in exchange for a full disclosure" of the crimes concerned (Tutu 1999: 34). Herein lies their originality, and also their significance as platforms for the performance of memory as healing. Truth commissions, ideally, avoid victor's justice or even victim's justice. Retribution takes a back seat; driving the whole process is trust in the conciliatory potential of comprehensive confession, testimony, dialogue, and discourse. Truth commissions aim to overcome silence and forgetting; amnesties or reduced sentences are pronounced not to encourage amnesia, but on the basis of confessions which anchor deeds in collective memory. Such collective therapeutics are designed as internal measures for post-conflict societies where previously opposed or warring factions need to be united in the domestic interest—a need reflected in the very names of governments, such as Rwanda's Government of National Unity, or South Africa's (1994–9). Historically grounded, ongoing tensions between different countries, such as Ukraine and Russia, North and South Korea, cannot be addressed through such commissions.

TOO MUCH MEMORY? THE HOLOCAUST

Despite the memory work of transitional justice, and despite the firm establishment of Holocaust memory around the world, doubts have been raised as to whether cultivating memory of past events is necessarily always such a good thing. In his provocatively titled book *In Praise of Forgetting*, David Rieff reminds us of the inevitability that everything will be forgotten at some point in any case (Rieff 2016a: 5), that memory of the past usually comes with a degree of deformation (2016a: 22–42), and that collective memory may be overrated as a measure of a society's coherence (2016a: 57). Elsewhere, Rieff has gone so far as to suggest that memory might be counterproductive. "What if collective historical memory, as it is actually employed by communities and nations," Rieff writes, "has led far too often to war rather than peace, to rancor and resentment rather than reconciliation, and the determination to exact revenge for injuries both real and imagined, rather than to commit to the hard work of forgiveness?" (2016b). Rieff cites the examples of the Palestine/Israel conflict, the former Yugoslavia in the 1990s, and the current and recent situation in Syria and Iraq respectively. Memory, for Rieff, can be destructive, a point raised at the beginning of this chapter in relation to Nazi Germany.

In another recent book which takes issue with the value of memory, Christian Meier points out that, right through to the twentieth century, it was usual for political systems to want to put pasts behind them, not make them the subject of enduring memory. Two days after Caesar was murdered on March 14, 44 BCE, Cicero held a speech in which he asked the Roman Senate to "eradicate all memory of discord through eternal forgetting" (Meier 2010: 10). Already in 403 BCE, the Athenians famously issued an amnesty to prevent any future strife emerging from the civil war (Meier 2010: 10). Meier goes on to provide his readers with countless examples of similar amnesties—originally, the term simply meant "not remembering"—such as the Edict of Nantes (1598), according to which the memory of "all things" was to be erased, the 1648 Peace Treaty of Westphalia which ended the Thirty Years' War and called for "perpetual oblivion," amnesty, and pardon, and Charles II's imposition of an "act of free and general pardon, indemnity and oblivion" following his return to England in 1660 (Meier 2010: 41–2). Meier identifies moments in the twentieth century when the idea of forgetting also seemed to take center stage: in the Treaty of Lausanne (1923), for instance, or in Churchill's speech of September 19, 1946 in Zurich, in which he called for a "blessed act of oblivion" (Meier 2010: 10).

Both Rieff and Meier would seem to be pleading for a degree of forgetting, but Rieff's arguments are based in part on a misconception. The problem in the case of Israel and Palestine, for instance, is not memory itself, but its imbalance. While Israeli politicians routinely recall the Holocaust, they ignore Nakba (the 1948 Palestinian exodus). Palestinian leaders routinely remember Nakba, but generally struggle to acknowledge the Holocaust, although Hamas has made an effort in recent years (Naeem 2008). What we need is more mediation and negotiation between one-sided memories to create a fuller and prejudice-free understanding of past events: *more memory*, not less, is the answer here. Memory imbalance still plays a significant part in the constitution of state identities, as in the case of post-Soviet states seeking to create distance to Russia: the example of Estonia, explored earlier, demonstrates that. But this imbalance is caused by the political instrumentalization of selective forgetting, not by any kind of surfeit of memory. And while Meier is able to provide significant historical examples of traditions of forgetting by fiat, he does not tell us whether such decisions to forget and move on actually worked. In any case, amnesties—prior to the introduction of confession-based amnesty through the South African Truth and Reconciliation Commission—often functioned in the interests of protecting perpetrators or at least the complicitous. Is that to be preferred to ignoring the victims?

Meier certainly acknowledges that the twentieth century, in essence, marked a turning point in memory terms. Firstly, because after the end of the First World War, the Allies refused to countenance amnesty, given that this war—which they blamed on the Germans—constituted, at least according to French prime minister Georges Clemenceau, "the greatest crime against humanity and the freedom of peoples" (Meier 2010: 43). And, secondly, because of Auschwitz: the enormity of the Holocaust made memory, so Meier argues, inescapable. If this is true, then the unfortunate and damning corollary is that previous atrocities in world history (and there are plenty of extreme examples) were more easily forgettable—including, presumably, what Clemenceau considered to be "the greatest crime against humanity." Meier writes a book apparently defending histories of amnesty, only to then admit that it took the indiscriminate slaughter of 6 million people to wake the world up to the need to remember. Toward the end of the book, however, he returns to traditions of sanctioned forgetting—implying that the reckoning with the East German past after 1990 was more severe than it really needs to have been (Meier 2010: 129–56).

At this point, I return to an idea I hinted at the start of the chapter: namely that there is a connection, albeit one which could not be proven conclusively, between recent interest in memory studies in "forgetting" and an increasing degree of skepticism surrounding the efficacy of memory. In 2003 already, Andreas Huyssen was asking if memory might not be getting out of hand, ousting history in determining our relationship to the past; he warned against a "hypertrophy of memory" (Huyssen 2003: 3). This skepticism stands in contrast to ideas of memory's moral fertility which memory scholars have been expressing over the last two decades. Responsible for this optimism is their faith in the power of memory of the Holocaust. According to what is surely by now a well-established narrative, after the Second World War, the Holocaust played little part in collective consciousness, indeed the term "Holocaust" did not really enter our vocabulary until the showing of the TV series *Holocaust* in America and Europe over the 1979–80 period (Doneson 2002, and see also the chapter by Kansteiner in this volume). Gradually, the Holocaust came to acquire iconic status as the stand-out event of the twentieth century. In January 2000, at the turn of the millennium, forty-six governments in Stockholm agreed on a fundamental statement of commitment to Holocaust memory and education, given that the Holocaust, according to the declaration, had "challenged the foundations of civilization" (Allwork 2015). Since then, we are repeatedly urged to "never forget." On Holocaust Memorial Day (HMD, usually January 27), countries unite in recalling the Holocaust, and, increasingly, other genocides, appealing to their citizens to remain vigilant. The belief is a clear one: by remembering the Holocaust, we can help to ensure that such a crime will never happen again.

There is indeed an at times almost limitless faith in what Holocaust memory can achieve. It has been claimed by Daniel Levy and Natan Sznaider that there has been a shift from national memory, to memory that is more global and cosmopolitan in character (Levy and Sznaider 2005; Levy and Sznaider 2002: 88). Levy and Sznaider even felt so confident as to proclaim that the "diffusion of human rights norms during the last six decades" represents the "distillation of changing modes of Holocaust memory" (Levy and Sznaider 2004: 143). In an influential book, Michael Rothberg put forward the theory that Holocaust memory, far from crowding out memories of other forms of violence in an unseemly competition, actually encourages the articulation of these memories, and enables them to gain purchase in collective consciousness. Memories interact in a "productive, intercultural dynamic" that Rothberg calls "multidirectional memory" (Rothberg 2009: 3). Similarly, Max Silberman has put forward a theory of what he calls "palimpsestic memory," exploring the connections between memory of the Holocaust and of colonialism in French and Francophone fiction and film (Silverman 2013). Others, often with the Holocaust in mind, refer to memory's transnational scope (De Cesare and Rigney 2014).

While evidence is adduced for these claims, it would be possible to make counterclaims, and to suggest that memory scholars, sometimes at least, are more interested in recommending multi-directionality and cosmopolitanism than they are in proving it exists. In that sense, we are dealing here with prescribed memory—this time by scholars, rather than states. There is certainly good reason to be very skeptical of the *effectiveness* of Holocaust memory. It appears so far to have been, and to be, of little practical value in stopping genocide. We now regularly remember Srebrenica, but the West did little to stop genocidal activities in Bosnia in the 1990s. "Only the most starry-eyed can believe," wrote Peter Novick, "that the universal version of 'Never again' [. . .] is a lesson American political leaders are willing to put into practice" (Novick 1999: 257). The same surely applies to leaders around the world. Part of the problem may lie in what Joshua Davidovich has called "the two pillars of how we deal with and relate to the Holocaust," namely "Never forget" and "Never again" (Davidovich 2017). In theory, "Never forget" enables us to learn for the present and future but staring into the past can also immobilize us. In theory, "Never again" enables us to act in the present and future, but if it becomes a mantra, there is a danger we will be satisfied with our high moral intentions without feeling obliged to actually do anything. In any case, for all the talk of multi-directionality (Rothberg 2009), there is little clear evidence that remembering the Holocaust really does sensitize us to the suffering of others, despite well-intentioned cultural comparisons; nor does empathy for past victims assure empathy for future ones. Not only that: as Wulf Kansteiner has pointed out, "it has become clear that a given society can cherish Holocaust memory and yet intentionally engage in serious human rights violations." Kansteiner even goes so far as to suggest that the presence of a "mature Holocaust memory regime" actually enhances "the risk for the illegitimate and unethical use of military force" (Kansteiner 2017b: 306). Rieff, in turn, in reference to the United States Holocaust Memorial Museum, warns against the dangers of using Holocaust memory as a defense of Zionism (Rieff 2016a: 82)—reminding us how readily recalling the horror of the Holocaust can be politically instrumentalized.

The claim that memory of the Holocaust has become cosmopolitan in character overlooks or at best underestimates the degree to which individual nations use it to mean whatever they want it to—usually in the interest of the nation, something which Holocaust memory, according to cosmopolitan theory, is supposed to transcend. Arguably, HMD in Britain is more about recalling British rescue efforts (such as the Kindertransport of mainly Jewish children from Germany, Austria, and Czechoslovakia in 1938/1939) and other acts of actual or supposed heroism than it is about remembering the Holocaust. "The 'national' character of the event even trumped its potential Jewishness," wrote one scholar in reference to the first HMD in Britain in 2001 (Macdonald 2013: 204).

Certainly, at this event, references were made to other genocides such as those that occurred in Bosnia, Cambodia, and Rwanda. But this appeared instrumental. Rather than being a truly cosmopolitan event, the 2001 HMD in Britain "showed an attempt to revise the nation itself *as* cosmopolitan" (Macdonald 2013: 204). The cosmopolitanism of Holocaust memory, ideally, is surely predicated on the capacity of individual nations to recognize past failings, but Britain has failed to confront its involvement in the slave trade, or even acknowledge its own black British history (Olusoga 2016), and shows little inclination to examine its own history of anti-Semitism. In fact, remembering the Holocaust can be a very good way of forgetting one's own crimes and histories of discrimination (Niven and Williams 2020). Often, Holocaust memory is simply grafted onto longstanding national traditions and renationalized. Poland is a good example. If Britain's heroic national self-conception effectively undermines the potential for a self-critical Holocaust memory, Poland's view of itself as historical victim has a similar effect. Poland's ruling Law and Justice Party (PiS) recently responded to well-founded historiography illuminating Polish collaboration in the Holocaust (Gross 2001; Grabowski 2013) by proposing a bill which called for imprisonment or a fine for anyone accusing the Polish state or Polish people of responsibility for Nazi crimes. The bill was passed by the Polish Senate in February 2018 (John 2018). Although it has subsequently been watered

FIGURE 8.5: Memorial at Choeung Ek, site of the most notorious of the Khmer Rouge "Killing Fields," Cambodia. Credit: Wikimedia Commons (Public Domain).

down following protests from Israel (Landau and Aderet 2018), it has not been abolished. Poland's PiS would like the nation to think of itself as a victim of allegations of complicity.

To date, the efficacy of memory of Nazi anti-Semitism and the Holocaust is also severely limited by domestic politics. During the current refugee crises, there have been plenty of well-meaning attempts to draw comparisons between the suffering of Jews under Nazism, and that of Syrian refugees: thus UNICEF created a video setting the fate of a Syrian today alongside that of a Jew under Hitler (Frazer 2017), while the United States Holocaust Memorial Museum now has a *Syria: Please Don't Forget Us* exhibition on its second floor (Tharoor 2017). Yet a 2016 Oxfam report revealed that the world's six wealthiest nations, including the USA, Britain, China, and Japan, had only managed to host some 9 percent of refugees (Myers 2016) between them. According to another 2016 Oxfam report, which compared the refugee intake of the world's twenty-eight richest countries, the UK had only taken in some 18 percent of its fair share—worked out according to relative GDP—and the United States only 10 percent. Germany, the exception, ranked first[t] among these countries at an intake of 118 percent (Roberts 2016). Even when memory was politically mobilized to support the intake of refugees, it rarely had a significant effect. Former Kindertransportee, Alf Dubs, for instance, was instrumental in bringing about the so-called "Dubs Amendment" to the UK's Immigration Law, an amendment designed to facilitate the immigration of unaccompanied child refugees (Dubs 2017). Yet the government backtracked on the plan to allow 3,000 refugee children to enter Britain under the terms of the amendment; instead, only some 350 were accepted. In the USA, where self-critical rather than self-celebratory memory was mobilized, the outcome was the same. References to the shame of the USA's failure to take in the Jews who had sailed to America on the *St. Louis* in May 1939 (e.g. Tavares 2017) made no difference to President Trump's determination to stop the USA turning into a "migrant camp" (Golshan 2018).

For all the talk of "universalizing" Holocaust memory, in practice it sometimes serves to hinder empathy for contemporary Middle Eastern refugees given that many of the latter are Muslims. Chiding the German government for its relative openness to admitting refugees, fashion designer Karl Lagerfeld opined that "one cannot [. . .] kill millions of Jews so you can bring millions of their worst enemies in their place" (Safronova 2017). He was criticized for his comments, but the view that Middle Eastern Muslims should not be allowed into Europe because some of them are anti-Semitic is widespread.

Yet none of the above problems associated with the culture of Holocaust memory is an argument against memory *per se*, or memory of the Holocaust specifically. This chapter has explored the shifting balance between memory and forgetting over the course of the twentieth century, and, particularly in the case of transitional justice, demonstrated how the emergence of suppressed, forgotten, or ignored memories has contributed to the negotiation of social and political change. In most cases, however, these memories emerged not *that* long after the events they recall. By contrast, Holocaust memory established itself only some thirty to forty years after the liberation of Auschwitz, often among people with no personal or family link to that event. Today, the generational and experiential distance to the Holocaust is enormous. Our relationship to Auschwitz is based almost entirely on the mediations of cultural memory (Assmann 2011), largely in the form of films, novels, memorials, and exhibitions. The only vital connection to the Holocaust is provided through the talks provided by survivors, and their number is dwindling by the day. In a desperate attempt to bridge the gap created by the anticipated loss of directly communicated memory, Holocaust centers such as the National Holocaust Centre (UK) and the USC

Shoah Foundation (USA) have resorted to virtual testimony projects—"The Forever Project" and "New Dimensions in Testimony" respectively (Sherwood 2016; McMullan 2016). Survivors are filmed in ways which suggest they are in the room with us, and which enable audiences to interact with their virtual representations. These projects are admirable, but they cannot hold up the transition to a time when Holocaust memory will be entirely dependent on cultural memory, rather than—as at present—mainly dependent. Virtual testimony, after all, is merely another form of cultural representation, the only difference being that it creates the illusion of spontaneity.

In terms of the living memory of those who experienced it, then, the Holocaust will soon be forgotten. Indeed, it is already the case that many survivors giving talks today had no experience of it—such as those who came to Britain on the Kindertransport. It is also the case that many survivors have themselves forgotten much of what they experienced, or adapted memories over time, often in response to cultural representations, audience expectations, the expectations of the institutions at which they speak, or their understanding of their own role. The question then is what today's generations are actually "remembering" when they "remember" the Holocaust, and the answer is sobering: not much, and even that

FIGURE 8.6: National Holocaust Centre and Museum near Laxton, Nottinghamshire, England. Credit: Wikimedia Commons (Public Domain).

they often get wrong. A recent survey by the Conference on Jewish Material Claims Against Germany came to the conclusion that many Americans lack knowledge of what happened, with this lack being particularly pronounced among "millennials" aged between eighteen and thirty-four. Thirty-one percent of those surveyed believed that 2 million Jews were killed in the Holocaust, while 41 percent could not say what Auschwitz was (Astor 2018). Cultural memory has to date often not succeeded in sustaining or creating an even basic understanding of the Holocaust. It is not clear either that films or novels wish to achieve this task. How much education can achieve is also questionable if novels such as *The Boy in the Striped Pyjamas* (Boyne 2006), which turns the Holocaust into a kind of playground entertainment, are taught in schools. Of course, we are all urged to see connections between the Holocaust and present-day events in order to make sense of whatever it is we "remember", but if that memory is flimsy, false or absent, how are we to make sense of anything?

CONCLUSION

In the end, then, discomfiture with "too much" memory is based on a misinterpretation. The problem, if anything, is that there is too little of it. In the case of the Holocaust, what memory there is, is built on second-hand or third-hand versions of what others think the Holocaust is, or they want to tell us about it. Much greater in scope is what we have forgotten, or, really, never known: it is all that which falls through the gaps in the cultural representations. Certainly, there are excellent history books which provide deep and comprehensive accounts of the Holocaust, but they are not widely read, and the debates they trigger—with some exceptions such as the "Goldhagen debate" around the book *Hitler's Willing Executioners* (Goldhagen 1996; Shandley 1998)—rarely extend beyond academe. There are publications, their titles predicated on the assumption that the Holocaust is widely remembered, but other atrocities not so much, which refer to "forgotten Holocausts" (Chang 2012; Lukas 2012). But in many ways the Holocaust itself is not less forgotten. The task for the twenty-first century, not least for museums, teachers, and organizations dedicated to Holocaust memory, will be to find ways in which cultural memory, appropriately informed by historiography, can translate into an approximation to lived memory, if the Holocaust is to sustain meaning.

Of course, more recent genocides and other acts of inhumanity, while fresher in our minds now, will soon face the same dilemma as the Holocaust. The twentieth century has been typified by two essential memory trends. The first has seen individuals, groups, as well as whole nations assert memories in the face of the will of others to forget and repress, a process in which the direct articulation of personal and group experience has fed into processes of moral and political renewal. A vital link between experience, expression, and transformation made this possible. The second has seen states and supranational organizations decide on the importance of remembering genocide as a means of strengthening the moral compass of today's citizens, particularly schoolchildren. Here, the vital link is replaced, or soon will be, by a symbolic one, in which past misdeeds are not personally remembered, but become part of a canon of loosely associated historical examples (the Holocaust, the Cambodian and Rwandan genocides, Srebrenica) of what needs to be avoided. On the one hand, such adjurations "never to forget" provide a constant moral impetus; on the other, as the events upon which they are based shrink in human memory to the status of a few key facts, their power to help us understand past violence, and how it might correspond to events in the present, is much diminished. In other words: we must try harder to remember what we must never forget.

NOTES

General Editors' Preface

1. https://www.memorystudiesassociation.org/ (accessed February 3, 2020).
2. Agenda-setting in this respect was Cesari and Rigney (2014). For a review, see Erll 2011: 4–18.

BIBLIOGRAPHY

14–18–Now (2016), "We're Here Because We are Here," online at https://becausewearehere.co.uk/ (accessed September 1, 2018).

Adorno, Theodor (1991), *The Culture Industry*, London: Routledge.

Adrian, Edgar (1932), "Nobel Lecture: The Activity of Nerve Fibres," Nobel Media AB 2014. Available online: http://www.nobelprize.org/nobel_prizes/medicine/laureates/1932/adrian-lecture.html (accessed July 9, 2018).

Adugbo, Daniel (2019), "Mixed feelings over oil discovery in the north," *Daily Trust*, October 19. Available online: https://www.dailytrust.com.ng/mixed-feelings-over-oil-discovery-in-the-north.html (accessed October 23, 2019).

Aguilar, Paloma (2002), *Memory and Amnesia: The Role of the Spanish Civil War in the Transition to Democracy*, New York and Oxford: Berghahn.

Ajayi, Rotimi (2018), "The Anticolonial Struggle in Nigeria," in Carl Levana and Patrick Ukata, eds, *The Oxford Handbook of Nigerian Politics*, 89–102, Oxford: Oxford University Press.

Alexander, Jeffrey (2004), "Toward a Theory of Cultural Trauma," in Jeffrey Alexander, Ron Eyerman, Bernhard Giesen, Neil J. Smelser, and Piotr Sztompka, *Cultural Trauma and Collective Identity*, 1–30, Berkeley: University of California Press.

Algazi, Gadi (2014), "Forget Memory: Some Critical Remarks on Memory, Forgetting and History," in Sebastian Scholz, Gerald Schwedler, and Kai-Michael Sprenger, eds, *Damnatio in Memoria: Deformation und Gegenkonstruktionen von Geschichte*, 25–34, Vienna/Cologne/Weimer: Böhlau.

Allier-Montaño, Eugenia and Emilio Crenzel, eds (2016), *The Struggle for Memory in Latin America: Recent History and Political Violence*, Basingstoke: Palgrave Macmillan.

Allwork, Larissa (2015), *Holocaust Remembrance between the National and the Transnational: The Stockholm International Forum and the First Decade of the International Task Force*, London: Bloomsbury Publishing.

Anderson, Benedict ([1983] 1991), *Imagined Communities: Reflections on the Origin and Spread of Nationalism*, London: Verso.

Anderson, B. (2017), "Towards a New Politics of Migration?" *Ethnic and Racial Studies*, 40: 1527–37.

Anderson, Mark Cronlund (2007), *Cowboy Imperialism and Hollywood Film*, New York: Peter Lang.

Antohi, Sorin, Balázs Trencsényi, and Péter Apor (2007), *Narratives Unbound: Historical Studies in Post-Communist Eastern Europe*, Budapest: Central European University Press.

Anugwom, Edlyne Eze (2019), *Memory, Ethnicity and the State in Nigeria: From Biafra to the Niger Delta*, Lanham: Lexington Books.

Apter, Andrew (2005), *Pan-African Nation. Oil and the Spectacle of Culture in Nigeria*, Chicago: University of Chicago Press.

Aragüete-Toribio, Zahira (2017), *Producing History in Spanish Civil War Exhumations: From the Archive to the Grave*, Basingstoke: Palgrave Macmillan.

Assmann, Aleida (1999), *Erinnerungsräume: Formen und Wandlungen des kulturellen Gedächtnisses*, Munich: Beck.
Assmann, Aleida (2001), "History and Memory," in Neil J. Smelser and Paul B. Baltus, eds, *International Encyclopaedia of the Social and Behavioural Sciences*, vol. 10, 6822–9, Oxford: Pergamon.
Assmann, Aleida (2011), *Cultural Memory and Western Civilization: Functions, Memory, Archives*, New York: Cambridge University Press.
Assmann, Aleida (2013a), *Ist die Zeit aus den Fugen? Aufstieg und Fall des Zeitregimes der Moderne*, Berlin: Hanser.
Assmann, Aleida (2013b), *Das neue Unbehagen an der Erinnerungskultur*, Munich: Beck.
Assmann, Aleida (2016), *Formen des Vergessens*, Göttingen: Wallstein.
Assmann, Aleida and Sebastian Conrad, eds (2010), *Memory in a Global Age: Discourses, Practices and Trajectories*, Basingstoke: Palgrave Macmillan.
Assmann, Jan (1992), *Das kulturelle Gedächtnis: Schrift, Erinnerung und politische Identität in frühen Hochkulturen*, Munich: Beck.
Assmann, Jan (1995), "Collective Memory and Cultural Identity," *New German Critique* 65: 125–33.
Assmann, Jan (2008), "Communicative and Cultural Memory," in Astrid Erll and Ansgar Nünning, eds, *Cultural Memory Studies. An International and Interdisciplinary Handbook*, 109–18, Berlin, New York: De Gruyter.
Assmann, Jan (2011), "From 'Collective Memory and Cultural Identity'," in Jeffrey K. Olick, Vered Vinitzky-Seroussi, and Daniel Levy, eds, *The Collective Memory Reader*, 212–15, Oxford: Oxford University Press.
Astor, Maggie (2018), "Holocaust is Fading from Memory, Survey Finds," *The New York Times*, April 12. Available online: https://www.nytimes.com/2018/04/12/us/holocaust-education.html (accessed July 25, 2018).
Attwood, Bain (2005), *Telling the Truth about Aboriginal History*, Crows Nest: Allen & Unwin.
Avedin, Vahagn (2019), *Knowledge and Acknowledgment in the Politics of Memory of the Armenian Genocide*, New York: Routledge.
Baddeley, Alan, Michael W. Eysenck, and Michael C. Anderson (2015), *Memory*, Hove and New York: Psychology Press.
Bai, Ruoyun and Geng Song, eds (2015), *Chinese Television in the Twenty-First Century. Entertaining the Nation*, New York: Routledge.
Baker Jr., Houston (2001), *Critical Memory: Public Spheres, African-American Writing, and Black Fathers and Sons in America*, Athens: University of Georgia Press.
Balabanova, Ekaterina (2015), *The Media and Human Rights: The Cosmopolitan Promise*, New York: Routledge.
Bangert, Axel (2014), *The Nazi Past in Contemporary German Film: Viewing Experiences of Intimacy and Immersion*, Rochester: Camden House.
Baram, Amatzia (1983), "Mesopotamian Identity in Ba'this Iraq," *Middle Eastern Studies*, 19 (4): 426–45.
Barash, Jeffrey Andrew (2016), *Collective Memory and the Historical Past*, Chicago: University of Chicago Press.
Bartlett, Frederic (1932), *Remembering: A Study in Experimental and Social Psychology*, Cambridge: Cambridge University Press.
Baskett, Michael (2008), *The Attractive Empire: Transnational Film Culture in Imperial Japan*, Honolulu: University of Hawaii Press.

Bauerkämper, Arnd (2012), *Das umstrittene Gedächtnis. Die Erinnerung an Nationalsozialismus, Faschismus und Krieg in Europa seit 1945*, Paderborn: Schönigh.
BBC (2019), "Nigeria profile—Media," September 30. Available online: https://www.bbc.com/news/world-africa-13949549 (accessed October 23, 2019).
Beck, Ulrich (2006), *The Cosmopolitan Vision*, Cambridge: Polity.
Beck, Ulrich (2007), "The Cosmopolitan Condition: Why Methodological Nationalism Fails," *Theory, Culture & Society* 24: 286–90.
Becker, Annette (2005), "Memory Gaps: Maurice Halbwachs, Memory and the Great War," *Journal of European Studies*, 35 (1): 102–13.
Benjamin, Walter (1968), "The Storyteller. Reflections on the Work of Nikolai Leskov," in Hannah Arendt, ed., *Illuminations: Essays and Reflections*, 83–110, New York: Schocken.
Berger, Stefan (2003), *The Search for Normality: National Identity and Historical Consciousness in Germany since 1800*, Oxford: Berghahn.
Berger, Stefan (2008), "Von 'Landschaften des Geistes' zu 'Geisterlandschaften': Identitätsbildungen und der Umgang mit dem industriekulturellen Erbe im südwalisischen Kohlerevier," *Mitteilungsblatt des Instituts für soziale Bewegungen* 39: 49–66.
Berger, Stefan, ed. (2019a), *The Engaged Historian. Perspectives on the Intersection of Politics, Activism and the Historical Profession*, New York: Berghahn.
Berger, Stefan (2019b), "Industrial Heritage and the Ambiguities of Nostalgia for an Industrial Past in the Ruhr Valley in Germany," Labor 16 (1): 37–64.
Berger, Stefan and Christoph Conrad (2015), *The Past as History: National Identity and Historical Consciousness in Modern Europe*, Basingstoke: Palgrave Macmillan.
Berger, Stefan and Wulf Kansteiner, eds (2020a), *Unsettling Remembering and Social Cohesion in Contemporary Europe,* Basingstoke: Palgrave Macmillan.
Berger, Stefan and Klaus Weinhauer, eds (2020b), Making Sense of a Period of Global Revolutions, 1905–1934, Basingstoke: Palgrave Macmillan.
Berger, Stefan and Bill Niven, eds (2014), *Writing the History of Memory*, London: Bloomsbury Publishing.
Berger, Stefan and Paul Pickering (2018), "Regions of heavy industry and their heritage—between identity politics and 'touristification': where to next?" in Christian Wicke, Stefan Berger, and Jana Golombek, eds, *Regional Identity and Industrial Heritage*, 214–35, London: Routledge.
Berger, Stefan and Joana Seiffert, eds (2014), *Erinnerungsorte: Chancen, Grenzen und Perspektiven eines Erfolgskonzeptes in den Kulturwissenschaften*, Essen: Klartext.
Berger Stefan and Eric Storm, eds (2019), *Writing the History of Nationalism*, London: Bloomsbury Publishing.
Berger, Stefan, Mark Donovan, and Kevin Passmore, eds (2002), *Writing National Histories: Western Europe Since 1800*, London and New York: Routledge.
Berger, Stefan, Heiko Feldner, and Kevin Passmore, eds (2020), *Writing History: Theory and Practice*, London: Bloomsbury Publishing, 2020.
Berger, Stefan, Sean Scalmer and Christian Wicke, eds. (2020), *Social Movements and Memory*, Basingstoke: Palgrave Macmillan.
Berger, Thomas U. (2012), *War, Guilt, and World Politics after World War II*, Cambridge: Cambridge University Press.
Bergson, Henri (2004), *Matter and Memory*, Brooklyn: Zone Books.
Berwanger, Dietrich (1998), "The Third World," in Anthony Smith, ed., *Television: An International History*, 188–200, Oxford: Oxford University Press.

Bevernage, Berber (2011), *History, Memory, and State-Sponsored Violence: Time and Justice*, London: Routledge.

Bevernage, Berber (2016), "Tales of pastness and contemporaneity: on the politics of time in history and anthropology," *Rethinking History* (June 2016), 352–74.

Bevernage, Berber and Chris Lorenz, eds (2013), *Breaking Up Time. Negotiating the Borders between Present, Past and Future*, Göttingen: Vandenhoeck & Ruprecht.

Bignell, Jonathan and Andreas Fickers, eds (2008), *A European Television History*, Malden: Wiley.

Black November (2015), Jeta Amata, Entertainment One Films.

Blight, David (2001), *Race and Reunion*, Cambridge, MA: Harvard University Press.

Boas, Franz (1901), *Kathlamet Texts*, Washington: G.P.O.

Boddy, William (1998), "'Sixty Million Viewers Can't Be Wrong': The Rise and Fall of the Television Western," in Edward Buscombe and Roberta E. Pearson, eds, *Back in the Saddle Again: New Essays on the Western*, 119–40, London: British Film Institute.

Bodnar, John (1992), *Remaking America: Public Memory, Commemoration, and Patriotism in the Twentieth Century*, Princeton: Princeton University Press.

Bodnar, John (2010), *The "Good War" in American Memory*, Baltimore: Johns Hopkins University Press.

Bogumił, Zuzanna, and Marta Łukaszewicz, (2018), 'Between History and Religion: The New Russian Martyrdom as an Invented Tradition', *East European Politics and Societies and Cultures*, 32: 4, pp. 936–63.

Bond, Lucy, Stef Craps, and Pieter Vermeulen, eds (2017), *Memory Unbound: Tracing the Dynamics of Memory Studies*, New York: Berghahn.

Boole, George (1854), *An Investigation of the Laws of Thought, On Which are Founded the Mathematical Theories of Logic and Probabilities*, London: Whalton & Maberly.

Bordwell, D. et al. (1985), *The Classical Hollywood Cinema: Film Style and Mode of Production to 1960*, London: Routledge & Kegan Paul.

Borges, Jorge Luis (2000), "Funes the Memorious," in Donald A. Yates, ed., *Labyrinths*, 59–66, London: Penguin.

Borrows, John (2017), "Challenging Historical Frameworks: Aboriginal Rights, The Trickster, and Originalism," *Canadian Historical Review*, 98 (1): 114–35.

Bos, Dennis (2014), *Bloed end Barricaden. De Parijse Commune herdacht*, Amsterdam: Uitgeverij Wereldbibliotheek.

Bourdieu, Pierre (1984), *Distinction: A Social Critique of the Judgment of Taste*, trans. Richard Nice, Cambridge, MA: Harvard University Press.

Boyne, John (2006), *The Boy in the Striped Pyjamas*, Oxford: David Fickling Books.

Brass, Paul R. (2003), *The Production of Hindu-Muslim Violence in Contemporary India*, Seattle: University of Washington Press.

Browning, Christopher (1992), *Ordinary Men. Reserve Police Battalion 101 and the Final Solution in Poland*, New York: HarperCollins.

Brubaker, Rogers (2002), "Ethnicity without groups," *Archives Européennes Sociologiques* XLIII (2):163–89.

Brunnbauer, Ulf (2004), *(Re-)Writing History: Historiography in South-East Europe After Socialism*, Münster: Lit.

Bruzzi, Stella (2015), "Re-enacting Trauma in Film and Television: Restaging History, Revisiting Pain," in Claudia Wassmann, ed., *Therapy and Emotions in Film and Television: The Pulse of Our Times*, 89–98, London: Palgrave Macmillan.

Bull, Anna Cento and Hans Lauge Hansen (2015), "On Agonistic Memory," *Memory Studies* 9 (4): 390–404.

Bullock, Alan and Oliver Stallybrass (1977), "Genetic Memory," in *The Harper Dictionary of Modern Thought*, 258, London: Harper & Row.

Butler, Judith (2004), *Precarious Life. The Powers of Mourning and Violence*, London: Verso.

Buzan, Tony (2009), *The Memory Book: How to Remember Anything You Want*, London: BBC Active.

Cajal, Santiago Ramón (1894), "The Croonian Lecture: La Fine Structure des Centres Nerveux," *Proceedings of the Royal Society of London*, 55: 444–68.

Carruthers, Mary (2008), *The Book of Memory: A Study of Memory in Medieval Culture*, Cambridge: Cambridge University Press.

Caussimont, Gérard (1980), "Diez años del 'Centre de Recherches Hispaniques' de la Universidad de Pau," in Manuel Tuñón de Lara et al., eds, *Historiografía Española contemporánea*, 3–43, Madrid: Siglo XXI.

Chakravarty, Anuradha (2016), *Investing in Authoritarian Rule: Punishment and Patronage in Rwanda's Gacaca Courts for Genocide Crimes*, New York: Cambridge University Press.

Chakrabarty, Dipesh (2000), *Provincializing Europe: Postcolonial Thought and Historical Difference*, Princeton: Princeton University Press.

Chakrabarty, Dipesh (2007), "History and the Politics of Recognition," in Keith Jenkins, Sue Morgan, and Alun Munslow, eds, *Manifestoes for History*, 77–88, London: Routledge.

Chakrabarty, Dipesh (2011), "The Muddle of Modernity," American Historical Review, 116 (3), 663–75.

Chan, Felicia (2017), *Cosmopolitan Cinema. Cross-cultural Encounters in East Asian Film*, London: Tauris.

Chandra, Bipan (1986), "Nationalist Historians' Interpretations of the Indian National Movement," in Sabyasachi Bhattacharya and Romila Thapar, eds, *Situating Indian History*, Delhi: Oxford University Press.

Chang, Iris (2012), *The Rape of Nanking: The Forgotten Holocaust*, London: Basic Books.

Chapman, Adam (2016), *Digital Games as History: How Videogames Represent the Past and Offer Access to Historical Practice*, New York: Routledge.

Chapman, James (2005), *Past and Present: National Identity and the British Historical Film*, London: Tauris.

Chapman, Audrey R. and Hugo van der Merwe, eds (2008), *Truth and Reconciliation in South Africa: Did the TRC Deliver?* Philadelphia: University of Pennsylvania Press.

Chartier, Roger (1982), "Intellectual History or Socio-Cultural History?" in Dominick LaCapra and Steven L. Kaplan, eds, *Modern European Intellectual History: Reappraisals and New Perspectives*, 30, Ithaca, NY: Cornell University Press.

Chartier, Roger (1998), "Introduction," in Roger Chartier, ed., *Cultural History. Between Practice and Representations*, 4, Cambridge: Cambridge University Press.

Cherlin, Andrew J. (2009), *The Marriage-Go-Round: The State of Marriage and the Family in America Today*, New York: Random House.

Chidgey, Red (2015), "'A Modest Reminder': Performing Suffragette Memory in a British Feminist Webzine'," in Anna Reading and Tamar Katriel, eds, *Cultural Memories of Non-Violent Struggles. Powerful Times*, 52–70, Basingstoke: Palgrave Macmillan.

Chotiner, Isaac (2017), "How should we remember the Confederacy?" *Slate*, May 9.

Choueiri, Youssef M. (2003), *Modern Arab Historiography: Historical Discourse and the Nation State*, London: Routledge.

Clark, Christopher (2012), *The Sleepwalkers: How Europe Went to War in 1914*, London: Penguin.
Clark, Phil (2010), *The Gacaca Courts, Post-Genocide Justice and Reconciliation in Rwanda: Justice without Lawyers*, Cambridge and New York: Cambridge University Press.
Clarke, David and Ute Wölfel, eds (2011), *Remembering the German Democratic Republic*, Basingstoke: Palgrave Macmillan.
Clarke, Jacquie (2015), "Closing Time: Deindustrialization and Nostalgia in Contemporary France," *History Workshop Journal* 79 (1): 107–25.
Classen, Christoph (1999), *Bilder der Vergangenheit: Die Zeit des Nationalsozialismus im Fernsehen der Bundesrepublik Deutschland 1955–1965*, Cologne: Böhlau.
Classen, Christoph (2013), "Unsere Nazis, unser Fernsehen," Zeitgeschichte-online. Available online: http://www.zeitgeschichte-online.de/film/unsere-nazis-unser-fernsehen (accessed July 7, 2017).
Cockett, Richard (1989), *Twilight of Truth: Chamberlain, Appeasement and the Manipulation of the Press*, London: Weidenfeld & Nicolson.
Confino, Alon (2010), "Memory and the History of Mentalities," in Astrid Erll and Ansgar Nünning, eds, *A Companion to Cultural Memory Studies*, 79–84, Berlin: De Gruyter.
Confino, Alon (2011), "History and Memory," in Axel Schneider and Daniel Woolf, eds, *The Oxford History of Historical Writing*, 36–52, vol. 5, Oxford: Oxford University Press.
Confino, Alon (2014), *A World without Jews: The Nazi Imagination from Persecution to Genocide*, New Haven and London: Yale University Press.
Connerton, Paul (2008), "Seven Types of Forgetting," *Memory Studies*, 1 (1): 59–71.
Connerton, Paul (2009), *How Modernity Forgets*, Cambridge: Cambridge University Press.
Cook, Robert J. (2017), *Civil War Memories: Contesting the Past in the United States since 1965*, Baltimore: John Hopkins University Press.
Coombes, Annie E. (2003), *History after Apartheid: Visual Culture and Public Memory in a Democratic South Africa*, Durham: Duke University Press.
Coontz, Stephanie (1992), *The Way We Never Were: American Families and the Nostalgia Trap*, New York: Basic Books.
Cooper, Frederick and Rogers Brubaker (2005), "Identity," in Frederick Cooper, *Colonialism in Question. Theory, Knowledge, History*, 59–91, Berkeley: University of California Press.
Corney, Frederick C. (2004), *Telling October: Memory and the Making of the Bolshevik Revolution*, Ithaca, NY: Cornell University Press.
Cornils, Ingo and Sarah Waters, eds (2010), *Memories of 1968: International Perspectives*, Bern: Peter Lang.
Coser, Lewis A. (1992), "Introduction," in Lewis A. Coser, ed. and trans, *Maurice Halbwachs: On Collective Memory*, 1–34, Chicago and London: University of Chicago Press.
Costello, Matthew J. (2005), "Rewriting High Noon: Transformations in American Popular Political Culture during the Cold War, 1952–1968," in Peter C. Rollins and John E. O'Connor, eds, *Hollywood's West: The American Frontier in Film, Television, and History*, 175–97, Lexington: University Press of Kentucky.
Craps, Stef, Rick Crownshaw, Jennifer Wenzel, Rosanne Kennedy, Claire Colebrook, and Vin Nardizzi (2017), "Memory studies and the Anthropocene. A Roundtable," *Memory Studies*, 11 (4): 498–515.
Crenzel, Emilio (2011), *The Memory of the Argentine Disappearances*, New York: Routledge.
Crone, Rosalind (2013), "Mass Media and the Transformation of Popular Culture," in Annika Mombauer and Rosalind Crone, eds, *National Europe, 1914–1933*, 254–61, Milton Keynes: Open University.

Crownshaw, Richard (2017), "Cultural memory Studies in the Epoch of the Anthropocene," in Lucy Bond, Stef Craps, and Pieter Vermeulen, eds., *Memory Unbound. Tracing the Dynamics of Memory Studies*, 242–57. New York: Berghahn.

Cubitt, Geoff (2018), "History of memory," in Marek Tamm and Peter Burke, eds, *Debating New Approaches to History*, 127–43, London: Bloomsbury Publishing.

Cull, Nicholas J. (2010), "Reading, Viewing, and Tuning in to the Cold War," in Melvyn P. Leffler and Odd Arne Westad, eds, *The Cambridge History of the Cold War, vol. 2: Crisis and Détente*, 438–59, Cambridge: Cambridge University Press.

Dahlstedt, Magnus and Anders Neergaard (2019), "Crisis of Solidarity? Changing Welfare and Migration Regimes in Sweden," *Critical Sociology* 45 (1): 121–35.

Dahlstrom, W. Grant (2014), "The development of psychological testing," in Gregory Kimble and Kurt Schlesinger, eds, *Topics in the History of Psychology*, vol. 2, 63–113, New York: Psychology Press.

Danziger, Kurt (2008), *Marking the Mind: A History of Memory*, Cambridge: Cambridge University Press.

Darian-Smith, Kate and Paula Hamilton (2013), "Memory and history in twenty-first century Australia: A survey of the field," *Memory Studies* 6 (3): 370–83.

Davidovich, Joshua (2017), "Between Never Forget and Never Again," *The Times of Israel*, April 24. Available online: https://www.timesofisrael.com/between-never-forget-and-never-gain/ (accessed July 12, 2018).

Day, Eric (2014), "Why We Don't Have a Holocaust Video Game and Why We Desperately Need One," overmental.com, May 5, 2014. Available online: http://overmental.com/content/why-we-dont-have-a-holocaust-video-game-and-why- we-desperately-need-one-1303 (accessed October 22, 2016).

Dayan, D. and Katz, E. (1992), *Media Events: The Live Broadcasting of History*, Cambridge, MA: Harvard University Press.

de Baecque, Antoine (2011), *Camera Historica: The Century in Cinema*, New York: Columbia University Press.

de Baets, Antoon (2019), *Crimes Against History*, London and New York: Routledge.

de Cesari, Chiara and Ann Rigney, eds (2014), *Transnational Memory: Circulation, Articulation, Scales*, Berlin: De Gruyter.

de Groot, Jerome (2009), *Consuming History: Historians and Heritage in Contemporary Popular Culture*, London: Routledge.

de Smale, Stephanie (2019), *Ludic Memory Networks*, Utrecht: GVO.

della Porta, Donatella, Massimiliano Andretta, Tiago Fernandes, Eduardo Romanos, and Markos Vogiatzoglou (2018), *Legacies and Memories in Movements: Justice and Democracy in Southern Europe*, Oxford: Oxford University Press.

Deleuze, G. (1992), *Cinema, vol. 1: The Movement Image*, Minneapolis: University of Minnesota Press.

Deneckere, Gita and Thomas Welskopp (2008), "The 'nation' and 'class': European national master-narratives and their social 'other'," in Stefan Berger and Chris Lorenz, eds, *The Contested Nation: Ethnicity, Class, Religion and Gender in National Histories*, 135–70, Basingstoke: Palgrave Macmillan.

Desaparacedos: *Lists of the Disappeared* (n. d.). Avaiable online: http://www.desaparecidos.org/arg/victimas/eng.html (accessed July 10, 2018).

Diawara, Mamadou, Bernard Lategan, and Jörn Rüsen, eds (2010), *Historical Memory in Africa. Dealing with the Past, Reaching for the Future in an Intercultural Context*, Oxford: Berghahn.

Dimendberg, E. (2004), *Film Noir and the Spaces of Modernity*, Cambridge, MA: Harvard University Press.

Doerr, Nicole (2014), "Memory and Culture in Social Movements," in Britta Baumgarten, Priska Daphi, and Peter Ulrich, eds, *Conceptualizing Culture in Social Movement Research*, 206–26, London: Palgrave Macmillan.

Dogramaci, Burcu and Fabienne Liptay, eds (2016), *Immersion in the Visual Arts and Media*, Leiden: Brill.

Dohe, Carrie B. (2016), *Jung's Wandering Archetype: Race and Religion in Analytical Psychology*, London and New York: Routledge.

Doneson, Judith E. (2002), *The Holocaust in American Film*, Syracuse: Syracuse University Press.

Dörner, Ralf, Stefan Göbel, Wolfgang Effelsberg, and Josef Wiemers, eds (2016), *Serious Games: Foundations, Concepts and Practice*, Cham: Springer.

Doward, Jamie (2017), "New Online Generation Takes up Holocaust Denial," *The Observer*, January 22. Available online: https://www.theguardian.com/world/2017/jan/22/online-conspiracy-theories-feed-holocaust-denial (accessed September 1, 2018).

du Bois, François and Antje Du Bois-Pedain, eds (2008), *Justice and Reconciliation in Post-Apartheid South Africa*, Cambridge and New York: Cambridge University Press.

Dubs, Alf (2017), "On Holocaust Memorial Day, Let Us Remember Our Duty to Child Refugees," *The Guardian*, January 6, online at https://www.theguardian.com/commentisfree/2017/jan/27/holocaust-memorial-day-child-refugees-kindertransport (accessed January 6, 2017).

Durkheim, Emile (1893), *The Division of Labor in Society*, trans. W.D. Halls, New York: The Free Press, 1997.

Durkheim, Emile (1895), *The Rules of Sociological Method*, trans. W.D. Halls, New York: The Free Press, 1982.

Durkheim, Emile (1912), *The Elementary Forms of the Religious Life*, trans. Joseph Swain, London: George Allen & Unwin.

Ebbinghaus, Hermann ([1885] 1913), *Memory: A Contribution to Experimental Psychology*, trans C. Bussenius and H. Ruger (*Über das Gedächtnis: Untersuchungen zur experimentellen Psychologie*), New York: Teachers College, Columbia University.

Ebbrecht-Hartmann, Tobias (2016), "German Docudrama: Aligning the Fragments and Accessing the Past," in Tobias Ebbrecht-Hartmann and Derek Paget, eds, *Docudrama on European Television: A Selective Survey*, 224–36, London: Palgrave Macmillan.

Echternkamp, Jörn and Stefan Martens (2010), *Experience and Memory: the Second World War in Europe*, Oxford: Berghahn.

Edkins, Jenny (2003), *Trauma and the Memory of Politics*, Cambridge: Cambridge University Press.

Edmundson, Mark (2007), *The Death of Sigmund Freud*, London: Bloomsbury Publishing.

Eksteins, Modris (1980), "War, Memory, and Politics: The Fate of the Film *All Quiet on the Western Front*," *Central European History*, 13 (1): 60–82.

Elkins, Caroline (2005), *Imperial Reckoning: The Untold Story of Britain's Gulag in Kenya*, New York: Henry Holt.

Elsaesser, Thomas (2014), *German Cinema-Terror and Trauma: Cultural Memory since 1945*, New York: Routledge.

Encarnacion, Omar G. (2014), *Democracy without Justice in Spain: The Politics of Forgetting*, Philadelphia: University of Pennsylvania Press.

Englund, Steven (1992), "The Ghost of Nation Past," *Journal of Modern History*, 64 (2): 299–320.

Erll, Astrid (2005), *Kollektives Gedächtnis und Erinnerungskulturen*, Stuttgart: J.B. Metzler.
Erll, Astrid, ed. (2008), *Cultural Memory Studies: An International and Interdisciplinary Handbook*, Berlin: de Gruyter.
Erll, Astrid (2011a), "Travelling Memory," *Parallax* 17 (4): 4–18.
Erll, Astrid (2011b), *Memory in Culture*, Houndmills: Palgrave.
Erll, Astrid and Ann Rigney, eds (2009), *Mediation, Remediation and the Dynamics of Cultural Memories*, Berlin: De Gruyter.
Ernst, Wolfgang (2013), *Digital Memory and the Archive*, Minneapolis: University of Minnesota Press.
Esterson, Allen (2001), "The mythologizing of psychoanalytic history: Deception and self-deception in Freud's accounts of the seduction theory episode," *History of Psychiatry*, 12: 329–52.
Etkind, Alexander (2013), *Warped Mourning: Stories of the Undead in the Land of the Unburied*, Stanford: Stanford University Press.
Evans, Richard J. (2014), "Michael Gove Shows His Ignorance of History–Again," *The Guardian*, January 6, https://www.theguardian.com/books/2014/jan/06/richard-evans-michael-gove-history-education (accessed August 21, 2018).
Featherstone, David (2017), "Anti-Colonialism and the Contested Spaces of Communist Internationalism," in Kevin Morgen, ed., *Legacies of October*, special issue of *Socialist History* 52, 48–58.
Feil, Georg, (1974), *Zeitgeschichte im Deutschen Fernsehen: Analyse von Fernsehsendungen mit historischen Themen (1957–1967)*, Osnabrück: Fromm.
Feindt, Gregor et al., "Entangled Memory: Toward a Third Wave in Memory Studies," *History and Theory*, 53 (February 2014): 24–44.
Ferrándiz, Franciso (2017), "Afterlife: A Social Autopsy of Mass Grave Exhumations in Spain," in Ofelia Ferrán and Lisa Hilbing, eds, *Legacies of Violence in Contemporary Spain: Exhuming the Past, Understanding the Present*, 23–43, London: Routledge.
Finney, Patrick (2013), "Vasily Grossman and the Myths of the Great Patriotic War," *Journal of European Studies*, 43 (4): 312–28.
Finney, Patrick (2017), "Politics and Technologies of Authenticity: The Second World War at the Close of Living Memory," *Rethinking History*, 21 (2): 154–70.
Fischer, Thomas and Rainer Wirtz, eds. (2008) *Alles authentisch? Popularisierung der Geschichte im Fernsehen*, Konstanz: UVK.
Flower, Wayne (2010), "Melbourne Family's Dance Video Spark [sic] Auschwitz Outrage," *Herald Sun*, July 13. Available online: http://www.heraldsun.com.au/news/melbourne-familys-dance-video-spark-auschwitz-outrage/story-e6frf7jo-1225891329631 (accessed July 21, 2010; link no longer active).
Fogu, Claudio, Wulf Kansteiner and Todd Presner, eds (2016), *Probing the Ethics of Holocaust Culture*, Cambridge, MA: Harvard University Press.
Forrester, John (2008), "1919: Psychology and Psychoanalysis, Cambridge and London—Myers, Jones and MacCurdy," *Psychoanalysis and History*, 10: 37–94.
Foundation for the Memorial to the Murdered Jews of Europe, ed. (2007), *Materials on the Memorial to the Murdered Jews of Europe*, Berlin: Nicolai.
François, Etienne and Hagen Schulze (2001), "Einleitung," in Etienne François and Hagen Schulze, eds, *Deutsche Erinnerungsorte*, vol. 1 9–24, Munich: C.H. Beck.
Frazer, Jenni (2017), "Twin Stories Link Holocaust and Syrian Refugees in UNICEF Video," *The Times of Israel*, February 16. Available online: https://www.timesofisrael.com/twin-stories-link-holocaust-and-syrian-refugees-in-unicef-video/ (accessed July 24, 2018).

Frei, Norbert (1996), *Vergangenheitspolitik: Die Anfänge der Bundesrepublik und die NS-Vergangenheit*, Munich: Beck.

Freud, Sigmund (1939), *Der Mann Moses und die Monotheistische Religion*, Amsterdam: A. de Lang.

Freud, Sigmund (2018), "Erinnern, Wiederholen und Durcharbeiten: Weitere Ratschläge zur Technik der Psychoanalyse II," in *Kleine Schriften I* (Chapter 18), projekt.gutenberg.de, online at http://gutenberg.spiegel.de/buch/kleine-schriften-i-7123/18 (accessed December 28, 2018).

Freud, Sigmund, James Strachey, Anna Freud, and Angela Richards (1966), *The Standard Edition of the Complete Psychological Works of Sigmund Freud*, London: Hogarth Press.

Friedman, Rebekka (2017), *Competing Memories: Truth and Reconciliation in Sierra Leone and Peru*, Cambridge and New York: Cambridge University Press.

Fritzsche, Peter and Jochen Hellbeck (2009), "The New Man in Stalinist Russia and Nazi Germany," in Michael Geyer and Sheila Fitzpatrick, eds, *Beyond Totalitarianism: Stalinism and Nazism Compared*, 302–41, Cambridge: Cambridge University Press.

Fuchs, Anne (2011), *After the Dresden Bombing. Pathways of Memory, 1945 to the Present*, Basingstoke: Palgrave Macmillan.

Fussell, Paul (2000), *The Great War and Modern Memory*, Oxford: Oxford University Press.

Gabriel, Teshome (1995), "Towards a Critical Theory of Third World Film," in Michael Martin, ed, *Cinemas of the Black Diaspora*, 70–90, Detroit: Wayne State University Press.

Gaines, Jane (1992), *Classical Hollywood Narrative. The Paradigm Wars*, Durham: Duke University Press.

Garrard, John and Carol Garrard (2012), *The Life and Fate of Vasily Grossman*, Barnsley: Pen & Sword.

Gaudreault, A. (2011), *Film and Attraction: From Cinematography to Cinema*, University of Illinois Press: Urbana-Champaign.

Gay, Roxane (2016) "The blog that disappeared," *The New York Times*, June 29. Available online: http://www.nytimes.com/2016/07/30/opinion/sunday/the-blog-that-disappeared.html?_r=0. (accessed October 21, 2016).

Gedziorowski, Lukas (2014), "Nazi TV," Fragmenteum: Splitter zur Kultur, July 18. Available online: https://fragmenteum.wordpress.com/2014/07/18/nazi-tv/ (accessed June 5, 2017).

Geisler, Michael (1992), "The Disposal of Memory: Fascism and the Holocaust on West German Television," in Bruce Murray and Christopher Wigham, eds, *Framing the Past: The Historiography of German Cinema and Television*, 220–60, Carbondale: Southern Illinois University Press.

Gentile, Emilio (1996), *The Sacralization of Politics in Fascist Italy*, Cambridge, MA: Harvard University Press.

Gentile, Emilio (2006), *Politics as Religion*, Princeton: Princeton University Press.

Gerrits, André (2016), *Nationalism in Europe since 1945*, Basingstoke: Palgrave Macmillan.

Gildea, Robert, James Mark, and Annette Warring, eds (2017), *Europe's 1968: Voices of Revolt*, Oxford: Oxford University Press.

Gienow-Hecht, Jessica C.E. (2000), "Shame on US? Academics, Cultural Transfer, and the Cold War—A Critical Review," *Diplomatic History*, 24 (3): 465–94.

Gienow-Hecht, Jessica C.E. (2010), "Culture and the Cold War in Europe," in Melvyn P. Leffler and Odd Arne Westad, eds, *The Cambridge History of the Cold War, vol. 1: Origins*, 398–419, Cambridge: Cambridge University Press.

Gitlin, Todd (1978), "Media Sociology: The Dominant Paradigm," *Theory and Society*, 6 (2): 205–53.

Gluck, Carol (2007), "Operations of Memory: 'Comfort Women' and the World," in Sheila Miyoshi Jager and Rana Mitter, eds, *Ruptured Histories: War, Memory, and the Post-Cold War in Asia*, 27–57, Cambridge, MA: Harvard University Press.
Glynn, Irial and J. Olaf Kleist, eds (2012), *History, Memory and Migration: Perceptions of the Past and the Politics of Incorporation*, Basingstoke: Palgrave Macmillan.
Goldhagen, Daniel Jonah (1996), *Hitler's Willing Executioners: Ordinary Germans and the Holocaust*, New York: Alfred A. Knopf.
Goldin, Ian, Geoffrey Cameron, and Meera Balarajan (2011), *Exceptional People. How Migration Shaped Our World and Will Define Our Future*, Princeton: Princeton University Press.
Goldmann, Lucien (1967), *The Hidden God. A Study of Tragic Vision in the Pensées of Pascal and the Tragedies of Racine*, 17, London: Routledge.
Golshan, Tara (2018), "Trump: The US Will Not Turn into a 'Migrant Camp' or 'Refugee Holding Facility'," *Vox*, June 18. Available online: https://www.vox.com/2018/6/18/17475512/trump-migrant-camp-refugee-germany (accessed July 24, 2018).
Gombrich, Ernst H. (1997), *Aby Warburg: An Intellectual Biography*, London: Bloomsbury Publishing.
Gould, Stephen (1977), *Ontogeny and Phylogeny*, Cambridge, MA: Belknap Press of Harvard University Press.
Grabowski, Jan (2013), *Hunt for the Jews: Betrayal and Murder in German-Occupied Poland*, Bloomington: Indiana University Press.
Graff, Bernd (2015), "Bestien wie du und ich," *Süddeutsche Zeitung*, April 30.
Gray, Ann and Erin Bell (2013), *History on Television*, London: Routledge.
Greimas, Algirdas Julien (1983), *Structural Semantics: An Attempt at Method*, Lincoln: University of Nebraska Press.
Gross, David (2000), *Lost Time: On Remembering and Forgetting in Late Modern Culture*, Amherst and Boston: University of Massachusetts Press.
Gross, Jan T. (2001), *Neighbors: The Destruction of the Jewish Community in Jedwabne, Poland*, Princeton: Princeton University Press.
Gumbert, Heather L. (2014), *Envisioning Socialism: Television and the Cold War in the German Democratic Republic*, Ann Arbor: University of Michigan Press.
Gunning, T. (1986), "The Cinema of Attraction: Early Film, Its Spectator and the Avant-Garde," *Wide Angle*, 8: 1–14.
Gunter, Joel (2017), "'Yolocaust': How Should You Behave at a Holocaust Memorial?", *BBC News*, January 20, https://www.bbc.co.uk/news/world-europe-38675835 (accessed November 20, 2019).
Gust, Onni (2016), "The Brexit Syllabus: British History for Brexiteers," *History Workshop*, September 5, http://www.historyworkshop.org.uk/the-brexit-syllabus-british-history-for-brexiteers/ (accessed 29 August 2018).
Gutman, Yifat (2017), *Memory Activism: Reimagining the Past for the Future in Israel/Palestine*, Nashville: Vanderbilt University Press.
Gutman, Yifat, and Jenny Wuestenberg, eds (2020), *The Routledge Handbook of Memory Activism*, London: Routledge.
Guynn, W. (2006), *Writing History in Film*, New York: Routledge.
Hage, Volker (2003), *Zeugen der Zerstörung: Die Literaten und der Luftkrieg*, Frankfurt am Main: Fischer.
Haigh, Thomas, Mark Priestley, and Crispin Rope (2016), *ENIAC in Action: Making and Remaking the Modern Computer*, Cambridge, MA: MIT.

Hajek, Andrea (2013), *Negotiating Memory of Protest in Western Europe: The Case of Italy*, Basingstoke: Palgrave Macmillan.
Halbwachs, Maurice (1925), *Les Cadres Sociaux de la Mémoire*, Paris: Presses Universitaires de France.
Halbwachs, Maurice (1950), *On Collective Memory*, trans. Lewis Coser, Chicago: University of Chicago Press.
Halbwachs, Maurice (1959), *The Psychology of Social Class*, trans. Claire Delavenay, Glencoe: The Free Press.
Halbwachs, Maurice (1980), *Collective Memory*, New York: Harper & Row.
Halbwachs, Maurice (1992), *On Collective Memory*, ed. and trans. Lewis Coser, Chicago: University of Chicago Press.
Hall, John R. and Patrick D. Joyce, eds (1997), *Reworking Class*, Ithaca, NY: Cornell University Press.
Hall, Katharina and Kathryn N. Jones, eds (2011), *Constructions of Conflict: Transmitting Memories of the Past in European Historiography, Culture and Media*, Oxford: Peter Lang.
Hall, Catherine, and Sonya Rose (2014), "Introduction: Being at Home with the Empire," in Catherine Hall and Sonya Rose, eds, *At Home with the Empire: Metropolitan Culture and the Imperial World*, 1–31, Cambridge: Cambridge University Press.
Hamilton, Paula (1994), "The Knife Edge: Debates about Memory and History," in Kate Darian-Smith and Paula Hamilton, eds, *Memory and History in Twentieth Century Australia*, 9–32, Melbourne: Oxford University Press.
Hamilton, Edith and Huntington Cairns, eds (1963), *The Collected Dialogues of Plato*, Princeton: Princeton University Press.
Hansen, M. (1991), *Babel and Babylon: Spectatorship in American Silent Film*, Cambridge, MA: Harvard University Press.
Harrigan, Pat, Matthew Kirschenbaum, and James Dunnigan, eds (2016), *Zones of Control: Perspectives on Wargaming*, Cambridge, MA: MIT Press.
Harris, Frederick C. (2006), "It Takes a Tragedy to Arouse Them: Collective Memory and Collective Action during the Civil Rights Movement," *Social Movement Studies* 5 (1): 19–43.
Hatherley, Owen (2016), *The Ministry of Nostalgia*, London: Verso.
Hartney, Christopher, ed. (2014), *Secularisation: New Historical Perspectives*, Cambridge: Cambridge Scholars.
Hartog, François (1996), "Time, History and the Writing of History: The Order of Time," in Rolf Thorstendahl and Irmline Veit-Brause, eds, *History-Making. The Intellectual and Social Formation of a Discipline*, 85–113, Stockholm, Almqvist & Wiksell.
Hartog, François (2015), *Regimes of Historicity: Presentism and the Experiences of Time*, New York: Columbia University Press.
Hartog, François (2016), *Croire en l'histoire*, Paris: Flammarion.
Hayden, Robert (1994), "Recounting the Dead. The Rediscovery and Redefinition of Wartime Massacres in Late and Post-Communist Yugoslavia," in Rubie S. Watson, ed., *Memory, History and Opposition under State Socialism*, 167–85, Santa Fe: School of American Research Press.
Hebb, D.O. ([1949] 2002), *The Organization of Behavior: A Neuropsychological Theory*, Mahwah, NJ: Lawrence Erlbaum Associates.
Henderson, John (1999), *Memory and Forgetting*, Abingdon and New York: Routledge.
Heonik Kwon (2008), *Ghosts of War in Vietnam*, Cambridge: Cambridge University Press.

Hepworth, Andrea (2016), "Site of Memory and Dismemory: The Valley of the Fallen in Spain," in Simone Gigliotti, ed., *The Memorialization of Genocide*, 463–85, London: Routledge.
Hermann, Irene and Franziska Metzger (2012), "A Truculent Revenge: the Clergy and the Writing of National History," in Ilaria Porciani and Jo Tollebeek, eds, *Setting the Standards: Institutions, Networks and Communities of National Historiography*, 313–29, Basingstoke: Palgrave MacMillan.
Hervieu-Léger, Danièle (2000), *Religion as a Chain of Memory*, trans. Simon Lee, Cambridge: Polity.
Herwig, Holger H. (2003), "German," in Richard F. Hamilton and Holger H. Herwig, eds, *The Origins of World War I*, 150–87, Cambridge: Cambridge University Press.
Hewitt, Leah D. (2008), *Remembering the Occupation in French Film: National Identity in Post-War Europe*, Basingstoke: Palgrave Macmillan.
High, Steven (2003), *Industrial Sunset: The Making of North America's Rustbelt, 1969–1984*, Toronto: University of Toronto Press.
High, Steven, Lachlan MacKinnon, and Andrew Perchard, eds (2017), *The Deindustrialised World: Confronting Ruination in Postindustrial Places*, Vancouver: UBC Press.
Highmore, Ben (2017), *Cultural Feelings: Mood, Mediation and Cultural Politics*, New York: Routledge.
Himka, John Paul and Joanna Beata Michlic, eds (2013), *Bringing the Dark Past to Light: The Reception of the Holocaust in Post-Communist Europe*, Lincoln: University of Nebraska Press.
Hirsch, Marianne (2012), *The Generation of Postmemory: Writing and Visual Culture after the Holocaust*, New York: Columbia University Press.
Hixson, Walter L. (2008), *The Myth of American Diplomacy: National Identity and US Foreign Policy*, New Haven: Yale University Press.
Hobsbawm, Eric J. (1994), *The Age of Extremes. The Short Twentieth Century 1914–1991*, London: Penguin.
Hobsbawm, Eric J., and Terence Ranger, eds (1983), *The Invention of Tradition*, Cambridge: Cambridge University Press.
Hodgkin, Alan (1979), "Edgar Douglas Adrian, Baron Adrian of Cambridge. 30 November 1889–4 August 1977," *Biographical Memoirs of Fellow of the Royal Society*, 25: 1–73.
Hogea, Alina (2010), "Coming to Terms with the Communist Past in Romania: An Analysis of the Political and Media Discourse concerning the Tismăneanu Report," *Studies of Transition States and Societies*, 2 (2): 16–30.
Holtmaart, Anthony and Karel Svoboda (2009), "Experience-dependent structural synaptic plasticity in the mammalian brain," *Nature Reviews Neuroscience*, 10: 647–58.
Horkheimer, Max and Theodor W. Adorno ([1944] 2002), *The Dialectic of Enlightenment: Philosophical Fragments*, trans. Edmund Jephcott, Stanford: Stanford University Press.
Hoskins, Andrew (2009), "Digital Network Memory," in Astrid Erll, Ann Rigney, and Laura Basu, eds, *Media and Cultural Memory: Mediation, Remediation, and the Dynamics of Cultural Memory*, 91–106, Berlin: De Gruyter.
Hoskins, Andrew (2014), "The Right to be Forgotten in Post-Scarcity Culture," in Alessia Ghezzi, Angela Guimarares Pereira, and Lucia Vesnic-Alujevic, eds, *The Ethics of Memory in a Digital Age: Interrogating the Right to be Forgotten*, 50–64, New York: Palgrave.
Hoskins, Andrew, ed. (2017a), *Digital Memory Studies: Media Pasts in Transition*, London: Routledge.

Hoskins, Andrew (2017b), "Memory of the Multitude: The Ende of Collective Memory," in Andrew Hoskins, ed., *Digital Memory Studies. Media Pasts in Transition*, 85–109, Oxford and New York: Routledge.

Hoskins, Andrew (2018), "The restless past. An introduction to digital memory and media," in Andrew Hoskins, ed., *Digital Memory Studies. Media Pasts in Transition*, 1–18, New York: Routledge.

Ho Tai, Hue-Tam (2001), "Remembered realms: Pierre Nora and French national memory," *American Historical Review*, 106 (3): 906–22.

Hunt, Lynn (1989), "Introduction: History, Culture, Text," in Lynn Hunt, ed., *The New Cultural History*, 19, Berkeley: University of California Press.

Huntemann, Nina and Payne, Matthew, eds (2010), *Joystick Soldiers: The Politics of Play in Military Video Games*, New York: Routledge.

Husserl, Edmund (1936), *The Crisis of European Sciences and Transcendental Phenomenology: An Introduction to Phenomenological Philosophy*, trans. David Carr. Evanston: Northwestern University Press.

Hutchings, Stephen and Vera Tolz (2015), *Nation. Ethnicity and Race on Russian Television*, New York: Routledge.

Hutton, Patrick H. (1997): "Mnemonic Schemes in the New History of Memory," *History and Theory* 36 (3): 378–91.

Huxley, Thomas (1882), "On the Method of Zadig: Retrospective Prophecy as a Function of Science," in Thomas Huxley, ed., *Science and Culture*, 134–55, London: Macmillan.

Huyssen, Andreas (2000), "Present Pasts: Media, Politics, Amnesia," *Public Culture*, 12 (2): 21–38.

Huyssen, Andreas (2003), *Present Pasts: Urban Palimpsests and the Politics of Memory*, Stanford: Stanford University Press.

Inglis, Ken (1993), "Entombing Unknown Soldiers," *Journal of the Australian War Memorial*, 23: 1–12.

Ingham, Tim (2009), "Call of Duty Series Tops 55 Million Sales," *MCV*, November 27. Available online: http://www.mcvuk.com/news/36680/Call-Of-Duty-series-tops-55-million-sales (accessed June 1, 2011) (link no longer active).

Iordachi, Constantin and Péter Apor, eds (2019), *Occupation and Communism in Eastern European Museums: Re-Visualizing the Past*, London: Bloomsbury Publishing.

Jackson, Julian (1999), "Historians and the Nation in Contemporary France," in Stefan Berger, Mark Donovan, and Kevin Passmore, eds, *Writing National Histories: Western Europe since 1800*, 239–51, London: Routledge.

Jacobs, Jason (2003), "Early Television in Great Britain," in Michele Hilmes, ed., *The Television History Book*, 69–72, London: British Film Institute.

James, William ([1890] 1950), *The Principles of Psychology*, vol. 1, New York: Dover.

Jarausch, Konrad, Christian F. Osterman, and Andreas Etges, eds, (2017), *The Cold War: Historiography, Memory, Representation*, Berlin: De Gruyter.

Jimeno, Roldán (2018), *Amnesties, Pardons and Transitional Justice: Spain's Pact of Forgetting*, London and New York: Routledge.

Jin, Jingji and Stephen Maren (2015), "Prefrontal-Hippocampal Interactions in Memory and Emotion," *Frontiers in Systems Neuroscience*, 9, article 170.

Jinks, Rebecca (2016), *Representing Genocide: The Holocaust as Paradigm?* London: Bloomsbury Publishing.

John, Tara (2018), "Poland Just Passed a Holocaust Bill that is Causing Outrage," *Time*, February 1. Available online: http://time.com/5128341/poland-holocaust-law/ (accessed July 24, 2018).

Johnston, Elizabeth (2001), "The Repeated Reproduction of Bartlett's," *Remembering. History of Psychology*, 4: 341–66.

Jones Stephen F. (1994), "Old Ghosts and New Chains: Ethnicity and Memory in the Georgian Republik," in Rubie S. Watson, ed., *Memory, History and Opposition under State Socialism*, Santa Fe: School of American Research Press, 149–72.

Jones, Sam, (2018) "Franco's Family Fights PM over Removal of Dictator's Remains," *The Guardian*, July 20, https://www.theguardian.com/world/2018/jul/20/franco-family-refuses-facilitate-removal-dictator-spain (accessed August 29, 2018).

Jordan, Raul (2008), *Konfrontation mit der Vergangenheit: Das Medienereignis Holocaust und die politische Kultur der Bundesrepublik Deutschland*, Frankfurt a.M.: Lang.

Judt, Tony (2002), "The past is another country: myth and memory in post-war Europe," in Jan-Werner Müller, ed., *Memory and Power in Post-War Europe. Studies in the Presence of the Past*, 157–84, Cambridge: Cambridge University Press.

Judt, Tony (2005), *Postwar: A History of Europe since 1945*, London: Heinemann.

Jugo, Admir and S.E. Wagner (2017), "Memory Politics and Forensic Practices: Exhuming Bosnia Herzegovina's Missing Persons," in Z. Dziuban, ed., *Mapping the "Forensic Turn": Engagement with Materialities of Mass Death in Holocaust Studies and Beyond*, 195–213, Vienna: New Academic Press.

Jung, C.G. ([1946] 1976), *Psychological Types. Collected Works*, vol. 6., trans. Gerhard Adler and R.F.C. Hull, Princeton: Princeton University Press.

Jung, C.G. ([1936] 2018), "Der Begriff der kollektiven Unbewussten," in Lorenz Jung, ed., *C.G. Jung, Archetypen: Urbilder und Wirkkräfte des kollektiven Unbewussten*, 55–69, Ostfildern: Patmos Verlag.

Kandel, Eric (2006). *In Search of Memory: The Emergence of a New Science of the Mind*, New York: W.W. Norton.

Kaes, Anton (1989), *From Hitler to Heimat: The Return of History as Film*, Cambridge, MA: Harvard University Press.

Kandel, Eric (2001), "The Molecular Biology of Memory Storage: A Dialogue Between Genes and Synapses," *Science*, 294: 1030–8.

Kandel, Eric (2006), *In Search of Memory: The Emergence of a New Science of the Mind*, New York: W.W. Norton.

Kansteiner, Wulf (2002), "Finding Meaning in Memory: A Methodological Critique of Collective Memory Studies," *History and Theory*, 41 (2): 179–97.

Kansteiner, Wulf (2004a), "Genealogy of a Category Mistake: A Critical Intellectual History of the Cultural Trauma Metaphor," *Rethinking History: The Journal of Theory and Practice* 8 (2): 193–221.

Kansteiner, Wulf (2004b), "Postmoderner Historismus: das kulturelle Gedächtnis als neues Paradigma der Kulturwissenschaften," in Friedrich Jäger und Jürgen Straub, eds, *Handbuch der Kulturwissenschaften, Band 2: Paradigmen und Disziplinen*, 119–39, Stuttgart: Metzler.

Kansteiner, Wulf (2006a), *In Pursuit of German Memory: History, Television, and Politics after Auschwitz*, Athens: Ohio University Press.

Kansteiner, Wulf (2006b), "Losing the War, Winning the Memory Battle: The Legacy of Nazism, World War II and the Holocaust in the Federal Republic of Germany," in Richard Ned Lebow, Wulf Kansteiner and Claudio Fogu, eds, *The Politics of Memory in Post-War Europe*, 102–46, Durham: Duke University Press.

Kansteiner, Wulf (2017a), "Film, the Past, and a Didactic Dead End. From Teaching History to Teaching Memory," in Mario Carretero, Stefan Berger, and Maria Grever, eds, *Palgrave Handbook of Research in Historical Culture and Education*, 169–90, London: Palgrave.

Kansteiner, Wulf (2017b), "Transnational Holocaust Memory, Digital Culture and the End of Reception Studies," in Tea Sindbæk Andersen and Barbara Törnquist-Plewa, eds, *The Twentieth Century in European Memory: Transcultural Mediation and Reception*, 305–43, Leiden: Brill.

Kansteiner, Wulf (2018a), "The Holocaust in the 21st Century: Digital Anxiety, Transnational Cosmopolitanism, and Never Again Genocide without Memory," in Andrew Hoskins, ed., *Digital Memory Studies: Media Pasts in Transition*, 110–40, New York: Routledge.

Kansteiner, Wulf (2018b), "Unsettling Crime. Memory, Migration, and Prime Time Fiction," in D. Bachmann-Medick and J. Kugele, eds, *Migration. Changing Concepts, Critical Approaches*, 141–66, Berlin: De Gruyter.

Kansteiner, Wulf (2019), "Hidden in Plain View. Remembering and Forgetting the Bystanders of the Holocaust on (West) German Television," in Christina Morina and Krijn Thijs, eds, *Probing the Limits of Categorization. The Bystander in Holocaust History*, 266–90, New York: Berghahn.

Kaplan, Ann (1997), *Looking for the Other. Feminism, Film and the Imperial Gaze*, New York: Routledge.

Kappell, Matthew and Elliott, Andrew, eds (2014), *Playing with the Past: Digital Games and the Simulation of History*, New York: Bloomsbury Publishing.

Kaschuba, Wolfgang (2010), "Iconic Remembering and Religious Icons: Fundamentalist Strategies in European Memory Politics," in Małgorzata Pakier and Bo Stråth, eds, *A European Memory? Contested Histories and Politics of Remembrance*, 64–78, Oxford: Berghahn.

Kattago, Siobhan (2016), *Memory and Representation in Contemporary Europe: The Persistence of the Past*, Abingdon and New York: Routledge.

Keightley, Emily and Michael Pickering (2013), *Research Methods for Memory Studies*, Edinburgh: Edinburgh University Press.

Keilbach, Judith (2008), *Geschichtsbilder und Zeitzeugen: Zur Darstellung des Nationalsozialismus im Bundesdeutschen Fernsehen*, Münster: LIT.

Keren, Michael and Holger H. Herwig, eds (2009), *War Memory and Popular Culture: Essays on Modes of Remembrance and Commemoration*, Jefferson: McFarland.

Khiabany, Gholam (2016), "Refugee Crisis, imperialism ad pitiless wars on the poor," *Media, Culture & Society*, 38 (5): 755–62.

Kim, Mikyoung (2015), *Routledge Handbook of Memory and Reconciliation in East Asia*, London: Routledge.

Kingsepp, Eva (2017), "Experiencing and Performing Memory: Second World War Videogames as a Practice of Remembrance," in Patrick Finney, ed., *Remembering the Second World War*, 217–33, London: Routledge.

Klein, Kerwin Lee (2011), *From History to Theory*, Berkeley: University of California Press.

Kleinberg, Ethan (2017), *Haunting History. For a Deconstructive Approach to the Past*, Stanford: Stanford University Press.

Kleist, Olaf and Irial Glynn, eds (2012), *History, Memory and Migration. Perceptions of the Past and the Politics of Incorporation*, New York: Palgrave Macmillan.

Kline, Daniel, ed. (2014), *Digital Gaming Re-imagines the Middle Ages*, London: Routledge.

Klein, Norman (1997), *The History of Forgetting. Los Angeles and the Erasure of Memory*, London: Verso.

Klymenko, Oksana (2018), "Constructing Memoirs of the October Revolution in the 1920s," in Agnieszka Mrozik and Stanislav Holubec, eds, *Historical Memory of Central and East European Communism*, 260–73, London: Routledge.

Koselleck, Reinhart (1985), *Futures Past: On the Semantics of Historical Time*, trans. Keith Tribe, Cambridge, MA: MIT Press.
Koselleck, Reinhart (1993) "Bilderverbot. Welches Totengedenken?" *Frankfurter Allgemeine Zeitung*, April 8.
Kovács, Friederike Kind and Jessie Labov, eds (2012), *From Samizdat to Tamizdat: Transnational Media During and After Socialism*, Oxford: Berghahn.
Kritz, Neil J. (1995), *Transitional Justice: How Emerging Democracies Reckon with Former Regimes*, Washington: United States Institute of Peace.
Kroeber, Alfred (1920), "Totem and Taboo: An Ethnologic Psychoanalysis," *American Anthropologist*, 22: 48–55.
Kubal, Timothy and Rene Becerra (2014), "Social Movements and Collective Memory," *Sociology Compass* 8 (6): 865–75.
Kushner, Barak (2006), *The Thought War: Japanese Imperial Propaganda*, Honolulu: University of Hawaii Press.
LaCapra, Dominick (1998), *History and Memory after Auschwitz*, Ithaca, NY: Cornell University Press.
Lacy, Joyce and Craig Stark (2013), "The neuroscience of memory: Implications for the courtroom," *Nature Reviews Neuroscience*, 14: 649–58.
Lagerkvist, Amanda, ed. (2019), *Digital Existence. Ontology, Ethics and Transcendence in Digital Culture*, New York: Routledge.
Lagrou, Pieter (2000), *The Legacy of Nazi Occupation: Patriotic Memory and National Recovery in Western Europe 1945–1965*, Cambridge: Cambridge University Press.
Lam, Tong (2019), "Ruins for Politics: Selling Industrial Heritage in Postsocialist China's Rustbelt," in Stefan Berger, ed., *Constructing Industrial Pasts. Industrial Heritage-Making in Britain, the West and Post-Socialist Countries*, 251–69, Oxford: Berghahn Books.
Lambert, Peter (2014), "Widukind or Karl der Große? Perspectives on Historical Culture and Memory in the Third Reich and Post-War West Germany," in Jie-Hyun Lim, Barbara Walker, and Peter Lambert, eds, *Mass Dictatorship and Memory as Ever Present Past*, 139–61, Basingstoke: Palgrave Macmillan.
Lambert, Peter (2017), "The Immediacy of a Remote Past: The Saxon Wars of 772–804 in the 'Cultural Struggles' of the Third Reich," in Peter Lambert and Björn K.U. Weiler, eds, *How the Past Was Used: Historical Cultures, c. 750–2000*, 181–200, Oxford: Oxford University Press.
Landau, Noa and Ofer Aderet (2018), "Netanyahu on Softening of Polish Holocaust Law," *Haaretz*, June 27. Available online: https://www.haaretz.com/israel-news/netanyahu-israel-welcomes-softening-of-polish-holocaust-law-1.6219584 (accessed July 24, 2018).
Landsberg, Alison (2004), *Prosthetic Memory: The Transformation of American Remembrance in the Age of Mass Culture*, New York: Columbia University Press.
Landsberg, Alison (2015), *Engaging the Past: Mass Culture and the Production of Historical Knowledge*, New York: Columbia University Press.
Landy, Marcia (2015), *Cinema and Counter-History*, Bloomington: Indiana University Press.
Lashley, Karl ([1950] 1966), "In Search of the Engram," in C. Evans and A. Robertson, eds, *Brain Physiology and Psychology: Key Papers*, 1–32, London: Butterworth.
Latour, Bruno (1993), *We Have Never Been Modern*, Cambridge, MA: Harvard University Press.
Lawson, Thomas T. (2008), *Carl Jung: Darwin of the Mind*, London and New York: Routledge.
Lebow, Richard, Wulf Kansteiner and Claudio Fogu, eds (2006), *The Politics of Memory in Postwar Europe*, Durham: Duke University Press.

LeCun, Yann, Bengio, Yoshua, and Hilton, Geoffrey (2015), "Deep Learning," *Nature*, 521: 436–44.
Lersch, Edgar and Reinhold Viehoff (2007), *Geschichte im Fernsehen: Eine Untersuchung zur Entwicklung des Genres und der Gattungsästhetik geschichtlicher Darstellungen im Fernsehen 1995 bis 2003*, Düsseldorf: Vistas.
Levy, Daniel and Natan Sznaider (2002), "Memory Unbound: The Holocaust and the Formation of Cosmopolitan Memory," *European Journal of Social Theory* 5 (1): 87–106.
Levy, Daniel, and Natan Sznaider (2004), "The Institutionalization of Cosmopolitan Morality: The Holocaust and Human Rights," *Journal of Human Rights*, 3 (2): 143–57.
Levy, Daniel and Natan Sznaider (2006), *The Holocaust and Memory in the Global Age*, trans. Assenka Oksiloff, Philadelphia: Temple University Press.
Lévy-Bruhl, Lucien (1910), *Les fonctions mentales dans les sociétés inférieures*, Paris: Les Presses universitaires de France.
Lichtblau, Eric (2013), "The Holocaust just got more shocking," *New York Times*, March 1, 2013.
Lochocki, Timo (2018), *The Rise of Populism in Western Europe. A Media Analysis on Failed Political Messaging*, Cham: Springer.
Lodge, Guy (2015), "Hollywood and Nollywood collaborate to underwhelming effect in Jeta Amata's impassioned but inert issue thriller," *Variety*, September: 1.
Loh, Christian, Yanyan Sheng, and Dirk Ilfenthaler, eds (2015), *Serious Games Analytics: Methodologies for Performance Measurement, Assessment, and Improvement*, Cham: Springer.
Loiperdinger, Martin (2004), "Lumiere's *Arrival of the Train*: Cinema's Founding Myth," *The Moving Image* 4 (1): 89–118.
López Saioa, Lucy van Dorp, and Garrett Hellenthal (2016), "Human Dispersal Out of Africa: A Lasting Debate," *Evol Bioinform Online*, 11 (Suppl 2): 57–68. Available online: doi:10.4137/EBO.S33489.
Lorenz, Chris (2004), "Blurred Lines. History, Memory and the Experience of Time," in Stefan Berger and Joana Seiffert, eds, *Erinnerungsorte: Chancen, Grenzen und Perspektiven eines Erfolgskonzeptes in den Kulturwissenschaften*, 73–90, Essen: Klartext.
Lorenz, Chris (2008), "Drawing the Line: 'Scientific History' Between Myth-Making and Myth-Breaking," in Stefan Berger, Linas Eriksonas, and Andrew Mycock, eds, *Narrating the Nation: Representations in History, Media and the Arts*, 35–55, Oxford: Berghahn.
Lorenz, Chris (2014), "Blurred Lines. History, Memory and the Experience of Time," *International Journal for History, Culture and Modernity*, 1 (2): 43–63.
Lorenz, Chris (2019), "Out of Time? Some Critical Reflections on François Hartog's Presentism," in Marek Tamm and Laurent Olivier, eds, *Rethinking Historical Time: New Approaches to Presentism*, 23–4, London and New York: Bloomsbury Publishing.
Lowenthal, David (1985), *The Past is a Foreign Country*, Cambridge: Cambridge University Press.
Loyle, Cyanne E. (2018), "Transitional Justice and Political Order in Rwanda," *Ethnic and Racial Studies*, 41 (4): 663–80.
Lübbe, Hermann (2007), *Vom Parteigenossen zum Bundesbürger: über beschwiegene und historisierte Vergangenheiten*, Munich: Fink.
Lukas, Richard (2012), *Forgotten Holocaust: The Poles under German Occupation*, New York: Hippocrene Books.
Lule, Jack (2016), *Understanding Media and Culture: An Introduction to Mass Communication*, Minneapolis: University of Minnesota Libraries Publishing.

MacDonald, David Bruce (2002), *Balkan Holocausts? Serb and Croat Victim-Centred Propaganda and the War in Yugoslavia*, Manchester: Manchester University Press.
MacDonald, Sharon (2013), *Memorylands: Heritage and Identity in Europe Today*, New York: Routledge.
Macdougall, Brenda (2017), "Space and Place within Aboriginal Epistemological Traditions: Recent Trends in Historical Scholarship," *Canadian Historical Review*, 98 (1): 64–82.
Madigan, Edward (2018), "Between the Poppy and the Lillya. A Century of Conflicted Irish Commemoration," paper presented at the conference "To End all Wars? Geopolitical Aftermath and Commemorative Legacies of the First World War," Ypres, August 22–25, 2018.
Maier, Charles S. (1993), "A Surfeit of Memory? Reflections on History, Melancholy and Denial," *History and Memory*, 5 (2): 136–52.
Majerus, Benoît (2014), "The 'Lieux de memoire' A place of remembrance for European historians?" in Stefan Berger and Joana Seiffert, J., eds, *Erinnerungsorte: Chancen, Grenzen und Perspektiven eines Erfolgskonzept in den Kulturwissenschaften*, 117–31, Essen: Klartext Verlag.
Majumdar, Rochona (2011), *Writing Postcolonial History*, London: Bloomsbury Publishing.
Makdisi, Ussama and Paul A. Silverstein, eds (2006), *Memory and Violence in the Middle East and North Africa*, Bloomington: Indiana University Press.
Mälksoo, Maria (2009), "The Memory Politics of Becoming European: The East European Subalterns and the Collective Memory of Europe," *European Journal of International Relations*, 15 (4): 653–80.
Mannheim, Karl (1952), "The Problem of Generations," in Paul Kecskemeti, ed., *Karl Mannheim, Essays on the Sociology of Knowledge: Collected Works*, 276–322, New York: Routledge.
Marcel, Jean-Christophe and Laurent Mucchelli (2008), "Maurice Halbwachs' mémoire collective," in Astrid Erll and Ansgar Nünning, eds, *Cultural Memory Studies. An International and Interdisciplinary Handbook*, 141–9, Berlin: De Gruyter.
Margalit, Avishai (2002), *The Ethics of Memory*, Cambridge, MA: Harvard University Press.
Margalit, Gilad (2010), *Guilt, Suffering and Memory: Germany Remembers Its Dead of World War II*, trans. Haim Watzman, Bloomington: Indiana University Press.
Marschall, Sabine (2013), "Collective Memory and Cultural Difference: Official vs. Vernacular Forms of Commemorating the Past," *Safundi: The Journal of South African and American Studies* 14 (1): 77–92.
Marx, Karl and Friedrich Engels (1848), *Manifesto of the Communist Party*, Moscow: Progress Publishers.
Masson, Jeffrey (1984), *Freud: The Assault on Truth*, London: Faber & Faber.
Masson, Jeffrey, trans. and ed., (1985), *The Complete Letters of Sigmund Freud to Willhelm Fliess, 1887–1904*, Cambridge, MA: Belknap Press of Harvard University Press.
Matten, Marc Andre, ed. (2012), *Places of Memory in Modern China: History, Politics and Identity*, Leiden: Brill.
May, Vivian M. (2015), *Pursuing Intersectionality, Unsettling Dominant Imaginaries*, London: Routledge.
McCabe, C. (1974), "Realism and the Cinema: Notes on Some Brechtian Theses," *Screen*, 1 (2): 7–27.
McCormack, Jo (2007), *Collective Memory: France and the Algerian War (1954–1962)*, Lanham: Lexington Books.

McCulloch, Warren and Walter Pitts (1943), "A Logical Calculus of the Ideas Immanent in Nervous Activity," *Bulletin of Mathematical Biophysics*, 5: 115–33.

McGregor, Katherine, Jess Melvin, and Annie Pohlman, eds (2018), *The Indonesian Genocide of 1964: Causes, Dynamics and Legacies*, Basingstoke: Palgrave Macmillan.

McMullan, Thomas (2016), "The Virtual Holocaust Survivor: How History Gained New Dimensions," *The Guardian*, June 18. Available online: https://www.theguardian.com/technology/2016/jun/18/holocaust-survivor-hologram-pinchas-gutter-new-dimensions-history (accessed July 25, 2018).

McVeigh, Stephen (2007), *The American Western*, Edinburgh: Edinburgh University Press.

Megill, Allan (2007), *Historical Knowledge, Historical Error. A Contemporary Guide to Practice*, Chicago: Chicago University Press.

Meier, Christian (2010), *Das Gebot zu Vergessen und die Unabweisbarkeit des Erinnerns: Vom öffentlichen Umgang mit schlimmer Vergangenheit*, Munich: Siedler.

Melgosa, Adrian Perez (2012), *Cinema and Inter-American Relations. Tracking Transnational Affect*, New York: Routledge.

Merrill, Michael (1976), "Interview with E.P. Thompson," in H. Abelove et al. eds, *Visions of History*, 20f, Manchester: Manchester University Press.

Merrill, Samuel, Emily Keightley, and Priska Daphi, eds (forthcoming), *Digital Media, Cultural Memory and Social Movements: Mobilising Remembrance*, Basingstoke: Palgrave Macmillan.

Messenger, David A. (2020), "The Bolshevik Revolution, Communism and Successor States after the First World War: Memory and Identity in Interwar Eastern Europe," in David A. Messenger, *War and Public Memory: Case Studies in Twentieth-Century Europe*, Tuscaloosa: University of Alabama Press, 45–60.

Miller, Barbara (2004), *The Stasi Files Unveiled: Guilt and Compliance in a Unified Germany*, Brunswick: Transaction Publishers.

Mills, Nicolaus (2011), "James Arness, Symbol of Power with Restraint," *The Guardian*, June 8. Available online: https://www.theguardian.com/commentisfree/cifamerica/2011/jun/08/james-arness-gunsmoke (accessed June 25, 2018).

Mombauer, Annika (2002), *The Origins of the First World War: Controversies and Consensus*, Harlow: Pearson.

Monk, Claire and Amy Sargeant, eds (2002), *British Historical Cinema: The History, Heritage and Costume Film*, London: Routledge.

Morgan, Kevin (2010), "Neither Help Nor Pardon? Communist Pasts in Western Europe," in Małgorzata Pakier and Bo Stråth, eds, *A European Memory? Contested Histories and the Politics of Remembrance*, 260–74, Oxford: Berghahn.

Morris-Suzuki, Tessa (2005), *The Past Within Us: Media, Memory, History*, London: Verso.

Moses, John A. (1975), *The Politics of Illusion. The Fischer Controversy in German Historiography*, Sydney: Prior.

Mosse, George L. (1975), *The Nationalization of the Masses: Political Symbolism and Mass Movements in Germany from the Napoleonic Wars through the Third Reich*, New York: H. Fertig.

Mosse, George L. (1990), *Fallen Soldiers: Reshaping the Memory of the World Wars*, Oxford: Oxford University Press.

Mouffe, Chantal (2013), *Agonistics: Thinking the World Politically*, London: Verso.

Moynihan, Daniel Patrick (1990), *On the Law of Nations*, Cambridge, MA: Harvard University Press.

MSA (2019), https://www.memorystudiesassociation.org/about_the_msa/ (accessed December 1, 2019).

Mühlhahn, Klaus, ed. (2017), *The Cultural Legacy of German Colonial Rule*, Berlin: De Gruyter.
Myers, Joe (2016), "The Richest Countries Take the Fewest Refugees," *World Economic Forum*, July 18. Available online: https://www.weforum.org/agenda/2016/07/richest-countries-fewest-refugees-oxfam/ (accessed July 12, 2018).
Naeem, Bassem (2008), "Hamas Condemns the Holocaust," *The Guardian*, May 12. Available online: https://www.theguardian.com/commentisfree/2008/may/12/hamascondemnstheholocaust (accessed July 22, 2018).
Nail, Thomas (2015), *The Figure of the Migrant*, Stanford: Stanford University Press.
National Holocaust Centre and Museum: Forever Project (n.d.). Available online: https://www.holocaust.org.uk/foreverproject1 (accessed July 25, 2018).
Navitski, Rielle and Nicolas Poppe, eds (2017), *Cosmopolitan Film Cultures in Latin America*, Bloomington: Indiana University Press.
Neier, Aryeh (2012), *The International Human Rights Movement. A History*, Princeton: Princeton University Press.
Neisser, Ulric ([1967] 2014), *Cognitive Psychology*, New York: Psychology Press.
Neumann, John von (1958). *The Computer and the Brain*, New Haven: Yale University Press.
Neumayer, Laure (2018), *The Criminalisation of Communism in the European Political Space after the Cold War*, London: Routledge.
Neveu, Erik (2014), "Memory Battles over May 68," in Britta Baumgarten, Priska Daphi, and Peter Ulrich, eds, *Conceptualizing Culture in Social Movement Research*, 275–99, London: Palgrave Macmillan.
Nie, Annie Hongping (2013), "Gaming, Nationalism, and Ideological Work in Contemporary China: Online Games Based on the War of Resistance against Japan," *Journal of Contemporary China*, 22 (81): 499–517.
Niethammer, Lutz (1972), *Die Mitläuferfabrik: Die Entnazifizierung am Beispiel Bayerns*, Berlin: Dietz.
Niethammer, Lutz (2000), *Kollektive Identität. Heimliche Quellen einer unheimlichen Konjunktur,* Rowohlt: Reinbek bei Hamburg.
Nietzsche, Friedrich (1999), "Unzeitgemäße Betrachtungen," in Giorgio Colli and Mazzino Montinari, eds, *Friedrich Nietzsche: Die Geburt der Tragödie/Unzeitgemäße Betrachtungen*, 157–427, Munich: DTV.
Niven, Bill (2001), *Facing the Nazi Past*, London and New York: Routledge, 2001.
Niven, Bill and Amy Williams, "The Dominance of the National: On the Susceptibility of Holocaust Memory," *Jewish Historical Studies* (January 2020), no pagination as yet.
Noakes, Lucy (1997), "Making Histories: Experiencing the Blitz in London's Museums in the 1990s," in Martin Evans and Ken Lunn, eds, *War and Memory in the Twentieth Century*, 89–104, Oxford: Berg.
Noakes, Lucy (2014), "'War on the Web': The BBC's 'People's War' Website and Memories of Fear in Wartime in 21st-Century Britain," in Lucy Noakes and Juliette Pattinson, eds, *British Cultural Memory and the Second World War*, 47–65, London: Bloomsbury Publishing.
Noiriel, Gerard (1996), "French and Foreigners," in Pierre Nora, ed., *Realms of Memory, vol. 1: Conflicts and Divisions*, New York: Columbia University Press.
Noon, David Hoogland (2004), "Operation Enduring Analogy: World War II, the War on Terror, and the Uses of Historical Memory," *Rhetoric and Public Affairs*, 7 (3): 339–64.
Nora, Pierre (1984–92), *Les Lieux de Mémoire*, 7 vols, Paris: Gallimard.
Nora, Pierre (1989), "Between Memory and History: les Lieux de Memoire," *Representations*, 26: 7–24.

Nora, Pierre (1992), "Comment ecrire l'histoire de France?" in Pierre Nora, ed., *Les Lieux de Memoire. III. Les France*, 11–33, Paris: Gallimard.

Nora, Pierre, ed., (1996–1998), *Realms of Memory*, 3 vols, New York: Columbia University Press.

Novick, Peter (1999), *The Holocaust in American Life*, Chicago: University of Chicago Press.

Nwakanma, Obi (2019), "The Nigerian Civil War and the Biafran Secessionist Revival," in Carl Levana and Patrick Ukata, eds, *The Oxford Handbook of Nigerian Politics*, 620–35, Oxford: Oxford University Press.

O'Brien, Dominic (2005), *How to Develop a Brilliant Memory Week by Week: 50 Proven Ways to Enhance Your Memory*, London: Duncan Baird.

Oduntan, Oluwatoyin (2018), *Power, Culture and Modernity in Nigeria*, London: Routledge.

Oldfield, R.C. (1954), "Memory Mechanisms and the Theory of Schemata," *British Journal of Psychology*, 45: 14–23.

Olick, Jeffrey K. (2007), *The Politics of Regret: On Collective Memory and Historical Responsibility*, London: Routledge.

Olick, Jeffrey K. (2016), *The Sins of the Fathers*, Chicago: University of Chicago Press.

Olick, Jeffrey K., Vered Vinitzky-Seroussi, and Daniel Levy (2011), eds, *The Collective Memory Reader*, Oxford: Oxford University Press.

Olusoga, David (2016), *Black and British: A Forgotten History*, London: Macmillan.

Oostindie, Gert (2009a), "History brought home: postcolonial migrations and the Dutch rediscovery of slavery," in Wim Klooster, ed., *Migration, Trade, and Slavery in an Expanding World*, Brill: Leiden & Boston 2009, 305–27.

Oostindie, Gert (2009b), "Public Memories of the Atlantic Slave Trade and Slavery" in Nicolas Pethes (2019), *Cultural Memory Studies: An Introduction*, Cambridge: Cambridge University Press.

Ostrand, Nicole (2015), "The Syrian Refugee Crisis. A Comparison of Responses by Germany, Sweden, the United Kingdom, and the United States," *Journal on Migration and Human Security*, 3 (3): 255–79.

Parikka, Jussi (2015), *A Geology of Media*, Minneapolis: University of Minnesota Press.

Parikka, Jussi (2017), "The Underpinning Time: From Digital Memory to Network Microtemporality," in Andrew Hoskins, ed., *Digital Memory Studies: Media Pasts in Transition*, 156–72, New York: Routledge.

Pasamar, Gonzalo (2010), *Apologia and Criticism: Historians and the History of Spain*, Berne: Peter Lang.

Paterson, Richard (1998), "Drama and Entertainment," in Anthony Smith, ed., *Television: An International History*, 57–68, Oxford: Oxford University Press.

Perry, Keith (2014), "Michael Gove Criticises 'Blackadder Myths' about First World War," *The Daily Telegraph*, January 3. Available online: https://www.telegraph.co.uk/news/10548303/Michael-Gove-criticises-Blackadder-myths-about-First-World-War.html (accessed September 1, 2018).

Peters-Little, Frances, Ann Curthoys, and John Docker, eds (2010), *Passionate Histories. Myth, Memory and Indigenous Australia*, Canberra: ANU Press.

Pogačar, Martin (2016), *Media Archeologies, Micro-Archives and Story-Telling: Re-Presencing the Past*, Basingstoke: Palgrave Macmillan.

Pogačar, Martin (2017), "Culture of the Past: Digital Connectivity and Dispotentiated Futures," in Andrew Hoskins, ed., *Digital Memory Studies: Media Pasts in Transition*, 27–47, New York: Routledge.

Pons, Silvio (2014), *The Global Revolution. The History of International Communism 1917–1991*, Oxford: Oxford University Press.

Ponzanesi, S., and M. Waller, eds (2012), *Postcolonial Cinema Studies*, London: Routledge.

Poole, Elisabeth (2002), *Reporting Islam. Media Representations of British Islam*, London: Tauris.

Portelli, Alessandro (1991), *The Death of Luigi Trastulli and Other Stories*, Albany: State University of New York Press.

Portes, Jonathan (2019), *What Do We Know and What Should We Do About Immigration?* London: Sage.

Presner, Todd (2016), "The Ethics of the Algorism: Close and Distant Listening to the Shoah Foundation Visual History Archive," in Claudio Fogu, Wulf Kansteiner, and Todd Presner, eds, *Probing the Ethics of Holocaust Culture*, 175–202, Cambridge, MA: Harvard University Press.

Pruitt, Lesley (2019), "Closed due to 'flooding'? UK media representations of refugees and migrants in 2015–2016 – creating a crisis of borders," *The British Journal of Politics and International Relations*, 21 (2): 383–402.

Qu, Xaofan and Xin Zhao (2019), "The Heritage of the Chinese Eastern Railway: Symbol of Colonization and International Cooperation," in Stefan Berger, ed., *Constructing Industrial Pasts: Industrial Heritage-Making in Britain, the West and Post-Socialist Countries*, 270–87, Oxford: Berghahn.

Reading, Anna (2016), *Gender and Memory in the Global Age*, London: Palgrave Macmillian.

Reading, Anne and Tamar Katriel, eds (2015), *Cultural Memories of Non-Violent Struggles: Powerful Times*, Basingstoke: Palgrave MacmIllan, 2015.

Renan, Ernest ([1882] 1990), "What is a Nation," reprinted in Homi K. Bhabha, ed., *Nation and Narration*, 8–22. New York: Routledge.

Renan, Ernest ([1887] 2018), *What is a Nation? and other Political Writings*, New York: Columbia University Press.

Rescorla, Michael (2015), "The Computational Theory of Mind," in Edward N. Zalta, ed., *The Stanford Encyclopedia of Philosophy* (Spring 2017 edition). Available online: https://plato.stanford.edu/archives/spr2017/entries/computational-mind/ (accessed September 20, 2019).

Reyes, G. Mitchell, ed. (2010), *Public Memory, Race and Ethnicity*, Cambridge: Cambridge Scholars.

Rhashkow, Ezra, Sanjukta Ghosh, and Upal Chakrabarty, eds (2018), *Memory, Identity and the Colonial Encounter in India*, London: Routledge.

Rice, Alan (2010), *Creating Memorials, Building Identities: The Politics of Memory in the Black Atlantic*, Liverpool: Liverpool University Press.

Richards, Jeffrey (1981), "The British Board of Film Censors and Content Control in the 1930s: Images of Britain," *Historical Journal of Film, Radio and Television*, 1 (2): 95–116.

Richards, Jeffrey (1982), "The British Board of Film Censors and Content Control in the 1930s: Foreign Affairs," *Historical Journal of Film, Radio and Television*, 2 (1): 39–48.

Ricoeur, Paul (2004), *History, Memory and Forgetting*, Chicago: University of Chicago Press.

Rieff, David (2016a), *In Praise of Forgetting: Historical Memory and its Ironies*, London and New Haven: Yale University Press.

Rieff, David (2016b), "The Cult of Memory: When History does more Harm than Good," *The Guardian*, March 2. Available online: https://www.theguardian.com/education/2016/mar/02/cult-of-memory-when-history-does-more-harm-than-good (accessed July 14, 2018).

Rigney, Ann (2018a), "Remembering Hope: Transnational Activism Beyond the Traumatic," *Memory Studies* 11 (3): 368–80.

Rigney, Ann (2018b), "Comment", in Marek Tamm and Peter Burke, eds, *Debating New Approaches to History*, 143–8, London: Bloomsbury.

Rigney, Ann (2018c), "Remembrance as remaking: memories of the nation revisited," *Nations and Nationalism*, 24 (2): 240–57.

Rippl, Gabrielle, ed., (2015), *Handbook of Intermediality. Literature–Image–Sound–Music*, Berlin: De Gruyter.

Ritterfeld, Ute, Michael Cody, and Peter Vorderer, eds (2009), *Serious Games: Mechanisms and Effects*, New York: Routledge.

Robbe, Tilmann (2014), "Benjamins Berlin. Gedächtnislandschaften zwischen memory boom und spatial turn," in Stefan Berger and Joana Seiffert, eds, *Erinnerungsorte: Chancen, Grenzen und Perspektiven eines Erfolgskonzept in den Kulturwissenschaften*, 91–101, Essen: Klartext Verlag.

Robbins, Bruce (1998), "Actually Existing Cosmopolitanism," in Pheng Cheah and Bruce Robbins, eds, *Cosmopolitics. Thinking and Feeling beyond the Nation*, 1–19, Minneapolis: University of Minneapolis Press.

Roberts, Rachel (2016), "The UK Has Taken in just 18% of its 'Fair Share' of Syrian Refugees, Report Shows", *The Independent*, December 16. Available online: https://www.independent.co.uk/news/uk/home-news/syrian-refugees-uk-fair-share-report-a7478891.html (accessed July 12, 2018).

Robertson, Adi (2015), "The virtual reality 9/11 experience is bad, but not for the reasons you'd expect," *The Verge*, October. Available online: http://www.theverge.com/2015/10/30/9642790/virtual-reality-9–11-experience-empathy (accessed October 21, 2016).

Robinson, Nick (2012), "Videogames, Persuasion and the War on Terror: Escaping or Embedding the Military—Entertainment Complex?" *Political Studies*, 60 (3): 504–22.

Robinson, Nick (2015), "Have You Won the War on Terror? Military Videogames and the State of American Exceptionalism," *Millennium*, 43 (2): 450–70.

Robinson, Paul (1993), *Freud and his Critics*, Berkeley: University of California Press.

Roediger, Henry (2003), "Bartlett, Frederick Charles," in Lynn Nadel, ed., *Encyclopedia of Cognitive Science*, vol. 1, 319–22, London: Macmillan.

Romano, Renee C., and Leigh Raiford, eds (2006), *The Civil Rights Movement in American Memory*, Athens: University of Georgia Press.

Rosenfeld, Alvin (1997), "The Americanization of the Holocaust," in Alvin Rosenfeld, ed., *Thinking About the Holocaust*, 119–50, Bloomington: Indiana University Press.

Rosenfeld, Gavriel D. (2009), "A Looming Crash or a Soft Landing? Forecasting the Future of the Memory 'Industry'," *The Journal of Modern History*, 81 (1): 122–58.

Rosenfeld, Gavriel D. (2015), *Hi Hitler! How the Nazi Past is Being Normalized in Contemporary Culture*, Cambridge: Cambridge University Press.

Rosenstone, Robert (1995), *Visions of the Past. The Challenge of Film to our Idea of History*, Cambridge, MA: Harvard University Press.

Rossington, Michael, and Anne Whitehead, eds (2007), *Theories of Memory: A Reader*, Edinburgh University of Edinburgh Press.

Rothberg, Michael (2009), *Multidirectional Memory: Remembering the Holocaust in the Age of Decolonization*, Stanford: Stanford University Press.

Rothberg, Michael (2010), "Introduction: Between Memory and Memory. From Lieux de Memoire to Noeuds de Memoire," *Yale French Studies*, 118/119: 3–12.

Rothberg, Michael (2019), *The Implicated Subject. Beyond Victims and Perpetrators*, Stanford: Stanford University Press.

Rothe, Anne (2011), *Popular Trauma Culture: Selling the Pain of Others in the Mass Media*, New Brunswick: Rutgers University Press.

Rothermund, Dietmar (2015), *Memories of Post-Imperial Nations: The Aftermath of Decolonisation, 1945–2013*, Cambridge: Cambridge University Press.

Roudometof, Victor (2016), *Glocalization: A Critical Introduction*, London and New York: Routledge.

Rousso, Henry (1991), *The Vichy Syndrome: History and Memory in France since 1944*, Cambridge, MA: Harvard University Press.

Rousso, Henry (2002), *The Haunting Past: History, Memory, and Justice in Contemporary France*, Philadelphia: University of Pennsylvania Press

Runia, Eelco (2006), "Spots of Time," *History and Theory*, 45: 305–16.

Runia, Eelco (2015), *Moved by the Past. Discontinuity and Historical Mutation*, New York: Columbia University Press.

Rush, Florence (1996), "The Freudian Coverup," *Feminism & Psychology*, 6 (2): 260–76.

Rutten, E., J. Fedor, and V. Zverewa, eds (2013), *Memory, Conflict and New Media*, New York: Routledge.

Sabrow, Martin, ed. (2007), *Wohin treibt die DDR-Erinnerung: Dokumentation einer Debatte*, Göttingen: Vandenhoeck & Ruprecht.

Sabrow, Martin (2009), *Erinnerungsorte der DDR*, Munich: C.H. Beck.

Safronova, Valeriya (2017), "Now Karl Lagerfeld Has Opinions on Migrants in Europe", *The New York Times*, November 14. Available online: https://www.nytimes.com/2017/11/14/fashion/karl-lagerfeld-migrants-angela-merkel.html (accessed July 12, 2018).

Saha, Anamik (2012), "Beards, scarves, halal meat, terrorists, forced marriage. Television industries and production of race," *Media, Culture & Society*, 34 (4): 424–38.

Saikia, Yasmin (2004), *Fragmented Memories: Struggling to be Tai-Ahom in India*, Durham: Duke University Press.

Sargeant, Amy (2002), "Do We Need Another Hero? Ecce Homo and Nelson (1919)," in Claire Monk and Amy Sargeant, eds, *British Historical Cinema: The History, Heritage and Costume Film*, 15–30, London: Routledge.

Sarkar, Samit (2014), "Chinese Game Lets Players Shoot Japanese War Criminals," *Polygon*, February 27. Available online: https://www.polygon.com/2014/2/27/5454928/chinese-game-shoot-japanese-war-criminals (accessed June 27, 2018).

Schacter, Daniel (1996), *Searching for Memory: The Brain, the Mind, and the Past*, New York: Basic Books.

Schacter, Daniel (2003), *How the Mind Forgets and Remembers*, London: Souvenir Press.

Schmidt, Jan (2013), "'Im Westen . . . Neues?' Deutsche Revolution und Arbeiterbewegung als Faktor in Ostasien am Beispiel Japans (1918–1920)," in Karl-Christian Führer, Jürgen Mittag, Axel Schildt, and Klaus Tenfelde, eds, *Revolution und Arbeiterbewegung in Deutschland 1918–1920*, 375–400, Essen: Klartext.

Schwartz, Joseph ([1999] 2003), *Cassandra's Daughter: A History of Psychoanalysis*, London: Karnac.

Scislowska, Monika and Vanessa Gera (2010), "Facebook a Virtual Memorial for World War II," *NBC News*, February 4. Available online: http://www.nbcnews.com/id/35235234/ns/technology_and_science-tech_and_gadgets/t/facebook-virtual-memorial-world-war-ii/#.W6IdYuhKjIU (accessed June 25, 2018).

Seaton, Philipp A. (2007), *Japan's Contested War Memories: the "Memory Rifts" in Historical Consciousness of World War II*, London: Routledge.

Sells, Michael A. (1996), *The Bridge Betrayed: Religion and Genocide in Bosnia*, Berkeley: University of California Press.
Semi, Emanuela Trevisan, Dario Miccoli, and Tudor Parfitt, eds (2013), *Memory and Ethnicity: Ethnic Museums in Israel and the Diaspora*, Cambridge: Cambridge Scholars.
Semon, Richard (1921), *The Mneme*, London: George Allen & Unwin.
Shandler, Jeffrey (1999), *While America Watches: Televising the Holocaust*, Oxford: Oxford University Press.
Shandler, Jeffrey (2017), *Holocaust Memory in the Digital Age: Survivors' Stories and New Media Practices*, Stanford: Stanford University Press.
Shandley, Robert R. (1998), *Unwilling Germans? The Goldhagen Debate*, Minneapolis: University of Minnesota Press.
Shaw, Julia (2016), *The Memory Illusion: Remembering, Forgetting, and the Science of False Memory*, London: Penguin.
Shenk, David (2001), *The Forgetting: Alzheimer's: Portrait of an Epidemic*, London: HarperCollins.
Shepherd, Gordon (2016), *Foundations of the Neuron Doctrine*, Oxford: Oxford University Press.
Shepard, Todd (2016), "The Birth of the Hexagon: 1962 and the Erasure of France's Supranational History," in Manuel Borutta and Jan C. Jansen, eds, *Vertriebene and Pieds-Noirs in Postwar Germany and France. Comparative Perspectives*, 53–69, London: Palgrave Macmillan.
Sherwood, Harriet (2016), "Holocaust Survivors' 3D Project Preserves Testimony for the Future," *The Guardian*, December 1. Available online: https://www.theguardian.com/world/2016/dec/01/holocaust-survivors-laser-image-project-preserves-testimony-for-the-future (accessed July 25, 2018)
Sherzai, Dean and Ayesha Sherzai (2017), *The Alzheimer's Solution: A Revolutionary Guide to How You Can Prevent and Reverse Memory Loss*, New York: Simon & Schuster.
Sierp, Aline (2014), *History, Memory and Trans-European Identity: Unifying Divisions*, London: Routledge.
Silverman, Max (2013), *Palimpsestic Memory: The Holocaust and Colonialism in French and Francophone Fiction and Film*, New York and Oxford: Berghahn.
Simić, Olivera, ed. (2017), *An Introduction to Transitional Justice*, Oxford and New York: Routledge.
Sitze, Adam (2016), *The Impossible Machine: A Genealogy of South Africa's Truth and Reconciliation Commission*, Ann Arbor: University of Michigan Press.
Slotkin, Richard (1992), *Gunfighter Nation: The Myth of the Frontier in Twentieth-Century America*, New York: Atheneum.
Smith, Anthony D. (1999), *Myths and the Memories of the Nation*, Oxford: Oxford University Press.
Smith, Kathleen E. (1996), *Stalin's Victims: Popular Memory and the End of the USSR*, Ithaca: Cornell University Press.
Smith, Leonard V. (2001), "Paul Fussell's The Great War and Modern Memory: Twenty-Five Years Later," *History and Theory*, 40 (2): 241–60.
Smith, Laurajane, Paul A. Shackel, and Gary Campbell, eds (2011), *Heritage, Labor and the Working Classes*, London: Routledge.
Sørensen, Mads and Allan Christensen (2013), *Ulrich Beck. An Introduction to Theory of the Second Modernity and the Risk Society*, London: Routledge.

Soro, Javier Muñoz (2016), "In Search of a Lost Narrative: Antifascism and Democracy in Present-Day Spain," in Hugo García, Mercedes Yusta, Xavier Tabet, and Cristina Clímaco, eds, *Rethinking Antifascism: History, Memory and Political Uses, 1922 to the Present*, 276–99, Oxford: Berghahn.

Speedtest (2019), "Global Index. Nigeria September 2019." Available online: https://www.speedtest.net/global-index/nigeria#mobile (accessed October 23, 2019).

Spencer, Herbert (1898), *The Principles of Sociology*, 3 vols, New York: D. Appleton & Co.

Spiegel, Gabrielle M. (2002), "Memory and History: Liturgical Time and Historical Time," *History and Theory*, 41 (2): 149–62.

Stamp, Gavin, ed. (2006), *The Memorial to the Missing of the Somme*, Profile Books: London.

Stan, Lavinia (2103), *Transitional Justice in Post-Communist Romania: The Politics of Post-Communist Romania*, New York: Cambridge University Press.

Starkey, David (2001), "The English Historians' Role and the Place of History in English National Life," *The Historian* 71: 6–15.

Stedman Jones, Gareth (1983), *Languages of Class: Studies in English Working-Class History 1832–1986*, 22, Cambridge: Cambridge University Press.

Stelzel, Philipp (2019), *History After Hitler: A Transatlantic Experience*, Philadelphia: University of Pennsylvania Press.

Stern, Fritz (2006), *Five Germanies I Have Known*, New York: Farrar, Straus & Giroux.

Stevens, Garth, Norman Duncan, and Derek Hook, eds (2013), *Race, Memory and the Apartheid Archive. Towards a Transformative Psychosocial Praxis*, New York: Palgrave Macmillan.

Stone, Dan (2014), *Goodbye to All That? The Story of Europe since 1945*, Oxford: Oxford University Press.

Street, Seán (2002), *A Concise History of British Radio, 1922–2002*, Tiverton: Kelly.

Sugrue, Tom (1996), *The Origins of the Urban Crisis: Race and Inequality in Postwar Detroit*, Princeton: Princeton University Press.

Sumartojo, Shanti and Ben Wellings, eds (2014), *Nation, Memory and Great War Commemoration: Mobilizing the Past in Europe, Australia and New Zealand*, Berne: Peter Lang.

Tamboukou, Maria (2016), *Gendering the Memory of Work: Women Workers' Narratives*, London: Routledge.

Tamm, Marek (2013), "Beyond History and Memory: New Perspectives in Memory Studies," *History Compass*, 11 (6): 458–73.

Tamm, Marek, ed. (2015), *Afterlife of Events: Perspectives on Mnemohistory*, Houndsmill: Palgrave.

Tavares, Laura (2017), "Text to Text: Comparing Jewish Refugees of the 1930s with Syrian Refugees Today," *New York Times*, January 4. Available online: https://www.nytimes.com/2017/01/04/learning/lesson-plans/text-to-text-comparing-jewish-refugees-of-the-1930s-with-syrian-refugees-today.html (accessed July 24, 2018).

Taylor, A.J.P. (1975), *English History, 1914–1945*, London: Penguin.

Taylor, Philip M. (1981), *The Projection of Britain: British Overseas Publicity and Propaganda, 1919–1939*, Cambridge: Cambridge University Press.

Taylor, Richard (2002), *October Октябрь*, London: British Film Institute.

Taylor, Richard and Ian Christie, eds (1994), *The Film Factory: Russian and Soviet Cinema in Documents, 1896–1939*, London: Routledge.

Teitel, Rudi G. (2000), *Transitional Justice*, Oxford and New York: Oxford University Press.

Teo, Thomas (2005), *The Critique of Psychology: From Kant to Postcolonial Theory*, New York: Springer.

Terrace, Vincent (2011), *Encyclopedia of Television Shows, 1925 through 2010, Volume 1: A–Ha*, Jefferson: McFarland.

Tharoor, Ishaan (2017), "The Plea of a Syrian Activist: Don't Forget Us," *The Washington Post*, December 8. Available online: https://www.washingtonpost.com/news/worldviews/wp/2017/12/08/the-plea-of-a-syrian-activist-dont-forget-us/?noredirect=on&utm_term=.27802f32d537 (accessed July 24, 2018).

Thioub, Ibrahima (2007), "Writing National and Transnational History in Africa: the Example of the Dakar School," in Stefan Berger, ed., *Writing the Nation: A Global Perspective*, 197–212, Basingstoke: Palgrave MacMillan.

Thompson, Allan, ed., (2007), *The Media and the Rwanda Genocide*, London: Pluto Press.

Thompson, Paul (2000), *The Voice of the Past: Oral History*, Oxford: Oxford University Press.

Todman, Dan (2005), *The Great War: Myth and Memory*, London: Continuum.

Todorov, Tzvetan (1984), *Mikhail Bakhtin: The Dialogical Principle*, Minneapolis: University of Minnesota Press.

Toews, John E. (1987), "Intellectual History after the Linguistic Turn: The Autonomy of Meaning and the Irreducibility of Experience." *American Historical Review* 92, 4 (Oct.): 879–907.

Tönnies, Ferdinand (1887), *Gemeinschaft und Gesellschaft*, Leipzig: Fues's Verlag.

Torpey, John (2001), "'Making Whole What Has Been Smashed': Reflections on Reparations," *Journal of Modern History*, 73 (2): 333–58.

Torpey, John (2006), *Making Whole What Has Been Smashed. On Reparations Politics*, Cambridge MA: Harvard University Press.

Tsai, Martin (2015), "Well-intentioned 'Black November' tends to overreach," *Los Angeles Times*, January 9.

Tulving, Endel and Fergus I.M. Craik (2005), *The Oxford Handbook of Memory*, Oxford: Oxford University Press.

Turvey, M. (2011), *The Filming of Modern Life: European Avant-Garde Film of the 1920s*, Cambridge, MA: MIT Press.

Tutu, Desmond (1999), *No Future without Forgiveness*, London: Random House.

Uhl, Heidemarie (1997), "The Politics of Memory: Austria's Perception of the Second World War and the National Socialist Period," in Günther Bischof and Anton Pelinka, eds, *Austrian Historical Memory and National Identity*, 6–94, London: Taylor & Francis.

University of Utrecht (2018), "ERC Advanced Grant for Ann Rigney: Remembering Hope: The Cultural Memory of Protest in Europe." Available online: https://www.uu.nl/en/news/remembering-hope-the-cultural-memory-of-protest-in-europe (accessed November 30, 2019).

USC Shoah Foundation: *New Dimensions in Testimony* (n.d.). Available online: https://sfi.usc.edu/collections/holocaust/ndt (accessed July 25, 2018).

Valuch, Tibor (2019), "'A Special Kind of Cultural Heritage: the Remembrance of Workers' Lives in Contemporary Hungary—a Case Study of Ózd'," in Stefan Berger, ed., *Constructing Industrial Pasts: Industrial Heritage-Making in Britain, the West and Post-Socialist Countries*, 242–50, Oxford: Berghahn Books.

Van Dijck, José (2013), *The Culture of Connectivity: A Critical History of Social Media*, Oxford: Oxford University Press.

Van Dijck, Teun (1991), *Racism and the Press*, London: Routledge.

Vieten, Ulrike (2018), "Ambivalences of cosmopolitanisms, elites and far-right populisms in twenty-first century Europe," in Gregor Fitzi, Jürgen Mackert, and Bryan Turner, eds,

Populism and the Crisis of Democracy, Vol. 2: Politics, Social Movements and Extremism, 101–18, New York: Routledge.

Vincent, David (2013), "The New Media: Television," in Rosalind Crone, ed., *Europe Reconstructed: 1945–1968*, 170–5, Milton Keynes: Open University.

Vinen, Richard (2018), *The Long '68: Radical Protest and Its Enemies*, London: Allen Lane.

Villalón, Roberta, ed. (2017), *Memory, Truth and Justice in Contemporary Latin America*, Lanham: Rowman & Littlefield.

Waddell, Kaveh (2016), "A Video Game That Lets You Torture Iraqi Prisoners," theatlantic.com, August 1, 2016. Available online: http://www.theatlantic.com/technology/archive/2016/08/a-video-game-that-lets-you-torture-iraqi-prisoners/493379/ (accessed October 21, 2016).

Wagstaff, Mark (2012), "Critiquing the Stranger, Inventing Europe: Integration and the Fascist Legacy," in Eric Langenbacher, Bill Niven, and Ruth Witlinger, eds, *Dynamics of Memory and Identity in Contemporary Europe*, 102–19, Oxford: Berghahn.

Wainwright, Martin (2019), *Virtual History: How Videogames Portray the Past*, New York: Routledge.

Walter, Stefanie (2017), *EU Citizens in the European Public Sphere: An Analysis of EU News in 27 EU Member States*, Wiesbaden: Springer.

Waters, Mary C. (1990), *Ethnic Options: Choosing Identities in America*, Berkeley: University of California Press.

Welch, David A. (2006), "Restructuring the Means of Communication in Nazi Germany," in Garth S. Jowett and Victoria O'Donnell, eds, *Readings in Propaganda and Persuasion: New and Classic Essays*, 121–48, Thousand Oaks: Sage.

Welch, David A. (2013), *Propaganda: Power and Persuasion*, London: The British Library.

Wellings, Ben and Chris Gifford (2018), "The Past in English Euroscepticism," in Stefan Berger and Caner Tekin, eds, 88–105, *History and Belonging. Representations of the Past in Contemporary European Politics*, Oxford: Berghahn.

Welsch, Wolfgang (1999), "Transculturality: The Changing Forms of Culture Today," in Armin Paul Frank and Helga Essmann, eds, *The Internationality of National Literatures in Either America: Transfer and Transformation: Cases and Problems,* vol. I/1: 287–308, Göttingen: Wallstein.

Wernecke, Klaus (2015), "1968," in Torben Fischer and Matthias Lorenz, eds, *Lexikon der Vergangenheitsbewältigung in Deutschland*, 188–93, Bielefeld: transcript.

Werner, Michael and Benedicte Zimmermann (2006), "Beyond Comparison: 'Histoire Croisée' and the Challenge of Reflexivity", *History and Theory* 45: 1, 30–50.

Wicke, Christian, Stefan Berger, and Jana Golombek, eds (2018): *Industrial Heritage and Regional Identities*, London: Routledge.

Wiesel, Elie (1978), "The Trivializing of the Holocaust," *New York Times*, April 16. Available online: https://www.nytimes.com/1978/04/16/archives/tv-view-trivializing-the-holocaust-semifact-and-semifiction-tv-view.html (accessed September 10, 2018).

Wieviorka, Annette (2001), *The Era of the Witness*, Ithaca, NY: Cornell University Press.

Wijermars, Marielle (2019), *Memory Politics in Contemporary Russia. Television, Cinema and the State*, New York: Routledge.

Wilke, Jürgen (2004), "Die Fernsehserie 'Holocaust' als Medienereignis," Zeitgeschichte-online, March. Available online: http://zeitgeschichte-online.de/thema/die-fernsehserie-holocaust-als-medienereignis (accessed July 6, 2017).

Wilson, Keith, ed. (1996), *Forging the Collective Memory: Government and International Historians through Two World Wars*, Oxford: Berghahn.

Williams, Melissa S. (1998), *Voice, Trust and Memory: Marginalized Groups and the Failings of Liberal Representation*, Princeton: Princeton University Press.

Winfield, Ann Gibson (2007), *Eugenics and Education in America. Institutionalized Racism and the Implications of History, Ideology and Memory*, New York: Peter Lang.

Winnerling, Tobias and Florian Kerschbaumer, eds (2014), *Early Modernity and Video Games*, Newcastle: Cambridge Scholars.

Winslow, Barbara, Temma Kaplan, and Bryan S. Palmer (1995), "Women's Revolutions: The Work of Sheila Rowbotham—a Twenty-Year Assessment," *Radical History Review* 63: 141–65.

Winter, Jay (1995), *Sites of Memory, Sites of Mourning: The Great War in European Cultural History*, Cambridge: Cambridge University Press.

Winter, Jay (2006), *Remembering War: The Great War between Memory and History in the Twentieth Century*, New Haven: Yale University Press.

Winter, Jay M. (2007), "Introduction. The performance of the past: memory, history, identity," in Karin Tilmans, Frank van Vree, and Jay M. Winter, eds, *Performing the Past. Memory, History, and Identity in Modern Europe*, 11–32, Amsterdam: Amsterdam University Press.

Winter, Jay (2017), *War Beyond Words: Languages of Remembrance from the Great War to the Present*, Cambridge: Cambridge University Press.

Wood, Nancy (1999), *Vectors of Memory: Legacies of Trauma in Post-War Europe*, London: Bloomsbury Publishing.

Worcman, Karen and Joanne Garde-Hansen, eds (2016), *Social Memory Technology: Theory, Practice, Action*, New York: Routledge.

Wright, Brendan (2018), "Divided Nation, Divided Memories," in Derek R. Mallett, ed., *Monumental Conflicts: Twentieth Century Wars and the Evolution of Public Memory*, 109–29, Oxford and New York: Routledge.

Wüstenberg, Jenny (2017), *Civil Society and Memory in Postwar Germany*, Cambridge: Cambridge University Press.

Yad Vashem (2018), "The Central Database of Shoah Victims' Names." Available online: https://yvng.yadvashem.org/ (accessed July 10, 2018).

Yang, Daqing and Mike Mochizuki, eds (2018), *Memory, Identity and Commemorations of World War II: Anniversary Politics in Asia Pacific*, Lanham: Lexington Books.

Young, Michael (2000), "The Sneer of Memory: Lebanon's Disappeared and Postwar Culture," *Middle East Report*, 217: 42–5.

Youngblood, Denise J. (2007), *Russian War Films: On the Cinema Front, 1914–2005*, Lawrence: University Press of Kansas.

Yoshida, Takashi (2006), *The Making of the "Rape of Nanking": History and Memory in Japan, China and the United States*, Oxford: Oxford University Press.

Zamponi, Lorenzo (2019), *Social Movements, Memory and Media: Narrative in Action in the Italian and Spanish Student Movements*, Basingstoke: Palgrave MacMillan.

Zamponi, Simonetta Falasca (2003), "Of Storytellers and Master Narratives: Modernity, Memory and History in Fascist Italy," in Jeffrey K. Olick, ed., *States of Memory: Continuities, Conflicts and Transformations in National Retrospection*, Durham, NC: Duke University Press, 43–71.

Zelizer, Barbie, ed. (2001), *Visual Culture and the Holocaust*, London: Athlone Press.

Zerubavel, Yael (1995), *Recovered Roots: Collective Memory and the Making of Israeli National Tradition*, Chicago: University of Chicago Press.

Zhu, Ying (2008), *Television in Post-Reform China. Serial Dramas, Confucian Leadership and the Global Television Market*, New York: Routledge.

Zhurzhenko, Tatiana (2015), "Shared Memory Culture? Nationalizing the 'Great Patriotic War' in the Ukrainian-Russian Borderlands," in Malgorzata Pakier and Joanna Wawrzyniak, eds, *Memory and Change in Europe: Eastern Perspectives*, 169–92, New York and Oxford: Berghahn.

Ziino, Bart, ed. (2015), *Remembering the First World War*, London: Routledge.

Zuboff, Shoshana (2019), *The Age of Surveillance Capitalism: The Fight for a Human Future at the Frontier of Power*, New York: Hachette.

CONTRIBUTORS

Stefan Berger is Professor of Social History and Director of the Institute for Social Movements at Ruhr-Universität Bochum, Germany. He is also executive chair of the Foundation History of the Ruhr in Bochum and an Honorary Professor at Cardiff University, UK. He has published widely on the memory of social movements, memory, and deindustrialization and the history of historiography and its relationship to identity building. Among his recent publications are *Constructing Industrial Pasts* (2020), *Social Movements and Memory* (2020), *Zeit-Räume Ruhr: Erinnerungsorte des Ruhrgebiets* (2019).

Patrick Finney is Reader in International History at the Department of International Politics, Aberystwyth University, UK. His recent publications include two edited volumes, *Remembering the Second World War* (2017) and *Authenticity: Reading, Remembering, Performing* (2018). He is Chair of the British International History Group and editor of the journal *Rethinking History*.

Wulf Kansteiner is Professor of History at Aarhus University, Denmark and has published in the fields of media history, memory studies, historical theory, and Holocaust studies. His research focuses on representations of history in film, TV, and digital media; the linguistic and narrative structures of historical writing; and the methods and theories of memory studies. He is the author of *In Pursuit of German Memory: History, Television, and Politics after Auschwitz* (2006) and, most recently, co-editor of *Probing the Ethics of Holocaust Culture* (2016). He is also co-founder and co-editor of the Sage-Journal *Memory Studies* (published since 2008).

Chris Lorenz is Professor Emeritus of German Historical Culture at VU University Amsterdam, The Netherlands and International Research Fellow at the Institute for Social Movements in Ruhr-University Bochum, Germany. His research themes comprise modern historiography, philosophy of history, and higher educational policies. His most recent book publications are: *Entre Filosofía e Historia. Volumen 1: Exploraciones en Filosofía de la Historia*, and *Volumen 2: Exploraciones en Historiografía* (2015); *Bordercrossings. Explorations between History and Philosophy* (2015); *Breaking Up Time. Negotiating the Borders between Present, Past and Future* (co-edited with Berber Bevernage, 2013); *Popularizing National Pasts: 1800 to the Present* (co-edited with Stefan Berger and Billie Melman, 2012); *Nationalizing the Past. Historians as Nation Builders in Modern Europe* (co-edited with Stefan Berger, 2010); and *"If you're so smart why aren't you rich?" Universiteit, Markt & Management*, (2008).

Bill Niven is Professor for Contemporary German History at Nottingham Trent University, UK. He has written widely on Germany's attempts to come to terms with the Nazi and GDR pasts, and, more recently, on European memory of the Holocaust. His monographs include *Facing the Nazi Past* (2001), *The Buchenwald Child* (2007), *Representations of*

Flight and Expulsion in East German Prose Works (2014), and *Hitler and Film: The Führer's Secret Passion* (2018). He is currently working on a history of the postwar reception of the Nazi film *Jud Süß*.

Jeffrey Olick is William R. Kenan, Jr. Professor of Sociology and History and Chair of the Sociology Department at the University of Virginia, USA. He is also Co-President of the Memory Studies Association (memorystudiesassociation.org). Olick is a cultural and historical sociologist whose work has focused on collective memory and commemoration, critical theory, transitional justice, postwar Germany, and sociological theory more generally. Forthcoming books include new translations and critical editions of two books by Maurice Halbwachs in collaboration with Sarah Daynes (UNC-Greensboro) (*The Collective Memory* and *The Legendary Topography of the Gospels in the Holy Land*). Further work, together with Christina Simko (Williams College), includes developing the outlines of what they call "tragic sociology."

Nick Tosh is a philosophy lecturer at the National University of Ireland, Galway, Ireland. He has published on the history of science methodology and on the interpretation of probability.

Jay Winter is Charles J. Stille Professor of History emeritus at Yale University, USA. He is an historian of the First World War, and the author of *Sites of Memory, Sites of Mourning: The Great War in European Cultural History* (1995), editor of *America and the Armenian Genocide* (2008), and editor-in-chief of the three-volume *Cambridge History of the First World War* (2014 and 2015). He has received honorary doctorates from the University of Graz, the Catholic University of Leuven, and the University of Paris—VIII. In 2017 he received the Victor Adler Prize of the Austrian government for a lifetime of work in history.

INDEX

aboriginal 29, 39, 112
Adugbo, Daniel 51, 52
Adorno, Theodor 56, 147, 151
Afghanistan, Afghan 28
Africa, African 9, 10, 12, 25, 28, 29, 39–41, 51–3, 71, 72, 107–9, 112, 126, 127, 160, 161, 164, 165, 167
Airikian, Paruir 25
Alfonsín, Raúl 162
Algeria, Algerian 8, 37–40, 108
Algerian War of Independence 40
Alzheimer 156
Amata, Jeta 51
Amazon Prime 51, 53
America, American 6, 9, 20, 25–7, 29, 62, 66, 89, 93, 97, 107, 108, 124–32, 134, 151, 167, 168, 170, 172
    African- 160, 161
    Civil War 160
    Irish- 152
    Italian- 152
    North 39, 43, 97, 103, 111
American Psychiatric Association 27
amnesia 59, 153, 165
    collective 157
    structural 157, 158
amnesty 25, 164–7
Amnesty International 25
ancien regime 157
Anderson, Benedict 71, 127, 147, 151, 156
Annales School 16, 17
anthropology ix, x, 104
anti-Nazism 5
antisemitism 5
Arabia, Arab 10, 18, 25, 33, 42, 80, 81, 85, 89
archive 19, 27, 36, 48, 68, 97, 98, 108, 132, 136, 137, 157
Argentina, Argentinian 25, 162, 163
    Dirty War 162
Arlington Cemetery 24
Armenia, Armenian 25, 26, 28, 49, 59, 66
army 20, 38, 89, 105, 158
    Red 5, 159, 160

Asia 12, 16, 59, 107, 126, 127, 151
Asian-Americans 151
Assassin's Creed 54
Assmann, Aleida 4, 19, 31–3, 39, 44, 45, 47–9, 116, 157, 158
Assmann, Jan 4, 19, 31, 48, 116
Athens, Athenian 166
Attwood, Brian 39
Auschwitz 24, 25, 43, 59, 64, 69, 70, 115, 136, 152, 167, 170, 172
    Trials 25, 42
Austria 29, 93, 99, 130, 168
Australia, Australian 29, 39, 98, 99, 102, 112
Azerbaijan 28

Babelsberg 55
Babylon 8, 18
Bakhtin, Mikhail Mikhailovich
Bali 17
Balkans 3
Baltic 5
Bangladesh 28
Basinger, Kim 51
Beck, Ulrich 53
Ben-Gurion, David 25
Benjamin, Walter 33, 140, 148, 152
Berlin 14, 15, 24, 27, 108, 118, 123, 160, 161
Biafran secession 52
Bible, biblical 6, 76, 129
Bitburg 27
black critical memory 10
Black November 51–3
Bloch, Marc 37
Bodnar, John 6, 132
Bollywood 55
Bolshevism, Bolshevikh 120
    revolution 19, 101, 102, 120
Bourdieu, Pierre 146
Borges, Jorge Luis 156
Bourgeoisie 120, 151
Borrows, John 39
Bosnia 33, 40, 105, 106, 168, 169
Braudel, Fernand 37

Britain, British 8, 20, 22–4, 26, 29, 86, 88, 89, 97–9, 102, 108, 111, 112, 115–18, 122–6, 131, 137–9, 168–71
Bronze Soldier, The 159, 160
Buchenwald 152, 160, 208
Buenos Aires
　Rio de la Plata 162
Burckhardt, Jacob ix
Burma 28
Byelorussia 11

Les cadres sociaux de la mémoire (Halbwachs 1925) 33
Caesar 166
Cambodia, Cambodian 9, 66, 169, 172
Cambridge 85, 98
　Psychological Laboratory 76, 82, 83
　School ix
Canberra 29
capitalism 53, 72, 109, 110, 127, 151
　electronic 151
　print 151
　surveillance 53
Cape Town
　University of 28
Caribbean 39
catholicism, catholic 103, 106, 107
cemetery 20–2, 24, 27
Cenotaph 22–4
Chakrabarty, Dipesh 13, 49
Charleston, SC 29, 160
Chartier, Roger x
Chile, Chilean 25, 163, 164
　Pinochet regime 163
China, Chinese 8, 10, 19, 59, 60, 101, 110, 111, 126, 131, 134, 151, 170
　Authorities 59
Chomsky, Marvin J. 7
church 19, 20, 23, 24, 29, 107, 122, 160
　Armenian Apostolic 28
　catholic 18, 107
　orthodox 28, 120
Cicero 166
cinema 9, 51, 53, 54, 56–9, 61, 65, 119, 120, 123–6
　of attraction 56
　first 58
　New German 57
　second 58
　third 58
class x, 3, 15, 16, 18, 20, 96, 101, 109–12, 119, 120, 146, 148, 149, 151
　consciousness 151

Clemenceau, Georges 167
climate 9, 53, 59, 152
　change 9, 59, 152
　death 53, 59
colonialism, colonial 9, 10, 12, 18, 34, 37, 39, 40, 47, 52, 58, 107–9, 126, 131, 168
　empire 39, 58
commission 20, 21, 156, 160, 162, 164, 165, 167
　truth 164, 165
commemoration 6, 7, 12, 17–19, 24, 47, 108
commonwealth 20, 21, 108
Comte, August 139, 141
computing 9, 19, 86, 89, 131
communalism, communalist 10, 109
communism, communist 5, 10–12, 14, 16, 18, 25–8, 43, 46, 100–5, 109–11, 115, 120, 126, 127, 131, 132, 135, 158–60, 165
　crimes 165
　party 18, 25, 115, 127
　Soviet 5, 127
　violence 160
communication 33, 48, 64, 68, 69, 88, 119, 157
communicative memory 19, 33, 48
CONDEP 162
Confederate States of America, Confederacy 24, 28, 29, 160, 161
Conference on Jewish Material Claims Against Germany 172
conflict 5, 9–11, 15, 17, 24, 28, 29, 39, 40, 42, 102, 118, 123, 130, 132–4, 137, 138, 157, 158, 164–6
　civil 157
Connerton, Paul 33, 157, 158
constitution, constitutional xi, 10, 11, 89, 101
consumption habits 146
contracts 146
Cook, James 29, 161
Coontz, Stephanie 148
Coser, Lewis Alfred 1
cosmopolitanization 43
cosmopolitanism 7, 16, 34, 42, 43, 52–4, 58–60, 64, 66, 68–73, 134, 167–9
crime 13, 17, 25, 27, 57, 60, 62, 64–6, 71, 134, 135, 156, 164, 165, 167, 169
　tribunals 164
Crow, Jim 161
Cuba, Cuban 19, 130
cult of the dead 145

culture, ix, x, xiii, 2, 6–13, 18, 28, 32, 34, 37, 39, 42, 46, 49, 51–6, 58–72, 95, 96, 99, 100, 105–13, 115–20, 122, 126, 127, 129, 130, 132–6, 151, 153, 157, 158, 170, 207
   digital interactive 55
   film 55, 56, 59
   high ix, 109, 115, 118
   memorial 8, 10, 42, 108–12
   of modernity 56
   national 10, 11
   popular 55, 64, 115–21, 129, 132, 136
   print 55
   visual 8, 54, 55, 64, 65
culturalization 49
cultural viii–xii, 1–3, 7–11, 13, 14, 16, 19, 31, 32, 34, 39–42, 45, 47–9, 53, 55–60, 63–7, 69, 72, 73, 75, 84, 93, 95, 102, 107, 109, 112, 113, 115–18, 122, 126–31, 134, 135, 137, 139, 142, 143, 146, 151, 152, 156, 168, 170–2
   Inheritance 143
capital 146
Czechoslovakia 168

Daily Trust 51, 52
Dark Web 152
Darnton, Robert ix
Darwin, Charles Robert 1, 76, 143
Davidovich, Joshua 168
decolonization 7, 8, 19, 28, 32, 39, 40, 95, 107, 110, 127, 131
De Gaulle, Charles 36
democracy ix, 14, 16, 17, 24, 25, 60, 69, 99, 102–4, 110, 119, 120, 122, 130, 132, 136, 155, 159, 160, 162, 164
democratization 17, 155, 159, 160
Derrida, Jacques 15
Los Desaparecidos 162
diaspora, diasporic 10, 34
dictatorship 18, 27, 111, 164, 165
digital 9, 19, 53–6, 59, 66–72, 88–91, 117, 119, 131, 132, 134, 136, 156
   games 56, 134
   memory 19, 53, 66, 68
Dinur, Yihiel 24
doctrine 88, 145
dogma 145
Dresden 152
Drug 9, 162
Dubs, Alf 170
   Dubs Amendment 170

Durkheim, Emile x, 33, 35, 37, 139, 141–6, 148, 149, 151, 153

East, Eastern 9, 10, 13, 20, 43, 71, 72, 99–101, 104, 110, 111, 127, 129–131, 135, 139, 160, 165, 167, 170
   Far 10, 99, 100
   Middle 9, 71, 170
Ebbinghaus, Hermann 1, 9, 75, 76, 80–85, 87, 91, 92
ecological disasters 53
ecology 72, 122, 145, 146
economy, economic viii–x, 33, 35, 37, 51–3, 71, 72, 86, 98, 110–12, 119, 127, 131, 132, 140, 149, 151
   exploitation 52
   globalized 53
   history x, 9
Edict of Nantes 166
Eichmann, Adolf 24, 25, 42
   Trial 25
Elementary Forms of Religious Life, The (Kant, 1912) 143
Eley, Geoff 156
Emanuel African Methodist Episcopal Church 29
empire, imperial 3, 7, 8, 10, 18, 20, 23, 26, 28, 31, 37, 39, 56, 58, 97, 98, 107–9, 111, 122, 125, 127, 130, 131, 134, 138
environment, environmental 1, 2, 35, 47, 51, 52, 59, 61, 66, 69, 102, 127
   crisis 52
   pollution 59
   socio-historical 1
Erll, Astrid 4, 31, 34, 39
Estonia, Estonian 9, 135, 159, 160
ethnicity, ethnic 5, 7, 10, 11, 13, 15, 34, 42, 52, 106, 111, 129, 151, 152
   cleansing 7, 13, 106, 152
ethics, ethical 52, 62–5, 69–71, 118, 156, 168
Europe, European 3, 5, 11, 12, 14–16, 18, 20, 26, 27, 29, 34, 39, 42, 43, 49, 51, 52, 56, 58, 60–4, 69–72, 76, 84, 98–106, 108–11, 118, 122, 124, 126, 127, 130, 131, 135, 136, 138, 140, 143, 149, 155, 163, 165, 167, 170
   Eastern 71, 72, 100, 101, 104, 110, 111, 130, 131, 135, 165
   Western 43, 100, 127, 130, 140, 143
   Welfare states 58
European Research Council 15

European Union 3, 12, 26, 100, 105, 108, 135
events
    forgotten 155
    neglected 155
exhibition 135, 136, 170

fascism, fascist 11, 12, 18, 26, 58, 60, 61, 98, 102–5, 109, 123, 125, 132, 159, 160
Feldman, Alexander Dmitrievich 25
film 53–61, 63–6, 68, 72, 73, 109, 116–27, 129–32, 134–6, 157, 168, 170–2
    culture 55, 56, 59
    experimental 55, 57, 58
    Francophone 168
    historical 55, 120, 121, 123, 124
First World War 1, 5, 13, 17, 22, 55, 58, 96, 97, 98, 99, 105, 117, 118, 119, 120, 125, 137, 138, 140, 141, 152, 155, 163, 167
Forever Project, The 171
forgetting xiii, 1, 6, 7, 33, 39, 55, 68, 75, 80, 81, 84, 155–9, 163–7, 169–71
    by annulment 157
    automatic 157
    complicit 157
    constructive 157
    defensive 157
    repressive 157
    sanctioned 167
    selective 157, 166
    therapeutic 158
Foucault, Michel 33
    Foucauldian 15
framing viii, 13, 32, 34, 39, 40, 44, 54, 113, 133
    national 40
France, French x, 2–4, 10, 20, 22, 24, 31, 33, 35–9, 45, 58, 70, 97, 101, 103, 106, 108, 109, 116, 125, 139, 144, 146, 157, 167, 168,
    Colonialism 37
    history of 33, 106
    Indochina 38
    military 38
    national politics 36
    New Wave 58
    Revolution 45, 101, 157
    Vichy- 37, 38, 116
Franco-German Studies 10
Franco, Francisco 18, 25, 103, 106, 164
Freud, Sigmund 1, 33, 75–81, 83, 86, 93, 94, 143
Funes el memorioso (Borges, 1942) 156

Gallocentric 39
Gemeinschaft und Gesellschaft (Tönnies, 1887) 141
gender 16, 20, 52, 96, 110, 112, 116, 119, 130, 151
genocide xi, xii, 7, 9, 13, 15, 26, 28, 33, 40, 43, 49, 52, 59, 60, 62, 64–7, 69–71, 118, 130, 135, 164, 167–9, 172
    Armenian 26, 49, 66
    in Bosnia 40
    Cambodian 172
    Nazi 40, 52, 64, 66, 130
    Rwandan 172
Georgia, Georgian 11
Germany, German ix, 4, 5, 7, 8, 10,a 13, 20, 22, 25, 27, 33, 42, 43, 58, 61–6, 70, 71, 73, 81, 82, 97–9, 101–3, 106, 108, 110, 115, 118, 119, 121–5, 130, 131, 137, 141, 155–7, 160, 164–8, 170, 172
    culture 157
    East 13, 160, 167
    Enquete Commissions 165
    postwar 130, 157
    reunification 43
    West 7, 25, 33, 62, 64, 103, 110, 160, 164
German War Graves Commission (*see* Volksbund Deutsche Kriegsgräberfürsorge) 20
German Federal Republic (GFR/BRD, *see* Germany, West)
Gettysburg 29
Glasnost 159
global ix, xii, 5–9, 12, 13, 16, 32, 34, 40, 42, 43, 47, 49, 52, 53, 57–60, 70, 72, 73, 93, 99, 101–5, 107, 109, 111, 126, 127, 131, 132, 136, 151, 155, 167
    village 151
    warming 47, 59
Goldmann, Lucien x
Goldhagen debate 172
Gorbachev, Mikhail 159
Graz, University of 29
Great War (*see* World War, first)
Greek 23, 91, 139
groups x, xi, 1–3, 6, 10, 11, 13, 15–17, 19, 22, 33–7, 39, 40, 48, 51, 57, 60, 66, 70, 71, 90, 95, 104, 120, 126, 132, 138, 141, 143–8, 151, 152, 159, 172
    collective identity of 35
    indigenous 39
guest-workers 58
Gulag 13, 25

INDEX

Habermas, Jürgen 16, 140
Halbwachs, Maurice xi, 1–3, 6–8, 15, 17, 31, 33–5, 37, 39, 41, 95, 143–9, 151, 152, 157
Hartmann, Geoffrey 27
Hartley, Leslie Poles 141
Hartog, François 31, 32, 44, 45, 47, 48
heritage 5, 14, 36, 47–9, 78, 110–12, 122
heroes of memory 13
Hervieu-Léger, Danièle 149
Hirsch, Marianne 4, 117
Hiroshima 43, 152
historia magistra vitae 45, 47
history viii–9, 13, 15–18, 24–6, 29, 31–3, 35–42, 44, 45, 47, 48, 51–9, 62–9, 72, 75, 77–80, 82, 90, 95, 98, 99, 102–9, 112, 117–20, 123, 129–31, 136–9, 141–3, 147, 148, 152, 155, 156, 159, 160, 163, 167, 169, 172
   of civil wars 8, 95
   claims of 41
   Colonial 108
   of concepts ix
   decolonization 40
   of decolonization 8, 95, 107
   of deindustrialization 8, 95, 110, 112
   Education 54
   European 5
   of everyday life ix
   of forgetting 155
   formal 37
   imperial 39
   of memory viii–1, 9, 15, 16, 18, 53, 55, 75, 117, 119, 139, 141, 142, 147, 155
   national 3, 6, 33, 36, 37, 39, 55, 98, 123, 131
   normal 44
   oral 4, 108
   professional ix, 8, 32, 54, 55, 62, 68, 69, 85, 95, 138
   real 47
   of revolutions 8, 95
   of surveillance 160
   of suppression 160
   wars 41
   Workshop ix
historical anthropology ix, x
historical ethno-symbolism 5
historical memory Law 164
historian ix–xi, 2, 4, 7, 8, 10, 14, 15, 18, 28, 31–3, 37, 39, 42, 48, 49, 55, 57, 76, 94, 95, 97, 98, 100, 103, 105–8, 112, 143, 148, 152, 156
   cultural x, 156
   film 57
Hitler, Adolf 5, 24, 99, 103, 122, 133, 156, 170, 172
Hitler's Willing Executioners (Goldhagen 1996) 172
Hollywood 53, 55–8, 124, 125, 129
holocaust xii, 7–10, 12, 13, 15, 24–7, 32, 33, 39, 40, 42, 43, 47, 48, 52, 54, 58, 60–73, 95, 98, 99, 115, 118, 119, 130, 131, 133–6, 155, 156, 162, 163, 166–72
   cosmopolitanism of 169
   Intergovernmental Conference on the, The 43
   studies 42
   survivor 26, 131, 136
Holocaust (TV-series 1978)
Holocaust Memorial Day, HMD 167
Holocene 59
Horizon 2020, Unrest (EU-Project) 16
Horkheimer, Max 151
Huizinga, Johan ix
humanities 4
human rights 7, 25, 44, 47, 49, 52, 53, 60, 65, 66, 69, 70, 71, 73, 98, 100, 132, 155, 164, 165, 167, 168
   discourse 44, 155
   movement 25
   Universal Declaration of 25
Hunt, Lynn x
Hussein, Saddam 8, 18
Huyssen, Andreas 15, 33, 167

Iberian Peninsula 3
iconography 20, 56, 66
identity 3, 10, 13, 22, 32, 33, 35, 36, 39–42, 47–9, 66, 73, 95, 98, 99, 105, 110, 122–4, 126, 131, 133, 144, 151, 157, 158
   collective 13, 32, 35, 48
   cultural 40, 48
   national 3, 99, 105, 123, 126, 131, 133
   personal 144
ideology, ideological 11, 12, 72, 115, 117, 120, 122, 124, 126, 129, 130, 134
imperialism 7, 10, 28, 107–9, 125, 127, 130, 131
   western 7

India, Indian 8, 10, 19, 28, 84, 85, 102, 109, 123
indigenious 18, 39, 56, 127
　first nations 39, 112
individualization 52
Indonesia, Indonesian 9, 17, 26, 109
industrial
　era 141
　heritage 14, 110–12
industrialization 5, 8, 52, 56, 95, 110–12, 140
inflation 152, 155
In Praise of Forgetting (Rieff, 2016) 166
intellectual history ix, x
internet 17, 19, 26, 52, 131, 136
Interwar Period 2, 12, 17, 24, 97
Iraq 53, 66, 166
Islam, Islamic 28, 52, 106, 107, 131
Israel, Isreali 10, 25, 42, 53, 73, 119, 162, 166, 170
　/Palestine Conflict 166
Italy, Italian 13, 14, 18, 24, 58, 98, 101, 125, 152
　Neo-Realism 58

Japan, Japanese 10, 28, 99, 101, 111, 125, 126, 131, 134, 151, 170
Jerusalem 24, 25
Jewry, 12, 70
Johnson, Lyndon Baines 29
Judaism, Jewish 6, 10, 20, 28, 62, 122, 168, 172
　Jewishness 10, 168
Jung, Carl Gustav 1, 2, 5, 143, 151
justice 7, 16, 25, 34, 47, 49, 51, 52, 127, 132, 155, 160, 161, 164–6, 169, 170
　corrective 164
　distributive 164
　social 16, 165
　transitional 161, 164–6, 170

Kamikaze 28
Kandel, Eric 9, 93
Kansteiner, Wulf 4, 7–9, 13, 16, 95, 99, 168
Kant, Immanuel 143, 152
KGB 28
Khrushchev, Nikita 159
Kindertransport 168, 171
King, Martin Luther 29
Klee, Paul 152
Kohl, Helmut 27, 28
Kollektivsingular 45

Kollwitz, Käthe 27
Konrad, Helmut 29
Korea, Korean 8–10, 19, 128, 151, 158, 166
　north 166
　south 9, 158, 166
　Civil War 158
　People's Army 158
Koselleck, Reinhart ix, 35, 45
Kosovo, Kosovan 33, 43, 133
Kosovocaust 43

labor 3, 14, 33, 72, 105, 141, 151
Lagerfeld, Karl 170
Landsberg, Alison 56, 117
language x, xii, 13, 18, 28, 57, 58, 63, 76, 94, 102, 121, 143, 145, 146, 151
　visual 57
Latin America, Latin American 9, 59, 66, 107, 126, 131
Latour, Bruno 44, 49
Lebanon, Lebanese 28, 164
Lee, Robert Edward 24, 161, 162
Leftist 36, 130, 159
　Revolutionary politics 36
Levy, Daniel 7, 31, 32, 42, 43, 167
Lévy-Bruhl, Lucien 1
liberalism, liberal 11, 16, 57, 72, 97, 98, 102, 110, 127, 128, 132, 142, 159
liberation 6, 12, 59, 64, 109, 159, 160, 170
Libya, Libyan 28
Lieux de mémoire (see Realms of Memory)
lifetime employment 151
linguistic turn x
local 7, 24, 34, 35, 36, 40, 43, 91, 92, 106, 111, 147, 151, 163, 164
Lübbe, Hermann 164
Lumiére brothers 54
lustration 164, 165
Lutyens, Sir Edward 22, 24

Mabo Decision 29
Macdougal, Brenda 39
McLuhan, Marshall 151
Maier, Charles S. 43
Malawi, Malawi 28
Mandela, Nelson 25, 28
Mannheim, Karl 1, 2
Margalit, Avishai 158
Marx, Karl ix, 139, 140, 150, 151
Marxism, Marxist iii, vix, x, 11, 15, 56, 101, 102, 120

INDEX 215

Marxist historiography ix
massacre 26, 36, 66, 109, 122
mass violence 61, 72, 152
May 1st 12
media xiii, 6, 9, 13, 34, 41, 52–6, 58–61,
    63–9, 71, 72, 93–5, 112, 116, 118,
    119, 121, 122, 129, 132–6, 138, 149,
    151, 161, 157, 159, 161–3, 166,
    169–71
  cultures 151
  digital 55, 59, 72
  Landscape 52, 61
  mass 34, 53, 55, 60, 64
  national 151
  platforms 55, 56
  social 9, 56, 63, 67, 69, 71, 119, 132, 136,
    138, 149
  technologies 56, 72
  theorists 151
  visual 53, 58
Meier, Christian 166, 167
melting pot 148
Memorial Day 28, 135, 167
memorial 7–12, 14, 15, 22–4, 28, 31, 36, 40,
    42, 54, 62, 64, 77, 95, 98, 100, 102,
    103, 195, 108, 109, 167–70
  confederate 161
memorialisation 7, 8, 22, 98, 112, 160
  guerrilla 161
memory, memorial
  activism 7, 13, 14, 15, 16, 54, 97, 112
  agonistic 7, 16, 39, 40
  alternative 158–9
  antagonistic 7, 16
  anthropcen, ic 53, 73
  authentic 37
  boom 3, 8, 20, 24, 26–9, 31–35, 44, 131,
    132, 136–8
  borders of 40
  chains of 149
  class 149
  collective 1–3, 5–8, 17, 19, 31–7, 39, 42,
    55, 58, 59, 60, 63, 95, 97, 104, 106,
    142–6, 148, 151, 152, 157, 165, 166
  colonial 39, 108
  communicative 19, 33, 48, 60
  of communist dictatorships 12
  continuous 145
  cosmopolitan 7, 16, 42, 43, 52–4, 60, 64,
    66, 68, 69, 71–3
  cultural xi, 1, 8–10, 19, 34, 39, 42, 47–9,
    55, 102, 116, 117, 170–2, 176

  cultural history of viii, xi, xii, 1, 9, 16, 75,
    139, 142,
  culture 8–13, 42, 51–6, 58–60, 63–9, 72,
    96, 99, 100, 105–7, 109, 110, 112,
    113, 205
  digital 19, 53, 66, 68, 183
  of disappearance 163
  of discrimination 155, 161, 169
  European 16, 43, 52, 63, 64
  false 148
  family 145, 148, 149
  frames of 34, 39
  functional 157
  genetic 1
  group 2, 3, 6, 33, 35, 144
  global xii, 73, 102
  globital 53
  Holocaust 7, 8, 12, 27, 32, 33, 40, 42, 43,
    60, 61, 63–5, 67, 70, 72, 73, 134–6,
    166–72
  historical 13, 37, 100, 109, 164, 166
  history xi, xii, 4, 6, 9, 35, 106
  human 9, 40, 48, 53, 75, 76, 81, 82, 92,
    94, 172
  hypertrophy of 15, 167
  inauthentic 37
  individual xi, 9, 143, 144, 163
  of injustice 160
  knots of 39
  law 12, 164
  loss 156
  of migration 10
  multi-cultural, transcultural 8, 10, 34,
    42
  multidirectional 31, 39, 40, 42, 168
  of murder 163
  national xii, 4–7, 10, 12, 13, 37, 39, 51,
    52, 53, 99, 100, 106, 112, 167
  non-traumatic 42
  official 6, 120, 160
  oral 39
  palimpsestic 168
  park 162
  places of 39, 142
  political 158
  progressive 58, 156
  project 6, 34, 39
  public 10, 15, 99, 102, 103, 106–10, 112,
    164
  racial 151
  real environments of 35
  recognition 40

regime 16, 18, 19, 57, 72, 168
regional 51
scholars xii, 6, 13, 15, 31, 33, 34, 39, 41, 45, 151, 167
science 9, 75, 76, 94
silence 158
sites of 6, 26, 31, 33, 34, 35, 36, 37, 39, 65
shared 145
social 37, 53, 67, 139, 143, 148, 151
social frames of 34
spontaneous 35
state 6, 7, 18, 158, 163
state-ordained 159
of struggle 151
struggle of 164
surfeit of 43, 166
surveillance 53
studies xi–xiii, 1, 2, 4, 5, 7, 9, 12–16, 31–4, 39–42, 44, 45, 49, 55, 64, 68, 115, 117, 167
strategies 58
technologies of xi, 56, 149
transhuman 53
traumatic 5, 13, 27, 42, 44, 161
trends 5, 172
twentieth century 7, 9, 59, 75, 94, 108, 139
unreal 36
vernacular 6, 11
of victimhood 99
of violence 9
wars 13, 29, 42, 96, 112
work 34, 40, 41, 59, 164, 166
Memory Studies Association xii, 4
methodological nationalism xii, 6, 40
micro-history ix
Middle Ages 35
militant 51, 52
    Islamist struggle 52
military 17, 18, 26, 27, 37, 38, 73, 124, 130, 134, 162, 168
migration 7, 10, 34, 38, 40, 41, 58, 59, 71, 72, 111, 131, 149, 151, 170
    background 40
    patterns of 149
    postcolonial 40
Missing of the Somme 163
mnemnohistory 33
mnemonic practices 118, 143
Mobilization (journal) 14
modernism, modernist xii, 5, 31, 48, 58

modernity, modern xii, 1, 4, 6–9, 31–3, 35, 36, 39, 40, 44–9, 52, 53, 55–8, 60, 127, 141, 148, 149
    world 47, 148, 149
modernization ix, 49, 107, 127, 141
moral compass 172
Moses and Monotheism (Freud, 1939) 143
Mosse, George 6, 18
Moscow 19, 130
movement ix, 3, 5, 11–16, 18, 19, 24–6, 29, 36, 58–61, 77, 82, 95, 98, 99, 102–7, 109–12, 122, 130, 132, 149, 151, 161
    1968 13
    civil rights 14, 29, 161
    labor 151
    revolutionary
    social 3, 11, 13–16, 61, 95, 102, 103, 110, 112
    student 13, 103
    womens' 3, 102, 112
    working-class 18
Moyn, Sam 44, 156
museum, museal xi, 7, 10, 26, 28, 36, 48, 54, 64, 68, 69, 116, 117, 122, 132, 134, 135, 144, 160, 168, 170–2
Muslim 109, 133, 170
Mussolini, Benito 24, 125

Nagasaki 43
nation, national viii, ix, 5–8, 12, 16, 18, 20, 22, 24, 31, 33–40, 42, 43, 45, 48, 51–3, 55, 61, 64, 97–103, 105–7, 109, 110, 112, 113, 123, 124, 126, 127, 129, 131, 133, 134, 136, 138, 144, 146–8, 151, 156–8, 160, 163–72
    exclusion 52
    first 39, 112
    French 3, 4, 33, 36
    supra- 34, 39
    traditions 169
    unification 52
nationalism, nationalistic xii, 2, 5, 6, 8, 12, 28, 35, 36, 40, 52, 60, 100, 109
narrative xi, 5–8, 13, 17–19, 24, 28, 29, 37, 42, 53, 55–62, 65–9, 71, 72, 80, 85, 97, 99–101, 103–5, 110, 111, 123, 129, 131, 132, 134, 158, 159, 167
    historical 5, 67, 100, 103, 110, 131, 134
    western-centric 58

Nazism, National Socialism 1, 5, 12, 15, 24–8, 30, 40, 42, 52, 54, 60–2, 64–6, 69, 70, 97–9, 102, 103, 109, 115, 116, 119, 121–5, 130, 133–6, 152, 156, 160, 162, 166, 169, 170
   past 30, 42, 54, 62
Neue Wache 24, 27
Neuzeit 141
new cultural history ix, x
New Dimensions in Testimony 171
New Orleans 29
New Left 42
Niger Delta 51
Nigeria, Nigerian 10, 51, 52
   activists 51
   corruption 52
   nationalism 52
   oil bonanza 52
Nigerian National Petroleum Corporation 51
Nobel Peace Prize 25
Nora, Pierre x, 3, 8, 10, 11, 15, 31–37, 39, 40, 41, 48, 95, 141, 147
nostalgia 57, 60, 132, 137, 148, 165
Novick, Peter 65
Nuremberg trials 24

Olick, Jeffrey K. 4, 8, 34, 44
Oostindie, Gert 40
Oxfam, Oxford Committee on Famine Relief 25, 170
   Report 170
On Collective Memory (Halbwachs, 1950) 31, 33, 37, 148

Pact of Forgetting 164
Pakistan 28
Palestine, Palestinian 8, 10, 19, 28, 53, 166
   /Israel Conflict 166
   Nakba 166
Panama 28
Paris 12, 22, 36, 42, 102, 142, 168, 170
Paris Commune 12, 36, 102
party (political) 17, 18, 25, 83, 85, 97, 105, 107, 109, 115, 127, 120, 169,
Peace Treaty of Westphalia 166
perennialism 5
Peru Truth and Reconciliation Commission 165
photograph 28, 53, 132, 149, 161, 162
pied noirs 3
Plato 1, 82, 91, 92, 94, 156
Pocock, John Greville Agar ix

Poland, Polish 5, 17, 26, 28, 65, 70, 102, 135, 136, 156, 169, 170
   Law and Justice Party 169
   Senate 169
political history viii–x, 98
political language x
politics x, xiii, 5, 6, 11, 13, 15, 16–19, 28–30, 34, 36, 41–5, 49, 53, 61, 62, 64, 67, 69, 71, 95, 98, 104, 107, 109, 113, 123, 124, 126, 132, 151, 160, 170
   reparation 34, 43
pollution 9, 47, 51, 58, 59
postcolonialism, postcolonial 9, 10, 32, 34, 39, 40, 58, 72, 107–9
   condition 39
   settler 39
post-Holocaust 32, 39
poststructuralist x
postmodern 36
   times 36
post-traumatic stress disorder 27
post-War 5, 38, 43, 54, 57, 58, 61–4, 75, 115, 119, 127, 130, 131, 157, 164
   consumerism 57
   immigration 38
poverty 9, 110
primordialism 5
presentism 45, 47
Principles of Sociology (Spencer, 1898) 139
proletariat 45, 102, 151
Proust, Marcel 48
Prussian 24
psychology 27, 58, 76, 77, 80–3, 85–7, 90, 92, 93, 95, 142, 156

racism, racist 1, 12, 16, 58, 72, 73, 136, 160
race 10, 28, 29, 96, 110, 111, 112, 151, 155
radio 17, 19, 60, 68, 72, 88, 119, 126, 127, 151
rationalization 84, 140
Realms of Memory (Nora 1984–92) x, 3, 10, 141
Red Square 19
refugee 58, 59, 70, 71, 106, 133, 149, 152, 170
   children 170
   crisis 152, 170
Regimes of Historicity. Presentism and experiences of time (Hartog 2015) 45

region, regional 3, 5, 7, 11, 34, 36, 40, 51, 92, 93, 110–12, 119, 126, 163
religion, religious xiii, 3, 6, 8, 17, 28, 33, 35, 48, 52, 85, 95, 106, 107, 112, 130, 132, 143–6, 148, 149, 151
  Jewish 6
  life 143, 149
  membership 149
  organization 149
  practice 145, 149
Remembering, repeating and working through (Freud 1914) 1
remembering xi, xiii, 1, 5, 7, 25, 33, 39, 60, 68, 71, 75, 80, 82–6, 94, 104, 116, 117, 144, 155, 156, 158, 166–9, 171, 172
  selective 158
remembrance 14, 17, 18, 20, 25–8, 34, 40, 41, 54, 56–8, 61, 66, 72, 105, 109, 110, 112, 134, 136
Renan, Ernest 39, 146, 147, 150
resistance 5, 17, 18, 24, 27, 52, 58, 60, 61, 72, 99, 100, 103, 116, 121, 126, 134, 160
revolution 7, 8, 11, 12, 17, 19, 22, 24, 36, 45, 52, 54, 68, 76, 86, 88, 95, 101–3, 107, 110, 112, 120, 123, 130, 132, 143, 157, 159, 160
  gender 52
Reynolds, Henry 29
Rhodes, Cecil 28
Rieff, David 166, 168
rights 7, 14, 25, 29, 44, 47, 49, 53, 60, 65, 66, 69–71, 73, 98, 100, 111, 112, 129, 132, 135, 155, 160, 161, 164, 165, 167, 168
  civil 14, 29, 129, 161
  human 7, 25, 44, 47, 49, 52, 53, 60, 65, 66, 69–71, 73, 98, 100, 132, 155, 164, 165, 167, 168
Rigney, Ann 4, 15, 31, 34, 39–41
ritual xiii, 6, 20, 53, 56, 68, 72, 117, 127, 139, 143, 145, 149, 164
Robben Island 28
Romania 131, 165
  post-Communist 165
  Presidential Commission for the Analysis of the Communist Dictatorship in Romania 165
Rome, roman 24, 122, 166
  senate 166
Reagan, Ronald 27, 129
Roof, Dylann 29, 160, 161

Rothberg, Michael 4, 31, 33, 38, 39, 40, 64, 72, 168
Rourke, Mickey 51
Rules of Sociological Method (Durkheim, 1895) 142
Runia, Eelco 44
Russia, Russian 11, 12, 20, 24, 36, 60, 70, 97, 101–3, 111, 121, 129, 160, 166
Russian Revolution 102, 103
Rwanda, Rwandan(ese) 9, 33, 60, 66, 164, 165, 169, 172
  International Criminal Tribunal for 164
  post-genocide 164
  Government of National Unity 165
  Hutu 165
  Patriotic Front 165
  Tutsi 165

Sabrow Comission 160
Sachsenhausen 160
sacred 36, 46, 143, 149
Saladin 18
Sakharov, Andre 25
Second World War 2, 5, 7, 10, 13, 17, 18, 24, 25, 26, 27, 28, 33, 43, 52, 59, 60, 61, 62, 64, 73, 89, 97–100, 102, 105, 107, 110, 115, 116, 118, 119, 125, 130–3, 136, 137, 167
scandal 64, 156
Scandinavia 3
Schacter, Daniel 156–8
secularization 107, 148, 149
Semon, Richard 143
shell shock 27
Shinto 28
Sieyès, Emmanuel-Joseph 139
Silberman, Max 168
Simiand, Francois 37
Singing Revolution 160
sins 51, 156
  of commission 156
  of memory 156
  of omission 156
Skinner, Quentin ix
slavery 6, 28, 29, 34, 37, 39, 40, 47–9, 67
social viii–xi, xiii, 1–4, 6, 8–16, 18, 20, 25, 33–5, 37, 39, 53–7, 60, 61, 63–9, 71, 72, 82, 95, 97–105, 109, 110, 112, 117–19, 123, 124, 126, 127, 129–33, 136, 138, 139–44, 146–9, 151–3, 155–8, 160, 164, 165, 170

INDEX

classes 2, 110, 144, 146, 149
conflict 9
evolution 157
facts 142
fragmentation 57
frameworks 143
history viii, ix, 98, 155
institutions 144, 149
media 9, 56, 63, 67, 69, 71, 119, 132, 133, 136, 138, 149
nature 143
organization 143
sciences 4, 139
Social Frameworks of Memory, The (Halbwachs, 1925) xi, 144
socialism, socialist 11, 12, 18, 25, 100, 101, 102, 103, 105, 109, 112, 127, 130, 131, 164
socialization 2, 144
society x, xiii, 1, 6, 7, 11–13, 15, 17–20, 24–6, 33–5, 37, 39, 42, 45, 51, 55, 64, 69, 71, 77, 78, 79, 98, 107, 110, 112, 117, 130, 134, 139–47, 153, 157, 160, 166, 168
classless 12
reconfiguration of 142
temporal 145
sociologist xi, 1, 4, 25, 112, 139, 140, 146, 149, 151, 152, 207
sociology 2, 95, 139, 141, 142, 143, 207, 208
solidarity 5, 16, 53, 59, 124, 126, 141, 144, 148, 151, 153
ethnic 5
South Africa, South African 25, 28, 112, 164, 165
Truth and Reconciliation Commission 164
Soviet 5, 11, 19, 25, 26, 28, 97, 104, 115, 116, 120, 121, 123, 127, 129, 130, 131, 135, 136, 156, 158, 159, 160, 166
Invasion of Poland 156
Foreign Minister 156
soldiers 159
Special Camps 160
Union 5, 11, 25, 28, 104, 115, 116, 120, 121, 130, 159
space xiii, 6, 12, 13, 23, 24, 27, 31–49, 53, 56, 58, 61, 86, 117, 118, 132, 133, 143, 145, 149
Spain, Spanish 9, 18, 103, 104, 105, 164
Civil War 104, 163, 164
Amnesty Law 164
Spencer, Herbert 139, 140, 142, 146

Spiegel, Gabrielle 44
Srebrenica 105, 168, 172
SS, Schutzstaffel 27
Stalin, Joseph Vissarionovich 17, 24, 46, 102, 120, 121, 130, 156
Stalinist 13, 115
De-Stalinization 159
Stalinism 159
Stasi (State Security Service) 160
Stedman Jones, Gareth x
stigmatization of forgetting 7, 156
stereotypes 58, 59, 62, 66
Stockholm 43, 135, 167
St. Patrick's Day 152
Strategic Arms Limitation Treaty 25
suicide 27, 152
supremacism, supremacist 29, 63, 72, 126, 161
symbol, symbols 2, 5, 19, 22, 23, 24, 33, 36, 43, 48, 49, 59, 102, 111, 120, 121, 143, 145, 152, 159, 160, 172
Syria, Syrian 28, 59, 70, 166, 170
Syria: Please Don't Forget Us 170
system, systems 8, 9, 45, 69, 75, 77, 86–93, 115, 128, 129, 151, 157, 159, 164, 165, 166
political 8, 159, 166
Sznaider, Nathan 7, 31, 32, 42, 43, 52, 99, 167, 168

teacher 82, 172
technology, technologies xi, xiii, 6, 9, 17, 19, 24, 26, 48, 51–73
technologies of remembrance 17
telegraphy 19
telephone 19, 88
television
experimental 55
commercial 55
public 55, 61, 65
terrorism 14, 152
Tessenow, Heinrich 24
Tönnies, Ferdinand 141
Thompson, Edward Palmer x
Theses on the Philosophy of History (Benjamin, 1940) 152
Thiepval Memorial 22, 163
Thirty Years' War 166
time xii, xiii, 1, 3–6, 8, 12, 13, 18–20, 24, 26, 27, 29, 30–49, 53, 58, 59, 63, 64, 66, 68, 75, 77, 80–3, 85–7, 89, 90, 94, 99, 100, 104, 107, 109, 115, 117, 123,

127, 128, 132, 140–9, 156–8, 160, 161, 164, 168, 171
   multidirectional 32, 44
Togo, Togolese 28
Tokyo 28
Tomb of the Unknown Soldier 22–4, 163
Torpey, John 31, 34, 43–5
touristification 14
Trade Union 3, 110
tradition, traditional viii–xi, 2, 5, 6, 12, 15, 18, 20, 28, 31, 32, 35, 36, 37, 40, 45, 48, 55, 58, 68, 75, 76, 82, 95, 100–3, 107, 109, 119, 128, 132, 140, 141, 145, 146, 149, 153, 161, 167, 169
   cultural 48
   non-western 58
   religious 48
traditionalism 141
transnational memory 7, 12, 13, 100, 110
transcultural 8, 10, 31, 34, 39, 41, 42
   memory studies 42
traveling 31, 41
trauma, traumatic xi, xii, 5, 8, 10, 13, 27, 42, 44, 47, 51, 52, 62, 64, 65, 73, 99, 119, 132, 152, 157, 161
Treaty of Lausanne 166
Treaty of Versailles 97, 124, 155, 156
Trump, Donald John 29, 60, 160, 168, 170
Tunisia, Tunisian 28
Turkey, Turkish 28, 101
Tutu, Desmond 165

Uganda, Ugandan 28
UK 65, 119, 170, 171, 208
   National Holocaust Centre 170, 171
   Immigration Law 170
Ukraine, Ukrainian 4, 11, 115, 130, 166
United States of America 9, 51, 107, 170, 171, 172
   Declaration of Independence 152
   Holocaust Memorial Museum 134, 168, 170
   USC Shoah Foundation 136, 171
Under the Dome (2015) 59
UNICEF 170
Unter den Linden 24
Unknown Warrior, The 23, 24
urbanization 140
utopia, utopian 12, 44, 137, 151

vergangenheitsbewältigung 34, 99
video game, video gaming 9, 59, 64, 66, 67, 69, 70, 118, 134
Vietnam, Vietnamese 18, 19, 27, 28, 129
   Army 38
   Dien Bien Phu 38
   War 27
violence 9, 10, 13, 19, 27, 54, 60, 61, 64, 65, 66, 67, 69, 72, 100, 106, 110, 125, 127, 128, 134, 152, 155, 156, 158, 160, 161, 163, 164, 168, 172
Virginia 24, 162, 207
virtual reality 9, 69
visual performance 55
Vittorio Emanuele II 24
Volksbund Deutscher Kriegsgräberfürsorge 20
Völkisch 1
Von Neumann, John 9, 87, 89, 90, 91, 93

war, wars
   civil 66, 103, 105, 106, 109, 110, 112, 158, 160, 163, 164, 166
   Cold 115, 119, 126–32, 136
   Great Patriotic 5, 115, 116, 129, 130
   nuclear 59, 112, 129, 148
   Six Day 42
   refugees 58
Warburg, Aby 2, 33, 143, 145
warfare 59
   tactical 152
   mechanical 152
Washington 29, 130
Way Things Never Were, The (Coontz 1992) 148
Westminster Abbey 22, 23
White, Hayden 15
Whitehall, London 22, 24
Winter, Jay 4, 6, 7, 8, 9, 21, 22, 23, 41, 95
workers 15, 57, 58, 110, 111, 120, 121, 151
Wright, Brendan 158

Yad Vashem, Israel 162
Yale University 27
Yasukuni Shrine 28
Yerevan 28
Yugoslavia 66, 103, 105, 106, 166

Zionism, Zionistic 6, 168
Zionist 25